Present at the Creation

PRESENT
AT THE CREATION

My Life in the NFL and the Rise of America's Game

UPTON BELL with RON BORGES

UNIVERSITY OF NEBRASKA PRESS I LINCOLN & LONDON

I wish to thank JoAnne O'Neill for her invaluable love and help all during this two-year process, as well as my friend, novelist William Martin, for his many suggestions and direction. My thoughts are of my son, Christopher, and my grandchildren, Peter and Jack, but most of all, Bert Bell and Frances Upton.—UB

To my wife, Nina, without whose love, understanding, and unwavering support I would never have done this or much of anything else. And to my parents, Jack and Helen Borges, who taught me to love and respect sports and words, but not in that order.—RB

CONTENTS

CONTENTS

Present at the Creation

1

On Any Given Sunday

To the best of my knowledge my father never knew Black Elk, the Holy Man of the Oglala Sioux who died on South Dakota's infamous Pine Ridge Reservation in 1950 at the age of eighty-seven, nor did Black Elk know him. Yet if anyone ever put my father's life in perfect symmetry, it was Black Elk, who once said, "The life of a man is a circle from childhood to childhood, and so it is in everything where power moves."

So it was with Bert Bell, the man who made the modern National Football League, and so it was with his son, who helped build the Baltimore Colts' Super Bowl teams and made his father's dream of returning to pro football ownership his own twenty-year quest. I should know. I'm that son.

My father was once the most powerful man in the NFL. He was the confluence of where power moved in pro football from 1946 to 1959, a visionary who in the words of Don Shula "saved the game" during his thirteen years as NFL commissioner. How did he do that?

He invented the NFL draft and made it in inverse order of the standings in an effort to create what has become known as parity. He did the same with the waiver wire.

He recognized the NFL Players Association, the players union, over the protest of many of the owners.

He organized the first player pension plan, which was eventually named the Bert Bell Pension Plan.

He negotiated the merger of the NFL with the All-America Football Conference in December 1949, admitting three AAFC teams:

Paul Brown's Cleveland Browns, the San Francisco 49ers, and the Baltimore Colts, who would come to mean so much to me.

He negotiated the first national television deal with DuMont Broadcasting with a weekly national game on Saturday nights. These were the first nationally televised, coast-to-coast prime-time NFL games, preceding ABC's *Monday Night Football* by seventeen years.

He insisted games be blacked out in local markets, successfully fighting a Department of Justice antitrust suit. The blackout rule would become a cornerstone of the marriage between NFL teams and national TV contracts.

He created the sudden-death overtime rule that led directly to the success of the 1958 championship game between the Colts and the Giants, which is considered to be the most important game in NFL history.

He was instrumental in the desegregation and reintegration of the NFL in 1946, beating Major League Baseball and Jackie Robinson by a year.

He was proactive in ensuring games not be tampered with by gambling influences after the legitimacy of the 1946 championship game was threatened by efforts to fix the outcome. He was the first commissioner to hire former FBI agents in every league city to monitor players and gambling influences and insisted on the creation of the weekly injury report to prevent gamblers from gaining inside information.

He created the schedule each year on his kitchen table using dominos representing each team. He insisted on the weak playing the weak early in the year—over the protest of the most powerful owners—to ensure the end of the season would have meaningful games and fan interest would remain strong.

Read that list and you can understand why Dick Vermeil, who coached the Eagles, Chiefs, and Rams and led St. Louis to a win in Super Bowl XXXIV, once said, "Before Bert Bell the NFL operated out of a closet, almost. Most of what you associate with pro football today began with Bert Bell."

Although he walked in many worlds, football circumscribed

his life, so it was fitting that on the day he died he was sitting in the stands at Franklin Field—the same field where he had quarterbacked Penn to the 1917 Rose Bowl—watching the two teams he once coached and owned through the Depression and World War II and where, as he sat there that day, he was serving what he secretly intended to be his final year as NFL commissioner.

My father was a human cannonball in his working demeanor, and by 1959 he resembled one. Short and stocky, he looked more like an aging pulling guard rather than the Rose Bowl quarterback he'd once been. His hair was always combed straight back and parted in the middle, and he was seldom seen in public wearing anything but his trademark starched white shirt, striped tie, and suit.

That's how he looked that last day in the stands at Franklin Field, a bear of a man stuffed into a stadium seat that seemed to have shrunk a bit as the years had passed.

An era in professional football would end before that day was over and my own would begin, although my entire life up to that point had been defined by the NFL, with an occasional diversion toward hitting Philadelphia nightspots and long jump shots for LaSalle College. Yet I had no reason to believe two days before my twenty-second birthday that this was going to be the case when the morning dawned sunny and humid, a difficult day to play football but a pleasant one to watch it. It was October 11, 1959.

After a night on the town, I was running late. Not so my father. He had by that point been widely and rightly credited for saving the NFL through its lean years between 1933, when he founded the Eagles, and the dawn of the modern age—the nationally televised 1958 overtime championship game between the Colts and the New York Giants that first turned America's sporting consciousness, and more important its growing television audience, toward pro football. It was my father who pushed that sudden death rule past the owners who saw no need for it and had little interest in the idea until it helped transform the game into a growing national obsession.

Baseball, boxing, horse racing, and college football ruled the sports landscape from the 1920s through the 1950s. The World

War II years between 1941 and 1945 only made an already difficult existence harder for struggling NFL franchises, as many of
the best players went off to war and most American households
had little discretionary money anyway. Many times players as well
as owners would meet with my father in our front parlor or talk
with him on the telephone that, to me, seemed to have been sur-
gically implanted to his ear.

Mostly they talked about their struggles to stay afloat. They
aired old grudges and fought change or demanded it, their position most often based on what was financially best for their team.
My father listened and often sympathized, but he focused on the
future and pushed to get them doing the same. Most often they
listened, although sometimes reluctantly.

By the time I got up that morning, my father had already dressed
in his trademark brown suit. It was the color of a football, which
was fitting, because pro football had finally begun to fulfill the
expectations he'd had for it.

I remember looking out my window around 7 a.m., seeing
four cars, all Fords of various ages, sitting in descending order
of repair in front of our house on 323 Haverford Avenue in Narberth on Philadelphia's Main Line. One was the family station
wagon; another was the convertible my father bought for me to
zip around town in. He always bought his cars from the same
salesman so his commission would be bigger.

My father sat in the car in the back of the line, ready for my
brother, Bert Jr., who was older than me, to drive him first to Mass
and then on to Franklin Field. It was the oldest car of the four
and the most worn out. It was the one he preferred and felt most
comfortable in. He couldn't care less about the age of his car as
long as it got him to the stadium on time.

I'd invited two of my closest friends, Joe and Bunny Ryan, to
the game, but by the time I got moving, everyone was gone and
so were my tickets. As commissioner, my father had a box on the
50-yard line, but he mostly spent his time in the stands, buying
his tickets in part because he still remembered the bad old days
he'd spent wishing someone would buy Eagles tickets.

When I finally got to Franklin Field, I knew where he'd be: in the box office talking with the president of the Eagles, Joe Donoghue. I went right to him, because had I asked someone from the Eagles for tickets I would have been in hot water with The Commissioner, which was not a place I, nor anyone in the NFL, wanted to be.

I asked him for three tickets and some cash to go to dinner after the game, and he teasingly hollered over to Donoghue, "I need three more tickets. Upton will be out to pay for them."

My father was a stickler about paying for tickets because when he owned the Eagles and co-owned the Steelers with Art Rooney, he had so much trouble selling them. I'm pretty sure he's the only commissioner in sports history who paid for his own box.

He never wanted to be beholden to any of the owners, because he understood nearly all of them had powerful personalities and personal ambitions that didn't necessarily coincide with what was best for the league. Because of that he wanted to be free to make decisions independent of their desires and whims, using the power he had been given when he agreed to take over the job from the former commissioner, Elmer Layden, after the war.

That led him to get into more than a few arguments with George Halas, who owned and coached the Bears; with the Maras, who owned the Giants; and with George Preston Marshall, the Redskins' mercurial owner. They had the league's most successful franchises and hence the most market power. My father well understood what could happen to the league's have-nots if they were not protected by the natural inclinations of the haves, a delicate balance he orchestrated like a symphony conductor.

A lot of times I'd be sitting in the commissioner's box, as I was that day, next to the visiting team's owner. I was an Eagles fan, of course, but I was under strict orders not to cheer. I was supposed to smile and be cordial and tell the visiting team owner how good his team was, even if it wasn't. I was the Commissioner's Son. He couldn't play favorites and, outwardly, neither could I.

"We're neutral," he used to tell me. That's implanted in my brain. "We don't root for anybody. We root for them all."

I've never been quite able to get over that. To this day I don't root for anybody unless I'm involved with the team. I'm Switzerland because my father told me I had to be.

The last thing I heard my father say was to one of his former players, John "Bull" Lipski, whom I'd known almost all my life. Bull was once a center for the Eagles who also babysat me and my brother when we were kids. One of the Eagles players was always our babysitter. My father would give them a few extra bucks for doing it. That's how it was in those days. I can't imagine any player today babysitting the owners' kids.

"Here you go, Bull, come see me tomorrow" are the last words I heard him speak. He was slipping an ex-player down on his luck a few bucks. That was the father I knew.

I still regret being in such a rush that day. I didn't say goodbye. You always wish that, don't you? That you'd said one more thing? Cracked one more joke? Asked one last question?

My father talked before the game with Art Rooney, commiserating about the league's haves (which they had never been as owners) and have-nots (whose problems they knew well). I don't believe Art had any idea my father was planning to resign as commissioner and buy back the Eagles, and neither did we.

He could always keep a secret. It's what made him a great commissioner. Heck, he converted to Catholicism only after the priest he studied with convinced him Catholicism made sense. No one knew it until he said he was going to get baptized!

At games my father was always moving around the stadium. He'd talk with reporters but not in the press box. It was at the top of the stands and there was no elevator, and by then that kind of walk had become too much for him.

He'd stand in the end zone, talking with coaches and players, and he always sat in the stands with the fans and his friends. In the end that's where he died, which I guess is about right. Perfect circle.

It was a hell of a game until the ending. If a man like my father had to go out that day, at least it was at a game that had Eagles fans roaring. The Steelers' quarterback was Bobby Layne, a future

Hall of Famer who played like one that day. He threw two touch-down passes, ran for a touchdown, and kicked a field goal and three extra points, even though the Eagles' defense kept chasing him all over the field.

The Eagles' future Hall of Famers, quarterback Norm Van Brock-lin and wide receiver Tommy McDonald, connected on an 18-yard touchdown pass that made the score 28–17 late in the fourth quarter. That proved to be the winning score, although Layne threw one last touchdown pass, a 17-yarder to Jimmy Orr near the game's end. Orr was someone who would play an important role in my life ten years later, but I never saw the catch he made that day, because McDonald's score came just about the moment my father was dying in the seats behind him. My father's friends said later that those two teams had been killing him for years.

As the Eagles were driving for that score, I noticed some com-motion up near the top of the end zone seats. Not in the upper deck but high up in the lower deck. I didn't think much of it.

Art Rooney wasn't in the box with us because he'd been sit-ting across the field with my father and the governor of Penn-sylvania, David Lawrence, in a special box, so it was just me and my friends. Governor Lawrence had just been elected in January after serving as mayor of Pittsburgh for thirteen years, so Rooney knew him well and so did my father. They had both gone to visit with him probably because they knew it never hurt pro football to have friends in high places.

My friend Joe Ryan was looking through my binoculars at all the commotion and he said, "It's somebody in a brown suit." That didn't register at first because I knew my father had been sitting with the governor, but then I remembered he often left his seat to go sit with his pals from Narberth in the end zone, so I nervously asked for the glasses. My palms had suddenly gotten sweaty, and not because of the humidity.

I could see people in the stands turning around. I saw a man slumped over. I knew immediately who it was.

At that point your mind makes you do things you'd never do. I was in a state of panic. I ran through the stands and jumped the railing and got down on the track that surrounded the field. It was the same track where I ran in the Penn Relays and the Meet of Champions when I was in high school. My father was there both times. Now I was running on it again and he was still there, and I believed in that way you do when you're young that if I could get across the field in time I could do something to save him.

I could hear people yelling, "It's Bert Bell!" Here I was, a college basketball player in great shape, but I felt out of breath after just a few strides. A guard came running over and I told him that was my father down in the stands and he started running with me. I don't know if he knew who I was or not, but he didn't stop me.

The game was still going on, so I'm not sure if I ran on the field or around it, but I didn't really care. What difference did this game mean now?

He seemed so far away. Like a mirage that kept receding. When I finally got to him his face was covered by an oxygen mask. People were yelling and when I asked how he was doing nobody answered. The story always was that the damn oxygen tank didn't work because they got it from the Steelers' bench. Nothing ever worked for the Steelers in those days.

You want to believe the only reason he didn't live was the oxygen didn't work, but he'd already collapsed in 1954 and had a heart attack earlier in 1959. Both times he ignored the advice of his doctors, who told him he had to reduce his workload and not go to football games. His response was if he couldn't watch football he'd already be dead.

As they were working on him there was a cheer, which seemed odd. I didn't even notice that McDonald had caught that touchdown pass from Van Brocklin.

In 1997 they installed the Bert Bell Historical Marker in front of Davis's store in Narberth, which is now Mapes 5&10. My dad used to come home, change into a gray sweatshirt, and walk down to Davis's to buy a newspaper and lean on a parking meter and talk with his cronies about football. Imagine the commissioner doing that today. It's where he said he learned a lot about what the league needed to do. He knew folks in Narberth would tell him the truth.

Tommy McDonald and Hall of Famer "Concrete Charlie" Bednarik were both at that dedication, and Tommy recalled how he felt when he caught that ball. He told a reporter from the *Philadelphia Inquirer*, "I had just scored a touchdown and saw that half the stadium was cheering but a whole mob of people on the other side of the stadium were yelling and running the other way. I learned later that Mr. Bell had had a heart attack."

They carried my father down through the stands with the game still going on. When they were putting him into the ambulance, flashbulbs were popping everywhere, and I remember thinking that a public man isn't allowed to die alone with just his family.

I climbed in with him, my brother, and my sister, Jane. I took his hand and it was cold as ice. They got to the University of Pennsylvania Hospital fast, but Art Rooney almost never got there. Years later somebody told me Rooney had almost gotten run over by a trolley while he was running up the tracks toward the hospital. Imagine if my father and his old partner had both gone down the same day! Pro football might never have been the same.

It was about five blocks to the hospital, but when they wheeled him in, newspeople were everywhere. I remember one of them asked somebody for the names and ages of his children, and I yelled, "It's not over yet!" It seemed like a rude question to ask, but it really was over and at some level I knew it.

It was over for us and it was over for that NFL, the one my father had created. Nothing would be quite the same again. A man hadn't just passed. An era of pro football had too. Something had been lost that couldn't be replaced: a time and a place in American sports.

Before they took his clothes away, I very quietly grabbed his money clip and his belt. I still have them, with "BB" on them. I just wanted something of his to take with me. Now the Hall of Fame wants them, but I don't know. Some things you keep. Some things you just never can let go.

Red Smith, maybe the greatest sportswriter who ever lived,

wrote the next day in his column, "Chances are he was enjoying himself. He was watching the Eagles, the team he created with his own sweat and tears, playing his other team, the Steelers, whom he operated with Art Rooney during the War. They were playing at Franklin Field, where 40 years earlier a little Penn quarterback had played the game that was to become his very life. It was almost as though he were allowed to choose the time and place."

No one can, of course. Not even my father. His circle from child to child, as Black Elk would see it, was complete at the age of sixty-four, but his plans were not, as we were about to learn.

Driving home along the Schuylkill Expressway that night, my great regret was that I forgot to kiss him goodbye when I left the Eagles' office with my tickets. I kept thinking of all the things we wouldn't do anymore. No more telephone on his ear at all hours. No more football people and show business people coming and going. I understood immediately they'd all be gone soon and we'd be left behind, but when I got home they hadn't left yet. It was a mob scene.

A friend of my father's, a landscaper named Eddie Dixon, was there looking after my mother, who hadn't gone to the game. A doctor came and gave her a shot. The phone was ringing off the hook. The first person to call was Toots Shor, the number one saloon keeper and sports fan in New York. He was in tears. Not long after that my future employer, Colts owner Carroll Rosenbloom, called and told me, "Your father was irreplaceable."

The president of the University of Pennsylvania, Gaylord Hartwell, came around to see my mother. He wanted to rename Murphy Field, Penn's big practice field, Bert Bell Field. My big brother said, "What happens to poor Murphy? The next time somebody dies you change it from Bert Bell Field to Whose Field?"

That was pretty funny at a time when not many things seemed to be.

The wake was at Bringhurst Funeral Home on Tuesday, which was my birthday. Jack Kelly, Grace Kelly's father, who was a very successful businessman and political operator in Philadelphia, was the first in line to pay his respects. When my father owned the Eagles in 1941, he recommended the league name Jack as commissioner after Arch Ward, a powerful sportswriter in Chicago, turned it down. Ward convinced some of the owners to name Layden instead. That's how the former Notre Dame fullback who was one of the famous "Four Horsemen" took over from the NFL's first commissioner, Joe Carr. Six years later my father replaced Layden. Pro football was a small world in those days.

The second in line was Eddie Gottlieb, who owned the Philadelphia Warriors NBA team. Toots Shor, the legendary New York saloon owner who had worked for my father as a bouncer when he ran the rooftop restaurant at the Ritz-Carlton for my grandfather, was there too. Within a day or two, so was nearly everyone from the NFL. There was only one thing missing at the funeral: a phone.

My father should have been buried with a phone in his casket. There was a phone in the bedroom. A phone on the landing. A phone on the first floor. A phone in what he called his office. You could just about kill yourself on those long extension cords he had running all over the place. He'd be walking back and forth, a cigarette in his left hand and a phone in the right, talking to owners like George Preston Marshall, and if you weren't paying attention you'd walk in, trip, and be on the floor.

Marshall came up from Washington to pay his respects but he did it in an odd way, which was typical of him. The owners of all twelve NFL teams were honorary pallbearers, but Marshall refused to go to the wake or the funeral. He said he wanted to remember my father when he was full of life. He was quoted in the papers saying, "They will never find a commissioner as good as Bell, no matter whom they pick."

The funeral procession stretched for blocks, and Narberth had every light turned green. We figured it was Eagles green. I didn't speak at the service, but if I had I would have told them how my father took me to see the movie *Pride of the Yankees* when I was a kid. At the end, when Lou Gehrig is dying of ALS, I was crying but I didn't want my father to see me. I peeked up at him, and he had tears on his cheeks too. I would have told them I held his hand that day, which I didn't do very often. The two of us sitting and crying in Mastbaum Theatre over a great first baseman's tragic grace.

I would have told them how Bert Bell worked seven days a week to make the NFL grow. How he put the schedule together on the kitchen table, fought the owners to create parity by having the weak play the weak and the strong play the strong early in the season so there'd be interest in the games at the end of the season, even though the powerful teams wanted to play each other early to attract big gates and bring some money in.

I would have told them how he never refused to take a phone call, even at dinner, which drove my mother crazy, but if my brother, sister, or I wanted to go somewhere, he'd tell whatever important people were on the line he'd call them back. If I had a basketball game or a track meet, the NFL had to wait.

I'd have told them about the day my basketball team at Malvern Prep lost the league championship against Haverford in a heartbreaker. We were driving home afterward and I was pretty quiet. All of a sudden his voice came out of the dark, saying, "Upton, life is full of disappointment. I know how hard this is but you'll get over it." He had been born into money, but he understood losing.

I would have told them his grandfather had been a congressman, his father had been state attorney general, his older brother (my uncle Jack) had been governor and chief justice of the Pennsylvania Supreme Court, and my father had been named DeBenneville but always thought of himself as just plain Bert. My grandfather was once asked if my father would be going to Penn, as was the family tradition. He snapped back, "He'll go to Penn or he'll go to hell." He went but it didn't totally take.

My father didn't follow in the family footsteps. He coached football at Penn and Temple and was a bon vivant in the Roaring Twenties who fell in love with a game, not business or politics or the law. Even when he finally gave in and went to work for my grandfather running the rooftop nightclub at the Ritz, after going broke in the stock market crash of 1929, all he really wanted to do was find a way to get back to football. For a long time, I felt the same way. The game fascinated us both.

My father was a fighter and a tough competitor, but he knew losing was as much a part of life as winning. Despite his upbringing, he had an understanding of the underdog because his teams, first the Eagles and then the Steelers, had been toothless ones. Because of that, when he became commissioner he understood that for the NFL to flourish the weak had to be protected from the strong and the field had to be leveled.

Finally, I would have told them about Ray Krouse, a fine defensive end for the Detroit Lions whose family suffered a tragedy back home in Baltimore and how my father forced the Lions to trade him to the Colts in 1958 so he could be in Baltimore full time. Bert treated football people the way he treated his family because in a way they were family.

· Winning at any cost may be today's mantra, but the National Football League was built on a different vision, largely my father's, and it prospered because of it. His NFL recognized that fierce competition instincts have their place only amid an ethos of cooperation and fairness. That's what Westbrook Pegler meant when he wrote after my father's death that Bert Bell typified America. He certainly typified that America, the one he helped build and the one I grew up in, a nation that would change radically as the game changed with it in the turbulent '60s and '70s. Society was turned upside down in those years and so was pro football. I know because I was in the middle of it.

What I would not have told them about was what came next, because I had no idea it was coming. The day after the funeral, my brother got a call from the Philadelphia National Bank. That's when we learned my father had been preparing to buy the Eagles.

The financing was in place and the deal had been negotiated. He intended to revive the team he'd founded in 1933 when he borrowed $2,500 from my future mother, his then fiancée, Frances Upton, who was a popular musical comedy actress and member of Ziegfeld's Follies at the time, to take over what had been the

Frankford Yellow Jackets along with a former Penn teammate named Lud Wray and some other investors. Within three years the franchise went bust, and my father bought it out of bankruptcy for $4,500 and took over as coach. Thankfully he was a better commissioner than he was a coach, as his 10-44-2 record from 1936 through 1940 made clear. Bert Bell wasn't a charter member of the first class of inductees into the Pro Football Hall of Fame because he could coach.

Although he hadn't told any of us of his plan, I should have known something was up. That year I can't tell you how many times on Monday nights Bill Campbell, the Eagles' play-by-play announcer, and Norm Van Brocklin would come to our house to talk. I remember wondering more than a few times, why are these guys here? What are they doing here all the time? It never hit me until after my father's death.

If Bert Bell had lived and taken over the Eagles, who would have been the coach? Van Brocklin. My father never said it, but the night Van Brocklin won the Bert Bell Award as Player of the Year in 1960 he told me my father had promised him that job. The Eagles reneged after my father died.

It all made sense. Buy the team. Take care of his kids. Come back to what he always wanted to be—a club owner. He had his coach, who was a quarterback just like he'd been. A perfect circle in an oblong game.

I think the love was always there to be an owner. One reason he had so much power in the NFL is he was one of them first. He thought like them. He could see ahead of time the pitfalls when an owner would make a decision out of panic or anger or short money, and he could step in and stop him.

He'd tell them, "I've been here, guys. I've lost the money. I understand what it is." He would never talk down to them as commissioner. He talked to them like another owner, and they listened because he was one of them.

Today Roger Goodell can't talk to owners like that because he's not one of them. None of these commissioners are. They're all renters and the owners know it. But my father knew money and he knew having no money. He knew not having enough players. He knew desperation. So he knew how the owners felt.

In 1943, in the middle of World War II, I was only six, but we all knew the Eagles were losing money. We knew Art Rooney was sending my father money in envelopes to keep the team going. Nearly every owner's belt was cinched tight, but at a league meeting where they were considering closing down until the war ended, my father said if they did, no matter how bad it was, they'd never reopen. He was right.

They kept urging him to agree as one of the owners to shut the league down because everyone was losing money, but he refused. He understood that if the NFL suspended play during the war, another league might form and, when the war ended, would take control of a game he fervently believed would eventually become the American obsession it is today.

In 1946 the All-America Football Conference was founded with Paul Brown and Otto Graham in Cleveland. If the NFL had shut down and was restarting when the AAFC began, Paul Brown and Otto Graham would have been the guys, not the NFL.

It's funny how things work out. If my father had lived through 1959 and bought the Eagles and stayed on until they found another commissioner, Pete Rozelle would have remained general manager of the Los Angeles Rams and taken terrible heat for the Ollie Matson trade. He could have been fired, because the Rams were struggling when Rozelle traded eight players and a 1959 second-round draft pick to St. Louis for Matson, and the deal hadn't helped. Matson ultimately went to the Hall of Fame, but at the time the trade was considered a bust. If Pete got fired because of it, he would never have become commissioner, and if Bert Bell hadn't been commissioner two years earlier, Pete wouldn't even have been in pro football.

My father is the one who got him the GM job with the Rams after Tex Schramm, who later built the Dallas Cowboys into America's Team, quit in 1957 because the owners were feuding so badly. The Rams had two warring partners and were such a fractured franchise they agreed that my father would break any ties on any club issue if they couldn't agree. When Tex left, my father recommended they hire Pete, who was a former Rams public relations director who'd left the team and was working for a PR firm that marketed the 1956 Olympics in Melbourne, Australia. My father had no idea that he was bringing in his replacement.

But now my father was gone and so was the deal to buy the Eagles. If it hadn't come as such a shock, maybe we could have stepped in and done something. The bank knew if he signed to borrow $950,000, he was good for it, but I was barely twenty-two and my brother was twenty-three and pretty soon would be assisting Austin Gunsel, the NFL treasurer who replaced my father until Pete was elected on the twenty-third ballot three months later. No banker was going to let two kids sign a note like that. Who could blame them? They just called as a courtesy to tell us it wasn't going to happen.

My brother always says, how could you have a greater ending? The two teams you used to own playing an exciting game on the field where you were (Penn) captain, last two minutes of the game with your team driving for the winning touchdown. I don't feel that way. I felt it was just cutting off the life of someone so vibrant and so much a part of my life.

A few days later I went back to LaSalle, but I couldn't wait to get out of college and go to my first real football job. I ended up on academic probation and couldn't play basketball because of it. I played my freshman and sophomore years and set a freshman record for the most field goals in a game one night when I scored 33 points, but that was over now too.

I never graduated. Philadelphia was over for me. My life was going in a different direction. It was 1961 and I had a $65 a week job offer in Baltimore.

I was off to a life in football with the Colts. If my father had lived and told me to finish up at LaSalle, I would have because he would have owned the Eagles and I would have known I had a football job waiting for me; but when he died, I decided I had to get going.

Who's going to give you a job in football in a few years? Who's going to remember Bert Bell? If Carroll Rosenbloom, who owned the Colts then, was going to give me a job picking up towels and eventually picking his players, I'd better get down there and get started.

2

A Long Ride to Baltimore

I was born at Presbyterian Hospital in Philadelphia on October 13, 1937, but the truth of it is I was really born in a huddle. Or at least into one.

The huddle is home for a football player, and it was home for me and for my father. He is credited by those who knew him with saving the National Football League after World War II, when frankly things could have gone either way for the NFL, strange as that sounds today. He was its first visionary, but he wasn't alone.

My mother, Frances Upton, who was one of the country's most popular Broadway actresses of her time, saw pro football's future even before my father did. More important, she financed his effort to buy the Eagles in 1933, which was really the start of it all for him and, in a sense, for me. In fact, while they were dating, she was the one who told him to forget his fixation with college football and his alma mater, Penn, and turn his attention to the pros.

As a celebrity showgirl her social circle in New York included pro football players. She'd watched the Decatur Staleys play in Chicago, she'd seen the Canton Bulldogs with Jim Thorpe, and of course she'd seen the Giants, who played at the Polo Grounds in those days.

Once she began dating my father, he'd take her to Penn games in Philadelphia, but she told him the college game didn't compare to the pros. He could never convince her otherwise and eventually she won the debate, because she was right.

At the time they met, my mother was much more famous than

my father and her life far more glamorous. She'd been discovered when she was sixteen working at the perfume counter at Macy's. A talent scout from Shubert Brothers, which was a big name on Broadway, noticed her, and soon after she was working as a chorus girl and actress in *Pins and Needles* and *Little Jesse James*.

In 1923 she signed a three-year contract with the Ziegfeld Follies and became one of America's biggest vaudeville stars. One year she was voted America's most beautiful woman. She was often on stage with W. C. Fields, Will Rogers, and Bing Crosby at the Palace Theatre, which was the premier vaudeville house in New York at the time.

By 1927 she was garnering rave reviews for a musical review for Ziegfeld alongside Eddie Cantor. The musical director was Irving Berlin, who was already one of America's greatest songwriters. He wrote the score for nineteen Broadway shows and eighteen Hollywood films, so my mother was in the right place at the right time.

Her career really took off when she costarred with Eddie Cantor on Broadway in *Whoopee!* Her rendition of the song "Makin' Whoopee" helped make it the nation's No. 1 hit. She was twenty-four when the play opened at the New Amsterdam Theatre on Broadway on December 4, 1928. The play also costarred Ruth Etting, who would become her one-time roommate and lifelong friend. Etting later married a Chicago gangster named Moe "The Gimp" Snyder, and a hit movie of their life story was made starring Doris Day and James Cagney called *Love Me or Leave Me*. The Gimp didn't like Cagney's portrayal. My mother was happy to learn no one got shot over it.

Makin' Whoopee closed on November 23, 1929, for good reason. It was four weeks and two days after Black Tuesday, the Wall Street crash that saw the market lose 25 percent of its value in forty-eight hours. It was the dawn of the Great Depression, which would cause misery throughout the country until World War II revived the economy.

Even for a popular young actress these were difficult times, but she continued to find work, appearing on a shortwave NBC radio show that was broadcast to Admiral Robert Byrd's expedition to the South Pole in 1929 and starring in one of the first experimental television broadcasts with Gertrude Lawrence and the former heavyweight champion Primo Carnera.

By that time, she'd also signed a contract with Pathé Exchange, a film company in Hollywood, and costarred in a popular movie of the day with Eddie Quillan and Sally Starr called *Night Work*, in which she played a perfume counter girl not unlike the one she'd once been. She soon tired of Hollywood, however, and returned to Broadway, which would be a fortuitous development for my father.

In the spring of 1932, Frances Upton would cross paths for a second time with a man she first met at a party in New York, someone now running the Rooftop Club at the Ritz in Philadelphia. That person was my father, who, after he had lost a small fortune in the stock market crash, had been given the job by his father, John C. Bell.

My father was a successful football man with a vision for what the game would become, but he was not often a success in the real business world. If he had been, though, he might never have met my mother, so in a sense those losses led to his greatest victory.

After stints as an assistant coach at Penn and Temple, he decided to try his hand as a stockbroker, but his timing wasn't quite as good as it had been when he was quarterbacking Penn to the 1917 Rose Bowl. He lost $100,000 in the great Wall Street crash, which today would be the equivalent of about a million dollars. My grandfather was not amused, which is how my father ended up working at my grandfather's hotel when Frances Upton, Broadway star, showed up one night to sing.

At the time, she was engaged to Bernard Baruch Jr., the son of the Wall Street financier Bernard Baruch (known as the original Lone Wolf of Wall Street), who had his own seat on the New York Stock Exchange and left it to advise Presidents Woodrow Wilson, Franklin Roosevelt, and Harry Truman. Bucking the conventions of the day, they planned to marry despite the fact Baruch was Jewish and she was Catholic.

Undaunted, my father pursued her, even after she informed

him she had no interest because of his freewheeling lifestyle. He contacted her repeatedly as she traveled the country singing and performing. She was the only person who could ever say no to Bert Bell, but even she could only keep that up for so long. He wore her down with the same charm and persistence that later made him successful as an NFL commissioner. She began to see him more and more. He kept asking her to marry him and she kept responding in the negative, but he always looked at that type of situation as a challenge or an opportunity to succeed.

In those days, I guess you could say he was a man about town. He didn't have any money in his pocket, except his father's, but he knew how to live as if he did. In other words, he liked to party and he liked to gamble and he liked to have a drink. He also liked football—just not pro football.

The same year he met my mother, George Preston Marshall, who owned the Redskins and was someone my father got to know during the summer horse racing season at Saratoga Race Track in upstate New York, tried to convince him to buy the rights to an NFL franchise, but he thought the idea was ridiculous. At that point college football was still his focus, but my mother's influence would soon change that.

Over time my father's powers of persuasion began to penetrate my mother's resolve the same way they later would the NFL owners he managed during thirteen years as the league's commissioner. About a year after he first heard her voice at the Ritz, during a dinner in Margate, a beach town on the Jersey shore near Atlantic City, she finally relented. Sort of.

She told him if he gave up drinking, she'd consider marriage. She told him he had six months to show her he could stay sober. My mother always said he didn't hesitate, which he never did when he really wanted something.

"All right," he told her. "I've had my last drink." And that was it. He never took another drink. That was my father.

On September 25, 1933, my mother costarred in her last Broadway show, *Hold Your Horses*, which opened at the Winter Garden Theatre. Nearly fifty years later, the Winter Garden would become the home for one of the longest-running musicals in history, *Cats*, which ran for 7,485 shows and eighteen years. *Hold Your Horses* wasn't as fortunate, not that that upset my father.

The show closed on December 9, and they were married in Chicago a month later, January 4, 1934—secretly, because Flo Ziegfeld prohibited his actresses from marrying. By then they were more than secret life partners. They were also partners in pro football, the game I was now about to join.

After being tipped off that my father had snuck into town to visit my supposedly ailing mother, a Chicago newspaper head-line read, "Millionaire playboy visits stricken actress girlfriend in Chicago." I later learned that my "playboy" father was practi-cally broke as well as secretly married to my mother at the time. When I asked her why she gave up one of the wealthiest young men in America to marry somebody who had to have his father bail him out so many times, she'd just say, "I had a feeling about your father I didn't have about anybody else. They might have had the money, but something about him made me feel I didn't have to worry."

I don't know how she came to that conclusion off his track record, but she turned out to be right. As I found out later, we lived in many fine houses, but they all were rentals until he finally bought a house in Narberth, on the Main Line in Philadelphia, in 1950. When we moved in, she put a statue of the Blessed Vir-gin in the front yard with a spotlight on it. Imagine a kid look-ing out the window seeing that, knowing all your friends did too, because the property was a corner lot right at the entrance to town. Driving down the road, you could see the Blessed Virgin all lit up from the top of the hill. It wasn't that my mother was so holy. It was just the hard times she'd come through.

She never forgot that her big break came at someone else's expense. One day she was at Macy's perfume counter, and a few years later she filled in for a woman with the Ziegfeld Follies and got the lead part. She told me once that one day you could be star-ring on Broadway, meeting Bob Hope and all these show business people, and the next you're on your knees praying for your next acting job.

She hadn't come from money, like my father. The Bells were one of the wealthiest families in Philadelphia. My grandfather had played football at Penn, where he was their first great end from 1882 to 1884. Later he became a successful lawyer, the Philadelphia district attorney, the state attorney general, a Penn trustee for life, and a member of the Walter Camp Rules Committee for college football.

It's been said my father was born with a silver spoon in his mouth, and who could argue? They had maids and butlers. He even had his own horse!

As a kid my father used some of the help to practice tackling in a mansion about a mile from the Penn campus, but that was nothing compared to when summer came. Then the Bells would head off to an eleven-acre property in Radnor, on the Philadelphia Main Line, with its own lake. It wasn't a country club, but if they had put out a shingle that said "Bell Country Club," nobody would have questioned it.

Although my grandfather never felt football was a vocation, he did help form the NCAA to save college football at a time when President Theodore Roosevelt was threatening to shut the game down because of the rash of head injuries. If that sounds familiar, it should, because the game is battling a similar problem today with the concussion epidemic that has seen young players in their prime, like twenty-four-year-old 49ers linebacker Chris Borland, choose to retire. Borland left a $540,000 salary on the table after one season in today's NFL and agreed to pay back a signing bonus of $617,436, out of fear that the problem that got my grandfather involved in creating the NCAA was now running rampant in the NFL.

Yet as involved as my grandfather became with college football, he never understood how my father thought the game was something to make a living at. To him, the pro game wasn't something to aspire to. It was a low-brow imitation of the collegiate game.

As things turned out, boy, was he wrong, because today's game is one of the most successful business models in the country. *Who knew?* Frances Upton, for one.

Unlike my father, my uncle Jack was just as successful as his father. He became both lieutenant governor and briefly governor of Pennsylvania and later chief justice of the Pennsylvania Supreme Court. My father? He was a football coach who fell in love with a game that would eventually make him famous, but it wasn't what the Bell family expected.

My father was the starting quarterback on the 1916 Penn team that went 7-2-1 and played in the 1917 Rose Bowl game, throwing the first forward pass in Rose Bowl history, but they lost to Oregon, 14–0. The next season, 1917, with war clouds hanging over the country, he led the Quakers to a 9-2 record that fall and then went off and enlisted in the army the day after Penn shellacked Cornell, 37–0, on Thanksgiving Day at Franklin Field. Seven of the team's eleven starters left for war at the end of that season.

Joining my father at boot camp was someone who became his lifelong friend and a future triple Olympic gold medalist in rowing, John B. Kelly. You may have heard of his daughter Grace, who became an Academy Award–winning actress before marrying Prince Rainier of Monaco in 1956.

At 3 a.m. the day after the Cornell game, Bert Bell was sworn into University Base Hospital Unit 20. That night he was elected captain of the 1918 Penn team, but he would be unavailable: he was going to war.

My father was cited by General John J. Pershing and the French government for bravery as a medical officer who aided wounded soldiers during a German shelling of their position. He returned to Penn on March 26, 1919, and captained the football team that fall, but he withdrew before he graduated and began a life in football. Forty years later, I was about to do the same thing at LaSalle, leaving college without a degree for the uncertainty of pro football. Black Elk was on to something: life is a circle.

With my mother's encouragement, my father was finally convinced to take up Marshall's offer in 1933 and buy an NFL franchise if he could find one. The NFL was thirteen years old at the time and not selling T-shirts in China as it does today. The league had enough trouble just trying to sell tickets in America, but my father knew what he wanted and she supported him. She also had a fatter pocketbook from her stage career and footed the bill.

My mother had grown up differently from my father. Her father was a New York police detective who often worked undercover. In her early days as an actress in New York, he used to meet her at the stage door after the show ended to walk her home. She was never sure she'd recognize him, because he was often in disguise. That was her world before she entered the more glamorous one of show business.

The thing you have to realize is it was my mother who kept telling my father that pro football was the game. "Why do you keep playing around with college football?" she'd ask him. "It's the pro game." She gave him the seed of the idea and then the seed money to buy what would become the Eagles in 1933. If he hadn't been able to win her heart, he might never have found his other love, because she then loaned him the money he needed to buy the Frankford Yellow Jackets out of bankruptcy, after his father refused to give him a nickel for such a foolish venture.

He joined up with an ex-teammate from Penn, Lud Wray, and four Philadelphia businessmen, each putting up $2,500 and assuming $11,000 in debts and a league prerequisite that he get the Pennsylvania blue laws altered. My father lobbied to get them changed and Governor Gifford Pinchot concurred, signing a bill allowing pro sports teams to play on Sundays. Who would have imagined that half a century later the NFL would own Sunday more firmly than religion would?

The NFL was born on August 20, 1920, at a Hupmobile dealership in Canton, Ohio, originally calling itself the American Professional Football Association. It began with eleven teams, but only four finished the 1920 schedule, setting the tone for the difficult road ahead.

The league was up to twenty-two teams the following season, but many were unstable financially and short-lived, even after the league was renamed (today they'd say rebranded) as the National Football League on June 24, 1922.

Red Grange's decision to sign with the Chicago Bears and launch a barnstorming tour in 1925 helped the league gain some stability, but it was not yet a factor in the national sports scene. It was an afterthought at best, if anyone thought of it at all.

Pro football was considered a rough-faced black sheep, an undignified stepson when compared to the college game. So it was for the Yellow Jackets, who hosted the first pro football night game in 1931 at Municipal Stadium in Philadelphia. By then they had lost their home field in northeastern Philadelphia to a fire and were playing in three different stadiums, with minimal attendance in all of them. With ownership weakened by the Great Depression, NFL commissioner Joe Carr terminated the franchise and made it a traveling team for the remainder of that season.

Unable to find a buyer, the franchise was returned to the league, and Carr began searching for new investors. The Depression had created havoc for the NFL by then. In 1926 the league had twenty-six teams. By 1933, when my father bought in, it was down to ten. To get them to an even number, he convinced his friend Art Rooney, who would later become his partner in the Eagles in 1941, to buy a franchise in Pittsburgh for $2,500 as a personal favor, a deal that was finalized on July 8, 1933. One day later, my father owned the Eagles.

What my father actually bought on July 9, 1933, was not the Yellow Jackets but rather the NFL rights to Philadelphia. The Eagles never claimed any of the Yellow Jackets' history, including its 1926 NFL championship team, and so are considered a 1933 expansion team in the league's record book.

The day the deal became official, my father was walking down Chestnut Street in Center City Philadelphia. When he got to the corner of Chestnut and Broad Street, Philadelphia's major thoroughfare, he saw a billboard promoting President Franklin Roosevelt's National Recovery Act. The symbol looking down at him with a hungry eye was a bald eagle. At that moment, the Philadelphia Eagles were born.

That first season, things went the way they seemed to so often for my father when it came to business. By the team's first road trip, he was broke. Still, on November 12, 1933, the power of persuasion that had won over my mother, and would later win over American sports fans to his game, was on full display. That Sunday the Eagles played in Philadelphia, five days after Governor Pinchot's signature had altered the state's blue laws. They still kept most businesses closed on Sundays, but the doors at pro football stadiums in Pennsylvania were now open.

The Eagles were not winning very often and not selling many tickets, but Bert Bell wasn't worried. He was in pro football and, more important, on January 4, 1934, he and my mother married. That was a secret that didn't last long.

On April 4, their marriage was revealed by Walter Winchell, the most influential newspaper and radio gossip columnist in the country. My father confirmed his report and a month later, on May 6, they made their marriage official at St. Madeleine Sophie Catholic Church. He was thirty-nine when he took his thirty-year-old bride on a honeymoon to 6803 Atlantic Avenue in Ventnor, not far from Atlantic City. As honeymoons go, it wasn't quite what my mother expected.

While they summered on the Jersey shore, so did the Eagles, who trained on the beach and lived in their rented mansion. That was the life my mother shared for the rest of my father's days, the one I grew up with first as a spectator to history and later as an active participant in the NFL for twenty years. The Eagles may not have been quite family, but often enough, many of them were in the bedroom next to mine.

The thing I learned from my parents is they were both chance-takers. Her father came over from Ireland and became a detective who wore disguises and disappeared for weeks at a time. He was one of the people who went into the Black Hand neighborhoods, because he spoke Italian as well as four other languages. He'd be gone for two or three weeks and show up suddenly and frighten her whole family, because they thought he was dead.

My parents weren't afraid of life, whether they had money or not. A lot of my mother's success came during hard times. My father certainly knew hard times for many years running the Eagles and later when he and Art Rooney partnered to keep their franchises alive during World War II. I became the same way. I was always willing to take chances, especially if it was a chance to keep me in pro football.

If the talent scout doesn't show up at Macy's that day, my mother isn't a Broadway star. If my father doesn't meet her and his father doesn't bail him out a few times and put him at the Rooftop Club, there's no Eagles. There's no partnership with Art Rooney and the Steelers. He doesn't become commissioner. There's no NFL draft. Maybe the league goes down.

It's always impressed me that much of what happened to get my father and me into the NFL was chance. You had to be in the right place. I think because that generation went through so many hardships with the Depression and two world wars, they appreciated more how lucky you had to be to make it. My father recognized the importance of luck, and so do I.

I had lost the most important person in my life that afternoon at Franklin Field, but I'd been lucky to have him and lucky that someone like Carroll Rosenbloom owned the Colts. Whatever anyone wants to say about Carroll, he gave Bert Bell's kids an opportunity in the football business. That all went back to the fact they'd known each other since Carroll was a running back at Penn and my father was coaching him in 1927. He and another coach had differences over the football future of Carroll and another back, Marty Brill, and the two of them grew discouraged and disgusted and eventually went to talk with Knute Rockne, the head coach at Notre Dame, about transferring.

Rockne agreed to take them, but Carroll's father did not agree. He told Carroll he hadn't sent him to Penn to be a running back, so he was staying. Brill left and in 1930 returned to score three touchdowns against Penn in a 60–20 Notre Dame rout. He got his revenge. I got my football benefactor.

Carroll stayed at Penn, and my father's encouragement and support convinced him to keep playing. He became a solid running back, and some twenty-five years later, my father convinced him to buy a ragamuffin team out of bankruptcy called the Baltimore Colts. He did it with reservations, but later he'd say it was the greatest business decision he ever made. He wasn't kidding. It cost him $13,000 and in four years was worth a million.

In August 1960, ten months after my father passed away, Carroll suggested I go down to training camp to work for the summer for his two-time NFL champion Baltimore Colts. The team was getting ready to leave to play in the College All-Star Game, and he felt it was a way for me to break in, working a summer job for $65 a week with the understanding I'd have a full-time job after I graduated from LaSalle.

I think that all went back to when they lived four blocks from each other during the summers in Margate. My father would walk over to Carroll's place to drink coffee and talk. He used to say to him, "Remember, I want a piece of that team for my kids." I don't think he was kidding, because he wanted his family to be taken care of after he was gone. After all, my father picked Carroll to take over in 1953 at the time Baltimore was suing the NFL to have the franchise returned to the city.

Originally the NFL put them there when my father engineered the merger with the All-America Football Conference in 1950, absorbing three AAFC teams: the Cleveland Browns, the San Francisco 49ers, and the Colts. But the Colts failed at the box office and lasted only one year. The NFL dissolved the franchise on January 18, 1951, after the owner, Abraham Watner, illegally turned the club back to the league during a meeting at the Blackstone Hotel in Chicago. He took $50,000 from the remaining owners for the assets, which included the players and their helmets. Twenty-eight of the players were taken in a distribution draft, but all the helmets were snatched up by the Green Bay Packers, which says something about those Colts . . . and the Packers too.

The NFL's New York Yanks franchise had been struggling financially for several seasons before owner Ted Collins (who made his fame and much of his fortune as the agent for the popular singer Kate Smith) returned the franchise to the league after the

1951 season. The Yanks' roster was then sold to two young Dallas businessmen, Giles and Connell Miller, on January 30, 1952, and the team became the Dallas Texans. Although technically a transfer of the Yanks, it was ostensibly a new franchise in Dallas, but the Texans were a far cry from America's Team, as the Cowboys would become two decades later. The Texans' only NFL season was 1952, and they were one of the worst franchises in league history. Unable to meet payroll by early November, the owners also returned the franchise to the league (do you see a trend here?) on November 14, with five games remaining. It was moved to Hershey, Pennsylvania, but while the team trained in Hershey, it became a homeless "traveling team" that played its final two "home" games in Akron, Ohio, and Detroit. But the Texans' failure wasn't all bad.

My father knew the city of Baltimore had a strong legal argument that its franchise had been unfairly taken and understood the city didn't want financial reparations. It wanted a football team, and here was the chance if he could find the right local owner.

He told Rosenbloom he needed someone who had money and was based in Baltimore. Carroll fit the bill, even though he was then spending much of his time in New York. He was understandably leery of the NFL and wary for a lot of other reasons, one being that the city's lawsuit was being handled by William D. Macmillan.

Macmillan worked at a prestigious law firm, Semmes, Bowen & Semmes, and represented Whitaker Chambers in the famous libel suit involving Alger Hiss. Hiss had been accused by Chambers of being a member of the Communist Party and sued for libel several years earlier. Among the trial's oddities were the "Pumpkin Papers," sixty-five pages of copied State Department documents and five strips of microfilm, allegedly copied by Hiss, that Chambers hid at one point inside a pumpkin.

That story became a national hysteria and made Macmillan one of the country's most famous lawyers of the time. He was also someone who loved Baltimore and thought he could build a case to get the Colts back. I kept hearing my father talk about it on the phone and I could tell he began to think Macmillan was right, so he made a deal.

He would give Baltimore its franchise back if it could sell fifteen thousand season tickets in the six weeks leading up to Christmas. If so, the city would get its franchise back and he would be given the power to find an owner, general manager, and coach. My father knew where to go first.

He was looking for a stable owner. It wasn't like today when any millionaire can step in and become an overnight billionaire. It was a risk owning an NFL franchise then, a gamble that often didn't pay off. In those days people used to say, "You know how to make a million dollars in the NFL? Start with ten million." That would change by the end of the decade, but in 1953 it wasn't easy finding someone to buy the Baltimore Colts.

My father didn't want someone from the outside because in his mind the owner had to be part of the city. He didn't want absentee ownership, and Rosenbloom was a Baltimore guy he trusted, a millionaire, and a Penn man of whom he had firsthand knowledge.

Several times I heard my father almost pleading with him on the phone to buy the team. It took quite a lot of convincing, which seems ironic now considering he paid only $13,000 for 51 percent of the team. His four partners paid the remaining $12,000 because, although the total purchase price was $200,000, the league only asked for $25,000 upfront. Imagine that! Today it's worth a billion.

The remaining $175,000 was to be paid in nine installments. My father made it easy for Carroll by prorating the payments over an eight-year period, but they did so well so quickly the debt was paid off in three years.

Finally, on January 10, 1953, Carroll gave a "qualified" yes: he said he'd agreed to the deal out of a sense of civic duty, but he didn't have the time or the inclination to run the team's daily operation. It was up to my father to come up with a general manager, and he settled on, surprise, another Penn man.

That's how Don Kellett became the Colts' general manager and my future boss. He'd been a basketball coach at Penn at one time and a three-sport athlete there. My father first met him when Kellett came to him with a suggestion for how to handle the struggling Dallas franchise.

Kellett was directing operations at WFIL-TV in Philadelphia when he read how the Texans were like a ship without a rudder. He called my father and asked for the rights to the homeless franchise, suggesting the league rename them the All-Americans and have them play in eleven different cities across the country.

Television was in its infancy but Kellett, being in that business, saw its potential. He wanted to make the "All-Americans" a traveling TV team, taking them to a different city each week with the game on national television. He calculated the uniqueness of that would likely allow them to at least cover expenses, and TV rights could be sold for several hundred thousand dollars.

By then the move back to Baltimore was in the works, so my father rejected the idea, but he was impressed enough by Kellett to suggest him to Carroll. Carroll had him vetted and the deal was done, but Kellett wasn't about to give up a secure TV position in Philadelphia to enter the precarious world of pro football. What convinced him was an offer not only of a contract but also of 25 percent of the profits, which would come in the form of stock options at the end of that first season. Before the end of January, Rosenbloom owned the Colts, and Kellett was running them from a downtown office at 2013 North Charles Street.

My father wasn't the type of person who would say, "If I get you in, I want a piece of this for my kids," but he did ask Carroll to look out for us, and Carroll did. He never had anything in writing, and he had his own sons and his daughter to be concerned with, but he kept his word.

My brother and I both ended up there. When my father died, we could have been in the position of ending up nowhere. When I first learned my father had been trying to repurchase the Eagles, I wanted to stay with them but was told Philadelphia might not be a stable franchise. The Eagles were going to be sold to somebody, but not to the Bell boys. Carroll took care of us and I never forgot it.

I had just turned twenty-two and was still at LaSalle, in body but not in mind. I was going into my senior year but my mind was on the practice field, so I went to Baltimore that summer with the idea I was returning to the Colts after my senior year whether I'd graduated or not. Made no difference to me. Turned out it was "or not." I was about to follow the same path my father did when he left Penn without a degree to coach football.

This was essentially the first time I was leaving home on my own. The times were a lot different than they are today. People didn't move around as much. Many of the writers used to say, "You never saw Bert Bell without one of his kids with him," and it was true. Now he was gone and I was leaving Philadelphia for the first time for Baltimore. I saw it as the beginning of the end of the family, and that was somewhat sad. We were never together again as a family.

It was wrenching to realize when I got in the car that August that this was the end, but it turned out it wasn't. While it was the end of the life I'd known watching my father operate in pro football, it was the beginning of a new football life filled with hope but also uncertainty. It could be tremendous or it could be disastrous. How would I know?

Today those kinds of moves are easier to make. Nobody stays in the same place for ten minutes. But sixty years ago it was a big deal to drive away from home and the life I'd known. It would never be the same again in Philadelphia or in the league. That life with my father was gone. If I wanted a life in pro football, I would have to make it on my own.

Mentally, I think it was the longest journey I ever took. In those days there were no real super highways, so it was three and a half or four hours in the car to Western Maryland College, which was in the middle of nowhere. There was a lot of time to think and a lot to recall.

I thought about how my father had struggled to get into pro football and how my mother made it possible. My first thought was how unselfish my father had been in his first year as commissioner when he went to Chicago and took his sons to the Bears' training camp with him. I was nine and Bert Jr. had just turned eleven, so somebody had to look after us while my father was off at meetings. It was usually Joe Labrum, who was the NFL's PR director, or Shorty Ray, the supervisor of officials who was inducted into the Hall of Fame in 1968. If I'd just become the NFL commissioner at such a crucial time, just coming off World War II, the last thing I would have said is, "I want to take my two boys with me." But that was my father.

In those days you'd get on a train at North Station in Philadelphia and take the overnight to Chicago. For a kid it was so exciting. All the sounds and smells and people. The dining car. The constant rattle of the train as the landscape flew by.

Today you just fly over everything and then you land. In those days you watched things pass by and you heard people talking to each other. Not like today when everybody is staring down at their iPhone or their laptop or reading on a Kindle, off in another world somewhere with their digital friends.

Even if you didn't know anybody, there was constant conversation to pass the time. That's how society ran. Things were slower, and the train was the way to go.

It was better than Christmas that first time heading out to training camps. Now I was going off on my own, but then I had the commissioner and Shorty Ray and Joe and my brother and all those great football players like Sid Luckman in Chicago, whom you'd heard of but seldom saw. This was before TV took over. The radio was what connected America then—that and the pictures you made in your mind.

My first training camp, we visited the Chicago Bears before the College All-Star Game in 1946. That game was bigger than the NFL Championship Game in those days. The Rams were beaten 16–0 in front of 97,380 fans at Soldier Field, and I was one of them for the first time. It was unbelievable.

Shorty was to take us to St. Joseph's College in Rensselaer, Indiana, where the Bears were training. The Monsters of the Midway were *it* back then, but they were a mystery too, almost a myth. If you told someone back then you were going to the Chicago Bears' training camp, you'd get a look of disbelief.

You painted a picture of them in your head from what you'd heard on the radio, and there were no real televised pictures to alter it. You knew of these people who were your heroes, but you needed to use your imagination to see them. It made you less cynical than today because you didn't know every wart.

If you can see it all the time on television, you get used to it. *So what?* But when you only get to see these people once, you remember them for a long time. They remain vividly in my mind to this day.

What my father didn't realize that trip was that Shorty Ray was colorblind. We were going through red lights and stopping at green. Bert and I were in the back, scared out of our minds. At that age you don't want to say, "Mr. Ray, you're going through the lights!"

We finally got there in one piece somehow and were given a room. St. Joseph's was a Catholic college, so there were priests walking around all over the place.

Before we got there, my father had rehearsed us. Now that he was commissioner, he didn't want either of his kids to say, if someone asked, that the Eagles were our favorite team. So he told us to say, "We don't root for anybody. We're neutral." I heard that for weeks leading up to the trip.

"We're neutral." I'll take that to my grave. If St. Peter is waiting at the Pearly Gates and he asks, "Upton, are you for Jesus?" I'm sure I'll say, "I'm neutral." And down I'll go.

Being kids, we each had an autograph book. We'd wait until the end of practice and stand outside the locker room of the Bears or the Redskins, or the Green Bay Packers, or the Chicago Cardinals, whatever training camp we were at, and get all these great players to sign. Don Hutson. Charlie Trippi. Luckman. Kenny Washington, one of the first African American players in the league with the Rams in LA. They all signed my book. I wish I could find it.

I remember my brother and me sitting on a tackling dummy at one of our first practices with the Bears. This was the glamour team so it was really exciting, but then all of a sudden there's George Halas, the coach and owner, giving this expletive-laden tirade. Here I was, nine years old, a Catholic kid taught by the nuns. I was hearing this and wondering, what are those priests walking around here thinking? But Halas was the god of gods in football, so he could say what he wanted, even at a Catholic school.

One thing that stuck out was that Halas let my brother and me come into the night meetings with the coaches. He didn't treat us like kids. He wasn't patronizing. It wasn't, "There's Bert's kids." It was, "How you doing? Sit down and listen."

I watched him and his assistant, Clark Shaughnessy, diagramming plays on the chalkboard. It was fascinating to me. There was input from all his coaches. You could see there was respect for each other's opinion, but Halas was the boss. There was a maturity there I didn't always see later when I was running the Patriots or over in the World Football League. These were men who'd served in World War II. They'd come through the Depression. They were men addressing each other as men.

Shaughnessy in many ways changed pro football. He created the T formation and later created the defense to combat it. He also created the position of flanker, which today is wide receiver. When I listened to him that summer, I was exposed to something revolutionary. I didn't know everything they were talking about, but when he started drawing on the board, I recognized there was something different up there, a different game. It would turn out to be the game that changed pro football: the passing game.

This wasn't the brutal game I was used to watching, slogging it out at the line. It was like football in 3D. "What is this?" I wondered.

My father was off in Chicago at the Blackstone Hotel, where he was dealing with Arch Ward, the sports editor of the *Chicago Tribune*, who hated the NFL. Ward founded the All-America Football Conference and was the most powerful sports editor in America at a time when that really meant something. He was ESPN in one person—the worldwide leader. He had that kind of power.

Ward invented both the baseball and football all-star games, and that game was so important to the NFL. He and my father respected each other, but I think they both sensed danger there too. Bert needed Ward for him to do his business. It was his first year as commissioner and he had to promote that game. It was the biggest game in the country at the time.

I remember the next year the Bears lost to the College All-Stars by the same score, 16–0. There were 105,480 people at Soldier Field. I'd never seen that many people in one place. The game was growing.

Maybe it's a young boy's memory, but there was nothing like what that game was then, because college football was still bigger than pro football. There was genuine excitement, not pumped-up hype from eight hours of pregame shows. The people were rooting for the College All-Stars to win, and don't think Arch Ward wasn't rooting for that too, because the more competitive the game was, the more tickets they sold. People wanted to know if these kids could beat the pros. And in those days they could.

After a few days of settling in with the Bears that first summer, I was watching some of the players outside one day after practice when I got my first lesson about managing a football team. There was a big tree and they were all trying to throw full beer cans over it. They'd get a running start and let it go. The player who won was named Mike Jarmoluk. He was about six feet five inches and 230 pounds, which was a giant in those days. He played defensive tackle, but today he'd be a small linebacker or a big safety. That's what life is. Some things evolve but others never really change, as I was about to learn.

A few days later I was sitting in Halas's office as he was meeting with the coaches. They were cutting down the team. One of them said, "This guy has a lot of ability, but I think he's a problem." It was Jarmoluk.

In my mind Jarmoluk was Paul Bunyan clearing that tree with a beer can, but to them he was a problem. Who knows if he was or not, but when I got back home, the word was he'd been cut and now he was with the Boston Yanks. Two years later he was with the Eagles.

Years later I heard the same sort of thing in personnel meetings with the Colts talking about Big Daddy Lipscomb, the great but troubled defensive tackle. Coach Weeb Ewbank said, "He's a disruption. He disrupts the team." A year later they traded him to Pittsburgh for wide receiver Jimmy Orr and defensive tackle Billy Ray Smith, which shocked the city because he was a great player and a popular guy. "How many Big Daddys do they think there are?" is what they were saying in Baltimore, but the Colts got good players out of the trade. When it happened, I thought of Jarmoluk and that meeting with Halas.

What I learned that day is there's nothing new under the sun— just how it's packaged. They may use different terminology. It may be refined. They may use more computers and analytics. All the tools of technology today make things faster and information more readily available. But judging players, the art of judging players, hasn't changed. How you scout, how you view tape, how you prepare reports may have changed, but how you view players? That's pretty much the same. The eye still decides. The eye and the mind.

It's the same when you're deciding when to get rid of a player. The eye and the mind decide. Look at Johnny Manziel. Greg Hardy. Ray Rice. You become a problem? You become a distraction? Somebody is watching and the clock is ticking. One day you wake up and you're Jarmoluk. You're gone.

I think those early times in those training camps gave me a head start when I got to Baltimore. I had begun to learn the terminology and the strategy of building a team, but I'd learned more about people and players and the dark side of pro football. It can be a hard-hearted business. Today Patriots coach Bill Belichick may be the master of that. There's no emotion. You make a financial decision or a decision based on declining talent and you say goodbye. I learned that the ones who do that the best, and sadly maybe the coldest, are the ones who win.

The following year, 1947, we left Chicago after the All-Star Game and headed to Los Angeles on the *Los Angeles Limited* train. You felt like you were on a wagon train. It was a forty-five-hour train trek to get to California. When you're a kid and you have that much time on your hands, you come up with some funny ways to pass it.

When the train was crossing the Mississippi, my brother and I were in our compartment, and I told him I thought it would be a good idea to take a piss in the Mississippi River. So there we were with the window open, standing up on the seat with our flies down when the door slides open, and it's my father with a famous actor he wanted us to meet. And there Bert and I were, pissing out the window. My father just slid the door closed, and we could hear them laughing over the train noise.

Finally we pulled into LA and saw palm trees. It's a different world from Philadelphia. We went out to the Rams' training camp and there was Bob Waterfield, their great quarterback. He was married to Jane Russell, who a few years earlier was the most talked-about actress in America after starring in the one-time banned movie *The Outlaw*. We also saw Kenny Washington and Woody Strode, who later played in the movie *Spartacus*. They broke the color line in pro sports a year before Jackie Robinson got to the Major Leagues.

Kenny was in the same backfield with Jackie at UCLA and had been an All-American running back, but he was denied a chance to play in the NFL until the Rams moved to LA and it became a requirement if the team was to play in the LA Coliseum. No black player had been allowed in the NFL from 1933 to 1946, but Kenny ended that when he signed a contract on March 2, 1946.

I can still see him walking out in shorts, carrying his cleats over his shoulder. He was a good-looking man: tall, slim, my idea of an athlete. If he'd played earlier he might have been an all-time great, the way he could cut and move, but he was denied his chance. His best days were behind him, but later, when I was scouting in the South for the Colts, I was looking for players who reminded me of Kenny Washington.

The Rams were getting ready to play an exhibition game against the Redskins that summer, and Washington was already out in California training too. That was when I first saw Sammy Baugh up close. I don't think I ever saw anyone throw a football as hard as that man did. How does someone in 1946 throw that water-melon they were using for a football as hard as Marino and Elway did or as accurately as Tom Brady?

Dan Reeves owned the Rams at the time, and he'd convinced my father and the other owners to let him move from Cleveland to LA after the 1945 season. The war was over, and the country was growing. He had a strong argument, the same kind some owners are still making today.

He told them he'd won the championship in 1945 and still lost money, and he believed the NFL needed to take the game across the country. He was right. That move helped solidify the NFL as a national league. How can you be a national league if you're not in LA?

It's amazing to me the league wasn't there for twenty years (1995–2016) in the midst of the game's explosion. Going from Chicago to LA that summer was like going from black-and-white to Technicolor.

Seventy years later, the league is finally back there. What that tells me is the original idea to go there was the right one and going to St. Louis was the wrong one. Two NFL franchises haven't made it in St. Louis—the Cardinals who moved there from Chicago and are now in Arizona, and the Rams.

The thing with LA is you have to give them a decent product. You have to win. They don't go to a bad movie out there. Same with a sports team. Bad act? People don't show up. It's show business.

So why did the Rams and Raiders leave in 1995 if there was a solid fan base? It's the same thing that's plagued the league and threatens it today: greed. The Rams got a better deal in St. Louis, and the Raiders got guaranteed sellouts in Oakland whether the fans came or not.

Of all the franchises, the one that should never have left was the Rams in LA. It's the second biggest TV market in the country, even if they have only ten people in the stands, but they walked away from that for twenty years for St. Louis? That was Carroll Rosenbloom's wife, Georgia, who did that. We'll get back to her later.

Now look how they go back to LA. By screwing St. Louis! They ended up screwing San Diego too. And what are they coming back to play in? Disney World in a stadium. That's the plan. It's not just a football team now. It's part of an exposition.

I'm not negative about that. It's just what it is. You've gone from an era where football was first and foremost with owners to where it's now about multiplexes and club seats and development rights around the stadium with the football team only part of the production. Today the team is like an anchor store. It's an important part of the mall but it's not the whole mall. Build a stadium, but make sure you have all these other things around in case your team isn't doing well. Pro football is becoming Disney World.

Things were different in 1950, when I first saw one of the greatest teams ever assembled. The NFL had fought the AAFC to a stalemate after four years of financial warfare, finally agreeing to merge and add three of their teams in 1950. The Cleveland Browns were the best of the lot, having won the AAFC championship all four years of its existence. They were also the best in the NFL, but no one in the league believed it.

I didn't either until I first laid eyes on them that summer. What I saw was a shock. It was a game and a team with which I was not familiar.

My father made a point of going out to the Browns' camp that summer, their first season in the NFL. Cleveland was not only the AAFC champion, it also had a four-year record of 52-4-3, including 5-0 in playoff games. The Browns were all but unbeatable, but many people dismissed them because they hadn't done it in the NFL.

The minute I got there, seeing that Browns team and how it played the game was like Moses parting the waters and coming out on the other side of the Red Sea. This was totally different from anything I'd ever seen before.

They had playbooks like textbooks. They had a lot of talented African American players who had been missing from the NFL. They had this force at fullback, Marion Motley. They had Otto Graham. They had great receivers like Dante Lavelli, Mac Speedie, and Dub Jones and a great line led by Bill Willis and Len Ford.

They had future Hall of Fame tackle and kicker Lou "The Toe" Groza, whom Brown considered Cleveland's greatest weapon. And they were organized. I had never seen a team more talented or more disciplined.

Even my father, who never went overboard with the press, told them we all had better watch out for the Browns. I came home to Philadelphia at the end of the summer and told my friends, "Those guys are going to kill the Eagles." They all laughed at me because the Eagles were the defending NFL champions and were opening the season against Cleveland. They laughed because they hadn't seen them.

When the teams met in the season opener, the Browns killed the Eagles, 35–10. They were a mystery until that game, but they dominated the NFL the same way they had the AAFC, going to ten straight championship games and winning seven between 1946 and 1955. Those Browns teams would have been great in any era.

So looking back, what is the big picture from 1946, when a nine-year-old kid went with his father to training camps, to a twenty-two-year-old young man headed to the Colts' camp in Western Maryland, to today? History is a circle.

That summer of 1960 is when I joined the circle for good. It's why I jumped into a two-tone Ford coupe and drove away from 323 Haverford Avenue in Narberth, headed for Western Maryland College the summer after my father's death.

I was off to make my own way in the NFL, I hoped, leaving everything I'd known behind. In some ways, I might as well have landed on the moon.

3

Welcome to the Colts

Considering that Carroll Rosenbloom was rumored to be a well-known gambler back in the days when you could be a well-known gambler and still own an NFL franchise, it is fitting that my ten years with the Baltimore Colts began with a bet—a winning one for me.

A few weeks before I left for Western Maryland College and my first training camp with the Colts in the summer of 1960, I'd gone to visit Carroll at his summer home on Pembroke Avenue in Margate, on the Jersey shore, to talk about a job. It was only a few blocks from the summer retreat my father maintained at 110 South Union Avenue and a few short strides from the ocean. Both houses faced the water, so the two of them knew when the tide was running in and running out. For the NFL, it was starting to rise, but seven years earlier, my father had to convince Carroll of that.

My father used to spend time over there talking with Carroll about politics, football, and finances, which didn't always go hand in hand in the early years of the NFL, although they did for Carroll from the moment my father convinced him to buy the Colts franchise out of debt in 1953.

The war years were over, and the game and American leisure time were growing. More important, so was television, although it wouldn't be until 1958 that Carroll's Colts would directly marry the NFL and television to the American public in the sudden-death overtime championship game against the New York Giants, which has been called "The Greatest Game Ever Played." That was the league's pivotal moment, December 28, 1958. I was there watching with my father, and Carroll was part of it. But things had already begun to change before World War II stalled the NFL's growth for a while.

On December 14, 1941, a week after the attack on Pearl Harbor, 43,425 fans gathered at Wrigley Field to watch the Bears play the Green Bay Packers in the playoffs. A week later only 13,341 showed up at Wrigley to watch the Bears and Giants in the NFL Championship Game in nearly zero temperature. The weather had something to do with deflating attendance, but the war would be as rough on the NFL as it was on the country in general.

The game's problems reflected the times, as they still do today. Today it's about the ravages of excess. Back then it was about the perils of shortages. Money was tight and men were missing. Rosters were depleted, with 638 NFL players in the military by 1945. My father had to merge the Eagles with Art Rooney's Steelers, forming the Steagles in 1943, to stay afloat. The following year Rooney would join forces with the Chicago Cardinals in a similar marriage of necessity.

The Brooklyn Dodgers football team went out of business, and the owners of the then Cleveland Rams, Dan Reeves and Fred Levy, suspended operation in 1943 because both were in the service and the team was rudderless and losing money. Reeves and Levy had purchased the Rams two years earlier for $135,000. It had only been in existence for six years and had never made a nickel.

The Cleveland Rams had fewer than a thousand season ticket holders at the time and no television revenue. It was the ultimate gamble to pull up stakes and head west, but it was in the American spirit too, and it would turn into a massive profit center when Reeves moved to Los Angeles in 1946. To do it, he had to first convince my father he had no choice because the Browns had won the league championship in 1945 with a one-point victory over the Washington Redskins, 15–14, and still lost $50,000. That was an argument a former team owner like my father could sadly relate to.

In 1945 the NFL was twenty-five years old. It had ten teams, but only four had shown a profit. More than forty franchises had folded since the league was originally formed in that car dealership in Canton, Ohio—twelve in one star-crossed season of unwise expansion. So who could blame Reeves for seeking to make a move?

Certainly not his fellow owners, who knew similar financial struggles themselves in most cities. They approved the move west on January 12, 1946, at the annual owners' meetings. On January 23, the LA Coliseum Commission approved the Rams' use of the 103,000-seat Coliseum, home of USC football. As part of the conditions, Reeves agreed to reintegrate pro football, which had silently but effectively banned black players since 1933 when the final two African Americans, Joe Lilliard and Ray Kemp, left the league.

Thus, in one move, the NFL had become the first to place a major league professional sports franchise on the West Coast and beaten Major League Baseball to integration, giving black athletes an opportunity a year before Jackie Robinson arrived in Brooklyn.

My father's decision to fight the owners who wanted to shutter the NFL during the war years to save money proved to be a wise one, because in 1944 the formation of the All-America Football Conference was announced with six franchises. My father had told them if they closed the league down, it might never open again. Baltimore was originally supposed to be an AAFC franchise, with former heavyweight champion Gene Tunney heading the operation, but he agreed to move the team to New York after the league's original New York franchise folded because owner Ray Ryan had oil business interests to deal with. Ray saw no reason to ignore them so he could lose money on pro football.

On September 6, 1946, the AAFC began operation as a rival of the NFL. The Cleveland franchise, named after their soon-to-be-legendary head coach, Paul Brown, took over Cleveland Stadium, former home of the Rams, and drew 60,135 fans to the league's inaugural game against the Miami Seahawks. The Seahawks, as things turned out, would soon become the Colts.

The Seahawks never drew at Miami's Burdine Stadium (later the Orange Bowl), their largest crowd being less than 10,000 and the smallest 2,250. The final straw came when the local sheriffs locked the Orange Bowl's gates because the Seahawks hadn't paid their bills. By then they'd had two games postponed due to hurricanes, which seemed like an omen of what was to come.

On December 20, 1946, the franchise was expelled from the AAFC for not paying its players or its bills, and the league took it over. The early history of the NFL was being repeated.

Yet a group led by Robert Ridgeway Rodenberg and Maury Nee, who had met in the army in Calcutta during World War II (when Rodenberg was an agent for the CIA's forerunner, the OSS), believed Baltimore was ripe for pro football. They bought the franchise for $50,000, and that sent Redskins owner George Preston Marshall into a fury.

Marshall's team had begun playing exhibition games at Municipal Stadium in Baltimore and was drawing healthy crowds. On February 9, 1946, he'd signed a six-year deal to play his Variety Club Charity game there, and on September 22, a week before the 1946 season was to begin, the Redskins played the Bears in Baltimore in front of 45,580 people, a stadium record at the time.

Now a year later, an AAFC franchise was in Baltimore and Marshall was envisioning a territorial loss. In the end he was right, but there wasn't much he could do about it, and for a time it looked like it wouldn't be a problem.

Rodenberg had recovered from a bout with malaria that struck him while he was in the service in Burma, and at thirty-eight he was flush with the high expectations of youth. He ran a contest to name Baltimore's new team, with the winner getting two season tickets, a $50 bond, a lamp, and an autographed football. He favored the name the Whirlaways, after the famous race horse that won the Triple Crown in 1941, believing it spoke to the history of Baltimore and the Preakness, which is the second leg of the Triple Crown. He was half right. The public rejected the "Whirlaways" but ran with the "Colts."

Three people submitted that name, and Charles Evans's entry won. He got his picture in the papers and a small place in Colts history. An office was established on Howard Street, and tickets costing $3.50, $2.75, and $1.50 went on sale. The ticket office was not stampeded.

The team lacked talent and ticket sales, but a love affair of sorts began that year with the writing of the Colts' Fight Song and the establishment of the Colts Marching Band. The band would remain in existence even after the team left in 1951 and 1952, and again years later after owner Robert Irsay sold out the city and moved the Colts under cover of snowy darkness to Indianapolis in 1984.

One problem with the AAFC was something my father had found a way to address in the NFL. The AAFC lacked parity, and that adversely affected attendance. My father worked the schedule to get the weaker teams playing each other early each season in an effort to make late-season games more meaningful. What the AAFC tried was more obvious. It asked the strong to give to the weak.

That's how future Hall of Fame quarterback Y. A. Tittle came to the Colts in 1948. Paul Brown knew the kind of talent Tittle had, but he also knew he had Otto Graham, so there was little chance Tittle would play. AAFC commissioner Jonas Ingram convinced Brown and the owners of the New York Yankees to allow some players to be moved to the lowly Colts. Try that today and see what happens, but it was 1948. No players union was there to fight it, no collective bargaining agreement to prevent it. Just a sense that the league needed help and something had to be done.

That April, Tittle and several others were notified by letter from Ingram that they were going to Baltimore, where Tittle became Rookie of the Year and led the Colts to a tie for the Eastern Division championship. The AAFC's parity plan was successful but in an odd way.

The Western Division was a close race between the Browns and the San Francisco 49ers. On November 14, they were both undefeated when they squared off at Cleveland Stadium in front of 82,769 fans. The Browns won, 14–7. Two weeks later they faced each other again in San Francisco's Kezar Stadium in front of 59,785 fans, and Cleveland won another close game, 31–28, to win the Western Division. The 49ers would finish the year 12-2 but miss the playoffs, because there was only the championship game in those days. Some nineteen years later I'd be running the Colts' personnel department and see the same thing happen to us in a 1967 season where we went 11-1-2.

Back east, it was a different story but a surprising one in Baltimore. With Tittle at quarterback, the Colts and the Buffalo Bills finished tied at 7-7. The Colts lost a playoff game to the Bills a week after ending their regular season by beating them, thus avoiding the embarrassment of what happened to Buffalo. Cleveland shelled them, 49–7, to finish the year 15-0.

But the playoff game between the Bills and Colts nearly never came off. The Colts had lost $549,500 in two years, and the ownership group had restructured. Rodenberg was out, and although attendance was up 30 percent, things did not improve financially even with Tittle's arrival. The Colts drew 224,502 fans, but with player costs driven up due to the war with the NFL, the team still lost $47,036.36.

When the extra game was announced to decide who would represent the East, the Colts players understood one thing. Their contracts didn't call for them to be paid for a game that hadn't existed when they first signed. They refused to play if not given a cut of the gate. Baltimore's owners said they would forfeit first and the players ultimately voted to play, but dissension split them. They lost, 28–17, in front of 27,327 fans, several of whom got onto the field and threatened the officials. A year later that same team would win only one game, and although the team would average over 23,000 fans in six home games, it lost nearly $100,000. The end was in sight for the Colts.

While the NFL was creating parity and teams like the Eagles, the Rams, and the Chicago Cardinals were rising up to challenge the dominant teams of the 1940s—the Bears, Redskins, Packers, and Giants—the AAFC was struggling with two teams dominating their league. Yet both leagues were hurting financially, in part because the talent war was driving up player salaries, just as it would in the 1960s when the NFL and AFL did battle for nearly a decade. The result in each case was a merger.

My father thought he had that done after the 1948 season because nearly every team in both leagues was now losing money. Peace talks began but fell through when the AAFC insisted on four teams merging with the NFL, while the NFL only wanted to add the Browns and 49ers. The AAFC walked away from the table until December 9, 1949, when a merger was finally agreed to that allowed three teams—the 49ers, Browns, and Colts—into the NFL.

Some felt Buffalo should have been added instead of the Colts because it had stronger ownership and better attendance, but the size of the city (only Green Bay was smaller among NFL franchises) and the fierce climate doomed the Bills. George Preston Marshall was not initially happy to see a team returning to Baltimore, but his concerns were assuaged by a $150,000 fee paid him to waive his territorial rights to Baltimore. The Colts were in. Just not for long.

With an uneven number of teams now in the NFL at thirteen, Baltimore became the "swing team," playing every team in the league once instead of home-and-home rivalries. They played twelve league games and seven exhibitions, including at one point three games in six days, which was more often than fans wanted to see them in a week.

Their lone win came on November 5, 1950, in Baltimore over the Packers, 41–21. Attendance tumbled to 94,992, and the new principal owner, Abraham "Shorty" Watner, was not willing to absorb the kind of financial losses that followed.

Watner was someone who had a unique understanding about financial losses in Baltimore. Six years earlier, he'd been talking to Marshall on the phone in his office when a strong breeze blew through his windows and sent $10,000 in cash streaming into the air and out on to Baltimore Street. Only $200 was returned. It was a better return than he was now getting from the Colts.

Within a year after Tittle's arrival, the Colts folded after having gone 1-11 in their final AAFC season in 1949 and 1-11 again in their inaugural year in the NFL. Less than a month after that season ended, Watner sold out the Colts for $50,000, returning the franchise to the league. But Baltimore was a relentless city with an inferiority complex. Because of that, the people didn't take no for an answer.

Due to William Macmillan's strong legal argument that the franchise had been illegally dissolved because Watner didn't have the consent of the full ownership group to make such a deal, my father chose to avoid a battle he believed the league could not win. He first tried to convince the New York Yanks franchise to come to Baltimore, but they found a better deal and sold to interests in Dallas, forming what would become another failed franchise, so Macmillan filed suit.

Finally, on December 3, 1952, with a legal battle looming, my father told the Advertising Club of Baltimore at a luncheon that he would return the team to Baltimore and find them a local owner if they could sell 15,000 season tickets in six weeks. The cost was $25.00 for a box seat and $19.80 for the grandstands. That's for the season, not for a game. A lot of people ended up with Colts season tickets for Christmas, and the deal was completed in four weeks. A month later, Carroll agreed to buy in.

Although Rosenbloom received what was left of the Texans—including a future Hall of Fame defensive lineman named Art Donovan, who became and remained a beloved Baltimore legend until the day he died—the Colts are considered in NFL history as a 1953 expansion team. Whatever they were then, by the time I was sitting in Carroll's house by the beach in 1960, they were two-time defending NFL champions and the best organization in pro football.

When I arrived to speak with him, Carroll was playing a dice game with a man he called "Colonel Gottlieb." I have no idea if he was a colonel or a Gottlieb, but Carroll kept taking his money playing Shut the Box. It's an old English pub game in which there are nine numbered tiles on hinges so they can be flipped up or down. You roll two dice, add the dots, and using the total in any workable combination equal to your total, you can shut down a box. For example, if you roll a 2 and a 7, you can shut down those two boxes or any other combination of them equal to 9. You roll until you can't shut down any more numbers and then add up the total of the numbers that remain "open." Then the next player does the same. The lowest score wins unless someone "shuts the box," meaning he gets all the numbers closed.

I was mystified at what was going on. Dice were rolling, money was changing hands, and Carroll was talking through the whole thing. I was just there to watch and get a job.

The money was flying mostly in Carroll's direction, as it usually seemed to, I would learn later. At the same time we were watching the Democratic National Convention, which had begun that July week in Los Angeles. Carroll was a friend of Joseph Kennedy, the father of the soon-to-be-nominated Jack Kennedy, for whom he was also a confidant, so while they played he was giving us an insider's perspective on presidential politics.

There's Carroll, rolling dice, dissecting a presidential race, giving Colonel Gottlieb the needle, and talking to me about a job for the summer. At first he wanted to send me to the Atlantic City Race Track, which was owned by his friends John B. Kelly (Grace's dad) and Sonny Fraser, a New Jersey politician who also owned the Atlantic City Country Club. Carroll kept saying I could make a lot of money over there parking cars. Meanwhile, he's telling us how the Kennedys cut the deal with Lyndon Johnson to run as vice president even though JFK's brother Bobby hated the idea. I remember him saying, "Jack will be president, but Bobby's the tough one. And the young one, Teddy, he's the best politician in the family."

Today you'd say he was multitasking. He's telling me inside information about what happened at the convention, talking about a job, and getting on Gottlieb, and all of a sudden he says, "I don't think so. Forget the race track. Go down to training camp." That's how I got into pro football, with the owner of the Baltimore Colts playing Shut the Box for cash.

I was there for a couple of hours before he said it. Then he swept up the cash, counted out $400, and said he'd split it with me. I was embarrassed to take it. I'd gotten what I was after. I was in pro football, but that was Carroll. If he liked you, he took care of you, so I left with $200 in my pocket and a summer job that he told me would become full-time after I finished up at LaSalle that winter.

A few weeks later, I headed off to training camp, and all I knew was that I was supposed to find Fred Schubach, who was the equipment manager. I'd never met him, but I knew his father because he was the Eagles' equipment manager for years. I remembered his dad best for pulling up to our new house in Narberth in a green truck that said "EAGLES" on the side, the truck full of our furniture. That's how we moved from our home on Montgomery Avenue to Haverford Avenue in Narberth: the Eagles moved us in.

Other than finding Fred, I had no idea what my duties were. I didn't care. I was being paid to work for the best organization in football. What I did didn't matter. I was in the game.

When I finally arrived, I couldn't believe how small the campus was. There was nothing out there in those days but the college. If you missed breakfast at the dining hall, it was lunchtime before you could find a restaurant.

I asked someone where the locker room was. When I found Fred there, he already knew I was coming. Carroll had called and explained everything to Don Kellett, the Colts' general manager.

I had more trepidation about leaving home than going to work. I looked at this as a stepping-stone. I didn't feel intimidated. It was a whole new world, but I was in a locker room, a place where I was always comfortable.

The Colts had just finished practice when I walked in. The first player I saw was Big Daddy Lipscomb, their star defensive tackle. He was a bigger-than-life character, and he was loud and telling jokes. Art Donovan walked over and put his arm around me and said, "Welcome to the Baltimore Colts."

It's ironic that the first place I went to was the locker room. I probably should have said, "Where's the office?" Instead I asked, "Where's the locker room?" That seemed natural to me. Sometimes I felt like I grew up in a locker room.

Raymond Berry, the great receiver who ended up in the Hall of Fame, was leaning over a sink, and it looked as though he was washing his practice pants. I'd heard that he did that but I never believed it was true until I saw it myself. He was obsessed with every detail of the game, including his uniform. It's what made him a Hall of Famer. That and the player throwing to him—Johnny Unitas.

Raymond came over and introduced himself too. Can you imagine that happening today? I was just some kid and he'd been All-Pro on two straight NFL champions, and he just came over as though he'd been waiting all day to see me. That's why Baltimore fell in love with the Colts. The players were their extended family. They were like home cooking.

Just watching these players interacting in their locker room after the first practice, I quickly got a feeling about them you don't always find. You got the feeling this was a team that was sure of itself. They weren't just winners; they liked each other.

I expected a very serious atmosphere. Not those guys—they were having fun. Maybe it was the confidence of having won two championships, but as I would learn later, it wasn't a feeling you found often or created easily. If you did, you had something. You had a bond that helped get you through the tough games and the down moments.

Fred told me where to get a key for my dorm room, so I went to the PR office and then to my room, which was a single on the third floor, the same floor as the players. The building had a slate roof that trapped in the heat. My room was like a steam bath, but so was everyone else's. No AC. Just fans and summer heat rising. I thought it was great.

Up in the dorm two of their top draft choices were living next to me. They were teammates from Auburn. One was Jackie Burkett, a linebacker the Colts took as a future pick in the first round who had a bad shoulder from college and missed the whole season but who ended up playing ten years in the league. The other was Zeke Smith, an offensive lineman who everyone thought was going to be great but who never made it. They were one of my first lessons about a scout's life.

Burkett looked like physically he might not last, but he did. Smith won the Outland Trophy and came in with a big reputation but only lasted two years. For all the time and effort I would later put into scouting and player evaluation, much of the time you are never totally sure. Some people try to make it sound like scouting is a science with weights and measures and testing, which are all good tools to have, but that doesn't make it science. It's a feeling. Sometimes you're right, like with Burkett. Sometimes you're not, like with Smith. If you want to stay around, you'd better be right more than you're wrong, especially if you're working for Don Shula as I would end up doing.

We were the same age and got along great—two rookies I could kind of talk to because I was a rookie too. We were all just hoping to make it in pro football.

My duties that summer were the best ones I ever had. I was in charge of getting room keys to the players on the road and giving out the meal money, which was very important to them in those days. A lot of them lived off it. The Colts fed them and they pocketed the money, so they loved to see me coming.

I'd check in every day with PR first to see if they had anything for me to do. Then I'd do the same with Weeb Ewbank and his coaches. The staff wasn't like it is today. Weeb only had four assistants, not four for each position. But it was a good staff.

Charley Winner (who was Weeb's son-in-law), Don McCafferty, and John Sandusky all later became NFL head coaches, and Herman Ball had been the Redskins' head coach in 1949, 1950, and part of the 1951 season. They all served Weeb well. You don't win as consistently as the Colts were doing without a sound coaching staff.

Weeb didn't have the typical demeanor of a head coach. He wasn't imperious or particularly threatening. He was short and stocky and always hunched his shoulders. He wore the baggy knickers-style football pants and looked like a little professor, which when it came to football he was.

I'd come to appreciate him more and more when I was around him. He was probably the perfect coach to handle Unitas. He believed in preparing his team, but then on game day the quarterback ran the show. That was Unitas's way of looking at it too.

Weeb was a detail man. I could see that the first summer in

the way he prepared the team. I learned that one reason the Colts wore white helmets with the horseshoe logo was that Weeb found their original blue helmets didn't lend themselves to sharp visibility on film, so he changed them to white. Like all great coaches, he took care of the little things because if you did, your team was always ready.

He also was a nice man. If he had a weakness as a coach, that was it. When the end came for him in Baltimore three years later, I know Gino Marchetti, the Hall of Fame defensive end and alpha male of our defense, felt it happened because Weeb was too nice a guy, and some players had started to take advantage of that.

I can't say every coach I was around was a nice guy, but I can say it about Weeb. He'd see me and say, "Uppie, how you doing?" I'm not sure he had any idea what I was doing, but he couldn't have been nicer to me. He hardly ever raised his voice, but when he talked to the players he was all business, and it worked for quite a while.

He also was a little slyer than he appeared to be. When he was first offered the Colts job, he was coaching for Paul Brown in Cleveland. Brown didn't want him to leave. I guess he thought it was disloyal somehow. Whatever his reason, Brown wouldn't allow him to leave unless he agreed to have no input into the draft. So he did it on the sly. He had a courier bringing notes to Keith Molesworth, who was the personnel director that I'd go to work for in a few years. It was never wise to underestimate Weeb Ewbank if you were competing against him, as we found out in Super Bowl III eight years later when he was coaching the Jets.

John Sandusky was loud and boisterous, a typical line coach. You could hear him from one end of the field to the other. He coached defense then with Charley Winner; then when Shula came in, Sandusky took over the offensive line. Charley was more like Weeb. Scholarly.

Don McCafferty would be considered the offensive coordinator today, although they didn't have those titles then. They were all just assistant coaches. When he took over as head coach in 1970, they started to call him "Easy Rider." That's how affable he was.

When I think of that first staff of five coaches, I really wonder about the ones they have today. Do you really need twenty coaches? I don't think so. Rosters were smaller, sure, but there were still only eleven positions on offense and eleven on defense. That hasn't changed. It was thirty-eight players then with five coaches. Now you have nearly as many coaches as you have positions, with two for the same position in some cases.

I agree you need more than four assistants because of the technology, but nearly as many coaches as you have positions? I don't see why you would, but all the way through until the World Football League team I owned in Charlotte went down fifteen years later, coaches were the same. The only word they know is "more."

Get me more players! Give me more coaches! Find me more technology! More, more, more. It's human nature. Every coach wants more people, but just because you have a huge amount of people doesn't mean you're any better. Sometimes it can make things too complicated.

Certainly technology and a lot they do today require more support staff, young coaches, whatever you want to call it—quality-control monitors and such. I'm not sure I believe it was better in the past, but I'm sure they have more coaches than they need now. Weeb certainly didn't seem to think he needed a dozen coaches, and that Colts team was as well coached and prepared as any I was around, so it's not the number of coaches that decides it. It's how well they can coach.

Would they play any less efficiently today if they lost five or six coaches? I doubt it. They're middle management. You lay it on and on and after a while there isn't much for them to do but get in the way of the people who are actually doing something. I always asked myself when I became a GM, is it the numbers I draft or the people I draft? If I get four quality people, isn't that more important than saying I got twelve bodies?

If I was running a team today, I would probably bring the head coach in and ask if we really need all these people or if they are getting in each other's way. What I saw as teams grew wasn't necessarily all positive, but what I saw that first summer in Western Maryland was.

The best part for me was that I went to every practice and became one of the guys who'd throw the ball to Raymond Berry. I thought it very odd at first because with all the teams I'd ever been around, everyone practiced together. At the Colts, Raymond ran his own private practice under a big tree for the first half hour or so.

The field was roped off and Raymond would be over by a tree with several ball boys throwing uncatchable balls to him. I became one of those kids—throwing balls at all angles so he could practice making diving catches and off-balance catches. Weeb never bothered him. Just left him alone.

Raymond never wanted you to throw him a good ball. He was wearing people's arms out, so they asked me to try it for a half hour or so. I started doing it every day. It was amazing to me that I was getting paid for this.

Raymond would strap a harness to the tree and run away from it. It was like what you see players doing today running with a parachute drag behind them. It's science now, but back then people thought he was nuts. Raymond really was ahead of his time.

He used to walk around squeezing silly putty to make his finger stronger. I think he finally patented it. I didn't think any of it was weird. I'd read as much as I could about the Colts before I got there, so I knew Raymond did some unusual things. I knew he had some strange habits like taking a scale on the road to check his weight, or when we'd go to the West Coast he'd start waking up on West Coast time days in advance so his body would be adjusted. They made him what he became, which was one of the game's greatest and most reliable receivers. He seldom dropped a ball he got his hands on because of the way he practiced.

Nearly every day after practice he'd be out there with Unitas, working on the precision of their routes. He used to say he'd developed eighty-eight moves to get by a defender, and by the end of that summer I didn't doubt it. He used to practice recovering his own fumbles, and he only fumbled twice in his career.

It's how they dissected the Giants in that '58 championship game. They knew each other so well because they put in that time after everyone else was gone. That was a lesson I learned that first summer with the Colts. The great players are usually the ones who work the hardest. There's a connection to their success and their desire.

Later, that was one thing I looked for as a scout. I wanted to see players in practice, not just games—to see what they did when they thought no one was looking. Did they take plays off or were they like Berry and Unitas?

At twenty-two, twenty-three, I was used to seeing strange things. Not quite as strange as watching Raymond practicing fumbling and then recovering his own fumbles, but I'd seen a lot with all the teams and camps I'd been exposed to. I was used to being around football players and coaches, so I wasn't awed by it too much. I just thought, "This is great. I'm throwing to Raymond Berry." Did I want to study game film with Weeb Ewbank or philosophy at LaSalle? The only degree I wanted was a degree in football.

Unitas was the one player everyone respected. He was the face of football. Everyone understood how great a quarterback he was. He knew everything that was going on, whether it was a play or a new kid showing up.

The first time he spoke to me, he just said, "You're Bell's kid. You'll enjoy this, Uppie." It was his way of welcoming me but at the same time letting me know he noticed everything.

They were such an interesting group of people. You're talking about a group that had won the championship two years in a row, but many of them were still working second jobs setting pins in bowling alleys, selling liquor, working as ironworkers at Sparrows Point. At one point there were twelve Colts working for Bethlehem Steel, and they weren't all in the management trainee program. Unitas was one of them. He worked with an acetylene torch. That isn't management.

At one point Jim Parker, who was as great an offensive lineman as the game ever saw, sold embalming fluid and cemetery plots for extra money. Later Art Donovan helped him get a liquor distributorship, and he opened a liquor store on Liberty Heights Avenue in northwest Baltimore. In a sense, he was still selling embalming fluid.

One of the most interesting players I encountered that summer was Alan Ameche. He'd been a No. 1 pick in 1955 after winning the Heisman Trophy at Wisconsin. The first time they handed him the ball he went 79 yards for a touchdown against the Chicago Bears. They didn't call him "The Horse" for nothing.

He led the league in rushing his rookie season, and by the time I arrived in 1960 he'd been named to four Pro Bowls in five years. But he was more than a runner. He was a Renaissance man. I only had to be at camp a couple days to learn that.

I was walking back to the dorm after completing my duties one night, and I heard opera music coming out of one of the rooms. It wasn't what you expected to hear in an NFL training camp but there it was, coming out of Alan's room. Later, after he and Gino Marchetti had built a chain of very successful restaurants they sold off for a big profit, he became a sponsor of the Philadelphia symphony orchestra. He was an interesting guy on a team of interesting guys, each in their own way.

I learned more than opera that year from Alan. I also learned pro football could be a cruel sport. That season he tore his Achilles and never played again. Every player lived in fear of that moment when his body would tear or snap and nothing would be the same. I knew about injuries, but Baltimore is where I learned what living with that kind of uncertainty really meant to a player as well as a team.

They were all different, but they fit together perfectly somehow. You could see that. You had Alan listening to the opera and Lenny Moore knowing more about jazz than you thought possible. You had Art Donovan from the Bronx, who had been a Marine in the South Pacific during World War II, next to Gino Marchetti, who at eighteen had lugged a machine gun around along the Siegfried Line in the Battle of the Bulge and then came home to become one of the greatest defensive ends in football history. And you had Big Daddy, who was orphaned after his mother was stabbed to death at a bus stop and by high school was working at a steel mill from midnight to seven and then going to school in the morning. All different, but they worked together so well.

Many of them, including Unitas, had been rejected by other NFL teams before they came to play for Weeb and together became champions, so they knew both sides of football. One of our linebackers, Bill Pellington, had been cut by the Browns and hitchhiked from Ramsey, New Jersey, to Western Maryland for a tryout in 1953. Hitchhiked! These were the kind of men I was exposed to that summer, and the greatest of them was Unitas, which we all knew.

Maybe the most important thing I learned was something I remembered all the years I was drafting players and building teams: I learned not to underestimate the players. They don't miss a thing.

If Freddie Schubach asked me to pick up towels and jocks, I would have done it, because if I acted like a spoiled kid, I knew how quickly that would have swept through the locker room. It was all part of the football life. It's jocks and socks and towels and showers. It's still that way. Even with all the technological changes, somebody has to pick up the laundry.

Reporting to Fred Schubach, what I saw was that he knew more than the GM and coach about what was going on in the locker room, and if you don't know what's going on there you won't be around long. I later hired Fred right out of the locker room to work in personnel for me with the Colts. These were the kinds of things I was absorbing that would serve me well years later running personnel departments at the Colts and Patriots.

I went to the exhibition games because it was part of my job. The first was the College All-Star Game in Chicago on August 12, which we won 32–7 in front of seventy thousand fans. That's when I took my first big trip on a DC-3. I found from that day to the very last trip I made with a team that the most interesting time for me was postgame on the plane coming home, win or lose.

You learned who's superstitious. Who's nervous? Who understood the game and who didn't? I learned a lot on those planes.

I looked upon the trips as a time to get to know your players and your team. You got a feel for who was disappointed after a loss or who cared more about how they played themselves.

I saw Carroll at the walk-through at Soldier Field the night before the game. He showed up with a couple of knockout women. I looked at him and started thinking this wasn't Rooney or Wellington Mara's NFL anymore. This was a colorful, interesting man surrounded by celebrities and beautiful women. There was nobody like Rosenbloom then. He was so smooth. The world was changing from black and white to color, and so was the world of pro football.

We also played in Dallas and Charleston, South Carolina, places where our black players couldn't stay with the rest of the team. Many years later John Steadman, who was the premier sports columnist in Baltimore for fifty years and for a few seasons the Colts' PR director, wrote about Alan Ameche's recollections of those exhibition games in the segregated South. He told Steadman, "We should have refused to play." It's easy to see that now, but in 1960 we lived in a different society—a segregated one that was about to change radically, although we didn't see it coming that summer.

We played six exhibition games and none were at home, because the people in Baltimore wouldn't buy those tickets. That became a problem years later and led to Carroll trading the Colts with Irsay for the Rams in 1972. That allowed him to move to Los Angeles and beat the capital gains taxes. He shut the box on the federal government with that move, but he left poor Baltimore to deal with Irsay, which would be a disaster.

It has been written many times that I picked up towels for $65 a week that summer, which made for a great story: the towel boy who became an NFL general manager. But it wasn't true. Never happened. Not that I wouldn't have done it if they had asked. I would have been glad to do it. It didn't make any difference to me what I did. What I was trying to do was absorb everything. That's why I tried to go into the locker room every day whether I had something to do in there or not. That's the place to learn about players.

Nothing was beneath me. Why would it be? I saw my father

doing it the same way, whether he was commissioner or the Eagles' owner. I was up in the press box with my brother, Bert, at the 1948 championship game in Philadelphia at Shibe Park, which was played in blizzard conditions. It snowed all day and the temperature was twenty-seven degrees. The owners wanted to postpone the game for fear there'd be no crowd, but it was the first televised NFL Championship Game, being broadcast by ABC only in the Northeast. Harry Wismer, who would later own the AFL's New York Titans franchise, was set to do the broadcast, and my father feared if the game didn't go off as scheduled, the league might never get back on TV, which he felt was going to be the key to growing the league's audience.

The grounds crew couldn't get the tarp up because it was frozen solid to the ground. Players from both teams came out in their helmets and foul-weather capes to help. They were all pushing it off the field when someone shouted, "Hey, isn't that Bert Bell?" I looked, and there's my father in a suit and a winter coat and hat, pushing the tarp with everyone else. No job was too small for him and certainly was not for his son.

At the end of the summer it was time to return to LaSalle, but I really never left Baltimore. Physically I went back to college, but it was all a blank. The only good thing about the rest of that year was that the Eagles were making a run for the championship for the first time in a decade, with Norm Van Brocklin at quarterback and Chuck Bednarik playing both ways at center and middle linebacker. Bednarik didn't miss a minute of the 1960 championship game win over Vince Lombardi's Packers. He was the last one to play both ways. They called him "Concrete Charlie" because he also worked part time for a concrete company. The irony was my father helped shape the trade that brought Van Brocklin to Philadelphia, which turned into the last championship the Eagles ever won.

After my father died, Jim Clark decided to keep the team for the time being, but it could have been my father's team and we would have won that championship. That would have been something.

As happy as I was for the Eagles, I wasn't connected to them anymore. I was a Colt in my mind. I went down to Baltimore a couple times that season to watch them play. I thought they were going to win a third straight championship, but that was the beginning of another part of my football education. Building a great team and maintaining it are two different things.

In 1959, when the Colts beat the Giants again for their second straight NFL title, they had eight All-Pros and nine Pro Bowlers, but a year later they had eight starters who were thirty or older. They were starting to unravel.

On November 13, 1960, they were 5-2 and in a fight with the Packers, who had yet to win a championship, for the Western Division title when they ran headlong into the Chicago Bears. It was a vicious confrontation. If it happened today they would have suspended so many players, neither could have fielded a team the following week. It was a more violent game in those days. After it was over, a lot of the players said it was the most brutal game they'd ever been involved in, and the proof was on their faces, most of all on Unitas's.

Unitas was driving the Colts toward the winning touchdown late in the game as he so often had when future Hall of Famers Doug Atkins and Bill George slammed him to the ground at Wrigley Field just after a 13-yard completion to Berry. Atkins's shoulder and forearm hit Unitas in the head, cutting his forehead, nose, and mouth. He required medical attention to staunch the bleeding, which was so profuse it took five minutes to get him repaired. At one point, referee Tommy Bell leaned in and said, "Take as much time as you need, John."

Unitas, in typical fashion, suggested Bell mind his business and just blow the whistle. He did, and after Unitas was sacked again for a 10-yard loss, he dropped back on 4th and 14 and lofted a 39-yard touchdown pass to Lenny Moore with seventeen seconds left to win the game.

When it was over, Unitas said of Atkins's hit, "He got me with his shoulder and forearm but I have no complaints. It was a clean hit."

In today's game, it would be felonious assault, which would cost

Atkins big money and the Bears serious penalty yardage. Again, different worlds back then, both inside the stadiums and outside.

That win maintained the Colts' half-game lead over the Packers and improved their record to 6-2, but they didn't win another game. No one fully realized it, but the era of those Colts was ending and soon a new one would begin, with Don Shula replacing Weeb and a twenty-eight-year-old man named Upton Bell finding the talent for his team.

My brother was still with the NFL office in New York working for Pete Rozelle, who had replaced my father on the twenty-third ballot in January as a compromise candidate who turned into a great commissioner. He got me tickets for the Eagles-Giants game that year in New York when Bednarik laid out Frank Gifford in what became an iconic picture of Bednarik dancing with one foot in the air and a doubled-up fist as Gifford was laid out cold in front of him. *Bam!* No flag. That was the NFL in those days.

I went to class occasionally, but I tried not to make it a habit. I was majoring in marketing, but I could have majored in underwater basket weaving. I'm not proud to say that nor would I recommend to anybody that you shouldn't finish college, but I knew what my life's work was going to be, and it was waiting for me in Baltimore.

When I made my decision to go to LaSalle, it was to play basketball. My whole mind was on basketball then. I loved basketball. In some cases I liked it more than football. Football was my life, but basketball was my game.

I went to the Palestra three nights a week. It was like going to a Broadway play every weekend. The greatest players came there from all over the country. Wilt Chamberlain, who was an All-American at Kansas, came from Overbrook High in Philadelphia. Then they had Wayne Hightower, Wally Jones, Ralph Haywood, Walt Hazzard. They all were stars there and went on to college. The three H's: Hightower, Haywood, and Hazzard, all at Overbrook. My God. There were so many players in Philadelphia in those days.

I played with Paul Westhead at Malvern Prep, and with George Raveling in summer leagues around Philadelphia. Paul went on to coach the Lakers, and George was PAC-10 coach of the year three times at Washington State and USC. The funny thing for me is there was talk I'd be offered a scholarship to LaSalle, but my father wouldn't take it. He said we didn't need it and someone else who did wouldn't get one if we took it. That was my father. Don't take what you don't need.

Had my father lived, I would have stayed in Philadelphia because that would have been easy. But I fell in love with the Colts and with the city of Baltimore. The minute the whistle blew at that first training camp, leaving home didn't bother me a bit. I was in love. But I wasn't going back in 1961 until after the summer basketball league ended.

The summer before, Raveling and I played together on a team that won the summer championship at the Narberth League, which was a pretty fast league around Philadelphia. It turned out that was where some of the fixers in the 1960s met the kids they were bribing in what would become a big scandal, but we didn't know a thing about it.

We made it to the finals and lost, and that was my last game playing in any type of college atmosphere. I'd told Carroll I would come down late that summer and I did. By that time, my brother, Bert, was working in the Colts' business office because he'd surmised that Rozelle wanted his own people in New York.

Bert wanted to go with a club anyway, so the timing was right. The league office was the league office. What influence was he going to have? Pete was bringing in his own people. Here was an opportunity to go with a club and be part of running one.

As we saw it, the power was no longer going to be totally in the commissioner's hands. The power was in Bert Bell's hands because of the circumstances and what he brought to the game, but Pete was a compromise candidate. Carroll was the one who suggested him. Pete was great for the NFL, but no matter how important he grew, he'd always be remembered as a compromise candidate, which meant the owners were going to have more and more say in running the league. I could see that coming just from listening to Carroll. Things were changing. My father's day was fading. It was a new league and a growing game, and I was headed back to Baltimore in 1961 to be part of it for good.

4

The Great Ticket Heist Was
My Kickoff in Baltimore

There has never been a relationship between a town and a team quite like the one between Baltimore and the Colts. I didn't know that until I got there in the late summer of 1961, but it didn't take long to understand the difference.

There are certainly cities that love their teams, especially when they're winning, but there's a difference between a city and a town, and the latter is what Baltimore was when the Colts were in their glory days.

Not only was it a town that was nothing like Philadelphia, it was a town with an inferiority complex . . . which made it even less like Philadelphia. Trapped along the Northeast corridor between Boston, New York, Philadelphia, and Washington DC, Baltimore was like a little brother always looking for attention but seldom receiving it until the Colts began to dominate pro football.

Until Johnny Unitas arrived, its football history was one of constant failure at the box office and on the field, and the significance of the Baltimore Orioles in baseball was no better. Baltimore's most famous resident lay at the bottom of an unmarked plot in Green Mount Cemetery. When the major reason to visit is to find the final resting place of John Wilkes Booth, the man who assassinated Abraham Lincoln, the residents tend to have some doubts about themselves.

Over my years in Baltimore I got to know well the leading sports columnist in town, a former Colts PR man named John Steadman. Steadman was the most influential voice in the media, although in those days it was called the press. He wrote a column six days a week for thirty years, first at the *News-Post* and then the *News-American*, which were the biggest newspapers in town for decades, back when people trudged home at night after a long day of hard labor at Bethlehem Steel or the Domino Sugar refinery near the Inner Harbor and picked up the evening paper. Late in his career, long after he'd engaged in a vicious battle with Rosenbloom over the owner's insistence that season ticket holders be forced to buy exhibition game tickets they had no interest in, John jumped over to the *Sun*, a morning paper that eventually became the lone newspaper survivor in town. Nobody loved the Colts more than Steadman, who went so far as to sit alone in the stands at an empty Memorial Stadium in 1984 after Robert Irsay, the owner of the Colts, had abandoned Baltimore for Indianapolis. It was the Sunday they would have played their first game that season.

John even chose to attend a Colts game rather than cover the Orioles in the 1970 World Series. Other writers were asking him what he was doing there, but he refused to miss a Colts game. That's the kind of feeling the whole town had when I arrived.

There are many ways to illustrate this, but here's one: In 1958 they played the Major League All-Star Game in Baltimore back when that was one of the biggest games of the year, because whatever league your city played in, the other league was a mystery you read about but seldom saw except for that game and the World Series. There were 48,829 fans who attended that game. Four weeks later, the Colts held an intrasquad game at Memorial Stadium to kick off summer training camp and drew 48,309—to a game without an opponent. That was Baltimore and the Colts.

Steadman described the town this way in his book *From Colts to Ravens*: "The citizens had a feeling of self-doubt. It was an inferiority complex of metropolitan proportions The condition dated back to the first half of this [the twentieth] century, a period when conservative Baltimore, rarely making a splash, was considered nothing more than a whistle stop. . . . [So] the town took its team's fate personally."

To say you loved Baltimore was, to borrow a line from its great philosopher H. L. Mencken, to "wink at a homely girl." A nice gesture, but you didn't really mean it. To say you loved the Colts, however, was a different story.

I compare it to catching a disease. Once you get it, you can't get inoculated to be rid of it. It's in your blood. I see it as the last great love affair between a town and a team before pro football took off and captured the whole country's imagination. Baseball was still king in most cities across America in 1961. The churches, not the NFL Network, still owned Sunday then. But in Baltimore pro football ruled. It was a vision of what was about to happen all across America. It took another decade or two, even longer in a place like New England, which was Red Sox country, but Baltimore was where it started. In that town the Orioles were second-class citizens, even when they began going to the World Series in the mid-1960s.

Now it's true everywhere in America, even during the off-season. The draft has become a four-day made-for-TV event, and fans watch the combine workouts as if they're scouts. They won't even run a presidential debate against *Monday Night Football*. But back in 1961, what they had in Baltimore was unique. Pittsburgh got that way in the 1970s once the Steelers started winning, but when the Colts came back to Baltimore in 1953, it was love at first sight.

Like all urban areas, Baltimore was a great melting pot, but its neighborhoods were clearly demarcated by ethnic clans, racial borders, and the proximity to the closest steel mill, dock, or industrial plant. It was a city of smokestacks, grime, and walking to work.

When I first arrived, I remember thinking, "This is a pretty dirty downtown." That's because it was an industrial town. There was a harbor then but no Inner Harbor like they have today, filled with shops and restaurants. It was a working harbor and a dingy one.

If the wind was right, the whole town smelled like cinnamon from the Domino Sugar refinery over on East Key Highway right off the harbor. It was odd but pleasant. If the wind shifted, it didn't smell like cinnamon; it smelled like a factory town.

The first time I brought my girlfriend down from Philadelphia, I met her at the train station and we walked over to the Sheraton Belvedere Hotel, which was the best hotel in town. It was where I stayed the night before the 1959 NFL Championship Game, the rematch with the Giants that established the Colts as the best team in pro football. My father had died and Rosenbloom invited my brother and me to the game. The Belvedere was the first building I ever saw in Baltimore.

I wanted her to fall in love with the city the way I had, but she looked at me and said, "You're kidding!" So much for love. I was trying to paint this beautiful picture, but there was no way to paint a beautiful picture of downtown "Bawlamer" then. I mean, the entertainment district was called The Block. It was full of porn shops and strip joints, a place where the biggest star in town other than Unitas ruled. That was Blaze Starr, a burlesque dancer who began working at the 2 O'Clock Lounge on East Baltimore Street in 1950 and eventually came to own it. She also became one of the city's most famous residents. Blaze was demure and self-effacing, at least by the standards of her profession, so she became beloved like Unitas, who had the same qualities but kept his clothes on when he worked. She ended up doing ads for the Baltimore Gas & Electric Company! That was Baltimore in the 1960s.

At one point the Bethlehem Steel plant at Sparrows Point was the largest in the country, employing over thirty thousand people during the war and well after it. Western Electric, Allied Chemical, Proctor & Gamble, and the GM plant known as Baltimore Assembly when it opened in 1935 all offered the kind of unionized industrial jobs that made buying Colts tickets a possibility for a lot of blue-collar workers who respected the players because they were blue-collar workers too.

Italians lived primarily in Little Italy. Greeks, Germans, and Eastern Europeans like the Slovaks and Poles lived on the east side. African Americans lived mostly in west Baltimore, and the Jewish population settled in the northwest part of town. Nearly all these neighborhoods were filled with row houses with white marble front stoops that people took pride in scrubbing clean on weekends and sitting on during steamy summer nights like lawn furniture without the lawn out front.

Many of those houses were covered with Formstone, an artificial stone used to seal leaky brick facades. It was often applied to row houses in Baltimore in the 1950s and 1960s to cover over the cheaply made porous brick used on some buildings in working-class neighborhoods. The acclaimed film director John Waters, who was raised in Baltimore and hit the big time with the film *Hairspray*, once called Formstone "the polyester of brick." That's the Baltimore I arrived at.

Eventually the makeup of the neighborhoods would begin to shift during the 1960s, with a growing black population taking over areas whites abandoned to flee to the suburbs. Even our great running back Lenny Moore experienced that when he moved into a home on Yosemite Avenue in northwest Baltimore. Not long after he moved in, he saw neighbors moving out. Not even being a Colt star and a future Hall of Fame running back could change some things, but he never spoke of it when I was there, so most of us never knew. To me, Baltimore didn't appear divided because it was a quiet division, like everything else in town.

It was a divide you might not notice, which I really didn't, but Maryland was a border state, more Southern than Northern. We were still mostly living in a black-and-white world, because the sixties hadn't really started yet, except on the calendar.

When they did start, they would shake up the country and the NFL, but in 1961 there wasn't much nuance. Television, politics, and a tumultuous social revolution would soon begin to color things differently, but no matter how much things changed, there was always one unifying force in Baltimore: the Colts. The team had black stars and white stars but worked like one unit. The Colts really were a melting pot and a meritocracy. They were more of a team than any I was ever around.

Everyone loved the Colts because nearly everyone knew a Colt. The players weren't royalty, like the Giants were becoming in New York and the whole league would become in a couple of decades. They lived in the same neighborhoods as their fans and many had second jobs, because pro football wasn't yet a full-time occupation for everyone involved.

Unitas once wielded both a football and an acetylene torch with equal flair, and the fans loved him for it, although it would be the former that made him one of those rarest of celebrities. All you had to say was "Unitas" and everyone knew who you were talking about. He was a working-class hero who became the face of the NFL when it started to explode. He was arguably its first true superstar.

That didn't change from the day I arrived at the ticket office at Memorial Stadium to the day he died in 2002. It's still true today. You say "Unitas" to someone and if they have a confused look on their face, they aren't from Baltimore and they aren't a real football fan.

What made him such an icon of the day can best be explained by his reaction to winning the 1958 NFL Championship Game at Yankee Stadium in overtime. After Unitas handed the ball off to Alan Ameche for the game-winning touchdown run, he just turned and walked off the field. No hands in the air or running around the field. In the locker room he was offered $750 to stay in New York to be a guest on *The Ed Sullivan Show*. That was big money in a country where the average working man was making $3,673.80 a year. He turned it down to fly home with his team.

Television wasn't fragmented like it is today either. There were three channels, and they didn't broadcast twenty-four hours a day. Turn on the TV at certain times and all you got was a test pattern. So the *Sullivan Show* was a cultural icon of the day. It was Sunday night family viewing across the country. Just two years earlier, Elvis Presley made his first appearance on it and 82.6 percent of all American television viewers watched. That's still the highest-rated show in television history, and nobody is going to approach it.

Ed Sullivan made stars but Unitas could care less, so Alan Ameche, the running back who scored the winning touchdown, did it for $500. Unitas flew to Baltimore with the Colts, and thirty thousand people jammed Friendship Airport, causing a near riot until he and a few other players got out and spoke to some of the fans.

When the players finally got back to the stadium, Unitas gave a ride home to Andy Nelson, a starting safety who lived near him. According to Nelson, Unitas never said a word until they got in front of Andy's house. As he was getting out, Unitas said, "See you tomorrow, Andy."

That was the kind of man people in Baltimore appreciated. You did your job and no matter how good you were at it, you didn't make a lot of noise about it. You didn't beat your chest; you beat your opponent. When the Colts started doing that with regularity, it created a bond that was best described by Gino Marchetti fifty-five years after the glory days had faded away, when he told *Sports Illustrated*'s Alexander Wolff, "We were like the great high school team in a small town."

That's exactly how it was. That great high school team the town never forgets even after the kids have gone to seed, old men now with gray hair and pot bellies, but not in the minds of those who were once so thrilled to cheer for them. That was Baltimore the day I showed up to my first full-time job in pro football.

I wanted to get right into the football part, but they started me at the bottom. Like everybody else, I started in the ticket office at Memorial Stadium, which was a letdown to me.

I was at the bottom of the totem pole. It was a long way from plane rides and handing out paychecks, but Don Kellett, the general manager, told me the most important place was the ticket office. My reaction was, "Really?" But it turned out to be the greatest lesson of them all.

Today the emphasis is on television partners, streaming video, social media, merchandise sales, and marketing. Teams have a river of revenue streams. But until the 1990s, the ticket office was the most valuable part of the team. I worked there for two years and when I left, the Colts were selling $1.65 million worth of season tickets. Their share of the league's new national TV contract in 1963 brought in just over $1 million. Television money wasn't driving profits like it does today. You dealt more directly with the public. That was how your franchise made it or didn't. You put fans in seats or you were gone, because if you couldn't keep the people in the stands happy, it directly affected the bottom line.

In those years the Colts sold more season tickets than just about anybody, but I knew if flow at the ticket office on Monday wasn't strong, it wasn't going to be a sellout that Sunday. I heard every story there was in life during those years, because Colts fans really did know everything about what the players were doing. I didn't need Twitter. Twitter was standing at the ticket window every day, listening. The fans who walked up and bought a ticket had heard what was going on with the team in bars and on side streets all over town from the players and the coaches, who were sitting right next to them.

They were all at Sweeney's on Greenmount Avenue or at Gussie's Downbeat, underneath a Chinese laundry on Eastern Avenue, or Lenny Moore's favorite jazz clubs. If you wanted to talk to a Colt after practice, you knew where he'd be. There was no VIP section between you and them.

For two years, that was it. I'd go out to camp in the summer to watch practice sometimes, but I didn't have duties there anymore. The ticket office was my job. When I became general manager of the Patriots a decade later, what I'd learn there was important. The Patriots didn't have any idea about what winning required. I'd tell people, "Do your job and stop bitching." They thought I was mean, but what does Bill Belichick say today? "Do your job!" That's how organizations win. Pro football has changed in a lot of ways, but not in the fundamentals of winning.

I lived around the corner from the stadium on Thatcher Street, right off Greenmount Avenue. If I stayed at Sweeneys until three or four in the morning, I'd go take a nap, stop at the diner for breakfast, then walk to the Stadium on Thirty-Third Street. My whole world was five or six blocks. That was my life and I loved it.

The Colts' main office was on Charles Street. That's where Kellett was, and scouting, which was only Keith Molesworth and a secretary then. Weeb and his coaches had offices there too. I didn't have to go there much until I got into scouting, but I'd walk down there because they had a great Chinese restaurant where a character named Wally Lee worked. He knew more than anybody about the Colts because he was always dropping food off for the coaches. He'd tell you things that were going on in the front office that I knew nothing about. Wally Lee knew more about who was coming or going and why than Carroll did.

The best thing about the job was I didn't always have to do it. There were many assignments that made it more palatable, although sometimes they could make a twenty-three-year-old guy uncomfortable. I was beginning to learn about parts of the world I hadn't been exposed to when my father was alive.

Whenever Rosenbloom called I was ready for action, whether it was taking stuff to the White House for his friend Jack Kennedy, like new footballs and sneakers for touch football games on the lawn, or driving his future wife, Georgia Hayes, to New York or wherever. Carroll also had a present wife at the time whom I'd known most of my life, and that made it kind of uncomfortable for me. They told me Georgia was a singer that Carroll was friends with, but I never heard her sing.

Joe Kennedy, the president's father, introduced her to Carroll in Palm Beach when she was some sort of television personality in Miami, and they hit it off. I'd pick her up at Friendship Airport and take her to the Sheraton Belvedere, maybe have lunch or dinner with her. Then Carroll would show up and it was time to leave.

I was twenty-three, twenty-four years old. She was thirty-two, thirty-three. Carroll was in his fifties. I figured out what was happening but it wasn't any of my business. I worked for the Colts and for Carroll Rosenbloom, but I knew it wasn't in that order. I'd been around owners all my life.

I'd already learned there are two kinds of people in the world. There are owners and renters. The owners make the decisions. The renters carry them out. I was a renter. The only problem I had was I was also friendly with Carroll's wife, Dolly, whom I liked a lot. I was very uncomfortable at times caught between two worlds.

You don't want to get involved in those things, and luckily I wasn't beyond doing the driving, but suppose there's a lawsuit?

I'm prima facie evidence. I'm picking her up and driving her into town. I'm driving her to New York for auditions. She was fun to be with and very nice, but ultimately she took the team away from Carroll's son, Steve, after Carroll drowned under what many people believe were questionable circumstances in 1979.

He did eventually divorce his wife and married Georgia in 1966, but by then I was out of the chauffeur business and now running the player personnel department, which was where I'd always wanted to be. Not long after they were married, he brought her to training camp one day and asked Don Shula, me, and a few others to come to a crab fest to celebrate their wedding. He had crabs brought from Obrycki's, a restaurant in Fell's Point with the best crabs in Baltimore. If you're dying and want a crab cake for your last meal, you'd get it from Obrycki's.

Carroll had acquired the Rams by trading the Colts franchise to Robert Irsay to beat capital gains taxes and get out to LA. Years later, after Carroll died and Georgia inherited 70 percent of the Rams team, she took control and Steve was cut out. I warned Steve many times this could happen. He ended up in New Orleans, where he worked for the Saints for a while. It wasn't right, but not everything is, even in pro football.

In my first years in Baltimore, I wasn't just in the ticket office. I was living life vicariously through Carroll Rosenbloom. I think he called on me and Bert because we were both single, and you don't want your son picking up your girlfriend at the airport. You don't want the GM or the assistant GM doing it either. So we were it. Carroll might call at any time and I'd be gone. Our ticket manager used to say to me, "You are here less than anywhere else!"

I didn't have a lot of interaction at work with the players those two years, but I'd see them at Sweeney's and Gussie's most nights. Every major sports figure who came into town knew where Sweeney's was. You never knew who would be there. It's where I met Sammy Goldstein, who ended up in the trunk of a car. People suggested it was the Mob. Who knows?

Those places were where I learned how players came down after a game. How they felt. The fears they had of an injury wiping them out. The money they had or didn't have. Family problems. Sooner or later you heard it all.

You learned what made players tick because they felt free to talk in those places, the way every working man talked about his troubles after work. One was at the steel plant. Another was at the Colts' plant. In those days the only difference came on Sundays.

Those experiences taught me the great fear players live with in football, more than in any other sport: the fear of one play ending it all, or of being cut without a trace or a penny.

Athletes die twice and they know it—once as an athlete and later as a person. That causes a lot of anxiety. You could always tell when cut-down time was coming. The chatter would increase. Are they going to keep me or not?

The biggest fear always was injury. It was true when I was in the NFL and it's just as true today. The money today changes it a bit financially, but these guys like to play. It's why they hide injuries. Always have, always will, which makes today's safety issues difficult to solve even if you're trying. Pro football has always been a pain business. That will never change. How you handle that pain is one of the ways you get evaluated. Can you still function? How fast can you come back? How much can you take? Part of ability in the NFL is availability.

It's why many players still hide concussions even knowing what they know today. They're athletes. They want to play the game and they're all afraid if they don't, someone else will be in there ahead of them, and who knows? Maybe the coaches like this kid who is playing cheaper than I am. They all understand that reality and they're fearful of it.

Today they do get more involved in outside businesses and making plans for the future, but Rosenbloom was always urging his players to stay around town and start a business too. He'd help any of them who asked, but in the 1960s the outlook of a player was more moment by moment. There was no great future planning. They didn't have agents and marketing reps. Hell, the teams didn't have marketing reps. The focus was what happened today at practice.

I always felt that was because of the dangerous nature of the sport. That fear of being wiped out was always there, just below the surface. It's why today's player still says he'd rather get a concussion than blow out a knee. Why? Because the impact of a knee injury on your career is often more immediate. The ravages of chronic traumatic encephalopathy (CTE), the debilitating brain damage caused by constant head-on collisions, which we've only begun to understand, is terrible, but that damage comes later. So players say they'd rather be hit high than low. It may not make sense in your world, but it does in theirs.

I really believe it was a more dangerous game back then. You didn't have the high-speed collisions then, but you also didn't have the equipment protection, the medicine, the improved surgical procedures, and the training methods they have today. It really hurt when you got hit in those days, and the fallout didn't fade away.

When I became the Patriots' general manager, I never used what I'd learned against players. I used it to understand them. Or try to. You didn't really need to make them fearful. They were playing for their lives. In most cases, they still are.

I remember flying back from Los Angeles with the team in 1962. We'd won two straight on the West Coast to get to 5-4, but the season had been a struggle. We were a team in transition from those championship teams of the 1950s, and it was starting to show.

A veteran linebacker, Bill Pellington, started talking to me about how he hoped Weeb would be coming back in 1963 so he'd have a better chance of staying. If someone new came in, who knew? And who wants to give up this life?

We lost three straight after that and finished 7-7. Weeb didn't come back. Pellington did.

Ernie Accorsi, who would later run the Colts, Browns, and Giants as their general manager, used to talk to me about being a kid in the stands in 1952 at the Eagles' training camp in Hershey, Pennsylvania, the day Steve Van Buren, the great Hall of

Fame running back, made a cut in practice and went down and everything stopped. Total silence. I didn't know Ernie then, but I was there that day too with my father and I remember Van Buren writhing in pain.

Van Buren led the NFL in rushing four times in eight years. He wasn't someone who expressed his fears, but I saw the look on his face, and you could see he knew it was over. You could see fear. This was someone I never thought knew anything about fear, but you saw it that day. What was he afraid of? The end. He never played again. He was thirty-one years old.

In other worlds, there's another job. In the NFL, once that happens, there's never going to be another job. Not like that one. In most cases, a career ends violently and abruptly at a time when most people are just starting theirs.

Are they going back to Alabama or Tennessee or Mississippi to a fabulous business? I don't think so. That's the reality of life in pro football I learned those years with the Colts. Once it's over, you're never coming back to the training camp, the training table, the locker room. You're not going to Sweeney's anymore. That part of your life is done and it can't be duplicated elsewhere.

What I also learned the hard way was when money is involved, problems follow. Strange things happen and you'd better be ready for that. That was never clearer to me than the day my boss at the ticket office, Mike Hofmann, didn't show up for work.

We didn't have computers tracking everything in 1962. We didn't have computers at all. We had a pen and pencil, which must seem quaint today.

Individual ticket sales were a cash business, the same as a liquor store. You took in the cash, put it in a box under the counter, and it was bagged up at the end of the day and deposited. If we'd had computers, Hofmann never could have gotten away with what he did in 1962. That was the year of the Great Ticket Heist.

Mike was hired after Carroll and Kellett fired the previous ticket manager at the end of 1961. We were told this great guy who had been in the navy for years was coming in highly recommended by Robert Kennedy, who was the attorney general, brother of the president, and a pal of Carroll's. It seemed like a pretty good recommendation.

He was a great guy. One of the nicest people I ever met. Full of shit but funny. When Carroll or Kellett would call, he'd holler, "Heavy artillery coming in from Charles Street! The *big cheese* is on the phone!" We'd all laugh.

Every season ticket holder had a card you'd put on a board. When they'd make a payment, you'd record how much they paid and when, and whether it was by check or cash, so you could keep track of when they had paid in full. You had to be very careful because it was the only record, and those tickets were like gold to the people who had them.

No one used credit cards then. At the end of the day you'd put the money and checks in canvas bags, and a Brinks truck would make a pickup. Late in the day Mike would come out of his office and holler, "*Bag it!*"—meaning, dump the cash and checks in those bags. Then they'd be taken to his office. He'd close the door and we'd close up. Who knew what he was doing. As it turns out, he was doing quite a lot.

He was selling the same tickets two and three times over and keeping the money. When he said, "*Bag it!*" he had a bag for the Colts and a bag for himself.

We didn't see a problem until seven days before the opening game against the Rams. Art Donovan was retiring that day, and there was a lot of excitement. There was a lot more excitement when Mike didn't show up for work and people began lining up saying they hadn't received their season tickets yet.

All we could say at first was, "What tickets?" It was a nightmare to figure out who was telling the truth. We had no idea what Mike had been doing. We were recording our sales, but we didn't know he was taking money for tickets we'd already sold. If there were computers, someone probably would have caught it, but it was just cash, checks, and handwritten notes.

The *Sunday American* ran a photo of me, Herb Wright, and Ray Gilland, who used to be the ticket manager, kneeling on the floor looking at a stack of papers and tickets as if we were trying to figure out the riddle of the Sphinx. That would have been easier. Even some tickets held by club officials like Kellett and the ones for the presidential box had been double sold. What do you tell the general manager? "Prove you paid"?

All we could do was go by the index cards and ask people to come in with an ID. That separated the season ticket holders from the imposters. We didn't have a record of people Mike sold tickets to, because those tickets didn't exist. And now neither did their money.

We always had a waiting list, and next to your children, a season ticket to the Colts was the most important thing in town. It gave you status. After all those years, you finally got two season tickets and now you found out you didn't? Imagine the anger!

Kellett even called Art Donovan and some of our other players and asked them to come to the stadium to try to calm down our fans. I was at the ticket window at the time and could see this might become a very ugly scene.

Rosenbloom brought in someone named Ben Small to try to straighten things out. He was Rosenbloom's "no" man. He was tough, so nobody liked him, but he knew all you could do was give the money back. But to whom?

Over $100,000 was missing, but the people didn't want refunds. They wanted to watch the Colts. The city ended up moving an additional 2,644 temporary seats into the stadium so we could accommodate the overflow. We didn't need a seat for Hofmann. He was gone. Poof! Like smoke over the Allied Chemical Plant.

He left his wife and eight kids behind and just disappeared for five weeks. They found over $30,000 under his mattress. There was a nationwide search that began four days after he disappeared. His wife turned over $20,350, and the police found another $16,000 in his house. She said Mike told her he'd won it betting on the horses.

Then one day he just reappeared, spent a night with his family, and then gave himself up. He was arrested the next day by the FBI, pled guilty, and went away. Everybody still liked him. It was the most amazing thing.

Meanwhile, Art Donovan, our great defensive tackle, was reluctantly retiring before the 2 p.m. kickoff. Everyone in town wanted to be there but Art. We'd gone 8-6 the year before and Art was still able to make plays, but the handwriting was on the wall. He was thirty-eight and Weeb wanted to go with a younger player, John Diehl, a defensive tackle from Virginia. It was something I'd see over and over. No matter how great you are, eventually night falls.

Art went to training camp, but he could see he wasn't getting the same chances and he knew what it meant. When Kellett called him to his house in north Baltimore, Artie knew what was coming. He'd seen it happen to a lot of players before him. It was August 30, 1962.

They asked him to retire. He didn't want to, but not many of them do. Very few of us really retire in the NFL. The team gets rid of you or makes it clear they're going to, and you realize it and leave. It's seldom pretty, but Art Donovan went out the way his teammates wanted. When he drove away from training camp for the last time, a cherry bomb went off under his car.

Diehl didn't work out, and in the end a player named John Colvin played left tackle on our defense. He started four years, but he wasn't Art Donovan. Nobody could be because Art was one of those players Marchetti was talking about when he said the Colts were the great high school team in the small town. Art was among the greatest of them, and because of his personality and the fact he'd been rejected by the NFL just like Baltimore but came back and won world championships there, he was beloved.

Art was usually hilarious, although not on September 16, 1962. That day he cried, and by then I can assure you no one was laughing in the ticket office. There were a lot of angry people. Carroll hired extra security because he was afraid of violence. We never totally sorted it out, but people accepted what they read in the papers. No one sued us, which is another way things have changed. Today everybody would be suing, even people who never met Mike Hofmann.

While all this was going on, there was also a problem with Art. There were 54,749 people packed in those stands and he wanted to go out wearing a coat and tie, but Lou Grasmick, who was head of the arrangement committee, insisted he wear his uniform.

Donovan saw no reason to wear pads just to take a walk, but he did what they asked and the crowd went crazy. They gave him a Cadillac, golf clubs, 70 pounds of potato chips and pretzels, because that was his number and he loved to eat, and a proclamation. He stood at the microphone and said, "There's a lady up in Heaven who wants to thank all the people of Baltimore for being so good to her boy, a kid from the Bronx."

Without another word, the last of the original 1950 Baltimore Colts turned and walked away with his head down, an old Colts cape over his shoulders, as the Colts' band played "Auld Lang Syne." The stadium was shaking from the reaction of the fans.

What none of them saw was what I saw after he got off the field. Here was this massive tough guy, who had earned a scholarship to Notre Dame but left after a semester to join the Marine Corps in 1942; who served in the Pacific Theater as an anti-aircraft gunner aboard the USS *San Jacinto* during the assault on Leyte in the Philippines; and who, after thirteen months of that, volunteered for the Fleet Marine Force that landed in the middle of combat on Okinawa.

He was hard as nails on the battlefield and the football field, but there he was alone, out of the view of the fans, with his hands bracing his body as he leaned against a concrete wall and wept. I'll never forget his shoulders shaking. It just meant so much to him to be on that team that had won over an entire town.

After the Great Ticket Heist, Carroll brought in one of the first computer programs in the NFL to track ticket sales. When I got to New England, I hired the man who put it in to come up with a scouting program for us. It was one of the first moves I made. Things were changing in pro football. It wasn't my father's NFL any more. No more making the schedule using dominos on our kitchen table. The computers were taking over and there was money to be made, as the Dallas Cowboys would soon prove.

I already saw myself as one day becoming a general manager,

and I was in a hurry to get going. The entry to that in those days wasn't personnel director. It was becoming a publicity director. Rozelle, Tex Schramm in Dallas, and Ernie Accorsi in Baltimore all went from being head of PR to being GMS, so originally I wanted to get into PR from the ticket office. But there was no room.

After two years I went to Kellett and told him I thought I'd learned as much as I could and wanted to move on. Don said maybe he could find something in personnel. That's what started me on the road to what I wanted to be—someone who would build championship teams.

5

A Scout's Life Is for Kit Carson
but Not for Everybody

In the early years of pro football's explosive growth in the 1960s and 1970s, the road to becoming a general manager wound through the PR office. It's where a lot of GMS came from, including Tex Schramm, who was the Rams' PR director before moving up to general manager and hiring a young PR man named Pete Rozelle. Rozelle later became one of the most successful commissioners in sports history, but before that he replaced Schramm in 1957 when Schramm moved to CBS. Three years later, Schramm would become the first general manager and president of the Dallas Cowboys and change the entire manner in which scouting was conducted, launching us all into the computer age.

A decade later, in 1970, Ernie Accorsi would begin in the PR office of the Colts before going on to becoming one of the finest GMS in football with the Colts, Browns, and Giants. In New York he built one team that reached the Super Bowl and laid the foundation for their Super Bowl XLII and XLVI championships with his aggressive maneuvering to acquire quarterback Eli Manning in a draft-day trade in 2004 involving the rights to Philip Rivers and two high draft choices. Understanding that if the PR office was where you learned the business of football, that's naturally where I wanted to go.

Often in life what you think is a bad break turns out to be your biggest break. So it was for me when GM Don Kellett informed me in 1963 there was nothing for me in the Colts' PR department. I had stayed in the ticket office another year after the Great Ticket

Heist but felt I'd mastered the art of making change and bagging the cash and wanted a bigger challenge. When Kellett offered me a chance to move into scouting, I took it.

Scouting began to evolve in the NFL right around that time, and I was fortunate to be there when it did. For years, many teams didn't scout for much but a good luncheonette to go read *Street & Smith's College Football Yearbook* and *College Football Illustrated* as preparation for the draft, but by 1963 the first scouting combine had begun and individual team scouting staffs would soon start to grow.

Today the drafting process is an annual multi-million-dollar industry for every NFL team. Everyone has seven or more area scouts, at least one national scout who serves as a cross-checker, as well as college and pro personnel directors and assistant directors. Every operation is computerized with both videotape and information available in an instant on team-issued laptops. Talent acquisition today is treated with the importance I believe it deserves.

In contrast, when I got to Keith Molesworth's office in September 1963, all we had was a secretary and some metal baskets. Actually, we didn't even have the baskets until I began scattering them around the room in order to sort out the reports coming in from the combine. Keith looked at me as if I'd lost my mind.

Our office was in the back behind the PR department. It was the size of a studio apartment, so small I didn't even have a desk. I had a desk chair surrounded by my baskets.

Don Shula had just replaced Weeb as head coach, a change that came about because even if you won championships for Carroll, you didn't get much of a grace period between them. We'd stayed competitive after the back-to-back titles in 1958 and 1959 but went 21-19 over the next three seasons. Mediocrity was not something Rosenbloom would long abide, so he fired Weeb, who was quickly hired by the Jets and would come back to haunt us five years later.

Although Unitas was still in his prime, the backbone of those championship teams had begun to age, especially on defense. Rosenbloom made a change that reminded everyone that in Carroll's Baltimore, you won or you disappeared, when he made Shula the youngest head coach in NFL history on the recommendation of Gino Marchetti and Bill Pellington, who'd played with Don in Baltimore and respected his defensive knowledge.

Only thirty-three, Shula was defensive coordinator of the Lions at the time and the architect of perhaps the greatest one-game resume ever written: when he came up with the game plan that resulted in the Lions' 1962 Thanksgiving Day Massacre of the undefeated Green Bay Packers. That day the Lions sacked Bart Starr eleven times, held him to minus 110 yards passing, and led 23–0 at halftime in a 26–14 victory that was not as close as that score implies. It was shocking the way they took the Packers apart.

What I learned from watching things unfold in Baltimore was you can't hold on to aging players hoping they have a year left. Weeb admitted later he'd done that and they got hurt in 1962, and we slipped to 7-7. Weeb later said he believed part of Carroll's decision was a result of his friendship with the Kennedys in Palm Beach. He saw them as big believers in youth, and Weeb and the team he put on the field in 1962 no longer represented that. I don't know if he was right, but the lesson I took from it was you can't stay the same in pro football. Age and injuries are always a factor to consider with players because the game is so punishing.

The other thing it reinforced was what I already understood about Carroll and pro football: you're only as good as your last game or your last draft. Weeb had gone down to the Senior Bowl in December and thought he had assurances from Rosenbloom that he wasn't thinking of making a change. When he got back, he was called into a meeting and was fired on January 8, 1963. They named Don the new coach the same day. That's the NFL— Not For Long.

Shula added two coaches to the staff but also kept McCafferty and Sandusky. A year later he would bring in Bill Arnsparger as a defensive assistant and in 1966 added Chuck Noll to the defensive staff. So we had both change and continuity. What we also had was a young head coach only a few years removed from playing with the men he was now coaching and having not played as well as they had. Don was aware of that and put the iron fist down early. Nobody doubted who was in charge.

It was shaping up as a year of upheaval in Baltimore. Barely four months later the town awoke to learn one of its most beloved Colts, Eugene "Big Daddy" Lipscomb, was dead from a drug overdose. In 1963 Baltimore that didn't happen. At least not to one of the Colts.

Big Daddy had been traded to the Steelers three years earlier because Weeb decided he'd become too much of a distraction. The man I'd seen at training camp marching around campus like a drum major with half the defense in single-file behind him turned out to be far more complicated than the good-hearted guy we saw on the surface.

When they traded him, I was reminded of Mike Jarmoluk, the player who threw the beer can over the tree years ago at the Bears' training camp. What Halas and his coaches said about trading Jarmoluk was what I was now hearing about Big Daddy. Those incidents confirmed for me that everyone has a shelf life. When your time is up, you're gone. We're all pebbles on the beach, as even Unitas found out at the end. When it's over, the game moves on without you.

But this was different. This was a real-world invasion of the sports world involving heroin and a seedy apartment in a broken-down section of Baltimore that Colt fans would not have associated with the Big Daddy they knew. Of course, that was the point. Fans don't really know the people they cheer for. Sometimes neither do the people coaching them or signing them.

Big Daddy never knew his father, who died when he was too young to have a memory of him. They'd moved to Detroit from Alabama as part of the great northern migration many blacks were part of in the war years because there were good jobs and personal freedom for them outside the South.

But life was still tough. When he was eleven, his mother was murdered, stabbed forty-seven times by a boyfriend while standing at a bus stop. The police knocked on the door and told an eleven-year-old boy who was cooking his breakfast what had happened. He was big for his age, so maybe they thought he was older, but how does a kid process that? Clearly he didn't. Big Daddy carried crime scene photographs with him the rest of his life, and one of his roommates, the offensive lineman Sherman Plunkett, used to tell stories about Big Daddy pulling his bed against the door at night and sometimes crying himself to sleep. Who knows why he carried those pictures? Maybe it was to remind him how tough life can be.

Big Daddy was raised by his maternal grandfather, Charles Hoskins, who was a hard man. He charged the boy rent and put his hands on him more than once. That meant Big Daddy needed a job. He began loading trucks and by high school was working the overnight shift at a steel mill in Detroit and then changing his clothes and going off to school. He didn't do well in school. It's obvious why.

He dropped out and joined the Marines, a kid haunted by fears of a side of life most of us thankfully never see. That's where Pete Rozelle found him in 1953, playing football at the Marine base at Camp Pendleton outside of San Diego, and signed him for the Rams.

He was huge by the day's standards—six feet six, 284 pounds—but more important, he could run like a man half his size. That was an unusual combination then as it is today, but if you have it there's a place for you in pro football.

Lipscomb played three years in LA, but off-the-field distractions led the Rams to waive him. The Colts claimed him for $100 on Labor Day weekend 1956. As with most things in life, there was some luck involved with him ending up in Baltimore.

The 49ers had first choice of anyone waived that year and the Colts had the second. The Niners sent a telegram to the league office, but because of the holiday it didn't get delivered for two days. The Colts called my father to make their claim, and he of course took the call. That's how Big Daddy got to Baltimore—somebody used the phone.

I remembered that when I got to the Patriots in 1971. One of the first things I did was hire someone from the league office who knew the waiver wire rules cold, because we had first claiming rights and needed players.

Big Daddy—who got that name because he often couldn't remember names, so he called most people Little Daddy—became a two-time All-Pro and three-time Pro Bowl defensive tackle playing next to Donovan and Marchetti. Everyone in town loved him, including the women.

He dressed well, drove a yellow Cadillac, loved kids, and was a fixture at jazz clubs and gin joints. He liked to party so much he was married three times, and when he died there were more women than that mourning his loss.

He was still living in Baltimore despite being traded in 1960 in a five-player deal that got us defensive tackle Billy Ray Smith and Jimmy Orr, the wide receiver who will always be remembered for what happened to him in Super Bowl III. Big Daddy had become too much of a distraction because he complained a lot and there was a stream of off-field problems.

Lenny Moore, our great running back, was close to him and years later said he thought they did it because they couldn't control him. He said somewhere that Big Daddy wouldn't tolerate blacks on the team being mistreated anymore. I never saw that, but certainly there was the discrimination of the times that all African Americans faced. When we'd travel to a game in the South during exhibition season, our black players had to stay at a different hotel. They finally went to Carroll about it and we stopped playing games in places like Birmingham. We never should have let that happen to them, but it was the law in the South in those days before the civil rights movement, and we accepted it without thinking of the consequences for those black players. That's no excuse, it's just an explanation. We shouldn't have gone to those places.

Whatever the reason for trading him, no one expected what they heard on May 10, 1963. The story was Big Daddy had played softball the night before, then went to a bar and began drinking. That's where a man named Timothy Black met him, and they ended up at his second-floor apartment on North Brice Street. Black claimed they scored a $12 bag of heroin and Big Daddy overdosed on five times the lethal dose. Later, Black claimed he went out for breakfast and came home and found Big Daddy dead. His story was as shaky as he was, and Big Daddy's friends never believed it.

Lipscomb was afraid of needles, everyone said, and why would a right-handed man shoot himself with his left hand? We never got any answers, and Black walked on a charge of possession of narcotics paraphernalia on a technicality after first being charged with involuntary homicide. Whatever really happened, Big Daddy was gone but not forgotten.

Thousands of people came to pay their respects at the Charlie Law Funeral Parlor. There were so many that when it came time to close at 10 p.m., the line was still so long that Law finally called Buddy Young's wife, Geraldine, and asked what to do. She said let them say goodbye. At midnight a woman showed up at Buddy's, a singer from Canada distraught at the news. Buddy had been a good running back and now worked for the Colts. He'd helped Big Daddy adjust to life as a star and understood how much he'd come to mean to so many people. He was a Colt for life. He was a Colt in death. Young could see he meant something to this woman too, so he took her to Charlie Law's funeral parlor and they let her in at midnight to say goodbye.

Big Daddy was a star because he could play defensive tackle better than anyone in the league for a while, but he was beloved in Baltimore because he treated so many people who were down and out with dignity. He helped strangers, buying clothes for little kids he could see had nothing, in the way he once had nothing. He understood pain and people loved him for it, but it ended badly for Big Daddy. It was a reminder that what you see on the field isn't often the whole story.

That fall I was a twenty-six-year-old refugee from the ticket office who moved into a cramped space on the second floor of the Colts office to begin looking for the next Big Daddy. It was a space I would share with Keith Molesworth for three years.

Keith had been a quarterback and running back with the Chicago Bears, playing in the same backfield with Red Grange and Bronko Nagurski. He also played baseball in the Orioles' farm system and in 1937 was half of the double-play combination of their top farm team, the Syracuse Chiefs. His double-play partner was a second baseman named Don Kellett.

Kellett named him the Colts' first head coach in 1953, but he was replaced the next season by Weeb in a shakeup that left Molesworth as director of personnel. Rosenbloom instructed him to build the best scouting operation in the league. The only problem was he didn't have any scouts.

Only the Los Angeles Rams and Cleveland Browns had their own scouts. Eddie Kotal became the first full-time scout in NFL history when the Rams hired him in 1946. He was a pioneer in what I believe is the game's most important element and belongs in the Hall of Fame, but he's been forgotten. That's a shame.

There are only two jobs in pro football that really count, in my opinion: the head coach and the guy who drafts. You can have everything else, you can sell all the commercials and all the tickets, but you don't win unless those two function well together. They don't have to like each other, but they have to respect each other's viewpoint and opinion. If you don't have that, you don't win, because if you give a coach a player he doesn't want, he won't give him a chance. Look at Walt Kiesling. He was the Steelers' head coach in Pittsburgh who didn't give Unitas a chance.

The general manager not only has to know about personnel, he has to know the personnel his coach wants, what fits his system, and what he can't abide. If he wants huge offensive linemen and huge linebackers, don't bring him 250-pound guards who can move or an undersized linebacker like Sam Mills. That doesn't mean Sam Mills wasn't a great player, but the coach has to give players that small a chance, and he usually won't.

Such was the state of scouting in the 1960s that most teams, including the Colts, mainly relied on "hired scouts." These were mostly college assistant coaches in the major conferences who would write reports for $50 and a team golf shirt. It was less than a decade since the Colts had returned from the West Coast on

December 12, 1954, at the end of their season with the first and third picks in the upcoming draft. Yet they thought so little of scouting that they left behind only Joe Thomas, a young coach who would later become a skilled talent evaluator with the Vikings and Dolphins, and later general manager of the Colts, to scout the Rose Bowl and East-West Shrine Game because he was single and wouldn't be ruining anyone's Christmas by his absence. The Colts ended up drafting Oregon quarterback George Shaw and Wisconsin running back Alan Ameche, so they did all right, but can you imagine what would go on today if a team held those picks?

My job was to read reports from our "paid scouts" and Moley. I wasn't really scouting anybody. We weren't in a scouting service yet either. That came the following year when we, along with the Browns, Packers, Giants, and Cardinals, joined CEPO (Central Eastern Personnel Organization), which later became known as United Scouting when the Falcons and Redskins joined, and then later as National Football Scouting. That meant more reports to read.

CEPO was a response to BLESTO-VIII, which had been originally formed by the Lions, Eagles, and Steelers to share scouting information and costs. It was LESTO then, but when the Bears joined they added a letter as well as a team and by 1971 it had added four more teams: the Vikings, Bills, Dolphins, and Colts.

This pooling of resources was done in different ways. Some, like CEPO, shared full information. If I watched spring practice somewhere, I'd write a report and it would go to everybody. Other scouting services only shared some information. I liked the latter idea because I thought some opinions you should keep to yourself, but we didn't.

In 1964 Dallas joined with the Rams and 49ers to form TROIKA, which became Quadra when New Orleans was added in 1967. It no longer exists, but any scouting organization that included the Cowboys was ahead of the curve. Today nineteen teams are part of National Scouting, and eight are with BLESTO. Then there are five that are non-affiliated, including the Patriots.

In 1963, though, there was just Moley and me, and he was gone most weeks from Thursday through Sunday, so I sat there reading scouting reports and making notes about who had to be seen. Then I had to figure out what to do with them, so I came up with twenty-six alphabetized wire baskets.

Finish a report, throw it in a basket. This was before computers. Only Dallas had computerized scouting, and that would soon change everything, but at the time no one understood their system, and with good reason. It came out of the Winter Olympics!

While Schramm was working for CBS Sports, he worked on the 1960 Winter Olympics broadcast and became intrigued by their use of computerized data. When he got back into football, he wanted to find a way to apply it to scouting to help find players others missed and avoid the kind of big mistakes that were so often prevalent.

He wanted to apply an objective method to a subjective choice, so he went to IBM to see if it was possible. In 1962 they figured out a way. Or, more accurately, a man named A. Salam Qureishi did.

No one in football remembers his name today, but he was an Indian-born computer programmer working for a company called Service Bureau Corporation, which was owned by IBM, and you could argue he changed scouting as much as anyone ever did. They sent him to Dallas to meet with Schramm. He had absolutely no idea about the game of football but he understood variables, and he told Schramm they had too many.

Together they boiled it down to five: character, quickness and body control, competitiveness, mental alertness, and strength and explosiveness. Scouts would give the players number grades based on the usual measurables of size and speed plus their own evaluation. Then the computer would work through the five variables and downgrade some who were missing what were considered significant assets and upgrade others who had them.

Bucko Kilroy told me when they ran a test of their system in 1964, the year before he got to Dallas, the computer picked Joe Namath, Dick Butkus, Gale Sayers, and Fred Biletnikoff as the top prospects coming out of college. They all ended up in the Hall of Fame. That computer kept the Cowboys ahead of the rest of the league for quite some time. It was part of what fueled their dynasty of the 1970s. It was a bit more advanced than wire baskets, but I went with what I had.

Dallas's computers changed the dynamics of scouting. You couldn't get by anymore just going to the top schools and a few historically black colleges, where we thought all the players were. You couldn't just read college football magazines or go by the All-America team or the All-Conference teams. Dallas was going everywhere. So you had to go everywhere too. Shula knew we had to ramp up.

Moley had just me, and at first he was the only one who went out and actually scouted the colleges. I respected him as a talent scout, but even if he was the greatest scout since Tonto, one person couldn't do it alone. Dallas used to keep me up until two o'clock in the morning. Did we miss someone?

By the end of the year we'd have fifteen reports or more on some players with grades from anyone who wrote a report. You can imagine the piles. There was no computer printout. Only Dallas had one. We didn't get them until CEPO started supplying them around 1964 or 1965. So I'd tell Moley the players I thought were important.

I finally convinced him to let me go out and see a couple of games. The first one was to scout a quarterback named Archie Roberts at Columbia. Not too many NFL quarterbacks had come out of there since Sid Luckman in the 1940s, so Moley wasn't taking any chances with me.

I came back and told him I knew it was Ivy League, but I thought he could be a good backup quarterback somewhere. He was a great athlete—finished seventh in the Heisman balloting his senior year, played on the varsity basketball team, and was an All-America shortstop. He was offered a Major League Baseball contract but was drafted by the Browns, and they let him stay on their taxi squad while he went to medical school, so he chose football. Imagine that happening today? Not likely.

He was traded to Miami in 1967 and was a backup for a year before deciding to move on. He became a great surgeon, and the irony is that thirty years later, one of the best profile pieces I ever did for television in Boston after I left football was on Archie Roberts, the great heart surgeon. He let me film during open heart surgery. Maybe he wasn't a great NFL quarterback, but he performed over four thousand heart surgeries before retiring. He was no surgical backup.

After that Moley began to send me out to more regional games. I wasn't doing the SEC, the Big 10, or the Southwest Conference, but I was back in football and I was happy.

Until I got there it was just Moley and his secretary. He was a terrific person. A gentleman of the old school. I really respected him, but as sometimes happens with change, we had a falling out pretty early.

He called me one day from the road and told me, "I don't know what you're doing, but I understand you're doing something with the reports." Maybe he felt threatened. Shula had just come in. Now here I was. Probably if I was his age and saw what happened to Weeb, I'd feel insecure too. Maybe Shula would want his own guy somewhere down the line. Maybe the secretary thought I was asking too many questions. Probably she was telling him I was there to take his job. I don't know what the cause was, but it led to a confrontation because there was just a bad vibe.

I finally said to him I didn't like the way it was going and I needed to go home and think about it. I'm a pretty straightforward person and I wanted a good relationship. Molesworth didn't say anything. I think he was taken aback that I brought it up.

So I walked out. I left the Charles Street office and walked home. I didn't want it to fester. Being a young man, I was not as cautious, so I picked up the phone and called Rosenbloom at his office in New York.

I explained the situation. I told him I didn't want to do something foolish but I felt I needed to talk to him. I didn't want to quit, but what did I know?

He told me he'd be down that Thursday because we were playing the Packers that Sunday, October 27. I'd only been in scouting about a month. He told me he'd see me before the game. I didn't speak with Shula because he wasn't really involved. His mind was elsewhere, and I didn't have a relationship with him then.

I laugh about it now. I called the owner to discuss something I should have settled myself. I didn't call to ask him to save my job. I called because I wanted him to know why I wasn't in the office in case it got back to him. It was the beautiful naïveté of youth.

With Rosenbloom then, if you had a problem you picked up the phone. That's how my father had operated as commissioner. So I called the man who paid everybody. Relationships then were different than they are in today's NFL.

Things get around fast on a team. I walked into the locker room before the game and Alex Hawkins, one of our running backs, hollered, "The Prodigal Son Is Back! I wouldn't put up with that bullshit." I guess my brother, Bert, told him, because they were friends. That's a locker room. Everyone knows what's going on.

Molesworth never called me. It was as if he was saying, "You want to walk out? Keep going." Today HR would have called ten times, but life was simpler in 1963. It was better, actually. You settled things and moved on.

Rosenbloom had a certain routine before the game. He'd walk through the locker room and then onto the field. He told me, "I'll talk to Don. You go back in there on Monday."

On game day I worked by the bench with a walkie-talkie conveying information to Harry Hulmes, the PR person who would later become general manager. If someone got hurt he'd call and I'd tell him what the status was. You did a lot of jobs in those days.

So Monday I walked back in. Moley and I didn't have a long conversation. I told him I was sorry about what happened between us but there's nothing there. That was the end of it. People didn't spend a long time then with agonizing discussions. Get to the point, which I loved. That was it. Relationships were so different then. Less than a month later, everything became different. The sixties began. It was November 22, 1963.

I was alone in the office that day. It was a Friday around 1:30 in the afternoon and I was reading reports when the phone rang and somebody said, "President Kennedy's been shot!" There was no TV set to turn on. No web to surf. Just an empty room and an empty feeling.

I immediately thought of Rosenbloom. The team had already gone to LA to play on the West Coast. Moley was off scouting. I was sitting in the office alone, working my baskets. I remember overhearing someone in PR saying Carroll wasn't going to the West Coast. He was headed to Hyannis to be with Joe Kennedy, the president's father.

They were friends from Palm Beach, and Rosenbloom used to fly some of the Colts up to Hyannis Port in the off-season to play touch football at the Kennedys' beachfront compound. Unitas and other players used to talk about it.

Unitas told me a story once about Bobby Kennedy, the president's brother, in the huddle at one of the games. Unitas wasn't sure if Kennedy didn't know who he was or just didn't give a shit. He told the greatest quarterback in football to run out for a pass. Unitas did it, but he always said the sisters were tougher than the brothers.

I walked out of the office kind of stunned, up Charles Street and over by the stadium toward home. I walked by the places I was familiar with. I needed to see those things.

I was sure the NFL would call the games off. When I got home I turned on the TV, and there was Walter Cronkite in tears. The president had been shot at 12:30 p.m. Dallas time and was declared dead a half hour later. This didn't happen in America. But it just had.

The AFL, our bitter rivals at the time, had canceled their games. Milt Woodward was the assistant commissioner, and he made the decision because Joe Foss was away and unreachable. Woodward waited until about 8 p.m. to see what we were going to do and to hear from Foss. He didn't hear from either, so he acted. Foss got credit for it, but he never knew until the decision was announced. The NBA, NHL, and most college football games were canceled too.

The Rams voted not to play, but come November 24 we played. Dallas was playing in Cleveland and they were afraid of what the fan reaction would be, because they felt like they represented the city that shot the president. But the oddest thing happened there. When the Cowboys ran out there was only silence. No booing. Just silence.

Rozelle claimed we played because he'd spoken with Pierre Salinger, JFK's press secretary, and he told him the president would want us to. I spoke with Salinger about that thirty-three years later when I had a radio show in Boston, and he told me, "That's true."

Rosenbloom later said he'd talked to the Kennedys and they felt the same way. It was the only big misstep Pete made in a brilliant career. One thing about him, he could anticipate reactions because he was a former PR person. That was one time he didn't. But the funny thing was in a lot of cities attendance went up. I guess some people just needed to get out of the house and away from the television, which was broadcasting nonstop news on the president's death and the alleged assassin, Lee Harvey Oswald.

On Sunday just after noon, I along with most of the country was watching on television as Oswald was being taken through the basement of Dallas Police Headquarters toward an armored car that was to carry him to the county jail. At 12:21 p.m. Eastern time, out of the crowd stepped Jack Ruby, a strip club owner and Kennedy admirer, who shot and killed Oswald on the spot. Oswald was officially pronounced dead ninety minutes later. That was the first reality TV show. By then the country was numb. It felt like the whole world was falling apart

No one was watching pro football that Sunday because CBS had canceled all regular programming, including NFL football telecasts, until after the president's burial. Instead the networks were running nonstop news broadcasts without commercials.

The end of my innocence came that Sunday. The end of a lot of people's innocence. That weekend was the end of the silent fifties and the start of the cacophonous sixties and a cultural revolution that not even pro football could avoid. The NFL wasn't going to be immune to the changes that were coming.

By January, things had certainly changed for me. Molesworth decided to let me go on the road to scout. I left in January and felt like I came back twenty years later, although it was only two or three months.

I rented a big white Lincoln Continental that looked like Moby Dick. If I was smart, I would have gotten Alabama plates, but you live and learn. I went through DC, out the Shenandoah Valley, into Tennessee, then down to Arkansas, Mississippi, and Louisiana, making sure I stopped at Grambling. That was one of the most important stops in the South in those days. Eddie Robinson, their legendary coach, had so much talent because college football in the South wasn't integrated yet.

Then I turned west and drove into Texas and headed for Houston, Dallas, Austin, West Texas, Oklahoma, New Mexico, and Arizona. Then I turned around and drove home. I think it was a relief for Moley to send me out there. Otherwise he had to do it. Our coaches went out in the spring too. They all had territories, but who wanted to drive to New Mexico and Arizona? Nobody but me. I would have driven across Siberia.

You're probably wondering by now what kind of training I had. Well, none. There's no formal training for scouts. You had forms you needed to fill out with name, height, weight, speed, a place for a grade and comments. Other than that they got you a car, and the secretary set up the trip. She got you a AAA Triptik, which was bound road maps that flipped over with your route outlined in blue ink on the map, and a "see you later."

I think that was a plus. It helped me that there were no preconceived notions. You made up your own mind. Moley wasn't telling me how to do it. Just get accurate information and have an opinion.

If we had any paid scouts at the school, you'd sit down with them first. I'd meet with the head coach and some assistants. The first coach I ever met was Joe Aillet at Louisiana Tech. They ended up naming the stadium after him. He was a legend down there.

I looked so young he asked if I was a student or the new PR guy. When I told him I was "Upton Bell of the Baltimore Colts," he eyeballed me curiously, but he set me off on the right path.

I think he could see I was somewhat nervous, and he couldn't have been nicer. That was very important for my confidence. I'll always remember the dignity of Joe Aillet and the way he treated me, this Boy Scout coming onto his campus. He took the time to talk with me about his players, and not everyone did then. They still don't. If the first coach I ran into had been Dan Devine at Missouri, I might have just kept driving to California and never come back.

I had business cards made up for a couple reasons. You leave them with the coaches so they remember you, but it was particularly important to have them in the South, since if you ended up stopped by the police and they thought you were down there without identification registering blacks to vote, someone might find your body ten years later. I know that sounds like an exaggeration, but that was the tension that existed in the South in the sixties. Especially if you were driving Moby Dick around with out-of-state plates.

A year later one of the strangest and biggest days of my life in pro football came unexpectedly. I was on the road most of the time. The baskets were behind me. Now I was writing reports but I still read all the others, so I had a full grasp of the players we were looking at.

The draft in those days wasn't a made-for-TV event. It was the Super Bowl for scouts and personnel men and always will be, but it wasn't a prime-time televised media festival. In fact, it was conducted during the season, before the college bowl games had even been played.

There was no combine and no pro days at colleges to help you get information. If your scouts didn't do their job in the spring, you were left in the dark reading college football magazines and hoping for the best. Dallas had made that a recipe for disaster.

My second season working for Moley we were playing back-to-back West Coast games when draft day came on November 28, 1964. We'd beaten the Rams and flown up to San Francisco with a 10-1 team headed for the NFL Championship Game a month later in Cleveland.

In those days the schedule was set up to save teams money on cross-country travel. You'd go out for the first game and then stay on the West Coast to avoid double plane fare, so we were staying in the Jack Tar Hotel in San Francisco while the draft itself was being held in New York.

It was a great hotel then. It was demolished in 2013, but in 1964 it was billed as the most modern hotel in America. It had a swimming pool and even an ice rink on the roof. If you had a car you could drive to your room and skip the lobby, which was a big deal but not as big as having closed-circuit TV in your room. That's how much the game had changed. Ten years earlier no one in the NFL except maybe the Giants could afford a hotel like that. They were lucky to be in a cold-water flat.

So we're ready to start and Moley says he's not feeling well. He looked terrible. In football you play hurt, but he couldn't. He was having a heart attack right there on Van Ness Avenue.

The draft had started but we hadn't made a pick yet when Moley slumped over. Shula said, "Moley, you okay?" He said he'd be all right, but you could see he wasn't well. They didn't cart him out, but the team doctor came and said he had to go to his room.

It turned out he'd had a heart attack earlier, but I never knew it. He was carried out, and I wouldn't see him again for months. He died less than eighteen months later, on March 3, 1966, while seeding his lawn.

So now what do we do? Our director of player personnel is gone. We don't have a room full of scouts, just our coaches. Shula just looked at me and said, "Well, Upton. You're in charge."

Nobody else said anything. I was businesslike and so were the coaches. We had to get on with it, although maybe a few of them were thinking, "We got this guy now?" But I was prepared. I knew the players. This was my chance to influence who we were going to take. I was running the draft room.

We didn't do mock drafts in those days. I didn't even know what Moley was thinking. But we were well stacked for the rest of the decade, so when we came up to the first round, I told Shula I liked Mike Curtis as a linebacker.

He said, "Upton, he's listed as a fullback." He played them both at Duke so I said, "I don't care what he's listed at. He's a linebacker, and someday he'll be terrific."

He kept saying he's listed as a fullback, which he should have said. Shula always questioned you and you had to have an answer. I said, "This guy may be a decent fullback but nothing special, but he could be a great linebacker." Somehow I convinced him. I don't think he would have taken him if I wasn't advocating for him because I'm not sure he knew enough about him. There were reports but not a lot of film. How would he know?

It was understood that I'd better be right, but he never said it. We were still fighting the other league too so we had to find him and sign him. It took a year to convince Shula totally he was a linebacker. He had him as a backup running back his rookie year, but I kept lobbying Shula and he gave him a chance. When he did, Mike became one of the best and most aggressive linebackers in football.

I'm sure Shula had his own feelings about it because we didn't pick anybody Shula didn't want. You had to convince him. You always have to, even if you have final say on personnel, but one great thing about Shula was you could convince him. You'd just better know what you're doing if you did.

On the second round, Ralph Neely's name came up. I said he's probably the most talented offensive lineman in the draft, but he was a lazy player at Oklahoma. He didn't have the best attitude. But I also said, "Look at his feet." Neely was really agile. We threw the ball a lot for the times, so I was interested in how quick his feet were. Shula said draft him. We took him but he wanted to play in Texas, so later on we traded his rights to Dallas, where he became a great player.

Why'd we trade him? Because we couldn't sign him. He wanted to be in Texas and he was ready to sign with the AFL. You'd rather see him playing in our league than the other league. We hated the AFL and they hated us. It was competition for talent, which began to raise the compensation for talent. When that started to escalate, the owners on both sides decided they liked each other more than they thought and merged.

That was a great draft for us. We took Curtis and Neely. Glenn Ressler on the third round, who became a solid offensive linemen for us. Marty Schottenheimer and Al Atkinson, who played in the AFL, and we got Roy Hilton out of Jackson State in the fifteenth round. If you can find a starting defensive lineman that late, you've accomplished something.

Somebody kept checking on Moley, but we weren't. It was too intense in that room. Rosenbloom was out there with us and kept coming in and out, but in all honesty I never gave a thought to who was there or why or even the shock of Moley getting sick. Of course we didn't know he'd had a heart attack. We just knew he didn't feel well. The only thing I was thinking about was who are the best players and how can I convince these coaches who may be saying, "You kidding me?"

For about eight hours I was in a zone. I never wavered or considered the outside elements. It was an occasion that comes along once in a lifetime and I knew it. So I knew I had to do the job, which I think I did. Shula must have too, considering that just two years later he and Rosenbloom made me the youngest personnel director in pro football after Moley passed away.

The draft went all day, but at some point Shula and the coaches had to go have their normal meetings with the team. After the first two rounds he came in and out, but he had to prepare the team. I think he saw how it was going and had reason to think I was up to the job.

The draft was a one-day deal then. Seventeen never-ending rounds. We had fourteen teams then, so you had a better chance of finding players. It was still possible to find someone no one else had on their radar, like a Preston Pearson playing basketball, or someone at one of the black colleges maybe other teams missed. You could do it in one day because there was no TV show attached. No ads to sell. No interviews to conduct or highlights to show of a kid never missing a block or throwing an interception. Just decisions to make, and to make them you needed more than numbers to crunch and medical information. You needed an eye for talent and an opinion you believed in.

6

The Making of an NFL Scout

What makes a successful NFL scout?

That depends on your definition. Many scouts are thorough. They gather all the string of heights, weights, medical reports, and character evaluations. They talk to the right coaches and wait for the trainers and plug all that information into a cogently written report. They may do all that and still not be a gifted scout like Gil Brandt in Dallas or Tony Razzano with the 49ers when he was building Bill Walsh's dynasty in San Francisco.

They may get everything down on paper and still not be astute in the way Lloyd Wells was in Kansas City and Bill Nunn and Art Rooney Jr. were in Pittsburgh or Ron Wolf in Oakland and Green Bay and Bobby Beathard in Miami, Washington, and San Diego or Joe Thomas was in Minnesota and Miami. That's because to be a great scout takes more than information.

Information is critical, of course. Without it you're flying blind, as they did for so long in the NFL during the days when teams drafted from those college football magazines and newspaper clippings. But to be a great scout you need a great eye and you need guts. You need judgment and the courage of your convictions while always having a willingness to listen to conflicting opinions and give them weight without going overboard in either direction.

You also need a thick skin because like great Major League hitters, you're going to swing and miss a lot. If you bat .300 in baseball you're a star. If you bat .333 in pro football talent evaluation the same is true, because it is not a science, even though Dallas tried hard to make it one.

I scouted and drafted pro football players for fifteen years. I helped build two Super Bowl teams and assembled one of the best scouting staffs ever constructed in New England, but I didn't get to finish the job we started there with Bucko Kilroy, Tom Boisture, Dick Steinberg, Mike Hickey, Peter Hadhazy, and Bob Turpening. George Young, Dick Szymanski, and Fred Schubach all worked for me, and I wish Ernie Accorsi had come to New England with me as I hoped he would. Every one of those men went on to run his own personnel department and was highly successful. So I think I know what makes a great scout. So what is it?

It isn't mastery of technology or coming up with a new algorithm like they're trying to do in Cleveland today. New technology and "advanced" statistics are helpful tools, but they don't make a great scout. Neither does watching video all night, unless you know what you're looking for.

I believe nothing has changed in player evaluation but the technology. You get the information quicker, but that doesn't make you a better talent evaluator. You either have the ability to look at somebody and see that he can play or you don't. I don't care where you come from. You can start out in PR and become a great scout like Ernie did, and you can be trained all your life by great scouts and not see what's in front of you.

To scout effectively, you need the long memory of a historian and the short memory of a great relief pitcher. Why? Long memory is when you're standing there and somebody says that player isn't as good as so-and-so. You have to remember that player and all the things you didn't put in his report but that are still in your mind so you can use them for comparison purposes. You have to remember what worked and what didn't and understand why.

When I saw something special about a player, good or bad, I could always remember it. As a kid I was constantly looking at players not for what they did but for the things that made them good or not. I was trying to learn what made a great player great. I was a scout, even then. I just didn't know it.

Short memory is a must because you must quickly erase your mistakes and move on. You can't dwell on the criticism. If you can't do that, turn in your pen, stopwatch, and reports. You're finished.

My belief is you can learn what it takes to make a cornerback or an offensive lineman or a linebacker or a quarterback (although this one is the hardest), but you either have that eye or you don't. I saw Sammy Baugh with my father and it was obvious to me his gift: he saw the whole field. He saw things others didn't and reacted immediately to them. Unitas, same way. Brady, same way. Lesser quarterbacks, not so much. It had nothing to do with their arm. That was a gift too, but it wasn't the magic.

Shula once told Jim Ward, one of our backup quarterbacks, to ask Unitas why he'd just thrown a ball where he threw it for a touchdown. Ward was young and Shula wanted him to learn. So he went over to Unitas to ask him what he saw. Unitas said, "How the fuck do I know? I just knew he'd be open."

Try to quantify that.

Assuming you have The Eye, the second thing is you must be able to make a decision. You have to not be afraid in the reports you write and especially in the pre-draft and draft day meetings to say what you believe and be ready to defend it.

When the head coach or general manager says—assuming he really wants your opinion—all right, we have so-and-so and so-and-so, who do you like and why, you must not be afraid to be in that position. A lot of scouts will hide to see what develops. You saw the player in practices, in games, on film. You can't be on the fence, even if you're wrong. Because you will be wrong some-times and you won't always know why it didn't work.

The fear of a scout is, if I'm wrong too much, I'll be out. Look, even if you're great at it, more than 60 percent of the time you'll be wrong. You have to accept that and not be cowed by it.

The hardest athletes to judge are football players. How do you explain Ralph Neely? He had all the ability in the world, but he probably would never be a great lineman because he appeared to take every other play off. What am I going to do when his name comes up?

You know the negatives, but in the end are you going to take him or not? Usually most scouts say, "I'm not really sure." I never was afraid to say to Shula or Chuck Noll what I believed, because that's really what a scout does. He's selling his beliefs. I believed in Neely's quick feet and I was right.

The coach gets fired or hired for wins and losses, but the scout is on the line as much as the coach. That's why I admire what Ernie Accorsi did in New York with Philip Rivers and Eli Manning. He always believed Eli was better. Many people liked Rivers more. But Ernie made his decision and stuck with it, made it happen. He'll tell you to this day it was the right decision, even though some people will say Rivers just hasn't been on a good-enough team. Perhaps. It happens. All I know is Eli won two Super Bowls for the Giants, which is what Ernie was hired to get done, and Rivers hasn't gotten the Chargers to any. Bottom line. So the great scout does two things: he sees something others do not, and he has the courage to put his name behind it and his reputation on it.

The thing that would drive me crazy, especially early on when I was looking at African American athletes at black colleges, were the naysayers who would argue, "Look at the conference he plays in." That was a bromide I kept hearing and I'd say, "So what? I just saw Otis Taylor on a dusty field at Prairie View where they serve sandwiches and orange juice for a pregame meal. I saw him run. I saw him catch. I turned on the film. That young man stood out. I don't care what the competition was."

You have to factor in the competition, of course. If you're in the Ivy League and you're going to play in the NFL, you have to dominate that league, in my opinion. But if you do, I don't want to hear about the competition he faced. The only question that matters is, can he play? At scouting meetings I used to tear out what hair I had left when scouts would hedge their bet behind that.

Here are the only things that counted to me: height, weight, speed depending on position, Wonderlic test to have some idea about decision making. That was it. That's as far as I wanted to go with all that kind of stuff. Vertical leap, broad jump, shuttle run time? Give me a break. I might want to talk to the player about body fat ratio, but please. In the end it's as simple as this: can he play football or not? You're guessing most of the time, but the clues are there on the tape.

Here are several examples that go against the measurable stuff. Ted Hendricks at Miami. The Mad Stork. He was six feet seven and about 195 pounds in college. Looked like a scarecrow.

We came to the second round in 1969. I'd seen him play. I said, "I don't care where you put him. We'll win with him." First off, he had the highest IQ of anyone I ever tested. That's an important variable. Then you put on the film and he's always making plays whether he's standing up or rushing the passer. He knows where to be and how to get there.

He went to the Senior Bowl, and Shula really liked him. I told Shula, I don't know where you play him but he's a player. The naysayers said, "Where's he going to play?" I told the Colts we projected him as a linebacker, and someone said, a six-foot-seven, 195-pound linebacker? Are you kidding?

But Bill Arnsparger was smart. He saw what Hendricks could be. He backed me up. He wasn't really talkative, but he had good judgment. He's the one who kept defending Roy Hilton, who was a six-foot-six, 220-pound defensive end from Jackson State we took on the fifteenth round the first draft I ran. Even I had doubts, but Bill saw something and he was right.

The other player was Larry Csonka. I'd gone to Syracuse to look at Floyd Little, who was a three-time All-American and is in the Hall of Fame and deservedly so, but my eye kept going to this plodding kid named Csonka. He'd started out there playing middle linebacker, but they'd switched him to fullback after his first year, and he eventually broke records set there by Jim Brown, Jim Nance, Ernie Davis, and Floyd by the time he was done.

He wasn't that player the first time I saw him, but when I put on the film, I tried to steal it so Dallas didn't get it. I saw this big hulk slow off the ball, but once he got there he carried five players with him. I told Shula he's not very fast and I don't know if he can catch, but if you watch, he keeps gaining yards. Maybe he was plodding along, but unlike most plodders, after he got hit he kept going, carrying players, until he plodded into the end zone.

If you looked at Csonka's measurables, you might say you're not sure about taking him on the first round. What's the most important thing for a running back? Quickness to the hole. Did he have that? No, but when he got to the hole, it opened when he hit it. He was a football player. Ted Hendricks was a football player. We took Ted and would have taken Csonka, but he was gone before the Colts picked. Ultimately, Csonka went high because by then he'd broken all those Syracuse records but there were still doubters who said he was too slow for the NFL. Well, he ran all the way to the Hall of Fame. It didn't matter what the stopwatch said about him.

In 1969 I liked Calvin Hill, but a lot of scouts kept saying "Ivy League." They were right, but he could have played in any league. As the picks went by, twenty-three teams passed on him. I thought we were going to get him, but Dallas picked ahead of us and took him with the twenty-fourth pick in the first round. He was a good runner on some great teams in Dallas. Shula used to say when he'd see me, "How'd we miss Calvin Hill?" I'd say, "You saw the film, but so did Dallas!" That damn computer.

But as effective as Dallas's computer was in the early days of scouting, the rise of analytics has gone too far. Now instead of leading you to a good player, they can lead you away. The scout's job isn't to find ways to reject a football player. It's to *find* football players.

Some of the new statistics are interesting, but a lot of them make me wonder what they are based on. Do they actually tell you anything useful or are they just a way to make it appear more scientific when, in the end, scouting is about your judgment? That's what happened with Tom Brady. Football people didn't see what he was because he didn't fit the numbers. They only saw what he wasn't.

When you miss on someone or if you pass over someone who becomes a great player, the personnel director hears it all year from the coaches. "Upton, you recommended this kid and he stinks. Your great prospect." You have to sit there when they cut him and listen to that.

If you've got rabbit ears, you won't survive. That can affect your judgment. Some scouts hesitate when it comes time to make a recommendation again. You have to have blinders. Doubt yourself and then you'll doubt your own eyes next time. You have to be disciplined and strong-minded. It helps if you also happened to be right a few times.

The other variable is, can you stand the life? It's a grind. I'd leave Baltimore in January when I was scouting for Moley and not come back until spring practices were over. In the fall, you were on the road every week from Tuesday to Sunday, then go to the Colts game if you could get there, then turn around and go out again.

The scout's family suffers from his absence. So does the scout, because he wants to be with his wife and kids as much as they want him to be. But the job's demands are ever present and so he often isn't.

My wife Anne and I lost our first child in childbirth, so I very much wanted to be there for the birth of our second child, Christopher, in 1967. Unfortunately it wasn't to be, because I got a call that he was born while I was at our final summer scouting meetings in Atlanta. That's the family life of a scout—too often on the road at the wrong time. Christopher has grown into a wonderful man, a successful attorney, and the father of my grandsons, Peter and Jack. I'm very proud of them all. None of them are likely to become pro football scouts.

Lack of sleep is what I recall about the road. You're up by 6 a.m. because you'd better be at those schools before 8, because their day has started. You spend the day watching film and practice and talking with people. Maybe you leave by 7 p.m. and it's back to the hotel to write reports or you're on to the next town. That's the routine and you'd better stick to it.

At night in the car you could get talk shows from all over the country. They kept you up on what was really going on. Without the radio I would have fallen asleep and been dead a long time ago. That's how Buddy Young died—on a lonely road in Terrell, Texas.

You want to arrive at a school sharp, able to concentrate. You don't want some college coach to see you falling asleep watching his players on film, because that kind of thing would get around and kill you with other coaches. It would get back to your team. You have to be excited to get to the next school and find the next player.

You can't be bored by the monotony. If you're bored, you're going to be out of work, because you'll miss things. Nighttime is the scout's enemy. Not much good was going to happen unless you were in your room writing reports at the Holiday Inn.

I used to stay in what was called a "down and out": first-floor room and out the back because it's quieter. At night you'd better be down and in. You'd better be writing those reports and getting enough sleep to find that gem waiting at the next school. The great scout always has the anticipation of that next player. That next school. Who knows what you might find there?

It's a lonely life. If you're twenty-five, thirty, maybe it's all right. If you're fifty, fifty-five, and have been on the road for twenty years, it's more difficult, especially if you have a family. Somebody who is twenty-five or thirty, it could be scary but it's an adventure. If you're forty-five or fifty, it could be torture. You had to love the search because it's the loneliest life. And in the sixties in the South, suddenly it wasn't just lonely. It could be dangerous.

When I first started out, my big fear in Texas and Oklahoma was tornados. I'd tell the man at the front desk, if you hear there's a tornado coming let me know—I'll be out of here in a hurry. You'd listen on the radio for tornado warnings. It was always a threat that was out there in that part of the country. But once the civil rights movement picked up steam and the voter registration drives and marches started, there was a whole different fear when you were driving around the South. The fear that something spontaneous could happen. I can't remember too often thinking about it consciously, but subconsciously it was always there.

The great dilemma for the scout hasn't changed in my mind. It's balancing talent against attitude. I always thought attitude was as important as the talent, but for coaches, I understood that if they saw someone like Bubba Smith, they'd say forget the attitude. What's the first thing you think as a coach? I can mold this man.

Coaches are all whores for talent. The honest ones will admit it. It's why a lot of them overrate the talent and underrate the attitude. It's also why a scout is the great buffer if he's willing to give you his true opinion. That's why when I was starting an organization in New England, I hired scouts first. I'd always do that, even before a coach. I want someone to give me his opinion on the talent, because if you don't have talent in football you've got nothing. I don't care who the coach is or who the owner is. Talent wins.

That's why attitude is important, assuming you have the base level of raw athletic ability a player must have or he can't play at the next level. We see it all the time. The great college player who can't make it in the NFL. Sometimes it's a deficiency in talent but not always. Sometimes it's his mental makeup, and a scout must understand that and factor that in.

How many players have you seen come into the league with talent but a terrible attitude? They don't succeed because talent isn't enough anymore. In the NFL everyone has talent. When some players realize they can't win with just their talent, they take plays off. Then they take games off. How many do we say that about? A lot. It's a tough sport.

That's why the good scout always spends time with the trainer. The trainer knows the players better than anybody. He knows who the malingerers are. Who recovers quickly and who doesn't. That's important in football. They know everything, physically and mentally. You have to develop relationships with them. Gil Brandt did that as well as anybody. He was a stickler for that and I became the same way. If they trust you, you'll get the truth about things you can't see on tape or the field.

Of all the sports, attitude is more important in football, because you're hitting somebody every play and someone is hitting you. In basketball, you can have a lousy attitude and still hit a jump shot. Baseball? That's the home of bad attitude. If you're Manny Ramirez you can sit in the back of the bus and tell the manager to go screw himself if you can hit the ball a mile. It's an individual sport, not a team sport.

That's where a scout differs from a coach. The coach sees raw talent and forgets the rest of it. A scout can't afford that. Why are mistakes made in the draft? One reason is it's hard to scout attitude. You can see talent or its absence. Attitude is more subtle but just as important. It's why Belichick always asks, "Is football important to him?"

I always tried to keep track of how many plays someone took off. If he's taking plays off in college, what will he do in the NFL? That's why I liked to watch practice. Does he practice hard? Does he put out or stand around? Where the instinct comes in is balancing that with game production. Some are practice players. Some are game players. They need the lights to come on. John Madden once admitted that Dave Casper, the Raiders' Hall of Fame tight end, started a year later than he should have because he wasn't a good practice player. Someone might dog it in practice and still be great in games. You have to make that judgment.

You also can't be blinded by raw talent. That's how Jeff George became a No. 1 draft choice and a bust. He had a great arm and a lousy attitude that killed teams and got coaches fired. It's why he was 46-78 as a starter in twelve years. Jay Cutler is the same kind of player. Great talent but something is missing. What? That's the great unanswerable, but you had better at least ask that question.

You must understand if the talent fits your coach and his system. You can be the right player in the wrong place. How would Joe Montana have fared on the Raiders, where they wanted to drop back and throw deep twenty-five times a game? How would Lawrence Taylor have fared in a tightly structured defense that didn't let him rush the passer all the time? That changes things and the scout has to understand that.

I remember going to Texas Western, which is now University of Texas–El Paso. They had a linebacker there named Fred Carr. I put the film on and thought I've never seen anything like it. He ran everybody down. But the more I watched, the more I wondered: Was he everywhere or was he undisciplined?

His coach told me, "We ask him to do a lot of things." When a coach says that, you should say, "Yeah, but within the game plan what does he do?"

Is he just a great athlete running around or does he have football intelligence? I went to the CEPO meetings and the Packers were in the group. Pat Peppler with the Packers was a friend of mine. I asked if he'd seen Fred Carr. I got up and said he was one of the best athletes I'd ever seen. Somebody said there's a question about his football intelligence. A red flag went up for me, like when you've fallen madly in love with a woman but know it will never work. He couldn't play for Shula.

If I'd fallen in love with his ability, I would have pushed for him because of that talent, but it probably wouldn't have worked. As it turned out, the Packers made him the fifth pick of the 1968 draft, and he went to three Pro Bowls in nine years. He played well but not up to his physical ability, because he could have done anything. Would he have played as well for us? I don't think so.

You always wonder about players you miss on who make it, and you should. Ernie told me he went through that with Brady. Brady was the 199th player drafted in 2000. Someone named Leif Olve Dolonen Larsen went before him. So did six quarterbacks. Even the Patriots passed on him six times. Ernie wanted to know why they missed him, so he went back over every report.

Turned out one of his scouts didn't miss him, but nobody had listened. He found a lot of scouting reports pointing out Brady's athletic deficiencies, but one was spot on. That scout saw everything Brady became. He talked about his intelligence, his confidence, his constant preparation and competitiveness. How he was a leader and someone who never flinched under pressure. He also noticed something the others missed. For all the talk of him being unable to beat out Drew Henson at Michigan (where they shared the position), it was Brady playing at the end of the game when it was being decided. That was ignored by the entire league because athletically he wasn't as gifted as some others. His arm wasn't as strong. He couldn't run.

That's the personnel director's dilemma. When do you find the outlier? When do you ignore the measurables? When do you listen to that one scout saying, "Curtis is a linebacker," or, "Brady can play"?

A scout's track record will have something to do with that. Sometimes you'll remember you had a scout who saw something and you'll go back and watch some more tape. Maybe you see it too. In Brady's case the truth is nobody saw it, or he wouldn't have gone 199th out of 254 players drafted. The whole league was wrong about the greatest quarterback of his generation. Some men don't look good in shorts, but you don't play the game in shorts. What did he do with the pads on?

That's the problem with the combine. Other than the medicals, the combine to me is the place you go to be talked out of drafting a good football player. You've been watching this person play for three or four years. You like him. He's been productive. Then you go to the combine and don't like the way he runs around some cones or did the vertical leap and you start to doubt him, which really means you're doubting yourself. If you're not careful, you make mistakes because the last thing you saw was negative. You let information overwhelm your eyes. That's how the gutless scout operates. He lives in a world of numbers, but in the end it's your eyes that will tell you the truth if they're open.

The other factor for a scout is the organization. A scout is only as good as the organization he works for. I remember when I came back from scouting USC in spring practice before the 1967 season. Ron Yary was the big tackle prospect there, but I came back and told Shula, "I've just seen the best back ever, but he's only a junior." It was O. J. Simpson.

All I could remember was this player making cuts and running away from everybody in a full-scale scrimmage. You could see he was special. Phenomenal. People forget how good he was because of all that's happened since then. So Buffalo took him No. 1 a couple years later, and in his first year with the Bills, the coach, John Rauch, didn't want to build the offense around him. He had him blocking and using him as a receiver out of the backfield. For three years he looked like a bust. That's how a scout gets screwed. You recommend a great runner, and some coach wants to make him a receiver. Everyone's looking at you and thinking, "You recommended that guy!"

There are so many things that can make you give up if you don't feel valued. You're out there on your own. If you want to throw in the towel, it's really easy. If you want to go back to your room and have a drink and say, "I'll write the reports when I get back," nobody will know it.

Now it's all on your laptop. The personnel director knows if those reports show up. When I was director, I didn't know if the scout filled it out until he got back.

One break for today's scout is at least they don't have to worry about splicing film. Now that's a lost art, thank goodness.

It's all video today, but when I was scouting, if you didn't know how to run a projector forward and back like Steven Spielberg, you ended up pissing off the coaches because the film would snap. You had to bring your own splicer and splice it back together if you snapped it. You could get a bad reputation at schools if you were cutting up their film.

Without a computer, one way I came up with to make it easier was I had these little books, like a prayer book. My player prayer book: a small three-ring binder. I had cards made up specific to each position, mimicking what was on the bigger report form.

At practice I'd put my remarks right in there along with the measurables. I had it all on those cards. The coaches laughed at me, but I told them it would make their life easier. I could write a full report on those cards. All I had to do was transfer it or give the card to the secretary and ask her to type it onto the report form. If you waited until you got back to the room to scribble down what you saw or thought about a dozen players, it was too late. What you saw in that moment on the field can be revealing, but you might not retain it.

Now what's the worst trait in a scout? That's easy. Being lazy and writing things your eye didn't show you or you really don't believe. That's something I learned on the road all those years.

You're on the Grand Tour with three or four other scouts from other teams, going from school to school. That can help with the loneliness, but if they start talking about a player you haven't seen yet and you're not careful, you go in with a preconceived notion. If Gil Brandt tells you the young man can play, then I guess he can. You start believing what people tell you instead of what you see. Every review says that *Ben-Hur*'s the greatest movie ever made; next thing you know, that's what you say, even though you don't like chariot races.

You sit at the personnel meetings and two or three scouts are saying this person can't play and you're thinking yes he can. What do you do? Do you go along with the crowd because you're afraid to look stupid, or do you tell them what your eyes told you? When you're a personnel director or GM, you have to know who is going to give you their own opinion and who's going to be part of the crowd.

I can still remember Don McCafferty's report on Dick Butkus, the great linebacker at Illinois in 1965. He came back from spring practice and I looked at his report. "Radar nose No. 1! Take him." That was it. I went and asked where his report was. He said, "You don't need a report. Radar nose." And he walked away. I knew where he stood on Dick Butkus.

In Baltimore we knew who we were working for: Shula and Rosenbloom. There may have been petty jealousies but there was no jockeying for power. When it's not like that it can be a problem, because you want people to tell you what they really think. It is such a bottom-line business. Can he make it or can't he?

That's why I took equipment manager Fred Schubach into the personnel department, and why I had such respect for Ernie Accorsi. They understood players, saw talent, and were unafraid to tell you what they thought. For me, it always came down to this: please give me your opinion, even if it's wrong. In many businesses you can hide yourself in reports, but you can't hide when there's a football game every Sunday. That's the bottom line for the scout. You were right or you were wrong. It's all up there on the scoreboard.

7

Spy vs. Spy Settles NFL-AFL War

On the surface, the six-year war between the National Football League and the American Football League was about television contracts, revenue, and survival. In reality it was about talent. Acquiring it was my game, so beginning in 1963, I was smack in the middle of the real battlefield between the two leagues.

The war that led to the creation of the modern NFL was contested under college football goal posts and in hidden hotel rooms across America. It was a fight for the hearts, minds, and wallets of pro football fans through the hearts, minds, and wallets of the lifeblood of any sport: new talent. When Hall of Famer Gene Upshaw was running the players union, he once said during a work stoppage that without the players "all those owners own are a bunch of tight pants and jocks." He probably didn't fully understand how right he was.

Beginning in 1960, that meant more than finding new talent. It meant signing the talent, which the AFL with its scouts and deep-pocketed owners began to make difficult and far more costly. It was the latter that led directly to the merger of the two leagues on June 8, 1966, two months and two days after the NFL first approached AFL founder Lamar Hunt about a peace settlement. Getting to that point involved many moments of intrigue fitting of a John le Carré spy novel.

It was no longer enough to find hidden gems at historically black colleges or on basketball courts as well as football fields. You now had to keep them away from the AFL long enough to get their names on a contract. That's what led me to a manicurist in Atlanta in the fall of 1963.

Having struggled more than we expected to convince players we drafted to sign with our league the first few years of the AFL's existence, Rozelle came up with a plan before the 1964 draft called "Operation Babysitter." My brother, Bert, and I were two of the first.

The idea was the NFL would station scouts, coaches, front office personnel, ex-players, and businessmen friendly to the league around the country to locate and lock down the college players we'd targeted to keep them out of the clutches of the AFL until we could sign them. Each team submitted a list of players it was interested in, and people were sent out to "babysit" them. The AFL quickly became aware of this and did the same. Some might call this kidnapping. We liked to think of it as good business practices.

I was in my first year in scouting when Kellett told me I was flying to Atlanta to attend the Georgia–Georgia Tech game on November 30. It was the same day as the AFL draft and two days before our draft. With the AFL getting the jump on us, tension was high because Tech had four or five players that could have gone early, including their quarterback, Billy Lothridge, who finished second in the Heisman voting behind Roger Staubach that year. They had a tight end named Billy Martin whom the Bears would draft No. 1 and a linebacker I liked, Ted Davis, whom I talked Shula into drafting on the fourth round.

My job was to occupy them any which way we could until our draft. That meant Saturday, Sunday, and Monday, which was a long time to hold somebody who wasn't in handcuffs.

We were to do anything within, and sometimes beyond, certain legalities to convince these kids not to sign with the AFL. The league set it up territorially, using motels and hotels near college campuses arranged by the league office. Once we got to the hotel we were to call a central number and give them the number where we could be contacted. No cellphones then, so that complicated matters compared to how you could operate today, but the AFL was in the same boat. This was real espionage. Sometimes we'd move players two or three times if we found out the other league was on to them.

I knew who the players were because I'd read all our reports, but I'd never met any of them. Bert and I found them after the game and told them they were highly thought of by the NFL. We handed out brochures telling them how great it was to play in the NFL and gave them our hotel room number and asked them to come by . . . and please not sign with anyone until they spoke with us.

I called room service and filled the bathtub with ice and beer and got some food. They were smart Georgia Tech students. Free beer, free food, why not? They came and ate and drank right up to draft time, but we didn't know if they'd already signed with the AFL or not. They said they hadn't, but how did we know?

I believed they'd go with whoever the highest bidder was, even though in those days the NFL was considered really superior to the AFL. I thought they would listen to both sides, but money right in front of you is a stronger incentive than money that may come later, especially if you've never had any, like most of these players.

Years later, after free agency began, my old assistant George Young was running the Giants. He used to say, "The more they say it's not about the money, the more you know it's about the money." It isn't always. But if you bet on the highest bidder, you'll win a lot more times than you'll lose.

Every time the players would leave, you didn't know if they were coming back. That Sunday I got some intel that Don Klosterman, who was a great scout working for the AFL at the time, was in town, and the minute these players left our hotel they'd gone to see him. I'd heard Don was a great entertainer and a snazzy dresser. I didn't know him yet but I'd been told he could engage anybody and convince them of anything, which turned out to be true.

I got a report he'd taken our players and gotten them all steam baths. Somebody called me literally from outside the steam room and said, "Your boys are over here getting steam baths courtesy of Don Klosterman!"

Steam baths! The minute you hear that you panic. Holy shit! If they do that, they're going to sign and I'm dead. The league had entrusted me to keep these young men occupied, and they're in a steam bath with Klosterman! Your imagination runs away with you. Is he fixing them up with beautiful women? Is he giving them liquor? All I've got is a bathtub full of beer!

You have to understand in those days very few players had agents. They weren't asking us for anything. They were accepting the hospitality, the steam bath, whatever, but they didn't ask for anything.

The NFL thought it was the superior league, so we felt if all things were equal they'd sign with us. I won't call it arrogance, but I was confident if I could keep them occupied they'd sign with our league, but there were some crazy things going on around the country and it would get crazier. Steam baths?

At one point I got a call from Jim Carlen, an assistant coach on Bobby Dodd's staff at Georgia Tech. He just said, "This is all very nice, but don't you think this is a little too much for our boys?"

Word had gotten around we were entertaining these kids morning, noon, and night, and they were worried something was going on that would be bad publicity. Davis had already made headlines during the season for being suspended for kicking a player in the head. Tech didn't need any more bad publicity, and as a scout I needed people like Carlen not to be mad at me.

I told him nothing was going on. You have to remember the times. It was 1963. No lap dances that I knew of, but I was suspicious of what might have been happening at that steam bath. Within two years players were being whisked away on planes, but we hadn't gotten that far yet. I don't think those coaches particularly liked all this, but that's what things were becoming.

At some point during the draft, I had convinced Shula to take Davis, and he hollered at me, "Do you know what you're doing? You convinced me to take the guy and you better be able to sign him!" That was the young Shula. He was always challenging you. I hadn't got to know him that well yet, so I was figuring if I didn't sign Davis I might not have much of a future in scouting. So I told him it was under control . . . which it was not.

We drafted Ted and he agreed to meet me the next day. We'd gotten pretty friendly because we were about the same age, but I didn't sleep all night.

He finally came by, but he was taking the position that he's talking to everybody. In my mind I was seeing the headline in the *Baltimore Sun*: "Ted Davis Signs with Don Klosterman! Colts Lose Draft Choice!" It was a nightmare.

The league office called to see if I needed help. I told them no. I gave Davis the outline of the contract, which included a $12,000 bonus. That was a lot of money back then. Then I asked what else he needed.

He was kind of a vain person, and something just popped into my head and I said, "Would you go for a full manicure?" I don't know why I said it. I knew he'd been at the steam bath with Klosterman, so that was out. Desperate times call for desperate measures.

I wanted him to know we were willing to spend money on him. I got a check right there. I got the contract right there. Finally he said, "Make out the check and the contract, but where's the manicure?'

I called downstairs and got it arranged and told them to give him whatever he wanted. Toes, fingernails, whatever. Give him a massage too. That's how I signed him. Then I called Shula and told him. He didn't say great job. He just said, "Manicure? He's a linebacker!"

I said, "No, he's a Colt." Shula said, "Great," and hung up, which was Shula in those days. Not much for shoulder rubbing, but I'd gotten my man. The first player I babysat signed with us. Everybody I had babysat for that weekend signed that year with the NFL. I was so relieved I went to bed and slept for half a day.

Babysitting was particularly important because in the first AFL draft the Colts had lost everyone. They were the two-time defending NFL champions and didn't really feel they had to work too hard to sign their draft picks. The result was we lost four of our first five picks, and that contributed to the aging of the team that resulted in Weeb's being fired a few years later.

Carroll was mad about it. Weeb blamed Kellett. Kellett blamed Weeb. Nothing like that ever happened again to the Colts. We lost a few players but not many. Carroll didn't like to pay more than he had to, but he understood without talent we'd all pay a price, so he gave us what we needed. Even if it was a manicurist. But it would get harder after that.

"Operation Babysitter" went on right up to the merger and the first unified draft, but I didn't have to do it after Atlanta, because I soon began running the Colts' personnel department. If there was somebody I needed to hide I would have, but by then Rozelle had a network of businessmen in place all over the country. Ed King, an ex-Colt who was comptroller of the Massachusetts Port Authority and later would become governor, was one of the babysitters. It was an incredible network. We were doing a better job of hiding than the Witness Protection Program.

As I began to travel more for scouting, I became close with Ron Wolf, who was a young scout with the Raiders. He helped build their great teams in the '60s and early '70s, then set the foundation for the Tampa Bay Buccaneers' first playoff team in the late 1970s before getting fired unfairly. He eventually became the general manager who revived the Green Bay Packers by signing Reggie White and trading for Brett Favre. He was inducted into the Hall of Fame in 2015, and he earned it.

Ron worked for the slyest guy in pro football, Al Davis. The man was brilliant. He knew football because he used to be a coach. He understood talent and would do anything to get it. And he seemed to know things nobody else did. It was uncanny.

Ron once told me how he signed their first pick the following year, an All-American tackle out of Memphis named Harry Schuh, who would start on their first Super Bowl team two years later. Signing him was like a travelog.

Wolf was babysitting Schuh, whom they'd taken on the first round. Both leagues drafted on the same day that year, November 28, 1964. Memphis had finished its season the weekend before that draft, so Al decided to fly Schuh to Las Vegas. Wolf met him along with the wife of John Rauch, who was the Raiders' head coach. She was there babysitting Schuh's wife and young daughter, who were already out there.

The Raiders had about a half dozen rooms, and Wolf was feeling pretty good about their chances until Schuh came up from playing blackjack and showed him a business card from the Los Angeles Rams. The man next to him at the blackjack table gave it to him, and he wanted to know what to do.

Ron called Al and next thing he knew, one of their players left with Schuh and they ended up in Hawaii. He told me, "I wasn't sure where Jane took the wife and daughter, but all of a sudden I had six empty rooms in Vegas. Harry signed with us. It was very interesting to be walking around with a briefcase full of cash. You started plopping down money and you could open some eyes. There was a little stress to it, but Al Davis was way ahead of everyone else."

He was, but two years later I beat him to a player named Butch Allison, whom we drafted in the second round. They didn't lose many, because the Raiders didn't draft players they didn't know they could sign, but they didn't get Butch.

You'd be on the field when one of the college team's seasons had finished and the end zone would be full of men in ties and white shirts trying to sign players. The enemy is here and we're over there. There were a lot of contracts signed that were later negated because someone got to the kid before he got to the end of the season, just to be on the safe side.

I was at the 1965 Gator Bowl, and sitting right near me was a scout from the Houston Oilers. I was there to sign a defensive back from Georgia Tech named Tom Bleick. He was there to do the same thing, and we both knew it.

With about five minutes left in the game, the rush was on. I headed down to the field. So did the scout from Houston. We're standing behind the ropes around the field and there are a bunch of policemen there for crowd control, because Georgia Tech was leading Texas Tech by 10 and they thought the students might rush the field.

Weeb Ewbank used to use me sometimes to run 40s against players as a measuring stick, since I was a decent enough sprinter at Malvern Prep. The clock is now ticking down and I'm hoping that I'm still fast enough to beat a scout from the Oilers to Tom Bleick.

All of a sudden, the man from Houston slips under the rope and is running toward the Georgia Tech bench. He beat me out of the blocks! All I could think of was stopping this man, because if he signed Bleick I'd have to face Shula. So I started hollering, "Arrest that man! Arrest that man!" A police officer heard me, saw the man running "away," and flew over and tackled him.

While he was holding the poor scout from Houston, the gun sounded and I slipped under the ropes and signed Bleick. He played a year for us and a year for the Falcons. I probably should have signed the cop instead. It was a great tackle.

Those were the things that convinced Pete to start "Operation Babysitter." When the AFL began, Pete was still GM of the Rams and lost Billy Cannon, the Heisman Trophy–winning running back from LSU, to the Oilers. He'd signed him before the Sugar Bowl for $50,000. After the game, Cannon signed with the Oilers in the end zone for $99,000 plus a $10,000 bonus and a Cadillac for his father. Bud Adams, the Oilers' owner, was right there on television in the end zone shaking his hand.

The Rams sued but Judge William Lindberg ruled in Louisiana that Pete had taken advantage of "a provincial lad untutored and unwise in the ways of the business world." That's what the judge said, but I don't know about that. He was tutored enough to take money from both leagues.

In November 1959, the AFL held its first draft and soon after fired the opening shots in the war when they signed half the NFL's first-round picks, six of the twelve players drafted including three of the first four. Pete never forgot it. At least ten players signed contracts simultaneously with both leagues during the war years, six of them in the first, furious 1960 draft. That was when we lost Don Floyd, a good defensive end, to the Houston Oilers after he'd first been drafted by the then New York Titans but was worried about adjusting to life in a big city. The other involving the Colts was Tony Lorick, a fullback we drafted on the second round in 1964 out of Arizona State my second year in personnel. We'd taken him right behind Marv Woodson, a defensive back from Indiana and right before we grabbed Davis in the fourth round, as we had no third pick.

Unlike the legal fights in federal court over Cannon, Neely, and Cannon's LSU teammate Johnny Robinson and a University of Mississippi fullback named Charlie Flowers, our battle with the Raiders over Lorick ended quickly. Al Davis didn't press the issue even though he signed Lorick first, because by 1964 eight of the cases had been settled and, as Dan Daly quoted Al in his book *The National Forgotten League*, "The court will always side with the boy."

Maybe the greatest story from those days happened in 1965 when the Chiefs signed Otis Taylor right under the Cowboys' noses. Literally. By then the war was costing both sides a lot of money. Rookie salaries were out of control. Veterans didn't like it and the owners liked it less, but both sides needed talent, which brings us to Lloyd Wells.

An African American face in the NFL was still unusual in the sixties, especially if he wasn't in a uniform, but Lloyd went to work for Hank Stram and the Chiefs because he not only knew talent but knew how to sign it, and there was no more talented player in the 1965 draft than Otis Taylor. When I saw him at Prairie View A&M, it was like the first time seeing Baryshnikov dance. You knew he was a genius.

The Chiefs and the Eagles both drafted him, but because he was from Texas, the Cowboys had a stockbroker watching over him. They had him holed up at the Continental Inn in Richardson, Texas, just outside Dallas. In those days the AFL was pretty much every man for himself. They babysat players, but they weren't as cooperative with each other as the NFL, which was running a league-wide operation. Our emphasis was on someone in our league signing the player. We didn't really care who if the other option was the AFL.

It turned out Lloyd had been mentoring Taylor since he was in high school. He knew his family but somehow the Chiefs lost track of Otis, and he ended up outside Dallas with this stockbroker sleeping across the hall to keep an eye on the door.

Lloyd found out from Taylor's mother where he was, but the stockbroker wouldn't let Lloyd anywhere near him. That didn't bother Lloyd, who was a relentless recruiter. At some point he went to the back of the hotel and got Otis's attention, and Otis climbed through the bathroom window and was gone. He signed the next day with the Chiefs. We should have realized then how tough he was to cover, which became obvious in Super Bowl IV when he shook off a Minnesota tackler and ran for a 46-yard touchdown in the Chiefs' rout of the Vikings that evened the Super Bowls at 2-2 and ended the war with one last victory for the AFL.

I believe the last straw for the owners involved two separate incidents in 1966. The first was when the Packers drafted running backs on the first round two years in a row, Jim Grabowski and Donny Anderson, to replace their aging future Hall of Famers Paul Hornung and Jim Taylor. They took Anderson with a future pick in 1965 and Grabowski in 1966, which was the last draft before the merger and was held on November 27, 1965.

Anderson signed right after his final college game that fall, but Grabowski had been the Dolphins' No. 1 pick as well as the Packers' and had an agent named Arthur Morse, who had represented his former teammate, Dick Butkus, the year before. According to David Maraniss in his biography of Vince Lombardi, *When Pride Still Mattered*, Grabowski was in New York to appear on *The Ed Sullivan Show* with the rest of the All-American team, with an NFL babysitter from Chicago, a meat packing executive named Vern Buol, alongside.

Buol moved Grabowski from the Waldorf-Astoria, where the All-Americans were staying, to the Plaza to avoid the AFL, but Miami told Morse it was willing to trade Grabowski's rights to the Jets so he could play in New York with Joe Namath. Namath had signed the year before for an unbelievable sum of $427,000.

The Cardinals had also drafted Namath and thought they could sign him. I was laughing to myself because I didn't think St. Louis was big enough for Joe Namath. They thought it was because it was in the NFL. I thought maybe so, but it ain't Broadway. Namath agreed.

There were questions about his knees, so if there'd just been one league he might not have been taken on the first round at all. I'm not sure without the use of his name as a celebrity in New York—which made him an icon of the sixties—that the AFL would have made it. That was the genius of that move. Maybe St. Louis would have taken him on the first round anyway, maybe not. That was the difference the AFL made. They forced the NFL's hand time and again.

Grabowski was interested in the possibilities of playing with Namath in New York, but he agreed to fly to Green Bay first and sit down with Lombardi. He left a Packer and about $400,000 richer. The Packers were a publicly held company and hated to spend money, but they shelled out over $1 million to sign Anderson and Grabowski. In that final year before the merger, the two leagues spent over $7 million on rookie bonuses, and while both sides could have sustained that for a while, they realized it was bad business.

What made things worse and changed everything immediately came soon after Grabowski signed. Giants owner Wellington Mara announced on May 17, 1966, that he'd signed Buffalo Bills kicker Pete Gogolak, breaking an unwritten "gentlemen's agreement" between the owners of both leagues not to sign each other's veterans. The first thing I thought was if I was going to steal from the other league, it wouldn't have been a kicker.

Rosenbloom was really displeased. When Rozelle announced it at the owners' meetings, Carroll hollered at Mara that he would have given him a (expletive deleted) kicker. Rosenbloom would end up with many grievances real and imagined against Rozelle, but among the first was the decision to approve that contract. One could argue it led directly to the merger, which proved to be great for Carroll, both leagues, and pro football, but he still resented it—and when he felt that way he didn't forget.

Technically, Gogolak was a free agent because he'd played out his option in 1965, and certainly the Giants needed a kicker. Bob Timberlake was 1 for 15 the previous season before losing his job, and overall Giants kickers were 6 for 25. With a .500 team that had lost the back page of the New York tabloids to Namath and the Jets, Mara felt pressured to make a splash. As it turned out, he did more than that. He made a new NFL.

The AFL had already made clear it was on a war footing when it named Al Davis as its new commissioner a month earlier. Although Carroll and Bills owner Ralph Wilson had begun merger talks two years earlier, Al wanted war. So did Rozelle.

Pete was always an NFL man. He didn't believe we should take the other league in because he didn't feel in the end they could beat us. That may have been the only thing Al and Pete, who remained rivals the rest of their lives, ever totally agreed on.

When Rosenbloom approached Rozelle in 1964 with the outline of the merger deal he'd worked out with Wilson to end the financial carnage, the commissioner said it would cost the AFL $50 million to buy in. Infuriated and insulted, Wilson walked away and the bidding war went on for two more years; but after that costly 1966 draft, Dallas's Tex Schramm realized this could not continue, and he approached Hunt, asking for a private meeting at Love Field in Dallas.

They secretly met next to a statue of a Texas Ranger in the airport lobby and went to Schramm's car to talk. Thus began the formation of the most powerful sports entity ever created, today's NFL.

Although Schramm was close to Rozelle, the commissioner and several owners on both sides continued to favor war. The NFL's position remained one of arrogance. Al Davis's position was like that of a Mafia hit man. He wanted to shoot it out.

Three days after Gogolak signed, the AFL announced the Raiders had signed Rams quarterback Roman Gabriel for $400,000. Within days 49ers quarterback John Brodie called San Francisco owner Lou Spadia from a hotel in Houston to inform him he'd signed a three-year contract with the Oilers worth $750,000. Spadia had up to that point opposed a merger. He quickly got religion.

Davis had just begun. Almost immediately our league's best

tight end, Mike Ditka, signed with Houston too. Now even the opponents of a merger could see they were headed for a financial bloodbath. Pete was still holding out for war, but if there was a deal to be made to save money, Rosenbloom would make it.

Carroll had told his fellow owners that this was just getting needlessly expensive, and most of them agreed. Then he drove home the point as only an owner can. He told Schramm to tell his friend Rozelle the deal would be done "with him or without him." It was struck on June 8, 1966, but the fight was far from over.

For the first and only time, the NFL fully merged with another league, accepting all the AFL's teams and agreeing to expand to twenty-eight teams by 1970. But the AFL members were forced to pay an indemnity of $18 million over twenty years to the shared markets in New York and San Francisco/Oakland after a suggestion the Raiders and Jets move was rejected.

There was an immediate common draft, but there would be no regular-season interleague play beyond what became the Super Bowl until 1970. All teams were also forced to play in stadiums with at least fifty thousand seats, leading to a number of stadium shifts and constructions that helped expand the league's revenue.

For all this to happen, two things were necessary: three NFL teams needed to move into what would become the AFC in 1970, and Congress would have to exempt the merger from antitrust laws. The latter put Rozelle in the crosshairs of a New York congressman named Emanuel Celler, who was the head of the Judiciary Committee and had the final word on issues of antitrust legislation. He was harder for Rozelle to please than Carroll.

Celler was not a fan of corporate mergers, but he met with Rozelle in early September and wasn't necessarily opposed to the idea of only one pro football league. But he knew the reason for it was rooted in the monopolistic tendencies of big business, so he wasn't ready to rush into it either.

As negotiations dragged, Rozelle worried the agreement might unravel. To avoid that, he deftly ran an end around, quietly agreeing to give New Orleans an expansion franchise in exchange for the help of Senator Russell Long and House Majority Leader Hale

Boggs, two of the most powerful men in Louisiana politics at the time.

On October 14, 1966, an immunity amendment opening the door for the merger's approval was added to an obscure foreign investment act that sailed through Congress unnoticed. By the time Celler realized what had happened, it was too late to stop it. Eleven days after passage, it was announced the city of New Orleans would join the NFL for the 1967 season, becoming its sixteenth franchise.

Two huge hurdles remained in 1969 to complete the merger. Three NFL teams had to agree to join their longtime AFL enemies to form one of two fourteen-team conferences, and those conferences had to be divided regionally into three divisions each.

Originally it was suggested the two leagues remain intact with only a joint draft, a championship game, and some shared revenue constituting the new league, but Paul Brown—the same Paul Brown who had come in from the AAFC in 1950 and dominated the NFL with his Cleveland Browns—refused. Brown had paid a whopping $10 million fee to become the AFL's tenth team in 1968 when he formed the Cincinnati Bengals with the assurance the merger would go through. When it was suggested otherwise, he exploded, saying he hadn't paid $10 million to join the AFL.

I was always against three original NFL teams moving into what was effectively the old AFL and still am. Not that anyone asked me, but I thought each should keep their own identity, like the National and American Leagues in baseball, and end the season with a true Super Bowl. Maybe they were right, judging by the popularity of pro football today, but I still would have preferred to see things remain separate with the AFL adding three expansion teams instead stocked by players from both leagues.

The realignment process began in March 1969 in Palm Springs at the annual owners' meetings, and it was all the league could talk about. It took three separate meetings, the final one a twelve-day affair in New York beginning on April 29 that ended with owners sleeping on cots in the hallway outside a meeting room on May 10 before three teams finally agreed. We were one of them.

Carroll was actually the first to agree to move, and the reason seemed obvious to me. He understood it would be a lot easier to make the playoffs in the new AFC than in a conference with the Packers, Rams, and 49ers. He helped convince Art Modell in Cleveland, who had originally said he would never move the Browns. Modell suffered with a bleeding ulcer and was hospitalized as the negotiations were dragging on, but when Steelers owner Art Rooney came to visit him, Modell reluctantly said he'd move if Art went with him. Rooney did and it was done, with the Colts, Browns, and Steelers moving into the newly created American Football Conference leagues.

The fact Carroll was paid $3 million spread over the next five years to move didn't hurt, but the real motivation was that he saw us in a division with the Dolphins, Patriots, and Bills and knew that all but guaranteed a playoff spot.

He also saw Namath and the Jets, who upset us in Super Bowl III, twice a year and he wanted to crush them. Ernie Accorsi told me he sat next to Carroll the first time we played them in 1970. We led 26–5 in the third quarter and were tearing Namath apart. We intercepted him six times, but he hit us deep a couple times late and we had to hold on to win, 29–22. Ernie told me after we intercepted Namath the last time in the end zone to end the game, Carroll uttered a sound like he'd never heard before. He hated the Jets.

We beat them a lot in those days, and Carroll was right about the playoffs. The first year after the merger, we were in Super Bowl V, the combined league signed new four-year television deals with CBS and NBC, and ABC came in with a separate deal that launched *Monday Night Football*, putting the NFL regularly on in prime time television.

The new NFL was taking over the sports landscape, and Carroll's Colts were on top of the mountain.

8

The South Is Burning!

Much of my time scouting in the '60s and '70s was spent traversing an America I knew nothing about when I started. That America was known as the Deep South.

If you were in the Northeast or the Midwest or out on the West Coast, you didn't have that feeling. Some things were different but not that different. Sure, the sun was always out in California, it seemed, and there were no palm trees in Ohio, but the basic landscape of life was similar to what I'd grown accustomed to in Philadelphia and Baltimore.

The Deep South during the turbulent 1960s and early 1970s, however, was a land apart, although you couldn't really see that at first unless you knew where to look. When I drove off from Baltimore with my stopwatch and my scouting notebooks in 1964, the South I first encountered seemed like the beginning pages of *To Kill a Mockingbird*. Beautiful, sleepy towns filled with friendly people, big breakfasts with grits, and great college football players.

But there was a second South that was beginning to be exposed, a second country I discovered peering through the front windshield of a white, four-door Lincoln Continental that was as wide as a tugboat and just as reliable.

What I didn't realize at first was that I was going to find more than football players driving around the South and the Southwest for the next ten years. I was going to find a society fraying at the edges, a bifurcated land that would be rent apart along racial lines, causing turmoil that would sweep up pro football and its players right along with everyone else.

If I was going to define the moment I began to learn about American apartheid, it was when Cassius Clay beat Sonny Liston in 1964 in Miami Beach. I was twenty-seven years old and on the road scouting in Houston, so I bought a ticket to watch the fight on closed-circuit television and rooted for Clay. A day after he pulled off his great upset, he declared he was a member of the Nation of Islam, which was better known as the Black Muslims. It was considered a radical organization, but its message of standing up for black people and demanding their rights had a powerful appeal to young blacks who had seen themselves held back for so long.

That's how quickly things were starting to change in America. One day Cassius Clay wins the heavyweight championship and it's a great sports story, and twenty-four hours later it's not about sports anymore. It's a political story about a man named Muhammad Ali, someone about whom Jimmy Cannon, who was one of the most famous sportswriters in the country back when that meant something, wrote, "Clay is part of the Beatle movement . . . the boys with their long dirty hair and girls with the unwashed look and the college kids dancing naked at secret proms held in apartments and the revolt of students who get a check from Dad every first of the month."

Talk about the Generation Gap. There it was, right on the sports page. Much of that gap would be reflected on college campuses and in football locker rooms in the NFL, the AFL, and on the segregated football fields of the South where I'd begun to mine for talent.

The word *apartheid* was never used to describe segregation in those days, although it was appropriate. Used to describe the formal system of legislated racial segregation in South Africa that existed for decades, *apartheid* is an Afrikaans word that means "separateness" or "a state of being apart." That was the South I traveled through and the players I scouted there. For too long it was also part of the NFL.

My father helped end that in 1946 when he supported the Cleveland Rams' move to Los Angeles. To play in the Los Angeles Coliseum, which was publicly funded, the Rams had to agree to integrate their team. There hadn't been an African American NFL player since 1933, the last two being Joe Lilliard and Ray Kemp. The league has always denied there was a formal program of segregation, but the fact is black players disappeared for thirteen years, returning a year before Jackie Robinson integrated Major League Baseball only because the city of Los Angeles demanded it.

It wasn't until 1948 that a second team, the Detroit Lions, signed two black players, and none were drafted until 1949. The AAFC held far fewer restrictions. By the time it merged with the NFL in 1950, six of its eight teams had black players while only three NFL teams had followed suit, even though part of the reason for the Browns' dominance in the 1950s was the presence of black stars like Marion Motley, Bill Willis, and Len Ford.

Not coincidentally, the NFL followed a similar pattern during my early days in scouting. Black players were now scattered throughout the league, but not in the same proportion as in the AFL, which seemed to have no stigma against not only signing blacks but allowing them to flourish at every position. It is no accident that the first black quarterback of the modern era was not in our league but rather the AFL, where in 1968 Marlin Briscoe took over the stumbling Denver Broncos on October 6, 1968, and set a team one-season record for touchdown passes by a rookie (fourteen) that still stands, despite his having started only five games.

The AFL wasn't without its own prejudices, however. The following spring Briscoe got a call from a teammate asking why he wasn't at the off-season quarterback meetings in Denver. No one had asked him to attend. Angry to learn he would not be allowed to compete against the white quarterbacks, Pete Liske and Steve Tensi, Brisco demanded his release. He ended up with the Buffalo Bills and became a wide receiver because they already had two established quarterbacks as well as a highly regarded young black quarterback, James Harris. Briscoe would reach the Pro

Bowl in 1970 but never played quarterback again. That was the landscape a scout faced in those days.

By the time of the NFL-AFL merger, roughly 30 percent of players in the league were African American, and that number is approaching 70 percent today. Regardless of those numbers, I was in the talent business and didn't care where I found it, which is one reason I spent so many days and nights visiting historically black colleges. They were filled with talent, in part because college football in the South was totally segregated until the late 1960s.

The first black player in the Atlantic Coast Conference was Darryl Hill, who integrated the University of Maryland team in 1963 after first doing the same as a plebe at the Naval Academy. He was their only black player until his senior year and the first in any major conference in the South.

The Southwest Conference (SWC) didn't integrate until 1966 when Jerry Levias was recruited to attend SMU. He was at first reluctant, but it was a decision he made because, ironically, no historically black college offered him a scholarship. They all thought he was too small. Levias endured great prejudice but became All-SWC and later an AFL All-Star. He said in a documentary film called *Breaking the Huddle* that to this day he's still healing from the events of those times.

The Southeastern Conference did not have its first black player until 1967 when Nat Northington suited up for Kentucky. Alabama would not have its first until future No. 1 draft choice Wilbur Jackson and defensive end John Mitchell, who is today assistant head coach of the Pittsburgh Steelers, arrived in 1971, a year after USC came to Birmingham with an all-black backfield and ran Alabama off the field, defeating them, 42–21. It was a choice Alabama's legendary coach, Paul "Bear" Bryant, purposely made in hopes of showing the university and its fans what the future would become without black players. They got the message. By 1972 every SEC team had begun to recruit the great black athlete.

Politicians and businessmen can feel how they like about integration, but scouts and most coaches go where the talent is.

The day after the Liston fight, "Clay" met with reporters and someone asked if he was "a card-carrying member of the Black Muslims." His answer set the stage for a generation of change. He said, "Card-carrying? What does that mean? I know where I'm going. And I know the truth and I don't have to be what you want me to be. I'm free to be what I want."

That was the moment for me when it became clear the winds of change were blowing and it wasn't going to be a casual breeze. Change was coming whether people were ready for it or not. The phlegmatic fifties were over, and as a scout who worked the South and Southwest, I was more than a spectator for a lot of those changes.

What an education I got about football, about the fact that talent is where you find it, and about race in America. I saw firsthand that opportunity doesn't always knock, because it didn't always exist for African Americans, especially in the Deep South. That was true even on the football field, where great players were being denied the chance to show their skills at southern football powerhouses.

There weren't many super highways in those days, so I'd leave Baltimore and drive through the Blue Ridge Mountains into Tennessee and then turn south toward Kentucky, Alabama, Mississippi, and Louisiana. What first struck me was how nice people were and how good the breakfast was. But slowly you picked up on the feeling something else was going on.

Civil rights protests and the Freedom Rides that sent mostly young whites and blacks on Trailways and Greyhound buses across the South to try to put an end to segregated buses, lunch counters where they couldn't get so much as a glass of Coke on a steamy Sunday, and public bathrooms began in 1961 and quickly resulted in violent responses. There was very little public conversation about blacks and whites at that time, but you didn't need a conversation to know what the story was.

Baltimore was still segregated itself in some places, although not on the Colts. One reason we had a large number of black fans was the presence of stars like Lenny Moore, Jim Parker, Milt Davis, and Big Daddy Lipscomb. Baltimore remained more segregated than I realized, but the Colts were different, and you could see it in the locker room. Years later Lenny spoke about a deeper divide than I saw, and it came as a shock to me and most of his teammates. It was a reminder that the racial divide is wider than we thought.

I didn't think we were one big happy family, but what I remember was I never saw a team play better together as African Americans and whites than in Baltimore. The Patriots in 1971–72? Completely different. We nearly had a black rebellion there. I wasn't at the Patriots for very long before I saw there was a problem between the African American players and some of my coaches, whom I asked John Mazur to fire. He refused. There was nothing like that in Baltimore.

Lenny never expressed to me or anyone I knew what he was feeling back then. I was the same age as most of the players and around them a lot socially in places like Sweeney's and Gussie's Downbeat. When Lenny had his jazz club, I went there too. I saw what was happening in the South, but I didn't see a split like that on the Colts. Maybe there was one socially, as Lenny suggested. I'm not saying it wasn't there, but it was never in the locker room.

As much as you could say the white players wanted to be with the people they felt comfortable with, the same seemed true with the black players. It's still true today, although it's not as pronounced. If somebody had said there was a problem, I would have gone to Shula or Don Kellett. That never happened, so you can't assume a problem exists.

I remember in 1963 or '64, Kellett came to Bert and me and told us Carroll wanted to get Lenny a bonus, which wasn't legal at the time. He was going to write us checks, and we were to cash them and give the cash back to Kellett and he'd get it to Lenny. That was Carroll. He used to give bonuses to everybody until my father stepped in, but he found a way around it. That was how he treated all his players. I guarantee you when Lenny Moore wanted something from Carroll, he got it, but that doesn't take away from the issues Lenny raised. I guess I shouldn't be surprised by it looking back today.

Even in the dining hall, as close as I thought that team was, blacks ate with blacks and whites with whites. That was right out in the open. There was a lot of back-and-forth joking, but that's how it broke down. How did it affect the team? On the field it didn't. Those men put aside whatever discomfort they may have felt, if they were feeling any, and played together.

The bottom line was, could they perform together as a team? None I ever saw did that better. Whatever their experiences were in Baltimore in those days when they were in the locker room, they were all blue and white and that was it. For example, there was a problem when we played an exhibition game in Birmingham, Alabama. Our black players weren't allowed to stay in the same hotel. They spoke to Carroll about it and he said we'd never go back. We didn't.

But your feelings weren't on your sleeve, especially in football locker rooms full of players like Gino Marchetti, who'd carried a machine gun at the Battle of the Bulge at eighteen. Those men came from a generation that didn't discuss anything. Today things are more out in the open.

You didn't see many blacks in Sweeney's. None really. Same at Gussie's. Black players had their own places. You didn't think about it. I figured they liked their own hangouts, but looking back now I see things a little differently. If the black players were going wherever they wanted, why were there COLORED and WHITE signs in some places? Why didn't they sit at the lunch counter at Woolworth's and sip a Coke? I'm not naïve about anything, but I was like many people in 1964. I didn't totally see what was coming until I was scouting in the South.

As I moved from town to town, I saw those COLORED and WHITES ONLY signs on bathrooms and lunch counters. You knew it existed, so seeing it wasn't shocking, but it leapt out at you. Baltimore was a southern town and Maryland was a border state. There were whites-only places in the 1950s, but I can't recall ever seeing a sign in the time I was there. Now I was in the Deep South where the discrimination was much more public. The signs were right there on the wall.

It didn't take long to decide I needed to be careful. East Coast wisecracks were not appreciated. I was aware the Freedom Riders had been coming down to desegregate the buses and restaurants and to register blacks to vote, many for the first time. You didn't have to be a genius to understand a lot of folks didn't like the idea. All you had to do was see the pugnacious face of Theophilus Eugene Connor, Birmingham, Alabama's commissioner of public safety, to understand how it was. They called him Bull for a reason.

He made clear he didn't feel the need to protect the Freedom Riders, whom he saw as lawbreakers. Soon we all watched the carnage on television, mostly black protestors attacked by police dogs and hit by water from fire hose blasts so hard it knocked them over like bowling pins. In 1963 Dr. Martin Luther King was jailed by Connor during a sit-in, and the resulting protests led the Birmingham City Council to repeal its segregation ordinances, but that didn't change people's feelings—it hardened them.

In the midst of all this was a twenty-seven-year-old scout who looked like he was eighteen and was tooling around in a massive Lincoln searching for football players. It was quite a time.

When I wasn't watching practices, viewing game film, or talking with coaches and trainers, I was driving with the radio on. It was no longer just for entertainment on lonely rides. It was my own scout, one that regularly warned me about mob violence here and protests there, often leading me to alter my route between schools.

You couldn't be in the South in those days and just drive away from everything, because the South was on fire. Change had the Old South surrounded, although men like Bull Connor thought otherwise. They were trying to hold back a tide that had been rising for 350 years. You couldn't do it in football. You couldn't do it in baseball. And finally you couldn't do it in America anymore.

I began to see a few black scouts appearing, but some of the coaches at the historically black colleges weren't sure their players were getting a fair shake if teams were sending in a black scout. I know when I took over personnel in Baltimore in 1966 and hired Milt Davis to scout, I told him I wanted him to stay on the West Coast, where he was from. I wasn't going to ask him to go to the African American schools. I made a conscious decision. I went myself. I knew the coaches down there and I wanted the head coach to see the Baltimore Colts' head of personnel on his campus.

Milt was a very intelligent man. He earned a doctorate in education from UCLA and became a college professor, but before that he was a great defensive back who'd suffered in the old NFL. A few years before he died, he told the *Eugene (OR) Register* that he was drafted by the Lions in 1954, but when he showed up there after two years of military service, he was told they had no place for him.

"We don't have a black teammate for you to go on road trips, therefore you can't stay on our team" was how he recalled it in that article. "That's one of those slaps in the face. It hurt considerably, but I'd been hurt so many times, that was minor."

The Colts signed him off the Lions' taxi squad the next year, which broke a gentlemen's agreement among the owners that Kellett could care less about, and he started on our championship teams in 1958 and 1959 and led the league in interceptions twice. But he was troubled by the slights blacks faced back then. That included being refused service in certain restaurants and hotels, not only on the road but in Baltimore. In the same article he talked about how Alan Ameche was one of the players who stood up for him and refused to patronize places like that. That kind of thing was what made those Colts special, I think. I know this: Milt was a very good scout before he went off to teach. I'm sure he was great at teaching, but I would have preferred to have kept him scouting for me forever.

Most of the coaches at the historically black colleges loved the Colts because we had black stars like Lenny and John Mackey and Big Daddy. Everybody knew who they were, and remember this: Weeb Ewbank came from the staff of Paul Brown, who had so many of the first great African American players. He'd seen how they impacted a team. Weeb wanted those kinds of players for the Colts and so did Shula. Those coaches knew there were opportunities for their players in Baltimore.

I have more admiration for the coaches at those black schools and the players who played there then than for anybody, because they really knew hard times. They didn't have great equipment, didn't have the best practice facilities, didn't have the best stadiums, and if they went five or ten miles off campus they could be in danger. People today don't fully understand the civil rights movement and the things people were dealing with—the everyday tensions that were underlying their lives.

Schools like Prairie View or Grambling or Mississippi Valley State were not in big cities. They were in out-of-the-way towns. That's why the scouts knew more about life in some ways than the people they were working for back in New York or Chicago. You're out there on your own in the middle of all this seeing what life really was.

In 1965 I'd been scouting near Selma, Alabama, and was on my way to Montgomery when I heard a report that there was a problem at the Edmund Pettis Bridge. It was all over the radio that the police would be on one side of that bridge and Martin Luther King and six hundred demonstrators would be on the other.

Those demonstrators were marching the fifty-four miles from Selma to Montgomery to support the Voting Rights Act, which hadn't passed Congress yet. Lowndes County, between Selma and Montgomery, was 81 percent black but didn't have a single black voter registered. It was 19 percent white, and 118 percent of those 2,240 folks were allegedly registered. That's how it was. You can look those numbers up in the history books.

That demonstration actually became three marches. The first was Sunday, March 7. They called it Bloody Sunday because police attacked the demonstrators, who couldn't see them massed on the other side until they reached the top of the bridge. They beat those poor people half to death and turned them back.

Two days later, on what they called Turnback Tuesday, they were there again and this time the police let them pass over. Then they turned back because Dr. King had made a deal with the government to do so. That caused people on both sides to be upset, so there was a third march that began on March 21, and this one was different.

There were 2,000 federal soldiers and another 1,900 members of the Alabama National Guard protecting the way. A federal judge said the march was legal but stipulated while they could all march on the four-lane road when it narrowed to two in Lowndes County, only a few hundred could go forward. So that's how it went.

It took four days, but at the end they estimated twenty-five thousand people walked the final few miles to the state capitol steps. That's where Dr. King made one of his famous speeches, saying, "How long will it take? I come to say to you this afternoon however difficult the moment, however frustrating the hour, it will not be long."

That night a white civil rights worker from Detroit named Viola Liuzzo was murdered by Ku Klux Klan members while she was giving rides to people back to Selma. On August 6, Congress passed the Voting Rights Act. Those were the times we lived in.

While that was going on, I pulled into a gas station on my way to Montgomery and went to use the restroom, and I saw those signs: WHITE and COLORED. It wasn't like I hadn't seen them before, but for some reason they hit me, I guess because of all I'd been hearing on the radio about the march, and I said to the attendant, "That's terrible."

He looked at me hard and said, "Keep that up and you may get your brains blown out. If you don't think so, I got my gun in the office, mister." He told me, "Fill up and get gone." That was the level of tension across the South. You say the wrong thing and you didn't know for sure the consequences.

I didn't say another word. I just drove for about thirty miles, then pulled over, nearly in tears. I kept thinking, "This is not right." I'm twenty-eight years old, alone with the radio in a country that was foreign to me. I just sat there for half an hour and thought, "What is it going to be like? What is life like for blacks living here?" It suddenly hit me, the reality of their life in the South and how terrible it had to be.

If you were black down there, your life wasn't worth anything. What's life like even if you're a great football player? You walk into town from school and it didn't make any difference. Things haven't changed as much as they should have, but thank God it's not 1965 in Selma. Outside of that day, I don't know that I had another discussion about race in the South. I made a conscious decision about that.

You had to be conscious of what was going on. You didn't want to be driving somewhere and end up in the middle of a demonstration or a riot. You wanted to avoid being picked up because of the way you looked in some lonely town by some cop who might have thought you were there to register voters.

The older scouts didn't have that problem, but I did. I looked like I was eighteen and there was no reason for a white, eighteen-year-old driving a big car with Maryland plates around in the middle of Alabama or Mississippi at eleven o'clock at night if he wasn't a freedom rider. Those were fear-filled times, and they forever changed how I looked at life and particularly race.

I remember once driving down the Natchez-Trace, which is a 444-mile-long parkway that winds from Nashville to Natchez, Mississippi. I was driving to Alcorn A&M in Lorman, Mississippi, and heard on the radio that people were shooting at the police off the highway.

The Natchez Trace is one of the most beautiful places in America, but it's got no lights at night. I started thinking, What if they have no motels on this road? What am I going to do? You're driving and thinking, This is the kind of place where those kids disappeared (the civil rights workers killed in Philadelphia, Mississippi).

By 1967 protests were escalating. There was not only the ongoing civil rights movement but now the antiwar protests over Vietnam. There was looting and riots in a lot of American cities, not just in the South. Ali had been stripped of his heavyweight title for refusing induction into the army. There seemed to be no calm anywhere and that included in the world of a football scout.

That year I flew into Jackson, Mississippi, to scout a double-header between four of the black colleges, but that same night,

Southern was playing in Baton Rouge against Alcorn A&M, and I wanted to see those teams too. It was a chance to scout six of the best black college programs in one day if I could see the two games in Jackson, or at least the first half of the second one, and then get to Baton Rouge in time to see Southern.

So I called an airport and was told I could rent a small private plane to get there. I didn't have the authority, but I jumped in a cab and got out to this small private airport and told them I was with the Baltimore Colts and needed to get to Baton Rouge. I could have gotten fired, but I was young. You don't think about that. You just want to see the players.

They told me the price, and I had never turned in a bill like that, but I had to do it. A pilot comes over and we take off. I'm not sure we ever got 100 yards above the tree line, but we got to Baton Rouge in time.

I get to the ticket office and tell the attendant I'm with the Colts but I had to come to the game with my pilot. The man looks at me skeptically, as if to say, "Sure," but he lets us in.

The press box was on top of the stadium and we're the only two white people there. If I recall correctly, it was Lou Brock Night and we're walking through the stands and people are looking at us like we're aliens, which I guess in a way we were. It was a little uneasy feeling. I don't know why, because I'd been to many games at black colleges, but this seemed different.

I looked down on the field, and there was a fistfight before the game between the two head coaches. They're fighting, the band is playing, and the game hadn't started. At halftime, Lou Brock was riding around the field in a convertible. He was a graduate of Southern and they were honoring him because the Cardinals had won the World Series that October.

At halftime I got the feeling it was time to leave. That pilot, I guarantee you, had never been to a game at a black college. He couldn't wait to get out of there. Remember, students in these colleges were clashing with police, and here are two white men walking through the stands at night. The last thing they probably thought was that's a pro football scout and his pilot!

We flew to Atlanta the next day to watch the Colts play the Falcons. I never told Shula how I got there. I just told him I'd seen a lot of players in Jackson and Baton Rouge. When I submitted the bill, no one said anything. Of course, I was the personnel director by then, so I was submitting it to myself.

Think about the players who came out of those black colleges then. They were on an island, most of them, so as much as I was judging a player, I had to factor in the circumstances they were living in and the adjustment they would have to make.

In the NFL they had to compete against the best football players in the world, and they were coming out of an environment where everything was telling them they weren't good enough. That they couldn't compete. It's difficult to imagine how hard that had to be.

As players, they not only had the competitive nature of it but also that baggage to carry and overcome. They had to believe they were better than people who had constructed a system to keep them doubting that they were good enough. They had to be special people, not just special players, and many of them were. It was a revelation for a young scout to find them and finally understand all they had overcome to get that far.

That's why it's so great to see the Pro Football Hall of Fame has taken in the Black College Football Hall of Fame. There should be special recognition for those players, particularly the ones from the 1960s who went through all that and went on to play pro football. You were reminded your whole, young life that you were "inferior." Nearly everywhere you turned was a little reminder that you are less than, you are less than, you are less than. Everything was designed to reinforce that message.

The restaurants, the back of the bus, the water fountains where they couldn't take a drink no matter how hot it was, the separate bathrooms and schools. How different was it from the plantations? I never came back to Baltimore and expressed it, but those were my observations of life separate from football in those days, and it changed me forever.

Here were all these white scouts coming to those black colleges and judging their players. If I'm Eddie Robinson, what am I thinking? He not only could coach as well as anyone, his players were better than the ones down the road at LSU in Baton Rouge. Where's Grambling? It's out in the middle of nowhere. They had some of the best players in the country but had to prove it to a world that probably knew they were better athletes and was afraid of it.

It's completely different today. Now the great black player doesn't go to the historic black colleges. Those players are dominating the fields at Alabama and Mississippi and Georgia and Texas. That's where you'd find a Mel Blount today, but I remember the first time I saw him at Southern University. When I put on the film I came out of my chair. There was the reincarnation of "Night Train" Lane! What a player.

The film quality wasn't as good as it would have been across town at LSU, but you looked at it for a few minutes and shut it off. You didn't need to see any more. I can only recall three players with reports where you didn't have to say anything: Dick Butkus, Gale Sayers, and Mel Blount.

One thing you always had to remember when you were scouting was that you were competing with the Cowboys. Not only were their scouts everywhere, but they brought gifts and left with rolls of film so the rest of us couldn't watch it.

Dallas sent schools anything they wanted. You go to some of those smaller schools and they'd tell you they needed a new projector and maybe suggest you call the Colts and see what you could do. If you don't deliver and Dallas does, you get cooperation but not quite the same as they were getting. What are you going to say?

Once I took over the personnel department, I didn't have to talk to Shula about that kind of stuff. He was great. He didn't care how you did it as long as you did it. Before that, I'd call Moley and someone would say, "How much? Upton, we're spending a lot on scouting," when it was really nothing. Today they spend millions with about the same results.

Most of the college coaches were helpful, but some didn't want to talk to you about their players. The big-name ones were busy and some of them looked at the NFL as having a farm system without paying for it, which was true. But coaches at the black colleges would do anything for you.

They wanted to be sure their players were getting the same opportunity to be seen as at the big schools. I used to love to go to the African American schools. Partly it was because they had so much talent, but they also helped you do your job.

They'd let you work people out if you wanted. The film wasn't always the best, because they'd have some kid shooting it. You're watching a play and all of a sudden you see the cheerleaders. But you could always go to practice, which wasn't true at some of the bigger programs. Those coaches took a personal interest in their players. They felt if they did, a kid might go in the second round from their school, not the fifth.

As good as he was, do you think Mississippi Valley State gets Jerry Rice drafted in the first round in the '6os? Not happening then. Remember Otis Taylor? Taken in the fifteenth round by the Eagles and the fifth by the Chiefs in 1965.

Most of the scouts were twenty, thirty, forty years older than I was. I listened to them like they were the Great Elders. For a young scout it was like talking to the prophets from the Bible. They knew. They might be lying about some player at some school, but they knew what this life was. They understood the nuances.

One of them said to me once, "You don't ever tell anybody what happened at the last place you were at no matter what." I always remembered that. You get the reputation you're passing on secrets from one coach to another and you're off the information highway.

By going to LSU and McNeese State and then going over to Grambling, you began to see the talent difference. You'd go to Texas or Rice or SMU and then to Texas Southern and it was obvious a lot of the best players were at those black schools. The athletes were better. Quicker. Faster. They didn't have the same opportunities as the white players at the big schools like Texas, but it made me realize the talent was where it was, not where maybe you thought it was. Some years I could have made a draft and a good one just from the African American colleges.

Out west it was a different world. Things were fairer there.

Geography played into what players were where. The farther away you got from the South, the better the chance you had to see black athletes at bigger schools like Arizona State or on the West Coast.

What was West Texas State known for then? Mercury Morris and Duane Thomas. In the mid-1960s those players were in their backfield. They were not going to be in Maryland's backfield or South Carolina's. I remember their coach, Joe Kerbel, telling me about these black players he had. There was a real different attitude out there when it came to playing black athletes.

The University of Texas didn't have a black player on scholarship until 1969. By then Mercury Morris was in the NFL. At West Texas they could do that. You weren't going to find Thomas or Morris at Arkansas or Oklahoma. The color line wasn't broken there yet.

In the NFL things were changing too, but there was still a reluctance to draft black athletes to play quarterback, middle linebacker, and center. It's an insult, but those were considered the "thinking" positions and they were being pigeon-holed. The AFL began to draft blacks for those positions, but the NFL did not in much of the '60s. That's one of the ways the Chiefs built that great defense that won them Super Bowl IV. Right in the middle of it was Willie Lanier. Now he's in the Hall of Fame. You wonder how many players like that didn't get their chance because of the times they lived in.

A lot of times the coaches at historic black colleges would tell you their guy couldn't play quarterback. Whether they believed it or just felt it wasn't going to happen so they were trying to get them into the league at another position, I don't know. No one ever said to me, "We don't want a black quarterback or a black middle linebacker." Not Shula. Not McCafferty. Not Weeb, although I wasn't around him as much. Not even Klosterman the year he was general manager after Shula left in 1970. Klosterman came to us from the Houston Oilers of the AFL, so he would have put an African American at every position if we had them, I think.

I'm not saying it didn't happen. I know it was true with some teams. You'd hear, "Maybe he can play defensive back or wide receiver," or, "He's not a quarterback but he's a great athlete." That's the closest thing you'd hear, but you understood what it meant. We didn't have that in Baltimore, but you did on some clubs.

If you looked at our drafts, I never paid any attention to that. I could see the type of athlete the AFL signed that many teams in the NFL were ignoring. I noticed the difference. It made me want even more to go out and find the best players. I didn't care where. Maybe that's because I was in my mid to late twenties and so many of the NFL scouts were a lot older and had been looking in the same places. I can't say. I just know we always wanted to find the best players, and a lot of them were the great black athletes who have come to dominate pro football today.

I have no doubt AFL scouts went into predominantly black colleges and told the coaches the NFL didn't want their players. But they came to know I didn't listen to anybody. I made my own decisions on who could play, but the attitude of the club has a lot to do with it for a scout. I listened to a lot of those older NFL scouts. They knew talent, but if your team isn't going to take a black middle linebacker or a quarterback, what does it matter? No matter what I said, if Shula had said, "I'm not taking him," what was I going to do? That's my point when people criticize those older scouts back then. I heard what those men thought of the players they were seeing, but if your organization doesn't believe in those schools or in the black player, what does the scout do? The scouts didn't rule the draft.

Of all the years I spent scouting, 1968 is the one I'll never forget. I was at Memphis State the week Martin Luther King was shot. I watched some film and some spring practices but wanted to see some more because there were some players I wasn't sure about. I told one of their assistants I didn't feel I'd seen enough, so I was going to stay another day.

In those days they had twenty or thirty days for spring practices, so the colleges spread them out. The assistant told me staying over might not be the best idea, because there was a sanitation workers strike and Martin Luther King was coming to town to lead a demonstration, and there might be problems. It was all over the news.

I asked him if he really thought it would be a problem. I remember it clear as day. He said, "I'd go home." Nobody had ever said anything like that to me before. I'd been scouting the South for five years. I wasn't sure what to make of it, but it just gave me an uneasy feeling.

By then so many things had happened. People murdered. People attacked by dogs and water hoses. Students and black citizens demonstrating. Cops attacking them. Segregation still in effect in many places. Things were escalating to a breaking point. You could feel it.

Something told me maybe I'd better listen this time. I went back to the Holiday Inn and checked out and flew home to Baltimore that night. I got home and turned on the television and there it was: MARTIN LUTHER KING SHOT! Murdered on the balcony in front of room 306 at the Lorraine Motel on the edge of downtown Memphis.

It was as if the whole world erupted. There were riots in Baltimore. There were riots all over the country. Indianapolis was the only city that didn't blow up. Bobby Kennedy was there campaigning, and he announced Dr. King had been assassinated. He gave a speech on top of a car saying he knew how they felt because his brother had been shot by a white man. They knew he wasn't bullshitting them and went home.

That defined the era I was living in. Violence. Death. Loss. It wasn't just the South. Racism and discrimination was in the North and in pro football too. The difference was the South didn't try to hide it. It was pretty clear how everyone felt.

It hit me later that I had to go back down there. My scouting schedule wasn't finished yet. So I had to go back to an atmosphere where if I'm an African American, I'm pretty angry. Before Dr. King died, you mostly just had to worry about saying the wrong thing when you were on the white side of the dividing line in the South. Now you had to worry on both sides of that line. It wasn't easy to be a white football scout walking around black colleges then.

I had an incident at one school after that. It was at Alcorn A&M,

which was off the beaten track down the Natchez Trace. There was a lot of anger everywhere, and it was hard to contain or hide.

A couple older scouts told me I might want to skip it and send an area scout more familiar with the folks down there, but being young I didn't listen. I showed up. I wouldn't do it today but I thought I could do everything then.

There were eight or ten players I wanted to time in the 40-yard dash, so we're out on the field, which is down in a hollow. There are people up on the hill watching us. The first player runs and I say to one of the coaches, "He ran 4.8." He looks at me and says, "Don't look like 4.8 to me. I got 4.5." I think, "There's no way he ran 4.5, but okay."

Next player runs a 4.7. The coach says, "What you got, Bell?" I say, "4.7." He says, "I got 4.5, Bell." Okay.

The third kid runs and I start to get the message. His time is my time. Before he can say anything, I say, "What you got, Coach?" "4.5." I agree. "I got 4.5 too."

He was making a point. On that field, that day, he was in charge. I could go back and write whatever I wanted and I did, but on that field *he* was in charge.

That had never happened before. Maybe he was just thinking, "Those scouts and their stopwatches, they never get it right." Or maybe he was making a point. Or maybe it was just the times.

I remember after I got done there, I got back on the Natchez Trace and I had a couple hours' drive. I kept thinking about that coach and my stopwatch. Things were changing for the better, but progress was slow. Too slow if you've been waiting all your life, I imagine.

It's a beautiful ride during the day up the Natchez Trace but it was getting dark, and out there the dark is very dark. That night it was as dark as I could ever remember it.

9

Running My Own Show in Baltimore

When your team's owner takes over his family's business at the age of twenty-seven and turns it into one of the most successful producers of work clothes and later military clothing in the country, it probably should come as no surprise that the Colts under Carroll Rosenbloom became one of the youngest organizations in football after he replaced Weeb with Shula. I became part of that youth movement, but in a sad way.

I was out west scouting spring practice in 1966, which was a trip I always looked upon fondly, because the year before it was when I first learned that looking ten years younger than my age wasn't always a handicap when it came to college scouting.

Not long after Moley sent me on the road full time, I was in Austin in the spring of 1965 visiting the University of Texas. Darrell Royal was the head coach, and the Longhorns were loaded. They hadn't lost a regular-season game in two years and were coming off a national championship in which they destroyed No. 2–ranked Navy in the 1964 Cotton Bowl, 28–6. They'd go 10-1 in 1965 too and beat No. 1–ranked Alabama and Joe Namath in the Orange Bowl, so the question wasn't was their talent there but rather who did you like best.

Considering all that success, I expected Royal to be happy to see a scout from the Colts on campus. Boy, was I mistaken. What I found instead was a steaming Royal who was not interested in letting pro scouts watch his practices, because the New York Jets had just signed away his top wide receiver, George Sauer Jr., with a year of eligibility left.

The fact that George was going to the team where his father was the personnel director didn't help Royal's disposition or my case. What did was the fact Royal had no idea who the hell I was.

I'd come all the way to Austin to scout a couple of players, and I damn well intended to do it, so I took off my tie and jacket and sidled up to the bench as practice was going on to survey the situation. Coach Royal took one look at me and figured I was the new student manager and hollered for me to bring the water bucket out to the huddle. Gladly!

I ran out and stood by their huddle, ladle in hand, the rest of the practice. I saw everything I needed to see and got a good laugh as well. Scouts gather information however they can.

Things weren't as funny the next spring after I got a phone call from Bucko Kilroy, the Cowboys' super scout whom I'd known since his days as an ornery lineman with the Eagles when they won the NFL championship in 1948 and 1949. He asked me if I'd heard Keith Molesworth dropped dead on his front lawn.

It was March 12, 1966. That's a day I wouldn't forget. I thought Moley had recovered fairly well from his heart problems, but I was obviously wrong. He was only sixty years old. Thirteen years earlier my father had installed him as the Colts' first head coach. I'd been working for him less than three years. Now he was gone. That's difficult to process at twenty-eight.

I didn't know what to say but I knew what to do. My wife, Anne, was with me and about an hour later we were headed back to Baltimore. It was 1,366 miles from Dallas to our offices on Howard Street, and I drove straight through for nearly twenty-four hours because I didn't know what was going to happen. There was nobody in the office other than the secretary. Who was going to get the scouting reports? Who was going to replace Moley? Where would that leave me?

I didn't know, but I was sure I shouldn't go back on the road until things were settled. I knew something else too: I knew I could do the job.

I had no idea if I would get it, but I knew I wasn't going to sit around and hope to be discovered. I'd run the 1965 draft that got us a half dozen starters if you included Neely (who was unfortunately starting for the Cowboys) and Atkinson (who was playing for the Jets). I understood what needed to be done to modernize our scouting operation. All I needed was a chance and there was only one way to get it—ask.

The way to deal with Shula was directly, so I went in and told him I wanted the job and knew I could do it. I said I understood he probably had other people in mind, but I believed I would do a good job for him and the Colts. I knew he had gotten kind of disillusioned with Moley. Don understood we had to upgrade our scouting department to compete with Dallas. Now I had to convince him I was up for that challenge

I was waiting for him to say get in line, but he never said that. He said nothing. He was always a good listener but never revealed more than he wanted to reveal. In this case, not much, but he listened and didn't say no.

I wrote Carroll a letter too. I'd told Shula how I felt, but Rosenbloom owned the team. I understood Shula would make the decision but I also knew he was going to run it by Rosenbloom, and I didn't want Carroll to think I hadn't asked him.

You had to be careful with Carroll. He was like the Godfather: you had to kiss the ring. He could be good to you and he'd give you a chance, but I felt there had to be deference paid. He was the one who brought me to Baltimore, so I thought I owed it to him to ask.

I was very direct in my letter. I reminded him he was the second youngest of nine children yet was the one who took over his family's business. I reminded him how he used to tell me young people should be given a chance. And I told him I was sure a lot of people thought I wasn't old enough, but I felt I could do it. Two months later, on May 28, I got the job. Carroll never said a word about it.

He could be a lot like Howard Hughes when he wanted to. A

man of mystery. That's how he played it, I think to keep people off-balance and on their toes. What's he thinking? We never quite knew unless he was mad. Then you knew exactly. He could be tough, but he was fair.

Shula called me in and told me I was now the youngest personnel director in the league, so kindly don't screw up. Then he laughed. That was Don.

If he had any other candidates, I didn't know about them. I would assume he did, because he should have talked to other people. But he didn't make me sweat. There wasn't a parade of more experienced personnel men coming in and out. Maybe that's because he was only thirty-six himself. I don't know. Maybe the '65 draft showed him I could do it. I never asked and he never said. I was just glad to have the chance.

I told him I was going to make a lot of changes. I wanted to bring in more film. I wanted magnetic boards for each coach with all the prospects in the spring at their position the way I rated them. They could move them up and down, but it showed them how I rated them and how CEPO rated them.

Chuck Noll used to accuse me of sneaking in at night when he wasn't in his office and changing his board back to the way I wanted it. Maybe I did. Like Shula, I never said.

If I was Shula, I'm not sure I would have picked me, for a couple reasons. I had never run anything and it was only his third season, and there was a lot of pressure working for Rosenbloom. Don had done a great job in three years, but he wasn't on a long-term contract, and he was beginning to get this question asked that so many great coaches and quarterbacks face until they win the championship: Can he win the big one?

That was the result of what happened the previous two years. The year he replaced Weeb, we'd finished 8-6 by winning five of our last six games, then went 12-2 and were the dominant team in the league in 1964. In those days there was only one playoff game, the NFL Championship between the Eastern and Western Conference winners. We were supposed to crush the Cleveland Browns and we should have, but we just didn't play well.

It was 0–0 at halftime and Unitas was off. He ended up with only 95 passing yards and three interceptions and a quarterback rating of 32.3. Of course, they didn't have quarterback ratings in those days, but you didn't need one to know how he'd played, and John would have been the first to tell you. You only needed two eyes. He was the best quarterback in the league, but it wasn't his day.

We couldn't move the ball consistently and our defense got shredded in the second half. Gary Collins caught three touchdown passes from Frank Ryan, and we lost 27–0. Carroll was seething. He didn't say much but he didn't have to. All you had to do was look at his face.

In 1965 the league still decided the NFL championship with a single playoff game between the Eastern and Western Conference champions, but that year the Colts and the Packers finished the regular season tied at 10-3-1 atop the Western Conference, so a one-game divisional playoff game had to be added to find an opponent for the Eastern Conference champion Browns. We should have been in that title game again in a rematch with Cleveland, but the best referee in football, Jim Tunney, blew a call against the Packers and we were out.

That's the year we lost Unitas and his backup, Gary Cuozzo, in back-to-back games and had to go with Tom Matte, a running back, as our quarterback. We led the Packers 10–7 with 1:58 left in the tie-breaker playoff game when the Packers' kicker, Don Chandler, lined up a 22-yard field goal try and missed wide right. More than likely, the game was over.

Then Tunney's hands went up. Not even Chandler could believe it. The second he hit it, he rolled his head to the side like someone who'd just blown a putt in a $100 Nassau. He knew he missed. Everyone but Tunney knew, but he didn't miss a 25-yarder in overtime, and we were out.

That's how a coach gets a loser label. Shula won the big one, or at least the one before the big one, but they took it from us. The league was mortified when TV film and news photographs proved Tunney made a mistake. They extended the goal posts higher the next season and put an official under each goal post to make sure it didn't happen again. That didn't do us much good.

The good thing was Rosenbloom realized what happened. Unlike most of the owners today, he was a football man. He'd played. He understood in a game things can go wrong that are out of your control.

Today coaches are getting fired for going 10-6, and in my old draftee Marty Schottenheimer's case, 14-2 in 2006. Don, who proved to be one of the greatest coaches in NFL history, might have been fired after those playoff losses now.

It's a different type of owner today. The general managers and the coach ran the team, not analytics or someone with an MBA. If they hired a coach, they gave him time to win if they thought he had anything. Look at Tom Landry. It took him seven years to have a winning season in Dallas. He'd be fired twice today in the time it took him to win once then.

You could see Shula knew what he was doing, but because we lost those two games, people started saying he couldn't win the big one. You could see this man could coach and you knew he was going to win, and he did win. He got us to the championship game and it should have been two years in a row. That means something.

Still, he was dealing with that kind of pressure when he let a twenty-eight-year-old kid take over his personnel department. That said a lot about him. He wasn't trapped by conventional wisdom. If he thought you could do the job, you got the chance to prove it.

Shula did tell me he wanted to hire George Young as my assistant. George was the head coach at City College then, which was actually a high school program in Baltimore. He'd won six Maryland Scholastic Association championships and was working part time for us breaking down film, and we liked him.

So when Shula said that about George, I said fine. No disagreement. I was the first person with the Colts to hire scouts. I hired George, Milt Davis on the West Coast, and then Dick Szymanski when he retired, and I started using Freddie Schubach, our equipment manager. He later became the Colts' personnel director and did a good job.

Not many personnel directors would grab an equipment manager to scout, but I always felt Freddie knew more about the players than anybody. I asked Shula to let me send him out in the spring of 1968. That was my third year and Shula's last in Baltimore. I could see he was really smart and he understood players. Freddie would cut the team before the coaches and was usually right. I'd ask him why he liked a player, and he always had a reason.

I called George and told him he'd have a key. Come in any hours he wanted. Just break down the film and make a list of the top one hundred or two hundred players and a list of the rejects. A list of the people not to pay attention to was important. It saved you a lot of time.

The later rounds were more important than they are today. With sixteen teams instead of thirty-two, a fifth-round choice was like a third-round choice today. That's when the real rounds start for a good scout. You're supposed to find players in the first two or three rounds. If you can find them on the fifth through the seventeenth, you're doing your job.

Eleven days after my promotion, it was announced that the two leagues were merging and there'd be a combined draft on March 14–15, 1967. So the first draft I ran was the first common draft and we had the first pick. What a way to start.

That spring and fall I was all over the country looking at players. I'd come back and move my metallic boards, which were all over the walls of my office. I was constantly evaluating. George was sorting through the reports, and by then we were in CEPO, so we were getting computer reports too. The league was becoming a more sophisticated operation.

The TV money was growing, there were more and more sellouts around the league, and now with the merger there was constant talk about which league was better. That was driving up the value of franchises and generating interest in a growing league.

Of all the places I went that season, the one I was most fixated on was East Lansing, Michigan, on November 19, 1966. It was dubbed the Game of the Century, which seems to happen every ten years or so, but in this case it might have been.

Notre Dame and Michigan State were both undefeated and ranked No. 1 and No. 2 in the country, respectively. There was so much talent on that field that there were seven No. 1 picks out of that game. Michigan State had four of the first eight, including the top two, Bubba Smith and Clint Jones. I thought the best player on the field was George Webster, the Michigan State linebacker who, until he got hurt, was all but unblockable, but Bubba was a giant pass rusher, and coaches have a hard time ignoring that.

The game ended in a controversial 10–10 tie with Notre Dame running out the clock at the end rather than trying to win. Their coach, Ara Parseghian, was heavily criticized for it, but they had a game left with USC and he felt, correctly as it turned out, they could still win the national title. They both finished 9-0-1 and shared the MacArthur Trophy, but at the end of the game I remember Bubba and a bunch of the Michigan State players taunting the Non-Fighting Irish as they sat on the ball until time ran out.

We were playing in Detroit the next afternoon, and when I got there, all Shula wanted to talk about was the game and the players. I don't think another game in the history of college had more first-round draft choices in it than that one. Michigan State had fourteen players drafted off that team—eight that year and six the next. I'd predicted back in Baltimore that Notre Dame would win with its passing attack, but by the end I was thinking Bubba and Webster might be the two best players on the same team I'd ever seen.

I actually liked Alan Page, Notre Dame's defensive tackle, better than Bubba, but I didn't try to convince Shula to take Page. Bubba was so much bigger, and we hadn't had a top pass rusher since Gino retired. Bubba could have been that, but he wasn't because of what I talked about earlier. Attitude. Page had it, which is why he's in the Hall of Fame. Bubba had it when he felt like it, which is why he isn't.

I told Shula the problem with Bubba was it was a question of how many plays he would take off. There were doubts and a lot of debate between Webster, Jones, and Bubba going first. What changed everybody's mind was the Senior Bowl. Sitting with the coaches watching him destroy people that week, how could I argue? Shula was looking for a dominant pass rusher, and that week, against the best players in the draft, Bubba dominated.

To me the Senior Bowl is the most important game to scout. With pro coaches coaching them, that's where you get a chance to see where a player projects. Bubba went in there to show people who he was for a few days and when he did . . . unstoppable. But that was always the question in my mind. How often would he do it? I raised the issue, but after that week I couldn't object.

Shula and I went to dinner with Bubba and Clint and George and Gene Washington, their best four players. Shula told Clint he was going with Bubba because he was just so big and mobile. He reminded a lot of people of Big Daddy.

The months leading up to that draft had created a lot of uncertainty in the organization. Moley had died in March, I became the youngest personnel director in the league in May, and then on November 21, Carroll announced Joe Campanella was going to replace Kellett as general manager.

We all knew Kellett was likely to retire at the end of the 1966 season, but the announcement of his successor seemed premature. It made things a little awkward in a season that ended in the same fashion.

Some people thought my brother, Bert, should have gotten the job, but we knew that wasn't going to happen. Bert quit the following Friday, so it looked bad and people thought it was because of that, but it wasn't. He had other issues with Carroll and the way the league was headed and came out publicly saying the NFL was no longer my father's vision of pro football. It was becoming too commercial. I didn't agree with him at the time, but if you look around today, it's hard to argue that he wasn't right.

He was quoted in the papers saying, "I cannot condone the crass commercialism that is striking at the very heart of the game." He accused the league of "capitulating" to the AFL in the merger and claimed that "the new medium in the NFL is the almighty dollar."

Carroll was angry about that, but he didn't take it out on me. It probably actually helped me. Bert was now like the bad son criticizing the family business and biting the hand that fed him while I was the loyal son. I was still there, picking his players and helping Shula build a championship team. Almost a year later, my brother was back in the news.

Bert was a close friend of Alex Hawkins, a running back and receiver who became a Baltimore folk hero as a scrappy special teams player when he was sent out with the captains for a pregame coin toss. The referee introduced "Captain Unitas, Captain Marchetti," but then he was stumped so he looked at Alex and said, "Captain Who?" The people in Baltimore loved it. So did Alex. He had the kind of fun-loving personality you could fall in love with.

He was with the Colts from 1959 to 1965, then went to Atlanta for a season but was released on October 4, 1966, after three games, and we claimed him. He'd lived with Bert in Bert's place on Abel Avenue, a block over from Sweeney's and not far from Hooper's, where they used to go and order the same breakfast every morning. They were good friends and often played cards together, but on November 1, 1967, they played one time too many.

Baltimore county police rolled up on a barbershop at a suburban shopping center after some complaints came in about suspicious activity. There, in a backroom, they found Bert, Hawk, and eight other men playing cards and arrested them. Bert and Alex had their pictures in the *News-American* the next day under a headline that read, "Hawkins, Bell, Jr. Pinched in Poker Raid."

My brother always said the only reason they got caught was their lookout fell asleep. The fact the cops arrived at 4:45 a.m. might have explained why. The time and the fact we were playing the Packers that weekend didn't make the Colts feel any better about my brother, although everyone got off because it was just a penny ante game. Or so my brother always insisted.

Years later Bert told a Baltimore reporter named John Eisenberg that he'd walked in on Carroll that last season he worked for the team as Carroll was on the phone making a bet. Bert knew how vigilant our father had been against gambling on games, so that bothered him, but he told Eisenberg there was something more that kept gnawing at him.

"People thought I left because someone else was promoted to GM but I could never have worked as a GM under Carroll," Bert told Eisenberg. "I knew there would come a day when he would have asked me to do something illegal."

At the time, Campanella had more serious things to concern himself with than my brother's hijinks with Hawkins. He was a close friend of Shula's and had played for the Colts for six years, retiring after the 1957 season to go into the restaurant business with Gino, Alan Ameche, and Louis Fischer, a classmate of Campanella's from Ohio State. They opened a place called Ameche's Drive-In in Glen Burnie, outside of Baltimore, and it was an instant hit.

Fast-food hamburgers and chicken were just starting to take off, and they timed it perfectly. They expanded the Ameche's franchise, opened Gino's Hamburgers and Chicken restaurants, and got the franchise rights to Kentucky Fried Chicken in the Mid-Atlantic states. Campanella left for about a year to open five Rustler's Steak Houses but came back, and by the time they sold the entire enterprise to Marriott in 1982, they had 329 restaurants and a multi-million-dollar operation.

Joe didn't get to capitalize on all that success, though, because four months after he became general manager, he dropped dead playing handball with Shula at the Downtown Athletic Club on Howard Street just a few blocks from our office.

I was off playing basketball at the Towson YMCA as I often did that time of year. Shula encouraged everyone in the office to get out to the gym and play basketball or handball or exercise together. It was a normal thing. As I was leaving, Shula said he was going to play handball, and when I got back, I saw him and he didn't look good.

I asked what was wrong, and he just said, "Joe's dead."

They were playing handball, and Joe said he had to stop. He was having trouble breathing. Then he just collapsed. He was dead when he hit the floor.

It was devastating. Everybody liked Joe, especially Shula, who had been his teammate. I remember after he took over, I went to him and said I thought the scouting department should be auton-omous. Joe was Shula's dear friend, but he was also someone we all could really talk to.

Here I was, a year on the job, asking for something like that. It was insane, but he listened to my reasons and wrote them down. It was never going to happen, but I didn't know that. He kind of laughed and said he'd talk it over with Shoes.

It wasn't that I didn't want to answer to anybody, but I didn't want to have anybody tell me what to do. I'd already seen that everybody had an opinion when it came to players, but after we picked them, it was the personnel director whose ass was on the line. If that was the case, then I thought I should run scouting the way I saw fit. Shula was great to work for, but I never had that kind of autonomy. Frankly, at my age I probably shouldn't have had it, but no harm in asking.

The owners' meetings were to begin that weekend in Hawaii, and Joe was supposed to go with Carroll. Rosenbloom ended up taking Harry Hulmes, our PR director, and Harry did the same thing I'd done. He asked for the job and Carroll gave it to him.

Harry was a wonderful man and very competent, but it was clear when he got back how things would run. He was in charge of the business side, including signing veteran players, which Shula never wanted any part of. Shula ran the football side. Harry was the GM, but there were clear lines. I was respectful of Harry but I knew exactly who I was dealing with. Harry was the GM, but I answered to Don and Carroll. That's just how it was.

So going into the first common draft with the AFL, we had a new general manager and a new personnel director. It didn't matter, because we knew what we were doing and, more important, we were all pulling in the same direction. But it seemed like the fit-ting conclusion to 1967, because that was the oddest of seasons.

We only lost once, finishing tied with the Los Angeles Rams for the best record in the league at 11-1-2. We were second in the league in scoring and scoring defense, first in total offense and fifth in defense, and Unitas won his third MVP, leading the league in completion percentage while passing for 3,428 yards and twenty touchdowns. Yet we didn't even make the playoffs.

That's because we lost the season's final game to the Rams, 34–10, and tied our first meeting, 24–24. That point differential gave them the tiebreaker, the Coastal Division title, and the right to meet the 9-4-1 Packers, who smoked them 28–7. We'd defeated Green Bay 13–10 in the regular season and felt we would have beaten them again, although to be fair, by then Unitas was complaining about tennis elbow, which would bother him the following season as well. He threw eight interceptions and only three touchdown passes in the season's final five games, but all we knew was when it counted most, sore elbow or not, we liked our chances with Unitas under center. We never got that chance, because business interests had begun to overrule football ones.

The logical thing was a one-game playoff to determine the division champion, but that couldn't happen because the Super Bowl date was set in stone. There was no room for an additional playoff game, so the owners approved a tiebreaker rule based on points scored against each other, never really thinking it would come to that. Well, it did, so a team with the best record in the league never got into the playoffs.

With the season over, the front office changes completed, my metallic scouting boards on the wall, and Bubba Smith now the first player selected in the first combined AFL-NFL draft, Shula was getting ready to go out to talk to the press when he said to me, "Let's go."

I was already looking at reports and getting ready for the second round. I asked him, "What you talking about?"

He said, "You're coming with me. It's our pick." He made sure my first draft that everyone knew I was part of it. How many coaches today would do that?

One of the sportswriters, Bill Tanton, knew I liked Webster better than Bubba, but I understood what Shula was doing. That gesture said to me he was making sure they understood he didn't do it all. But I think there was more to it than that. It was also a test.

I was a great believer that once the decision is made, I'm on board with it. I might have said I liked Webster or Page, and Shula was good with that. You could disagree with him at times. He might get pissed off but that was the end of it. I don't remember him ever saying, "Don't go out there and tell people that." He didn't really care. We all understood who had the final say.

After we drafted Bubba, I started getting phone calls. I must have gotten calls from five different men saying they were Bubba's agent. They were all ready to negotiate. He had three agents, and Clint Jones, who went second to the Vikings, had none—he went in to negotiate with his mother with him. Bubba's people were calling every day. I finally told Shula, "This man's got three agents and maybe more!" Shula just laughed.

Bubba's father, Willie Ray, was a high school coach in Beaumont, Texas, who supplied a lot of players to Michigan State. Willie Ray got ahold of Rosenbloom and next thing I knew Willie Ray was working for us. A package deal.

I remember thinking this may be the beginning of a dreadful time because agents are going to take over and you won't be talking to the player anymore. That was good for the player but not for the team.

I think the scout was more important then than he is today. Today you go see a player and get information, and then the school has a Pro Day and your information isn't anything special. Back then you might find players not every team had seen. Today in the NFL, when it comes down to scouting and revenue sharing, it's genuine socialism. You can still screw it up, but the actual procuring of information has changed. It's pretty much communal in today's NFL.

Where's the sense of discovery today when a scout goes into a school? He's probably already seen these players on tape. When I went into a place like Tennessee State, I hadn't seen anybody. I might find someone I didn't even have on my list.

Back in the 1960s you were often discovering someone. Alvin Hammond on the nineteenth round. Roy Hilton on the fifteenth round. Preston Pearson in the same draft where we took Bubba. Pearson had never even played football. I saw him playing basketball. He couldn't shoot, but he could jump over the basket.

I was at the University of Illinois that winter scouting, and I went to a basketball game and saw him. I used to do that a lot because I'd been a basketball player and loved the game, but I was also looking for athletes. That winter of 1967 I found one.

When we drafted Pearson, a reporter called and asked why I'd draft a basketball player. I think he was implying I didn't know what I was doing. I told him, "Because he's better than half the stiffs playing college football."

Noll liked him as a defensive back, but Shula wanted him at running back. That's what he played for us. Noll traded with us to get him in 1970, and he became a starting running back there. He was in Pittsburgh five years, but when he became an outspoken union member during the 1974 strike, Noll released him and he ended up in Dallas in 1975, where he played another five seasons.

Altogether, that basketball player lasted fourteen years in the NFL, became a starting running back, and appeared in five Super Bowls, winning two. He was one of the best athletes I'd ever seen who never played a down of college football.

Finding those kinds of players is the thrill of scouting. Anybody can find Bubba Smith. All you had to do was find the field. Who wouldn't notice George Webster or Alan Page? But who saw Preston Pearson? That's when you sit up in your chair as a scout and feel a moment of great discovery.

There are exceptions to the above, of course, and those are the teams that really struggle. Some can't find players anywhere. Take the Cleveland Browns. They had six No. 1 picks between 2011 and 2014. None started for them in 2016. It's not a coincidence they went a collective 23-57 from 2011 through 2015.

My point? If you consistently can't find players at the top of the draft, you won't find them at the bottom. If you find them in both places, as we did in Baltimore from 1963 to 1970, you win consistently. That's never changed. Why? Because the whole basis for success in the NFL isn't your system. It's your players. Good ones win. Bad ones get you fired. Simple game, pro football.

But, as I was about to learn, when it comes to a single game, good ones can lose too. Even if you have the best players and it's one of the two biggest games in pro football history.

10

Worst Loss in the History of Losses

On January 12, 1969, I learned how Adam and Eve felt when God found them naked in the Garden of Eden. I was part of the National Football League's original sin. My team, the Colts I'd been so involved in building, lost Super Bowl III to the New York Jets.

Some things you never live down, at least not in the eyes of your peers or, more important, in the eyes of the man who owned the franchise and *his* peers. That's what happened to us.

Nobody remembers that the 1968 Colts went 15-1 and beat the Minnesota Vikings and Cleveland Browns by a combined score of 58–14 in the playoffs to win the NFL championship. Everybody remembers we were 18-point favorites to continue the NFL's dominance over the AFL, but they only remember because we didn't do it.

We would have beaten the Jets nine times out of ten. The problem was it was hard to convince some of our players that a tenth time existed. Hard to convince a team so far superior to its opponent that it could lose. Yet we did, and the reason wasn't all Joe Namath.

Broadway Joe was named Super Bowl III MVP, but for the life of me I don't know why. He was 17 for 28 that day for 202 passing yards and no touchdowns. He had a quarterback efficiency rating of 83.3. He did a good job running an offense that had little to do with what he did best. The truth is Joe Namath didn't beat us nor did he make us tremble, even though we all respected how well he could throw a football. That afternoon he spent most of his time handing it off to the player who did beat us and should have been MVP, running back Matt Snell.

Snell exposed our team's one defensive weakness. He tore the right side of our line to shreds because it was old and worn out. Defensive end Ordell Braase was in his final season, and outside linebacker Don Shinnick would barely hold on for one more. The Jets exploited that, or rather Snell did, running for 121 yards and a score and keeping us off-balance and our offense off the field much of the game. Snell controlled the clock better than Rolex. He wasn't unstoppable, but we made him look that way. Or, to be correct, our old coach did.

Weeb Ewbank, the little man across the field in the glasses, knew everything about us. He understood our strengths and, more important, knew our weaknesses because he'd coached many of our players for nine years, from 1954 to 1962. He was the one who first made the Colts champions—he and Johnny Unitas, of course.

When he went to the Jets in 1963 after being fired by our owner, Carroll Rosenbloom, he brought more than a few former Colts with him. More important, he brought an insider's understanding of our weak spot because the players in it were ones he'd coached.

When you're 15-1 and can boast about having the second-best offense and the No. 1 defense in the NFL, it's reasonable to assume that your team has no weaknesses, but the truth is every team has a weakness. Even Shula's '72 Dolphins, who went 17-0, had weaknesses. The key is whether your opponent can find and exploit them.

Weeb did. He understood the way to beat us was not to get into a shootout with the best defense in football, even if he did have Namath pulling the trigger. It wasn't wise to throw on us, Namath or no Namath. The way to beat us was to attack our weak spot and hope for the best.

Not even insider knowledge should have been enough for us to lose the biggest game in Super Bowl history, however. As badly as we played—and we played badly much of the game and unluckily throughout—we still should have won. That's how wide the talent gulf was between the Colts and the Jets, but we didn't win because of Weeb and because our quarterback, Earl Morrall, finally woke up from a season-long dream. The result was that one of the most important games in NFL history became a nightmare for me, one from which the Colts never fully recovered, and it all started two weeks earlier on the day we lived out a dream.

We arrived at Cleveland Municipal Stadium on December 29, 1968, to face the Browns in the NFL Championship Game, secure in the belief that the only reason we weren't undefeated was that in Week 5 Shula had suffered an uncharacteristic moment of sentimentality or blind faith. Some would later accuse him of panic that day, but that was not true. Don didn't panic. What happened on October 20 was just a reflection of what we all felt about Unitas. We had come to believe, collectively and individually, that John could perform miracles. We believed it because we'd seen it happen so often.

By the end of training camp, it was clear to all of us that Unitas's injured elbow had left him unfit to play. He'd been the league's MVP in 1967, but his arm was tired and already bothering him going into camp, so the plan was that his backup, Jim Ward, would take most of the snaps in preseason. But when Ward injured his knee, Shula knew he had to adjust his thinking, because Unitas's arm was aching from a severe case of tennis elbow.

Shula's mind was like a computer whirling through a mountain of football knowledge. He could see Unitas was no longer in his prime despite coming off an MVP season. In those days most of the defenses played man coverage and he couldn't get the ball in there quickly enough anymore, but everyone had so much confidence in Unitas that our players felt even if neither arm worked, he'd pull it out. It wasn't reality, but it's what they believed. I remember Alex Hawkins, one of our wide receivers, kept saying, "Next week John will be back." It was as if he was saying, "Jesus will walk on water."

Shula couldn't afford to think that way. He understood he needed to protect his team from the possibility John's arm didn't come around, and he remembered a New York Giants backup named

1. My father, DeBenneville Bert Bell, kicking at Franklin Field in 1919, was the captain, quarterback, and punter. Courtesy the Racquet Club of Philadelphia.

2. (*opposite top*) In 1959 (*left to right*): Bert Bell Jr.;
John Unitas, first Bert Bell Award winner from
Maxwell Club; Richie Lucas, quarterback for Penn
State and Maxwell Award College Player of the Year;
and Upton Bell. Courtesy Upton Bell.

3. (*opposite bottom*) Malvern Prep's Upton Bell
driving to the hoop, 1957. Courtesy Upton Bell.

4. (*above*) The Bell family: Bert Jr., Upton, Janie,
Frances, and Bert Sr. in Margate, New Jersey, 1948.
Courtesy Upton Bell.

5. President Harry Truman being presented an NFL Gold Pass by Commissioner Bert Bell and George Preston Marshall of the Washington Redskins at the White House. Source: Abbie Rowe, National Park Service; Harry S. Truman Library and Museum.

6. (*opposite top*) My first draft with head coach Don Shula and the director of player personnel, Keith Molesworth, 1963. Courtesy Upton Bell.

7. (*opposite bottom*) Colts training camp, 1967: Upton Bell (*left*) with his first player drafted, Bubba Smith (*on one knee*). Photo by Curt Boushey. Courtesy Upton Bell.

8. Rookie camp, 1967, with Don Shula; Tony Lorick, starting running back; Don McCafferty (*with hat*); Upton Bell; Ray Perkins, wide receiver and future New York Giants and Alabama head coach; Rick Volk, starting safety; and Jim Ward, backup quarterback to Johnny Unitas. Courtesy Upton Bell.

9. Upton Bell, player personnel director, Baltimore Colts. Courtesy Upton Bell.

10. Presidents Cup, Racing Day, Baltimore Colts staff at Bowie Race Track. Included in picture are owner Carroll Rosenbloom's sons Steve and Danny; Upton Bell; assistant coach Don McCafferty; Colts head coach Don Shula; scout and equipment manager Fred Schubach; coach Dick Bielski; and future Steelers and Hall of Fame head coach Chuck Noll. Courtesy Upton Bell.

11. Baltimore Colts scouts Dick Szymanski and Fred Schubach; Colts player personnel director Upton Bell; and George Young, 1968. Courtesy Upton Bell.

12. Colts scouting team: Fred Schubach, Upton Bell, GM Harry Hulmes, and George Young (future New York Giants GM). Courtesy Upton Bell.

13. Patriots GM Bell with first-round draft choice and Heisman Trophy winner from Stanford Jim Plunkett, 1971. Courtesy Upton Bell.

14. Patriots GM Bell with magnetic board of every NFL player, 1971. Photo by Paul Connell, *Boston Globe*. Courtesy Upton Bell.

15. Patriots training camp, press conference, 1971. Photo by Dick Raphael. Courtesy Upton Bell.

16. Patriots GM Bell with Howard Cosell and Curt Gowdy, 1972.
Courtesy Upton Bell.

17. Bell with Patriots president Billy Sullivan, before opening game at
Schaefer Stadium in Foxboro, Massachusetts, 1971. Photo by Dick Raphael.
Courtesy Upton Bell.

18. Bell with Miami Dolphins head coach Don Shula, winner of the Superman of the Year Award for the Dolphins' perfect season, 1972. Courtesy Upton Bell.

19. Opening Day at Schaefer Stadium, September 1971, Patriots upset Oakland Raiders. Patriots GM Bell with Patriots co-owner Danny Marr, Massachusetts U.S. senator Ed Brooke, and Patriots president Billy Sullivan. Courtesy Upton Bell.

20. Two-time Pulitzer Prize–winner Paul Szep's illustration of President Nixon applying for Upton Bell's job. Used with permission of the artist. Courtesy Upton Bell.

21. Upton Bell, owner and president, Charlotte Hornets, 1974–75. Courtesy Upton Bell.

22. Charlotte Hornets
program, September 6,
1975. Courtesy Upton Bell.

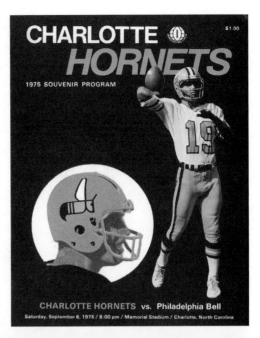

23. Val Pinchbeck (NFL League Office), Lamar Hunt (founder of the AFL
and owner of the Kansas City Chiefs), George "Papa Bear" Halas (owner
and founder of the Chicago Bears), Ernie Accorsi (GM—Baltimore Colts,
Cleveland Browns, New York Giants). Courtesy Ernie Accorsi.

24. Bell presents President George H. W. Bush with a World Football League football after their interview. Courtesy Upton Bell.

25. Bell at the dedication of the historical marker in Narberth, Pennsylvania, honoring his father, former NFL commissioner Bert Bell, 1997. Courtesy Upton Bell.

26. Bell shoots hoops with and interviews Boston Celtic superstar Larry Bird. Source: FayFoto/Boston.

27. *Sports Weekly*—Bruins GM Harry Sinden and Red Sox and Hall of Fame pitcher Dennis Eckersley with cohosts Upton Bell and Bob Lobel. Courtesy Upton Bell.

28. Bell with Bob Lobel in the Yankees' dugout at Yankee Stadium—Sox vs. Yankees, 1978. Photo by Frank O'Brien, *Boston Globe*. Courtesy Upton Bell.

29. Bell with actress
Angie Dickinson at
Boston Public Library
for publisher Houghton
Mifflin's anniversary.
Courtesy Upton Bell.

30. Host Upton Bell,
Sports Nightly on PBS,
1980–81. Photo by Bob
Greene, *Boston Globe*.
Courtesy Upton Bell.

31. WBZ Radio, *Calling All Sports*, Bell with Hall of Fame Cleveland Browns quarterback Otto Graham. Photo by and courtesy Bob Arnold.

32. (*opposite top*) Boxing dinner, New York City, 1982: Jose Torres, World Light Heavyweight Champion; Archie Moore, the longest-reigning World Light Heavyweight Champion of all time; and Upton Bell. Courtesy Upton Bell.

33. (*opposite bottom*) Bob Lobel, Bob Ryan, and Upton Bell of the original *Sports Beat* (missing from photo, original member Joe Fitzgerald of the *Boston Herald*). Courtesy Upton Bell.

34. (*opposite top*) Bert Bell commemorative coin.
Photo by and courtesy JoAnne O'Neill.

35. (*opposite bottom*) Coin toss at Franklin Field,
Penn vs. Harvard, 2016, commemorating the
one hundredth anniversary of Penn's Rose Bowl
appearance vs. Oregon, where Bert Bell threw
the first forward pass in Rose Bowl history.
Photo by and courtesy JoAnne O'Neill.

36. (*above*) Bell with statue of college and
NFL Hall of Famer Chuck "Concrete Charlie"
Bednarik at Franklin Field, 2016. Photo by and
courtesy JoAnne O'Neill.

37. At Franklin Field, Bell sits in the seat where his father, Bert Bell, died on October 11, 1959, watching a game between the two teams he owned, the Eagles and Steelers, on the field where he played college football as captain of Penn. Photo by and courtesy JoAnne O'Neill.

38. Upton Bell on Franklin Field on the one hundredth anniversary of his father, Bert Bell, leading the University of Pennsylvania to the Rose Bowl. Photo by and courtesy JoAnne O'Neill.

Earl Morrall whom he'd seen do some great things as a starting quarterback in Detroit when Shula was a defensive assistant
there, including leading a comeback win over the Colts with thirteen seconds left on the clock. That's the kind of thing that sticks
in a coach's mind.

The Giants had signed Fran Tarkenton the year before, replacing Morrall, who by now was seen by many in the league as an
aging former starter. In 1956 he'd been not only the San Francisco
49ers' No. 1 pick but the league's overall No. 1, but they traded
him to Pittsburgh and the Steelers later sent him to Detroit, which
turned out to be fortuitous for us and Shula. But he was thirty-
four by 1968 and had gone 1-5-1 in his last seven NFL starts for
the Giants in 1966 before breaking his wrist. He appeared to be
little more than a career backup playing out the string, but he fit
what Shula felt we needed. He wanted someone who could take
direction, not panic, and get along with Unitas, which wasn't
always easy.

Earl had a good attitude and grasp of the game, and Shula felt
he could be trusted with the offense if John missed a few games.
So on August 25 Shula informed us he'd dealt a six-year backup
tight end named Butch Wilson to the Giants for Morrall. We were
underwhelmed. Who knew we'd just acquired the man who'd
become the league's MVP? No one, including Shula, but we all
felt we'd improved our team just in case.

"Just in case" happened thirteen days later in the Cotton Bowl
in Dallas. In the final exhibition game of the summer, Unitas was
twisting to his left under pressure from the Cowboys' pass rush
and tried to throw a pass to his right. As he did he was hit and
heard his elbow go POP! To many it was the sound of our season
deflating like a pierced balloon.

He'd torn two tendons that held the upper and lower bones
together at the elbow joint. After that Unitas could barely throw
the ball across the kitchen with any assurance he'd hit the refrigerator. Pain is something you can't always overcome, even if your
name is Unitas. Our trainer, Ed Block, tried everything to get John
ready: ice, cortisone shots, heat. He even began to slather his elbow

with analgesic and wrap a plastic bag around it, tightly taping it to his arm during practice to keep body heat on the area. It looked like a massive turkey leg in a refrigerator bag. It also didn't help. What Unitas needed was what you never have enough of in pro football: he needed time and rest.

Block said it was an overuse injury common to thirty-five-year-old quarterbacks and jackhammer operators. You could have argued John was both for us, but now he was gone for an unspecified period. In the end he would complete only 11 of 32 passes all season. Earl Morrall was our quarterback, even though it was months before his teammates conceded the point.

What resulted from that serendipitous trade would have gotten Shula labeled a genius by today's hyperbolic media, but those were more understated, Twitterless times. Shula had simply made a move to protect his team that turned out brilliantly, at least until January 12, 1969. No one back then was comparing him to Albert Einstein for doing it, but with our defense Earl gave us a chance to win each Sunday.

We started off 5-0 because we were only allowing 11.5 points a game. Earl hardly reminded anyone of Unitas, but he had some big games, throwing four touchdown passes against Chicago, and three were for 66, 50, and 45 yards. But he was also still learning a new system different from what he'd run in the past, including a numbering system for the holes that was the opposite of what he'd run in Pittsburgh, Detroit, and New York. His former teams labeled the holes to the left of center with odd numbers and those to the right with even ones. We did the opposite and more than a few times Earl would take the snap, spin in one direction, and find no one to hand off to because the back had gone the other way. Habits, good or bad, are powerful things in sports and difficult to break.

Earl once told a story that he began to look at the fingers of our best running back, Tom Matte, when he'd call a play because Matte would twiddle them on one hand or the other as the play was called. Earl thought he was signaling him what direction the play was going. It took a few games for him to realize it was just a nervous habit.

Matte wasn't the only one getting nervous in the huddle at that point. As we prepared to meet the San Francisco 49ers at Kezar Stadium on October 13, Unitas was throwing lightly the week of practice. The players took it as a sign. John's coming back.

He did but only briefly, when Shula inserted him into that game to see what his readiness level was, even though Earl had thrown touchdown passes of 44 and 41 yards. Unitas threw three passes, completing one for a 6-yard touchdown to John Mackey late in the fourth quarter of a 42–14 rout, and another pass was dropped. We could sense what was next.

All season Earl was asked his feelings about replacing Unitas. The week after that game he told a *Sports Illustrated* writer named Bud Shrake something typical of Earl. It was the kind of thing that made him not only a wonderful teammate but also someone who could survive this kind of situation twice under Shula, in 1968 replacing Unitas and in 1972 when he replaced Bob Griese, after Griese broke his ankle in Miami's fifth game of what would become their undefeated season. Earl managed to get along with Shula and with Unitas in Baltimore in what could have been a tenuous relationship because he understood who he was and who they were. Earl was the keeper of the keys. He knew they were Unitas's keys. And he knew it was our defense that kept us winning.

"I know what will happen when John gets ready," he told Shrake after completing 13 of 23 for 188 yards, two touchdowns, and an interception against the Niners. "He'll be back in there. He should be."

Earl had no illusions and neither did the rest of us. There was only one Unitas. That's as true today as it was in 1968. John was the face of the game when it only had one face. There was no Brady-versus-Peyton-like debate. There was Unitas. Then there were the others.

John believed he was always what was best for the team, and in most respects he was. He had the greatest respect among his peers of anyone I've ever seen. He was like a great jazz man. He was playing the same notes as other musicians, but the song came run. It wasn't a suggestion. Run it! If you didn't you answered to him, and John didn't appreciate it.

That situation taught me a lesson while observing all of this as a young man who at the time would sometimes blanch when Shula was criticizing me about this or that. My first reaction was to think, "What's he telling me?" I'd think about it later and realize it wasn't personal. After a while I never took it personally when he'd criticize me or ask me if I knew what the fuck I was talking about. There were some real arguments over personnel decisions and drafting in the beginning, but he also understood if every time I went to make a move he overruled me, then I would be just a puppet. If he'd done that all the time to me, I'd have been as embarrassed as maybe Unitas felt when he called him out about a play or a refusal to run what Don sent in.

Weeb and Don both developed the game plan with Unitas, but it was different. Football was starting to change into a coach-run game rather than a quarterback-run game. It was just the beginning of that, but Shula was a disciple of Paul Brown, who called every play with his messenger guards and wanted to put electronic devices in the quarterback's helmets decades before the NFL finally did it. Shula wanted that control that head coaches have today, the control Unitas had always had.

John was the opposite. *He* ran the game. Shula used to tell Ward, our backup quarterback, to ask John when he came off the field why he'd done this or that so he could begin to learn. He'd ask John, "What did you see there?" More times than not Unitas just looked at him and said, "How the hell do I know?"

He just saw things and understood immediately where the ball had to go and was accurate and bold enough to put it where most people wouldn't or couldn't. He couldn't tell you the play he called or what defense the opponent was in, but at the moment of truth he *knew.*

The greatest players feel things. They have a sense of things that comes from preparation and a deeper understanding than the rest of us possess not only of how the game works but how *this* game is working on *this* day. After the '58 NFL Championship Game, the one you could argue created the modern pro game, John was asked why he'd thrown the ball to Jim Mutscheller on second-and-goal at the Giants' 6-yard line in overtime, one play before Alan Ameche's touchdown run won it. They were already within field goal range, so Dave Anderson, who would later win a Pulitzer Prize but was then a young reporter at the *New York Journal American*, asked Unitas, barely three years removed from working construction and playing sandlot football for $6 a game for the Bloomfield Rams, why he took the risk.

Unitas fixed him with an icy glare, as Anderson recalled it, before saying, "There is no risk when you know what you're doing."

That was Unitas even before he'd become the face of the NFL, which by 1968 he was. I remember a story about how the Colts were all in an airport on their way to the West Coast once when Clark Gable, the leading movie star of the day, heard the Colts were there and came over because he wanted to meet Johnny Unitas. That's how famous he was. Gable wanted to shake Unitas's hand, not the other way around.

The Colts of 1958–68 were the Dallas Cowboys without the phony hoopla. Everybody knew who the Colts were because everybody knew who Unitas was. All you had to say was "Unitas." He was famous in a time when it was a lot harder to become famous. John Mackey, our Hall of Fame tight end, once explained what it was like this way: "Playing with Johnny Unitas was like being in the huddle with God." Where'd that leave Shula?

Here's the quarterback who invented the two-minute offense. The quarterback who invented the checkoff at the line of scrimmage. The quarterback who won the game that changed football. The quarterback who'd already won two championships. He's the *ultimate* quarterback. Now this young coach comes in, a defensive genius by the way, and he's going to tell Unitas what to do and he's not going to be soft about it?

If you talked with Shula, the conversation was direct. He wasn't going to rub your shoulders. If Shula sent in a play and you waved it off, that pissed him off. If you pissed him off—and John did—he'd confront you. He confronted everybody. You could have a conversation with him that ended up in an argument pretty easily in those days, but when the argument was over, that was it. No carryover. John wasn't that way. He remembered.

And you can't minimize the fact Shula had been a teammate of John's in 1956, Unitas's rookie season. He was a backup defensive back whom John burned plenty of times in practice. Shula was waived the next year, just as Unitas was becoming a star. Now that guy is telling him what plays to call? He's thinking, "What does he know about football except that he couldn't play it like me?"

Shula was naturally more comfortable with Earl Morrall. There was no tension between them. Earl was an extension of Shula. It was like family. John wasn't. Shula had great respect for John because he'd seen what he could do, but it was different. Maybe the problem between them was they were too much alike. Or maybe it was because there was a new world out there, in football and out. A lot of things were changing, young people were challenging authority, and people have trouble with change. It was complex but John was black-and-white.

In some ways I don't blame either of them. I see John as the great quarterback who was becoming, like all of us, mortal. Not coming to an end, but 1968 was not the year for him. On the other hand, Shula was a young coach who wanted to do it his way. It was two strong-willed men with brilliant football minds locked in a battle for control of the offense's intellectual property. I understand how they both felt. I wanted to shake things up too. I had ideas. I wanted to do it my way. It's natural. How could you not have a clash?

People talk about Shula, Paul Brown, Belichick, all the great coaches, as cold men. That's what made them great. Cold men. We're moving on. But Shula was a little different. He'd been a player who had been told to move on. He understood what that felt like. It happened to him. Maybe that's why one of my jobs in training camp was to be The Turk. I was the person who went to players' rooms and asked for their playbook and told them the coach wanted to see them. Nobody wanted to see me coming. The most difficult thing in professional sports is to tell someone it's over. If the player is someone like Unitas, it's a lot more than difficult.

Luckily for Shula he didn't have to tell Unitas it was over, but he had to bench him. I think that was the most painful decision of his football life. He had to tell somebody who essentially made the NFL great to sit down, but to his credit he didn't sit him down for the whole year. He put him back in against the Browns on October 20, which turned out to be a disaster.

The week after the 49ers game, we were 17-point favorites to beat Cleveland at home. We were 5-0 and they were 2-3. It was a beautiful fall day, 64 degrees, light wind, crisp air. Perfect day for football but not for Earl, who struggled.

We were down 14–7 at the half and Shula made the switch to John. His first throw was intercepted at our 36, and eight plays later the score was 21–7. We got a couple of field goals to make it close again, but John threw two more interceptions in the fourth quarter and the game got out of hand. We were down 27–13 when he had a pass blocked at the line of scrimmage and intercepted by a defensive end, Bill Glass. Perhaps for the first time in his career at Memorial Stadium, John was booed. Cleveland kicked another field goal to make it 30–13 with ten minutes to play, and Shula sent Earl back in. Unitas had gone 1 for 11 for 12 passing yards with three interceptions. His arm was dead.

Bringing him in cost us the game, but it may have saved our season. Shula saw what happened and that was it. Now it was Earl's team. He wouldn't come out again until it was too late in Super Bowl III. The truth is we wouldn't have gone anywhere if we kept using John to relieve Morrall. We were going to sink or swim with Earl. In the end we did both.

We went undefeated the rest of the way and allowed only 32 points in the next seven games. Then we beat the Vikings pretty easily in the Western Conference playoffs, 24–14, to set up a rematch with the Browns for the NFL title. Cleveland had won eight straight after beating us, but we were now viewed as one of the greatest teams ever built. We were led by the Coach of the Year and the league's MVP, Morrall. We all knew this was the real Super Bowl. Whoever the AFL sent to Miami in two weeks wasn't going to stop the inevitable . . . and neither were the Browns.

We were 14-1 and all of us believed if we'd stuck with Morrall that day in October, we'd have been undefeated. Now we had a chance to prove it and we did. We didn't just beat the Browns, we obliterated them, 34–0, on their own field in front of 80,628 witnesses.

The highlight for me came before the game. We were down on the field and Carroll told me, "Uppie, your father, if he was alive today, would be proud of you." That meant so much to me, because Carroll was a dear friend of my father's. To hear that took a little edge off the tension for a minute, but not for long.

I was up in the coaches' box, which wasn't normal for a personnel director, but Shula wanted me there to learn. I stood most of the game, but as we began scoring more and more I remember thinking, "Does it get any better than this?" Unfortunately the answer was it didn't, but who knew?

That day I felt Shula had been vindicated for the loss in Cleveland. Everyone was shocked by the score, but Tex Maule of *Sports Illustrated* wrote the next week that the world championship had already been decided. Our defense was ferocious, limiting Leroy Kelly, who'd rushed for 130 yards in October, to 28 yards and forcing three turnovers. Their quarterback, Bill Nelson, completed only 11 of 26 throws and threw two interceptions, while Tom Matte, a kid who grew up in East Cleveland cheering for the Browns, trampled their defense for 88 yards and three touchdowns. When we flew back to Baltimore that night, it seemed like half the town was waiting for us.

It was as though all of Baltimore won, because that's the kind of city it was. Baltimore viewed itself as a poor stepchild sandwiched between New York and Washington. It was like a lot of America at the time. You went into a local bar and it was like *Cheers*—everybody knew your name. That was particularly true of my brother, Bert, who worked on the business side of the Colts for a while. He was great friends with some of the players and was often out with them, playing poker and enjoying life. I can assure you *everyone* knew Bert's name.

After we got back I ended up with a close friend of Frank Sinatra's named Sammy Goldstein, who owned a popular nightclub on The Block, a seedier part of downtown Baltimore, which at the time was lined with strip joints. Sammy was a great person with some nefarious friends, I guess, because about ten years later his dead body ended up stuffed in the trunk of a car. That was one of the great things about Baltimore. You could have a gangster on one elbow and a bishop on the other if the Colts were involved.

All the players used to go to Sweeney's or over to Gussie's Downbeat at 4713 Eastern Avenue, which was owned by a bookmaker named Constantine "Gussie" Alexander. It was located underneath a Chinese laundry. Fabulous place. No VIP area keeping the fans away from the players. We all lived together, worked together, and played together in Baltimore. We were neighbors. Baltimore was the Colts and the Colts were Baltimore, which is what made that time so special. Every gambler in town, including the one who owned the Colts, would settle up at Gussie's on Monday nights at some point. Gussie used to say, "Carroll Rosenbloom? Just another customer."

That night I ended up at the most famous bar in Baltimore, Sweeney's up on Greenmount Avenue and Thirty-Second, a few blocks from Memorial Stadium where we played, and I had Sammy in tow. I called my wife and told her to come meet us because we were all headed to Unitas's restaurant, The Golden Arm (naturally), which had just opened that year out in York Road Plaza, for a team party. Sammy came too, but they wouldn't let him in because he wasn't part of the Colts' official party. If he'd showed up with some of his influential friends like Sinatra, they wouldn't have had a choice; but he didn't, so Sammy had to go.

The euphoria all over the city was unbelievable. You would have thought it was Christmas. Nobody was thinking a bit about the New York Jets except Shula and maybe Bobby Boyd, our best defensive back and a partner in The Golden Arm. Boyd was extremely intelligent. He was like a Unitas on defense. Anything he said was prophetic. Unfortunately in this case.

Most of the players were unimpressed by the Jets, but Bobby told me when he looked at their backfield on film—no iPad video in those days—Matt Snell and Emerson Boozer would have beaten out our men, Tom Matte and Jerry Hill. He thought their receivers, Don Maynard and George Sauer Jr., were one of the best tandems he'd seen. Maynard was a burner who was an NFL reject but ended up in the Hall of Fame. He was hurt and didn't catch a pass in Super Bowl III, but his presence had a major impact on the game and our defense. And, of course, they had Namath.

At one point Alex Hawkins, a ten-year veteran whose career was winding down, told Boyd he felt the Jets' defense was the poorest he'd ever seen in pro football. He told Bobby we should score 50 on them. Bobby told him, "You may have to."

Our defensive coordinator was Chuck Noll, who would leave at the end of the season to take over the Pittsburgh Steelers, a team that had up to then been a perennial NFL doormat. He would not only transform them but write NFL history by winning four Super Bowls in six years there. Going into the Super Bowl, he recognized they had a dangerous offense. Neither he nor Shula said anything disparaging about the Jets, but I began to sense some of our players were growing beyond overconfident.

The Jets' defense was undersized and had a number of retreads from the Colts that Weeb brought over with him after Carroll fired him for not winning enough championships. Carroll told me later it was the toughest thing he'd ever had to do in football, because there was no real reason to fire Weeb. He just felt Weeb had run his course. Six years later there he was on the other side of the field looking like Yoda in a top coat and a buzz cut. He still had The Force with him, even though he didn't have Unitas anymore.

When I looked at the film, I thought they had a good offense, but we had the best defense in football. We'd only given up 144 points, which tied the 1963 Chicago Bears for stinginess, and we'd scored 402. Looking back, I never would have shown our players the Jets' game films, because once they watched them they thought, "Are you kidding?" Many thought the game would be a rout, but the Jets were more than they appeared to be, and we picked the worst day of our lives to be a little less than we were.

We'd won twenty-six of our last thirty games over two years. We had two Hall of Fame coaches, Shula running our team, and Noll and Bill Arnsparger running our defense. We made one of the greatest pickups in NFL history. Looking back, it was so improbable we'd be seen as one of the greatest teams in NFL history going into Super Bowl III with a backup quarterback replacing Johnny Unitas. Earl being the MVP was maybe the most unlikely thing to occur in NFL history. Everything just came together. Until the last game it was like magic.

But from the time we got to Miami, things were just off. I met the team there on Thursday because I was off scouting, and the day before I arrived, Namath had "guaranteed" a Jets win at a Miami Touchdown Club awards dinner after someone in the crowd yelled out, "The Colts are going to kick your ass!" Namath took the microphone and said, "Hey, I got news for you. We're going to win Sunday. I'll guarantee you." The next morning the *Miami Herald* had a headline: "Namath Guarantees Jets Victory." Weeb was furious, but no one else wrote about it for two more days. Most of the New York papers except for *Newsday* didn't even mention it until game day. Can you imagine the feeding frenzy that would have caused on social media today? Twitter would have crashed.

A few nights earlier one of our players, our kicker and reserve defensive lineman Lou Michaels, confronted Namath in Jimmy Fazio's restaurant in Miami Beach about things he'd been saying about Earl, and it got pretty heated at first. Namath had said the Raiders' quarterback, Daryle Lamonica, was a better passer than Morrall, and when he was defending his prediction sitting poolside in a beach chair at the Galt Ocean Mile Hotel where the Jets were staying, he told a bunch of writers, "There are five or six better quarterbacks than Morrall in the AFL."

Lou said something to him about shutting his mouth, that Unitas never talked like that. Joe said, "Unitas is over the hill." I imagine he was joking, because everyone revered Unitas, including

Namath, who grew up in Beaver Falls, Pennsylvania, not far from where Unitas grew up in the Mount Washington section of Pittsburgh. Those two men, along with Joe Montana and Dan Marino, turned that part of western Pennsylvania into the cradle of quarterbacks, so my guess is Joe was just trying to get under Michael's skin, which wasn't that difficult, and he succeeded. Nobody talked like that in those days, but the times they were a changin'.

I wasn't sure any of this was a good sign for us, because we weren't that type of team. We confronted opponents on the field, not in press conferences or cocktail lounges, but that's what this game had become. It was a symbol of something bigger. Two cultures in conflict, the generational battle going on in the '60s in every walk of life, was going to be settled at the Orange Bowl.

We represented not just the NFL but the Establishment. Namath and the Jets were the Counterculture. He wore long hair, an occasional Fu Manchu moustache, and white shoes and guaranteed victory. Morrall wore a brush cut and guaranteed nothing but his best effort. Fathers rooted for the Colts. Sons—and daughters—rooted for Broadway Joe.

It was another example of a country in upheaval. Kids were rebelling against their parents and their government. African Americans wanted equality and were sick and tired of going to the lunch counter at Read's on Howard and Lexington in Baltimore, where they once were refused service, and still being handed a paper cup if they ordered a Coke so as not to "contaminate" the glassware. Everywhere you turned America was in turmoil, and that included in the Orange Bowl.

That game was the essence of the generation gap that was growing wider in America. It was the white bread NFL versus the AFL with all those black players from small colleges in the South playing positions the NFL wouldn't let them play like middle linebacker and quarterback. They had players who boastfully guaranteed victory. We had a coach in Shula who was apoplectic with disbelief when he learned Namath had blown off a mandatory Tuesday photo day with the media to go to the pool. It was as though Namath was saying, "We're the future. You're the past."

Looking back on it, symbols of the changes America was struggling with were everywhere. If you were looking for a sign of the seismic size of the shift taking place, maybe the most obvious was that Namath was in room 534 at the Galt Ocean Hotel. It was the Governor's Suite. It was the same room they gave Vince Lombardi the year before when the Packers stayed there the week before Super Bowl II.

That week our whole routine was off. There was a party atmosphere around the game that didn't fit its demands. I remember my father's old friend, Norm Van Brocklin, who was now the Atlanta Falcons' head coach, telling some sportswriters in a buffet line during a Friday night party at the Doral that "Sunday Joe Namath will be playing his first pro game." He was widely quoted and didn't deny it. That's how sure everyone from the NFL was that this was a mismatch.

As the week wore on, there was more talk about Rosenbloom's planned victory party than about the game. He even invited Weeb, who respectfully declined. Our players were exhausted mentally by the time the game actually came around. They couldn't get away from all the talk of domination. We were mentally fried by the magnitude of it and we played like it, Earl in particular. We were used to playing at 1 p.m. but the Super Bowl wasn't until 3 p.m. We were waiting around all day to play knowing everyone expected us not to just beat them but to manhandle them.

On game day everyone seemed more interested in talking about Joe Kennedy, the father of John, Robert, and Teddy, being caught in traffic than they did about Joe Namath and the Jets. Vice President Elect Spiro Agnew wanted Richard Nixon, the president elect, to call in the first play for Shula. Agnew had been governor of Maryland and was a friend of Shula's, so he was in Miami. It was the first time the league called the game the Super Bowl (it had simply been the AFL-NFL Championship Game the first two years when the Packers crushed the Chiefs and the Raiders) and the first time it turned into a celebrity's convention.

Bob Hope and Jackie Gleason were on opposite sides of the field. I still don't know what that was about. The *Apollo 8* astronauts—

Frank Borman, James Lovell, and William Anders—had just gotten back to Earth December 27 after becoming the first to orbit the moon, and they were there.

Anita Bryant, a singer and former Miss Oklahoma, sang the national anthem, and the halftime entertainment was the Florida A&M Marching Band, which was famous in football circles. In a few years they'd be replaced by Michael Jackson, Whitney Houston, and Bruce Springsteen, but you had to start somewhere in the process of evolving from sport to spectacle.

By the day of the game, some of our players were talking about how tired they were. It was mental. The pressure was building like storm clouds over the Atlantic, and the magnitude of the thought we might lose just wore some of them down. That Sunday was the longest day I can remember.

As I said, in terms of talent we should have beaten them the way the oddsmakers predicted, but in the two biggest games in NFL history—the '58 sudden-death overtime game against the Giants and Super Bowl III—Webb won. He understood too many people tried to pass on us. He knew if they got the lead and pounded our right side with the run, we'd struggle. He understood the way to attack us was to run right at Braase and Shinnick and throw at the corner on that side, Lenny Lyles. They were players who were nearer to the end then our defensive statistics led most coaches to conclude, but Weeb knew it because he knew them. He understood their vulnerabilities.

Namath's dismissiveness of Earl may have had an effect too. He kept pointing out he was a backup only playing because Unitas was hurt. Hawkins wrote about that in his book and it was an interesting point. It was dime-store psychology, but it made a lot of sense, explaining why so many things went wrong for Earl that day.

Hawk claimed he was talking with Jimmy Orr, one of our best receivers, on the way to the game and Orr told him, "Senor, don't let Earl wake up today. Just let him sleep for three more hours." It was as though Jimmy knew Earl had been playing beyond his capabilities all season.

At halftime Hawk thought, "Whether the disparaging remarks previously levied at Morrall by Namath came into the picture, I have no way of knowing, but some recollection of his past with four different teams must have flashed through his mind. Jimmy Orr's and my own worst fear had been realized. Earl had awakened."

If that's true, it became apparent just before halftime. It was the kind of moment you only realize in retrospect has sealed your fate. It made it clear Cinderella had broken the glass slipper.

The flea flicker pass Morrall failed to complete just before halftime will always be the thing that totally turned the game around. We'd practiced it for weeks. Orr was always open and Earl always found him. I'm standing in the back of the coaches' box thinking the Jets led 7–0 but we'd been moving the ball up and down the field, so it was a matter of time before we broke through.

When Shula called the flea flicker, I thought it was perfect timing. Weeb said later he knew it was coming, but apparently he didn't tell his secondary, because Orr was 35 yards behind his cornerback, Randy Beverly, when Matte turned and flipped the ball backward to Earl. I saw Orr downfield behind the defense waving his arms and thought, "*He's wide open!*"

The lateral was a little bit off, so Earl had to reach for it. Maybe that's why he never looked to his left. Maybe that's why he never saw Jimmy. Or maybe, like Jimmy feared, he just woke up. To me it's one of the most iconic moments in NFL history—Orr frantically waving and Earl throwing to Jerry Hill and getting the ball intercepted by Jim Hudson at the Jets' 12-yard line.

Earl told people later he missed Orr because there was a sea of blue shirts in the stands behind the end zone and he didn't pick him up. Some people in the organization believed he just threw to the first blue shirt he saw even though it was our fullback, who was the fourth option on that play. In the end all that mattered was if he hit Orr, the game's tied at halftime, we settle down and stop making stupid mistakes, and, I believe, win by 20 points. But he didn't.

We'd run through them the whole half. Matte had just had a 58-yard run to the Jets' 16 on the previous drive. They couldn't stop us, but we kept stopping ourselves. In the last four drives that half, Earl threw three interceptions and Lou Michaels missed a 46-yard field goal. They weren't all Earl's fault, but it's what happened on his watch. He didn't cause the ball to hit Tom Mitchell, our tight end, in the arm and pop straight up into the air for an interception the first time we had the ball. After our defense stopped the Jets, we drove 54 yards in eleven plays to the Jets' 19, but Willie Richardson dropped a pass, Earl badly overthrew Mitchell on second down, then had to run to avoid being sacked on third down, and Michaels, who got into that beef with Namath early in the week, missed a 27-yard field goal. If we score we lead 3–0. But we didn't.

That was what I found myself thinking all day. Whenever we had a chance to change the game, we didn't. Earl had some bad luck, but you can't afford bad luck in the Super Bowl. If you watch the film and are dispassionate about it, he didn't have a bad game. He had an average game, but in the Super Bowl that's a problem.

There was no sense of panic in the coaches' box, but after Earl missed Orr, I had the most ominous feeling come over me. It just changed everything. I kept thinking either we come out in the second half and blow them out or this is going to be a long night.

To be fair, though, there were two other plays in the first half that have been pretty much forgotten for the past forty-seven years, but they were both critical for the Jets and symbolic of the kind of day it was for us. The first came on the fourth play of their second drive, first-and-10 on their 35. Maynard just ran right by Bobby Boyd and one of our safeties, Jerry Logan, but Namath overthrew him. I remember the crowd's reaction. It was like, "Wow!" I wondered if Namath was throwing that just to let us know he could air it out and beat us anytime he wanted.

We didn't know Maynard had a bad hamstring and almost didn't play. All we knew was he averaged 22.8 yards per catch that season and had sprinter's speed, so after he got behind us like that we made an adjustment. We rotated our zone coverage toward him, leaving our right corner, Lenny Lyles, one-on-one with George Sauer Jr. Sauer was one of eleven AFL All-Stars on the Jets, and he played like it that day.

He abused Lyles, finishing with eight catches for 133 yards, averaging 16.8 yards per catch. Even when he made a play early in the game that might have killed the Jets on another day, Sauer got away with it. Lyles unloaded on him late in the first quarter after a 3-yard catch, and he fumbled. Our linebacker, Ron Porter, recovered at the Jets' 12, but on third-and-4 at the 6, Earl took a three-step drop and threw that ball toward Mitchell on a slant. It should have given us a 7–0 lead and Earl some breathing room, but their linebacker, Al Atkinson, tipped it and it bounced off Mitchell's shoulder pad and arm and shot straight up, and Beverly intercepted it in the end zone. If you threw that ball in there like that a hundred times and it hit Mitchell in the arm like that, it would never bounce straight up like a pop fly, but this time it did and they grabbed it.

The other play came with the Jets backed up near their goal line in the second quarter. They were punting from the end zone and Hawk came in unblocked. He should have blocked the punt or tackled the punter, but he hesitated for a second and didn't do either. Normally that year we would have blown in there and made the play, but the magnitude of it all seemed to make us hesitate. Whatever caused it, the result was the punt went right under his arms when he put his hands up and he hit the punter, Curley Johnson, and was flagged for roughing the kicker. That penalty ended up being nullified because the Jets were called for illegal procedure as well and had to re-kick. This time Hawk was blocked. That's the kind of day it was.

Still, even with all the mistakes, we were only down 7–0, and our offensive line was opening up holes like you couldn't believe. We averaged 6.2 yards a carry (143 yards on twenty-three rushes) and in 1968 that meant something. The pass was taking over but it was still a running game, and we were doing that at will. Of course, so was Snell.

Unitas always claimed Shula told him in the locker room at halftime that he'd start the second half, but Shula told me later that would have been unfair to Earl. Even though he was the MVP, we all knew he was being watched very closely. You could feel it, so I'm sure he did too. Maybe the coaches feared the Big Game was too much for him. I sensed some of the players felt that way and Orr's comment proved it, but I always attributed that more to their confidence in John.

Whatever it was, Shula didn't feel that way four years later in Super Bowl VII when he started Griese ahead of Earl. Maybe he learned something from what happened to us. Whatever the reason, when we got the ball to start the second half, Earl was at quarterback. Shula had told the team at halftime it had stopped itself and just had to stop making mistakes. He was right, but the first play from scrimmage Earl hands off to Matte and he gets jumped from behind by Verlon Biggs, the Jets' best defensive end, and fumbles. The Jets recovered at our 33. Our defense held and they settled for another field goal, but the message was clear: we were still making mistakes.

It's a helpless feeling for a personnel director once the game starts. There's nothing more you can do to help your team. The players you picked must execute, and we weren't. We didn't do anything with the ball on the next drive and New York came back, but instead of running it, Namath threw on us, holding the ball for over four minutes before Jim Turner made another short field goal. We were down 13–0. It was time.

I looked up and suddenly it seemed like sunrise. Unitas was jogging toward the huddle with that oddly stooped shuffle of his, moving like a man whose feet were killing him. He wasn't walking on water but he was walking onto the field, and that was enough for anyone wearing blue and white to have hope.

He went three and out and Namath came back throwing again, twice hitting Sauer for gains of 11 and 39 on Lyles. The latter was the longest pass of the day, and it gave the Jets first-and-goal at our 10, but we held again and they settled for another field goal. The defense was more than holding its own considering all the problems our offense was creating, but now it was 16–0 with only 13:26 to play. We were running out of time and Weeb knew it.

Namath didn't throw another pass. He just kept hitting us with Snell on a play we called 19 Straight, chewing up the clock and our defense.

And then Unitas was Unitas, and it seemed anything was possible for the Colts.

It was thrilling to watch him drive the team downfield with a dead arm. He got us to the Jets' 25, but the shadow of himself he'd become was obvious on one play that drive. He saw Orr break open on a deep post and immediately let it go. He knew exactly where to put the football, but his arm couldn't get it there in time, and Beverly undercut the route and made his second interception in the end zone. There was 11:06 left. We still had time, but the clock was ticking on us and on Unitas's aching arm.

The Jets then ran the ball seven straight times, taking off another four and a half minutes. You could feel the life being sucked from us, but Unitas readjusted his game. Throwing only as far as his arm now allowed, he completed four passes, two of 11 yards, one of 17 on fourth down, and another of 21, the next time he got the ball. We got to the 1 but needed three tries before we scored, losing valuable time we no longer had.

You could see players on the Jets' bench start to rustle. Namath was up and watching. This was Unitas and everyone in the Orange Bowl knew what that meant, especially after an onside kick bounced off Sauer's hands and Tom Mitchell recovered it at the Jets' 44. John completed three straight passes, taking us to the Jets' 19. Johnny U was showing Broadway Joe what it meant to play quarterback in the NFL. He was going to save us from our great embarrassment. He was going to take us home . . . and then his aching arm hollered at him. And he didn't.

Three straight passes flew well off the mark, each by more than its predecessor. The final one was an overthrow well beyond Orr's reach, and we were done. The Jets ran six times, five surprisingly to the right toward Bubba Smith. Weeb was one of the first coaches to figure out how to play Bubba. The Jets didn't take him on. They took him down low, with cut blocks. It was a smart way to attack him, and it wasn't the only smart thing the Jets were doing.

WORST LOSS IN THE HISTORY OF LOSSES

They were twice called for delay of game, giving up yardage in exchange for time off the clock. By the time they were done, there were eight seconds glowering down at us on the scoreboard clock. The best team in football, maybe the best ever not to win a Super Bowl, had made history in the worst way.

We all knew Carroll was not happy and neither were his fellow owners. I came to realize later that an embarrassed owner is a very dangerous man to work for. He's worse than an angry owner. An angry owner gets over it. An embarrassed owner never does.

As I was walking to the locker, I ran into my friend Dan Rooney, son of Steelers owner Art Rooney, my father's longtime partner, and we started talking about all that was left—the future. I knew he was looking for a new head coach and I pitched Noll, as I had earlier in the season to his father. I felt Noll had everything it would take to succeed. I know that may seem strange at that great moment of disappointment, but like everything in life, when it's over it's over and you have to move on. I felt Dan would make the decision and I didn't know when I'd see him again, so I wanted to get Noll's name on his radar.

He and I talked about how embarrassing this was for the league, but I reminded him Noll's defense had performed well. Had our offense performed near its norm, we would have won. I must have been convincing, because years later I learned Dan interviewed Noll the next day and he got the job. The rest is history.

When I walked into our locker room, it was as silent as a monk's retreat. I'd never heard so loud a silence and never have again, thank God. Rosenbloom was standing there and the look on his face was frightening. If looks could kill, he would have been the only man standing. Rosenbloom never forgot defeat. He still remembered a 27–0 loss in Cleveland in 1964, in Shula's second year as head coach. It would come up from time to time. So you can imagine what that loss in Miami was like. It was like a funeral. A funeral for all of us but most of all for Shula, who was gone in two years.

Within three years we were all gone. Harry Hulmes, the acting general manager, was gone. Shula was in Miami. Noll left for

Pittsburgh. I left two years later for New England to become the youngest GM in football at thirty-three. George Young, who later was GM of the Giants and won two Super Bowls there, lasted until 1974, but he was finally fired by Joe Thomas after he became the Colts' GM, and George joined Shula in Miami. If we'd won that day I don't believe Shula ever would have left. He was much more a Baltimore man than a Miami man.

If we'd won we would have become a dynasty, and Carroll would never have swapped the team with Bob Irsay to move to LA to take over the Rams either, and the Colts would never have left for Indianapolis fifteen years later. NFL history would have been entirely different, but that's the domino effect of that kind of failure in life.

Carroll spoke to the team with Shula standing silently next to him. He didn't say anything about being proud of our effort or anything like that. He said he didn't hire people to lose. Bill Curry, our center, recalled it years later on an NFL Films documentary perfectly. He just about got every word painfully correct when he recalled Carroll saying, "Now men, I'm not in this business to be humiliated and embarrassed. To come in second place. Ever. I've already fired a coach who won two world championships for me. I want you to understand I'm interested in one thing. I'm interested in dominance and the world championship. Are there any questions?"

There were none. The less said, the better.

That speech was very unusual for an owner. I was thirty-one years old and had never heard anything like it. I can't remember another owner who ever did that in any locker room I was ever in right after a loss. I'd never heard an owner talk that way, but that was what I'd always heard about Rosenbloom from my father, the person who convinced him to buy the Colts in the first place. He was very demanding and brutally honest about his feelings. Sometimes I admired that. Other times I didn't. But you always knew where you stood with Carroll Rosenbloom, and that day we didn't stand in very good stead.

The feeling in the room was so oppressive I just couldn't stay in the midst of it any longer, so I walked into the shower area and saw my friend Hawkins shaving and went over to talk with him. Hawk had one of the best perspectives of a non-coach I ever saw. His perspective was of an oracle, so I went to get his take on what just happened.

Unitas was standing to Hawk's left and Hawk started talking about how we'd screwed up this and screwed up that, which we had. He wasn't making fun of anybody, he was just laughing at how outrageous it was the way things had gone. He was sort of saying it was a joke how badly things had played out. Unfortunately, our middle linebacker Mike Curtis heard him.

Curtis had been a running back and linebacker at Duke, and I'd begged Shula to draft him. He was skeptical at first but he did it, and Mike became one of the most intense players I'd ever seen. Years later he described the way he felt that day: "That was one of the best teams I ever played with, and we lost to a team we would have beaten eight thousand times after the Super Bowl. It was humiliation . . . to be kind."

It was how we all felt. Humiliated. Stunned. Angry. Angry in a way that was turning that room into an explosive address.

Curtis started shouting, "Shut up, you soв! Just shut up! You don't know what you're talking about!" Curtis thought Hawk was laughing about the loss, which he wasn't, but you could see we were at a flashpoint. I was sure the next move was a fistfight, but Hawk didn't say a word. He kept staring straight into the mirror. He could see Curtis with this demonic look on his face, and he just ignored it. Unitas didn't say anything either, and I damn sure wasn't going to. I was Curtis's friend, but I'd been around players enough to know there were certain ones you didn't say anything to when they were in a mood, and this was that player in that mood. The sound of silence got a little louder after that, plastic pads hitting the floor making the only noise until we all left to get on the buses and head back to the hotel.

I went back and met my wife and we got ready to go to Rosenbloom's victory party, which was no longer about victory or much of a party. The buses were late, so we didn't get to Carroll's house out at Golden Beach until around ten. By then I'd already learned when I was back at the hotel that the impossible had happened: things had gotten worse.

Several players asked me if I'd heard about Rick Volk, our safety. He'd taken a knee in the head from Snell on the second play of the game and probably got a concussion. He was in a fog the rest of the day but he came back and played. Years later he told the *Detroit Free Press* he'd actually gotten two concussions that game, so it's no wonder what happened to him.

When Hawk was leaving his room to meet Unitas in the hotel bar downstairs, he saw Volk's wife, Charlene, running down the hallway screaming for help. Rick was on the bathroom floor vomiting, his body quivering with convulsions, and he was swallowing his tongue.

Our team doctor, Dr. Norman Freeman, got up there and used a ballpoint pen to free Volk's tongue and somebody called an ambulance. They put him in a bathtub full of ice, and I was told when he regained consciousness in the hospital the first words out of his mouth were, "Who won?"

When we finally got to Carroll's place it wasn't much different from the scene in our locker room, except the food was better and there was music playing in the background. I've been to a lot of victory parties in my life. Then there was this party. The conversations were very low, like they are at any wake, which this was. On the invitation it said, "After midnight breakfast will be served." Before the game I read that and thought they'd be serving a lot more than breakfast after midnight, but now I had a different thought: nobody would be staying for breakfast.

There was a dance floor, but no one was dancing until Bubba Smith went out there with Rosenbloom's daughter, Susie. Shula was kind of off to the side, and Unitas wasn't there at all. He was back with Hawk drinking at the hotel, believing as we all did that if he'd gotten in the game sooner it would have been different.

One politician who was there was Senator Ted Kennedy, who along with his dad, Joe Kennedy, had been a guest of Carroll's at the game. At one point they were in a pretty animated conversation and Teddy kept saying yes, it was a terrible loss, when Carroll turned and walked toward a sliding glass door that led to the pool. Teddy followed him out and as he left, an aide of Kennedy's scurried after him, but he was a step too late. Carroll slammed the door shut and the aide walked into the glass and broke his nose. He just stood there looking through the glass at Teddy and Carroll outside talking, his nose dripping blood. Strange night.

When we got back to Baltimore the next day, there weren't thirty thousand people waiting for us at the airport. What were waiting instead were headlines like one in the *Los Angeles Times* that morning that read: "Broadway Joe Rings Down the Curtain on the NFL."

In the overall picture, it came out right for the whole league. Not for us but for the league. This was bigger than a football game. The Jets' winning legitimized the merger and the AFL. It was good for the owners too because it was good for business, but they didn't see it that way then, and we all suffered the fallout. Two days before the game, at the annual commissioner's press conference on Friday, Commissioner Rozelle suggested possibly changing the playoff format after the merger went into effect in 1970 so two NFL teams could play in the Super Bowl instead of those inferior AFL teams. He didn't say inferior, but we all knew what he meant. After that game he never brought it up again.

Two years later we'd be back in this position and things would be different, but nothing could absolve our sin. We'd forever be the first NFL team ever to lose to the AFL. Mike Curtis got what that felt like right. Humiliation . . . to be kind.

11

Some Things Can't Be Fixed

The Colts organization never fully recovered from Super Bowl III. Some things simply can't be erased. It was like a hangover for which there was no antidote.

The relationship between Rosenbloom and Shula deteriorated because Carroll blamed him for the worst loss of his life. He probably looked back at what happened against the Browns in 1964, when we lost the NFL title to Cleveland despite being heavily favored, and thought we were 27-3 combined those two years under Shula and we still lost both championship games. Carroll was a bottom-line person. He hated to lose. He didn't forgive you if it happened too often at the wrong time, and there's no worse time than in the championship game.

The next season we slipped to 8-5-1, which left us second in the Coastal Division of the Western Conference but out of the playoffs altogether. We lost our first two games, including a 52–14 shellacking in Minnesota, and for a time both our tight ends, John Mackey and Tom Mitchell, were hurt. So was Orr, and Unitas's elbow problems persisted.

John started twelve of our fourteen games but threw for only 2,342 yards and had more interceptions (twenty) than touchdown passes (twelve) . His production would drop off every year after that until he retired early in the 1973 season after being traded to San Diego. He would always be Johnny U, young, fearless, and wearing a crew cut, to fans of the Baltimore Colts, but he wasn't that player anymore.

Our fans remained as loyal as ever, though. That hadn't changed. The Colts Band was still marching; and Hurst "Loudy" Loudenslager was still Mr. Colt along with Bill Gattus, Reds Hubbie, and Willie "The Rooter" Andrews, among so many others. Loudy was a classic. He'd bring his portable record player with him to Friendship Airport to play the Colts' fight song ("Let's go you Baltimore Colts / And put that ball across the line . . .") whenever we went on the road and every time we came back to Baltimore, no matter how late we arrived.

Regardless of how we were doing, Loudy would be out there with his record player, win or lose. We knew no matter what else might happen in life, Loudy would be there. Michael Olesker was a reporter and columnist at the *Baltimore Sun* and the *News-American* for over twenty-five years. He's kind of the balladeer of Baltimore. In his book *The Colts' Baltimore*, about the city's love affair with the team, he said Loudy had sent 3,059 birthday cards and 3,797 Christmas cards to players and coaches during his lifetime. His wife, Florence, baked 726 black walnut birthday cakes for players, a tradition started in 1960 for Ordell Brasse because they felt he was so far from home. When Loudy died in 1989, the pallbearers were former Colts.

Loudy organized Colts Corral No. 2, which was the second of what became over thirty team fan clubs during the time I was in Baltimore. There was one in Hollywood with Clark Gable as its president, but the amazing one to me was Corral No. 954. It was in the Maryland State Penitentiary. At one point it had over 1,500 members.

I'd never heard of such a thing until I got to Baltimore, but I thought it was a great idea. Those Corrals were all over the city. What a phenomenon. They raised money for charity and each one had a big dinner every year, even after that Super Bowl loss. Most of the time I was in Baltimore, someone from the Colts attended their meetings. Not just the dinners but the monthly meetings. Even someone like Kellett went at some point.

Over at Gussie's Downbeat the routine was the same as always, too. Every Monday the local bookmakers showed to collect on the weekend's game. We'd all heard stories about Carroll's gambling, but none of us in the organization really knew. One man who always claimed to know was Gussie himself, Constantine Huditean, who co-owned the place.

I wasn't sure if he was a bookmaker or not at the time (turned out he was), but he knew them all. They were part of the woodwork in that place. Today the league wouldn't let us within a mile of Gussie's, but back then you could go mostly where you wanted. Innocence was bliss.

When it came to scouting, nothing much changed for me, but it wasn't for my lack of trying. Throughout 1968 I was doing more than scouting. I was trying to buy the Eagles.

Their owner, Jerry Wolman, had become the youngest owner in NFL history when he bought controlling interest in the team in 1963 for $5.5 million, but a couple years later he got in trouble with a one-hundred-story building in Chicago he was trying to put up, and things spiraled out of control. There were pilings and foundation issues that caused delays and cost him millions. One of his partners was Ed Snider, with whom he'd bought the NHL expansion Flyers and financed the Spectrum where they played.

Now he was in deep trouble and needed to sell the hockey team to secure enough foreign financing to stay afloat. Snider refused and he went under, and the team ended up in bankruptcy court, so I called my father's old partner, Art Rooney, in Pittsburgh for some advice.

I saw it as an opportunity to go back home and become what I'd always wanted to be: an owner, not a renter. I thought I could buy it with other people's money. I was taking after Al Davis . . . and my father.

I told Rooney I was looking for investors, and he said he might have some people for me. He also told me he was looking for a coach. I told him if he was he should look at Chuck Noll, who was still with us. As it turns out, my brother, Bert, had already told him the same thing.

Rooney suggested a Philadelphia millionaire named Herb Barness, a real-estate developer who would become a big-time Republican powerbroker. Art spoke with him and set up a quiet meeting. I told him I thought I had a chance to get the franchise, and he said he'd be interested. I thought the Eagles price would double or triple what Wolman had paid.

After the Super Bowl, I started to get an uneasy feeling about Barness. I wasn't sure if he was in or out. Little did I know he was also talking with Leonard Tose, a local trucking magnate who was also trying to buy the team. Some people would call that double dealing. Others would call it business.

At this point Rosenbloom didn't know this was going on, and I wasn't nervous about that. I never thought Art Rooney would tell Carroll but I didn't care if he did, because I felt Carroll would tell me that if I had a chance to go home, I should go ahead.

After the season, the team was still in bankruptcy court, so I called my uncle Jack, who was chief justice of the Pennsylvania Supreme Court, and told him I thought Barness might be up to something and the deal might not materialize. I asked if he knew anyone else who might partner with me.

At the same time, I'd been talking to Buddy Young, the former Colts running back who was now working for Pete Rozelle. He was the first African American hired by the league office, and I was asking him for a meeting with Pete.

I knew Pete, of course, but now he was commissioner and I thought I should go through proper channels. The NFL wasn't any longer like when my father was running it and you could just get the commissioner on the phone. There were bodies now between him and the rest of us, unless you were an owner.

Word was out there that Vince Lombardi might be trying to put a group together too, so I knew some people might think the idea of a thirty-one-year-old personnel director putting a group together was whacky. But my father bought the Eagles out of bankruptcy for $4,500, and now I was trying to get it back the same way, but for millions. Rozelle understood.

He told me if I could put a group together, the league would consider it. I knew Rosenbloom and the Rooneys would go to bat for me. I had to get a money man in the room, but I thought being Bert Bell's son wouldn't hurt if I had the right person behind me.

Pete didn't make a commitment to me. I wanted him to but he didn't, which was the smart way for him to play it. When my father was commissioner, like with Carroll, he would say, "You've got the team, now go do it," but those days were over. The NFL was becoming big business.

Uncle Jack was very prudent. He got back to me and said he'd spoken with Fitz Eugene Dixon, one of his friends. Dixon was listed by *Fortune* magazine as one of the four hundred richest men in America by virtue of his mother's family, the Wideners, who had amassed a fortune in the meat-packing business and streetcar lines as well as being involved in building U.S. Steel and the American Tobacco Company. Safe to say they were more diversified than the West Coast offense.

My uncle said he had arranged a meeting in his office, but "I cannot be there and I will not be there." The reason was obvious, because of his position as chief justice.

The funny thing was Fitz Eugene Dixon had once been assistant headmaster at Episcopal Academy, and during a basketball game with Malvern Prep where I was the starting guard, I'd threatened to punch him during our game when two players started pushing and shoving. When the stands emptied and it looked like there would be a riot, Dixon tried to break it up. He probably didn't remember but I pushed him out of the way. Now it's twelve years later and I'm hoping he doesn't remember me pushing him around on a basketball floor, and now I'm asking if he wants to invest $15 or $16 million in the Eagles.

I'm sure he didn't remember but he also didn't show up, which I should have expected. He sent two lawyers who handled all his properties. Before I went, I called Rosenbloom to tell him about the meeting and ask if I could I bring along Duval Farrar, a smart man who handled a lot of Carroll's contracts. He agreed and told me, "If you got a chance to go, go." That was Carroll.

I wanted a small percentage of the franchise, 5 percent or so, to run it. Dixon would own the rest. His lawyers said they'd consider it. Here I was with no money asking for 5 percent of an NFL team and the authority to run it. Audacious would seem to describe what I was proposing.

They were very sharp people, hired to protect Fitz Eugene Dixon, not George Upton Bell. They knew time was running out. Enter Jerry Wolman.

Wolman called me out of the blue. It's now the spring of 1969. Dixon's people can't agree on my percentage. They seemed somewhat on board but weren't sure they wanted to make a bid in the court, because it was a shooting match now.

I think Pete told Wolman what I was trying to do, but it could have been any of them. He was a likeable person, but he found out that when you're in trouble, nobody helps you. He asked, "Why didn't you call me? If I knew you were interested I would have helped you."

I told him I didn't want to be one of those people trying to shoot at him, but once the team was in bankruptcy, it was a different story. He said, "Well, you should have called me. We might have been able to do something." I was trying to do the honorable thing, which, sucker or not, I thought I did.

I'll never know what might have been had I called him. It was already in bankruptcy court, so it didn't make a difference. That's the mystery of life. All the "what-ifs." But I appreciated the call. A lot of people never would have made it in the situation he was in.

Just before the bids were to come in, I got another call. Dixon's people said, "It's gotten out of hand. We're going to pass." It was the same day I'd gone in to tell Shula I was trying to get my father's team back. I don't know if he knew or not, but he wished me luck.

In a sense they were right. We'd agreed to go as high as $15 million. Later I heard Tose somehow had a right of first refusal, so it wouldn't have made any difference what I bid. He would have always been able to get on top of us. He ended up buying the team on May 1, 1969, for $16,155,000, which was a record for a franchise at the time.

It turned out I had a Brutus by my side in Herb Barness. He

was relaying everything to Tose and ended up with 29 percent of the Eagles until 1978, when he sold out after a long court fight with Tose. Seven years later, in a bit of irony, Tose's gambling problems sent him into bankruptcy and he had to sell out as well.

I can't say Barness screwed me. It was just business. He was Brutus but that's how it goes. He got a minority interest and I got nothing out of it and went back to the Colts. Two years later, we won Super Bowl V, with seventeen of the forty players on our roster being ones I drafted. The Eagles are still waiting to win a Super Bowl. So they got the team and I got a ring. Unfortunately, I didn't get it with Shula.

By the end of the 1969 season, his seventh-straight winning season but a disappointment to us all, the tension between him and Rosenbloom was clear. To understand what that meant, you need to understand that as good as he could be to you, Rosenbloom could treat you just as cruelly. You only needed to read a sentence from Gene Klein's autobiography to understand what Shula was facing.

Klein owned the Chargers, and in his book *First Down and a Billion*, he said, "He always gave you the feeling that, if you crossed him, he was capable of slitting your throat, then donating your blood to the Red Cross blood drive."

That was true. If you ended up on the wrong side of Carroll, he would not only cut you loose, he'd cut you to ribbons if he could. I think Rosenbloom never got over his anger from losing that Super Bowl. I knew that day he'd never get over it and he didn't. He held it against Shula and it blinded him to what a great coach he had. I knew something bad was going to happen in Baltimore soon.

After the season, Carroll appointed Don Klosterman, my old AFL rival, as general manager while I was at the Senior Bowl. If he hadn't done that I believe Shula would have stayed because of the way things were set up. When Harry Hulmes was general manager, Shula was in charge of the football operation. It was a perfect setup.

Hulmes was good on the business side and a sweet, unassuming man. Klosterman was a flashy, fast-talking man. When Carroll brought in Klosterman over Harry, I knew it was all over. We'd gone from an organization of no bullshit to an organization that was all bullshit. I liked Klosterman, but if you were to pick someone totally the opposite of Shula, it was Klosterman. Those two would never get along.

Shula played it smart. The only time I saw him react was the night of the last draft he was involved in with us, on January 28, 1970. I'd prepared the draft board like always, but Klosterman kept coming in saying he'd just spoken to this college coach or that coach and this is who we should take. I liked Klosterman but I didn't think his opinion was worth much, and I showed it in some ways. I disregarded every one of his opinions. I wasn't purposefully going in the opposite direction, but I knew the players. I felt like saying, "Show me your reports."

I knew he didn't like it, but I felt I still answered to Shula. To me, fair or unfair, Klosterman was an interloper. Carroll put him there hoping he could lead us into a deal where the town would accept buying exhibition games as part of their season ticket package. It had nothing to do with football.

We had a good draft. We needed a back and got Norm Bulaich on the first round and two solid defensive tackles who started for us in Super Bowl V, Jim Bailey from Kansas on the second round and Billy Newsome from Grambling on the fifth. Plus we got Jack Maitland on the sixteenth round, who was an effective jack-of-all-trades, and third-round pick Jim O'Brien, who was a combination receiver and kicker, which was important then because the rosters were smaller and you didn't want to give a spot just to a kicker if you could avoid it.

After it was over we went to Unitas's place, The Golden Arm. Shula was there, and Rosenbloom's son, Steve, a great person whom we all liked, also came. We had a drink and Shula said he was going to Pellington's restaurant, The Iron Horse, to see a couple of his coaches. Right after he left, Klosterman walked in wearing a blue pinstriped suit, sat down, and next thing I know he smashes a glass on the table and says, "You kept me out of everything!"

I knew he was putting on a show for the owner's son and I was getting hot, but I didn't want to get lured into anything. Steve asked him to stop, and I left and went to find Shula.

When I told him what happened, that look you didn't want to see came over his face. Tight, jutting jaw. He said, "I'll talk to him in the morning. I don't like this."

A reporter heard about it and called them both. Nobody had ever done that before. I was upset. Was this what the future was going to be? It was drama right out of Shakespeare.

Around that time, Don got a call from a reporter for the *Miami Herald*, Bill Braucher, who had been a teammate of Shula's at John Carroll University. He was calling to see if Shula would consider coaching the Dolphins. Talk about perfect timing.

Carroll was overseas on vacation, so Shula asked Steve for permission to talk with Miami and he granted it. Don went down and met with the Dolphins' owner, Joe Robbie, and Robbie offered him a chance to be coach, general manager, and part owner. I never saw him again in Baltimore after he went down there to interview. I know he came back once and he called me from Miami to tell me he was leaving. It was one of the best-kept secrets of them all. Shula later learned that dealing with Joe Robbie wasn't easy either, but he never regretted the move. Why would he? Look at the success he had there.

He called Rosenbloom in Hawaii before it was announced on February 18, 1970, and Carroll was angry that Steve gave Shula permission to leave. He might have been happy if Shula left right after Super Bowl III, but now he was furious. In his mind, Don had crossed him. He hadn't kissed the ring.

Carroll, being ruthless and smart, realized our fans were up in arms about Shula leaving, so he saw both opportunity and a chance for face saving. He accused Miami of tampering.

He and Robbie started hurling insults back and forth. Now remember, the league's weren't officially merged until that fall, so there was still a lot of venom between AFL owners and NFL owners, and it all came out.

How can you tamper with a man who has permission to go

interview for a job? Carroll didn't care. He wanted draft choices out of it and he got Rozelle to award him Miami's No. 1 pick in 1971 to settle things. We turned that into a running back named Don McCauley, who would play eleven years for the Colts but only start twenty-five games. He was no Don Shula.

Now everything was changing. Noll had taken over the Steelers the year before. Don was gone. Soon Hulmes would leave for New Orleans and in a year I'd be gone too. Don never bad-mouthed Carroll publicly, which was smart. He'd moved on, and when you're dealing with someone like Rosenbloom you'd better be smart. But Don and Carroll remained bitter enemies for years.

The first time we played them that fall, Shula came over to me on the field before the game and put his arm around me and whispered, "Carroll is watching you." We both smiled. He knew that would irk Carroll no end.

To his credit, eventually Don Klosterman became the peacemaker. He went to Shula after his undefeated season in 1972 and asked him to meet with Rosenbloom at the league meetings. Don agreed and they kind of buried the hatchet, but it was more on Shula's side. I never got the feeling Carroll forgot anything.

It was a phony summit meeting to me, but that's what the league was becoming—more and more of a PR-driven operation than it had been in my father's day. Appearance counted more. That's become worse than ever now. When you become a powerful business like the NFL is today, you don't always worry about doing what's right. You do what's expedient and what sells. And nothing sells today like the NFL.

With Shula gone we needed a coach, but Carroll didn't seem to be in much of a hurry to hire anyone. A lot of us thought he'd promote someone from the staff, but nobody knew. He waited forty-four days before he named Don McCafferty. I always thought he waited that long to send Shula a message: Who cares who the coach is? I don't need him.

I was shocked when they named McCafferty. He couldn't have been more different than Shula. Shula was demanding and relentless. He pushed his players hard and demanded things be done right. Shula yelled louder ordering breakfast than McCafferty would have if his hair was on fire.

McCafferty was his offensive coordinator, but Don ran the offense when Unitas didn't. Shula prepared the quarterbacks. He and Unitas clashed a lot, although not in meetings, because they were both stubborn and smart. They were too much alike, really.

McCafferty, on the other hand, was quiet, patient. They called him Easy Rider, which was a name Ernie Accorsi came up with. He just seemed to placidly go along. That worked in 1970 because he was handed a hell of a team by Shula, but it didn't work long. In three years the Colts would slip to 5-9 and he'd be fired. He just didn't have the dominant personality a head coach needs.

There wasn't even a big press conference announcing his hiring. It should have been a major announcement, but it wasn't treated that way. The famous picture that came out that day was of McCafferty lighting Klosterman's cigarette. That told me everything.

At the time, I didn't care what they did. I thought it had gotten ridiculous, so I was just going to do my job. By then I'd developed a system that had been successful. I felt even if a new coach might want to change certain things, he didn't have the power to do so. Only Rosenbloom could do that. Since my drafting record was good, I didn't see it as a problem.

Today when a new coach or GM comes in, the whole organization seems to be at risk. If you did a good job in 1970, though, there weren't that many firings. You could be in jobs forever. I got the job at twenty-eight. Most of the people doing it were twenty years older than I was, so I wasn't worried. I'd drafted well, we had a good team, and I was only thirty-two. Who worries at that age about his job? I felt if I were going to be executed, it would be by Rosenbloom, not Klosterman, but I'd done a good job for Carroll and he knew it.

Klosterman never said a word to me about how to do my job. He might say he was going to some games, but I'm not sure he ever went. I had my full staff scouting and writing reports. Klosterman was the window dressing. I don't know how much he did after I left, but that year he'd come in and say, "They tell me this guy's good," but he never bothered me.

We were in our offices on North Howard Street across from the bus station, and I had the whole third floor. I had three times the size of what I'd had before. We put magnetic boards on the walls with all the team's personnel. Now we had computers. We had everything we needed. I don't think I ever saw Klosterman up there. I'd say Ernie Accorsi, the new PR person, was up there more than Klosterman.

McCafferty brought in Lou Rymkus and Hank Bullough as assistants. I knew Rymkus, who was old-school. They fired him three games into the season and took George Young out of my office to become offensive line coach. George was a good coach, but he'd never coached beyond high school. It worked out but I remember thinking, who hires an assistant and then fires him before the season starts? Does this man even know who can coach?

I didn't fight it when they told me they were taking George. I saw it as a fait accompli, so why argue? Besides, George was really a coach at heart. He never coached in college but he was a very competent coach. He stepped in with a veteran offensive line and did a very good job.

I didn't replace George, but I think that's when Ernie got the bug. He was up in my office quite a lot, so I finally took him to scout his first game. It was West Virginia against Penn State. I was interested in a fullback from West Virginia, so I told Ernie to write a report and I'd look at it. He wrote reports on several players, and I thought for someone with no experience he wrote very clearly what he thought and what he saw. He was a natural and I wasn't surprised years later when he became general manager of the Colts, the Browns, and finally the Giants.

I didn't have a problem after Shula left, but I'd come to realize there wasn't great loyalty in the NFL. I felt Rosenbloom would at least help me go somewhere else if that was necessary, but you'd better be able to produce. Two or three bad drafts and you're on the way out the door. I'd had good drafts so I concentrated on doing my job, but things were changing. I wasn't sitting in with the assistant coaches in the press box anymore like I had with Shula. Totally different operation.

The second game of the season, Kansas City beat the hell out of us, 44–24, on *Monday Night Football*, which was just in its first season. At that point I didn't think we were going anywhere. We were down 31–7 at halftime. Unitas was 5 for15 with two picks and McCafferty replaced him with Morrall, who was picked three times. Our quarterbacks were sacked seven times. Now what?

Halfway through that season, Fred Schubach, our equipment manager, told me John Mackey said they needed the whip put to them like Shula would have done. I knew McCafferty couldn't do that, but the team was still good enough that it could go on a run, and it did. You can get by relying just on the players, but that doesn't last for long.

We won six straight, tied Buffalo, and went to Miami and lost to Shula's Dolphins, 34–17, after having beaten them 35–0 three weeks earlier, but we closed with four wins and then swept through the playoffs and were set to face the Dallas Cowboys in the Super Bowl.

The game was back at the scene of the crime, in the same Orange Bowl where we'd lost to the Jets two years earlier. I certainly didn't believe we'd beat Dallas, but in that game everything that went wrong in 1968 went right this time.

Unlike three years earlier, there were no families at the hotel. They didn't arrive until the day before the game. We stayed kind of out of the way, in a hotel and practice complex at Miami Lakes that wasn't far from where Shula was living. A few of us snuck off to visit him, but everyone was careful about it because we were all afraid how Rosenbloom might react.

We were all business but we were also tight as a drum. So was Dallas. These were two teams who both had been branded as unable to win the big games. This time only one of us could, but we played like neither of us wanted to.

I sat in the stands. I have no idea why. Great seats on the 50-yard line with Dick Szymanski and our wives, but it wasn't much to watch.

There were eleven turnovers. It was one of those games where you had no feel for it. We threw three interceptions and fumbled five times, losing four of them. Dallas lost one fumble, which proved critical, and their quarterback, Craig Morton, threw three interceptions too. It was really one of the strangest professional games I've ever seen. A week later, *Sports Illustrated* dubbed it the Blooper Bowl.

If we had the 1958 or 1959 Unitas, the game would have been over by halftime, but his arm was gone. He was playing from memory. His mind was still intact but he couldn't deliver the throws like he once had. I also always felt he wasn't as good on turf for some reason. John was one of those players who when he backed up looked awkward. He looked worse doing it on turf.

He threw two interceptions before he was leveled in the second quarter by George Andrie and bruised his ribs. He was done for the day. It was like turning Super Bowl III inside out. This time it was Earl Morrall who came off the bench to try to save us. It was one of the few games where I was nervous, maybe because I knew the consequences of losing that game.

In a nutshell, here's the kind of game it was. The Cowboys take a 6–0 lead on two field goals after recovering a fumble at our 9-yard line and then getting it down to the 6 on their own, both sort of victories for us. Then Unitas throws a pass intended for Eddie Hinton. Hinton tips it and then it just hits the fingertips of Dallas safety Mel Renfro, but instead of popping into the air or falling on the ground, the ball bounces right to Mackey, who takes it 75 yards for a touchdown. Of course, we miss the extra point, so it's 6–6. That's the kind of Blooper Bowl that Super Bowl V turned out to be.

By halftime Dallas led 13–6, and we fumbled the second-half kickoff. Just as it looked like they were going to pull away, four of our players slammed into Duane Thomas, with whom I would soon have my own odd encounter the following year, at the 1-yard line and he fumbled. There was a mad scramble and Dallas's center, Dave Manders, came up with the ball, but our defensive end, Billy Ray Smith, kept hollering, "Colts' ball!" and the line judge,

Jack Fette, agreed. He awarded it to my draft choice, Jim Duncan, who was the same player who'd fumbled that kickoff. If Dallas had gone up 20–6, who knows how things would have ended, but they didn't.

Dallas also didn't throw the ball once the entire third quarter, but maybe that made sense, because when they finally had to, Morton went 4 for 10 for 27 yards and three interceptions in the fourth quarter, including the final one that won the game for us. Mike Curtis, the player Shula kept arguing was a fullback, not a linebacker, intercepted Morton and returned the ball to the Dallas 28. Three plays later my rookie kicker, Jim O'Brien, was lining up with a chance to break a 13–13 tie and win Super Bowl V.

He was so nervous he kept trying to pick up a blade of grass to throw it up and test the wind. Earl finally said, "It's artificial turf, kid. Just meet it square."

O'Brien was a straight-on kicker and the true trick-or-treat of life. He might come through, he might not. He might make it from 50 and miss an extra point, which he'd already done, or we'd be sitting on the ball and the lead. He'd barely made 556 percent of his kicks that year, and that would end up being his four-year career average, but he made that one from 32 yards, and we had finally won our Super Bowl.

We stole a game that day. I just sat in the stands numb. I didn't feel elation, just relief. O'Brien was leaping around as if he was on a pogo stick, but the image I remember was Bob Lilly, the great Dallas defensive lineman who's now in the Hall of Fame, trudging off the field and suddenly unbuckling his chin strap and throwing his helmet about 30 yards through the air. He left it there. I understood his despair.

I found Rosenbloom in the locker room and saw him hugging a writer, Bill Tanton, which I'd never seen before. Carroll was no fan of the writers, so you could see what that game meant to him.

We'd won the Super Bowl, but that didn't erase the past. Super Bowl III was supposed to be a coronation. We had the greatest team in history, and we lost. The coronation became a beheading. Super Bowl V could never heal those wounds, and it didn't.

Years later Curtis said in an NFL Films documentary on that game that he never wore the ring. He said it was in the pocket of one of his suit coats.

We had a party that night but it was at the hotel, not Carroll's house. The most famous gate crasher was Muhammad Ali. I found Ernie and told him I thought maybe it was time to go. I didn't have anything going and no real plan, but it just felt like it was time. Everything was changing. I had no idea how much, but I was about to find out not every NFL organization was organized.

12

Why Did You Ever Come Here?

The best explanation I can come up with for my decision to leave the Super Bowl champions on February 26, 1971, to become general manager of the most dysfunctional franchise in professional football is simply this: it seemed like a good idea at the time.

That's the day I stepped to a podium in the function room at the Hotel Sonesta in Cambridge, Massachusetts, to make it official. Unknowingly, I had crossed the river Styx without a paddle to become GM of the Boston Patriots.

There is a generation of football fans today who have no idea what the Patriots were before Bill Parcells and Bill Belichick arrived. They know them as perennial Super Bowl contenders and five-time Super Bowl champions, but when I arrived the Patriots were the laughingstocks of the NFL, a homeless team without a stadium of its own and without a history like the Colts.

For over a decade they had been unable to build an organization or a stadium to house it in. They moved around from Boston University's Nickerson Field to Fenway Park to Boston College's Alumni Stadium to Harvard Stadium. They even had a "home game" in Birmingham, Alabama, one year.

The season I arrived, we had to print tickets for three different venues because we weren't sure where we'd end up. At another point in their checkered past, the players dressed in a hotel before games because they couldn't use the locker room, and they were told not to sit on the beds because the team would only be charged half price if they didn't wrinkle the covers. After dressing, they'd walk to the stadium like some Division 3 college football team.

For a couple of years they fielded competitive teams, but typical of their history, the only time they made the playoffs in the first eleven years of their existence, their record was 7-6-1 and they got blitzed in the 1963 AFL Championship Game, losing 51–10 to the San Diego Chargers. That's the day their defense made Chargers running back Keith Lincoln a bigger name than Abe Lincoln by allowing him to rush for 206 yards on just thirteen carries and gain an additional 123 yards on seven pass receptions. Nobody suggested they might want to keep an eye on No. 22 at some point?

I was thirty-three when I arrived in Boston, the youngest general manager in the NFL, so of course I ignored all that. I wasn't there to read history, I was there to change history, which I thought I could do. What I was about to learn, however, is it's not easy to turn around an NFL *Titanic* when you're wrestling for the helm with the owner. Actually, owners with an "s," because they had more warring factions on their sixteen-person board of directors than Abraham Lincoln's "team of rivals" cabinet.

That was something I'd never seen in Baltimore. There you worked for Rosenbloom, but on football matters you answered to Shula. To be successful, it can't be any other way. Owners own the franchise. Football people run the team. That's how you win consistently.

A man who made his fortune in the oil business may know what 10w30 means, but he doesn't know why short arms are the death of a pass rusher or what the difference is between college speed and pro speed. Jerry Jones has found that out the hard way in Dallas. He won when his former college teammate Jimmy Johnson was running both the personnel department and the locker room, because Johnson was a great coach and a better personnel evaluator. Johnson left when he began fighting Jones for the helm of the Cowboys. They haven't won a championship in Dallas since Barry Switzer replaced Johnson and immediately won one more with Johnson's players. Since then, they can barely spell playoffs in Dallas.

I guess I should have known what I would be facing, though, when the first question I got that day came from Jack Clary, a writer for the *Boston Herald*. He didn't ask about our first draft choice, Heisman Trophy–winning quarterback Jim Plunkett. He didn't ask my plan for reviving the team.

"Upton," he said, "why in the world would someone like you, who has won championships with the Baltimore Colts, ever want to come to a franchise like this?"

Not a bad question, but not the first one I expected. I'd put together two Super Bowl teams in Baltimore. We'd won consistently and with a little bit of luck in the 1960s could have been the Team of the Decade instead of the Green Bay Packers. If the officials didn't blow that call on Don Chandler's missed field goal, we would have won that game and very likely the NFL championship, and who knows where we would have gone after that. If Shula had stayed I think I would have too. I don't know for sure, but I was really happy in Baltimore. We were winning and opportunities would have come that were better than the Patriots, but that's not how it goes in life. Usually events drive you, not the other way around. Isn't that the great lesson in life? In most cases nobody has a clear path.

An exodus had started in Baltimore. Shula was gone. Noll and Arnsbarger were gone. Kellett and Harry Hulmes were gone. My brother, Bert, was gone. Soon Unitas would be gone. McCafferty was on a short leash. Nobody told me I had to get another job but I knew it was over. You don't get to pick the perfect spot in life very often. I'd had it in Baltimore for a while, but it wasn't the same Baltimore anymore.

I had no doubt in my mind if I got to the right place we'd win. I had a plan I'd been developing my whole life about how to build a winning football franchise. I kept notebooks for years, writing down everything I'd learned from all the football people I'd been exposed to. What I learned from Paul Brown, George Halas, Weeb Ewbank, and Don Shula was there's no right way or wrong way to do it. There are a lot of ways, so it comes down to your plan. It works or it doesn't. I believed mine would. To this day, I still do, but you need time to implement it.

The first time I heard about the Patriots was two days before Super Bowl V when the *Boston Globe*'s football writer, Will McDonough, approached me at the commissioner's party and told me he'd recommended me and Ron Wolf to Sullivan. I didn't know Will then, so I didn't say much. Years later he and Billy would be at loggerheads but at the time they were close. Sometimes it felt like McDonough was running the team.

I had no idea then I'd be moving. I'd spoken with Al Davis at the Senior Bowl and told him I thought I was ready to run a team. He asked if I wanted him to make some calls. He thought he could get me something in San Diego but I wasn't really interested.

Back in Baltimore after Super Bowl V, Larry Harris, one of the veteran beat writers on the Colts, wrote a terrific article on me pointing out all the good drafts we'd had. I remember Rosenbloom calling and saying, "It's about time somebody wrote something good here. As long as it's not from Steadman." He knew Steadman liked me, and he hated him by then. They were already in a beef about Carroll wanting to force season ticket holders to buy exhibition game tickets as part of their package. That's standard operating procedure today but not then. Steadman felt the fans were loyal, working-class people who shouldn't have to buy tickets to phony games. In a way it was a precursor to what was about to happen. Business decisions were taking precedence over fans and eventually football, which is what you have today.

Carroll called me to his house a few days later and told me he'd spoken to Billy Sullivan, but the real connection was Phil Fine. Carroll had called Fine to get advice on how to finance a new stadium because Fine was the one who came up with Stadium Realty Trust, which paid for the Patriots' new privately funded stadium under construction in Foxboro, twenty-five miles south of Boston. It was supposed to open that season and was one of the fastest built—and cheapest made—in the history of stadium construction. That would come with its own issues later.

Next thing I know I'm on a plane to Boston to meet secretly with Billy and Phil at Boston's Logan Airport. It only took me about a day to prepare, because I knew the team and its personnel. We played them twice a year and I'd scouted most of their players. I explained that they needed to get younger and bigger personnel. They had to build up the scouting department. Without that they had nothing. No one disagreed.

Nothing was decided, but I could tell their present GM, George Sauer Sr., was on the way out. It didn't bother me that they were talking with me while he still had the job, because there was a reason they were getting rid of George. They'd had one winning season in six years and just finished 2-12, the worst record in the league. Billy hired a coach who literally went insane that year in Clive Rush and replaced him with John Mazur, who was not prepared to be a head coach. The NFL is a cold, bottom-line business. If they wanted to get rid of George, what am I going to say? Don't do it?

I'd been told George had no power. I was more interested in that than anything else. I wanted to know what the coach's contract was and my authority to hire and fire. I wanted the right to hire and fire everybody. I came from an organization where it was Rosenbloom who had the power, but he gave that authority to whomever he wanted. The owner is always the one who really hires and fires, but other than the owner's obvious power to overrule anything, I wanted to come in with full authority. If not, there's no use coming.

I have to give Billy credit. He learned something from watching J. Michael Curley, the Irish mayor of Boston they called the Rascal King, who got elected once while he was in federal prison. Billy was his own Rascal King. He could say yes and you weren't quite sure whether it meant yes or no.

He told me Mazur had a one-year contract because the board felt it was only fair after he stepped in for Rush. I'd hear, "The board made me do it," or, "Upton, we are a quasi-public corporation and the decision has to be made by the board," more times the next two years than I could imagine, but he assured me he and I would decide, which seemed reasonable because that's really how it is.

He was careful how he put it. You could take it however you wanted, and I took it to mean I had the authority. I understood I wasn't going to make any decision like that by myself, but I thought if I went to him and said we need this person, they'd back me. If he had just said, "You don't have that authority," I would have gone back to Baltimore and that would have been it, but I thought if I made sense it would work out. That was my first mistake, but the fact is there are only so many of those jobs, and I was being offered one. All you can do is take a man's word. I knew I was a renter, but I thought I was a renter with benefits. Turned out I wasn't.

Sullivan said he understood my concern, but anything like that had to be run by the board, which had more committees than Chairman Mao. It was the opposite of how the Colts worked or how Bob Kraft has run the Patriots since he bought them in 1994. He gives Belichick a lot of power. He's a committee of one. You listen to other people but in the end the football people make the football decisions or it doesn't work. Never has. Never will.

Two local developers, Dan and Bob Marr, plus Hessie Sargent, who was represented by her son Lee, were on the executive committee with Billy. Together they made the final decisions, but Billy, I found out later, usually got what he wanted.

Phil was very demonstrative at that point. He said to Billy, "Are you going to let this man run your team?" Billy got annoyed. I should have seen a red flag right there. You don't want to be hired after the coach is in place if you didn't pick him, because the question becomes, who has the authority? I went against my most basic belief, which was my crucial mistake. The coach is on a one-year contract and he's trying to survive while you're trying to build for the future. He thinks he has no future beyond that year and he's usually right, so he coaches for the moment.

You want young talent, he wants veterans who don't make mistakes. What does that mean? It means your team gets older.

That was one of the problems in New England. We had a similar problem when I went into the Colts' personnel department. We were getting older and Shula saw we needed to get younger. In less than two years at the Patriots, we took them from averaging twenty-eight and a half years old to twenty-five years old. We went from the oldest team to the youngest and replaced twenty-five of the forty players I inherited. They needed to get younger, faster, and bigger.

In my opinion, the team I inherited was almost devoid of the talent needed to play in the new NFL. Len St. Jean was a tough man and a good offensive lineman, but he was 5 feet 11. Those days were over. He had to block players like six-foot-seven, 295-pound Bubba Smith or six-foot-three, 270-pound Mean Joe Greene. Physical mismatches. Not his fault, but you couldn't win with those kinds of players anymore.

They weren't like Kansas City or Oakland, which was built to move into the NFL. We had to get healthy quick or it wasn't going to matter who the coach was. We'd all be gone. That's why I traded for Fred Dryer and Duane Thomas and they blew them both—Billy with Dryer and Mazur with Thomas.

Before I agreed to terms, I went back to Baltimore and spoke with Billy three or four more times, and he was getting more and more enthused. Sullivan saw I had an actual plan how to run the organization. I think he saw me as the ultimate solution. He was taking a lot of heat from the other owners because of his stadium problems and Clive Rush's illness that season, and he needed a sign there was going to be some stability.

I felt that as bad as it might seem up there, I'd work it out, but I didn't know how deep the chasm was between Sullivan and his partners. Ernie Accorsi advised me not to do it. A lot of people did, including Al Davis, but Shula wasn't one of them. He didn't say either way. He just told me Sullivan seemed like a league guy, meaning he did what was best for the NFL.

A couple weeks after that meeting, I was offered the job. The draft had already happened. I was involved with it from the Colts' perspective along with Klosterman, but I'd had Plunkett rated No.

1 between him, Archie Manning, and Dan Pastorini, so I thought New England made the right pick. I thought Pastorini had the best arm but Plunkett was the most ready to play.

That day in Baltimore, I drafted one of the first black quarterbacks into the NFL, Karl Douglas from Texas A&I–Kingsville, an NAIA school. We took him on the third round and I thought he could play, but I was concerned because I wasn't there to campaign for him. I convinced McCafferty to take him, but I'm not sure he ever believed in Karl or gave him a chance. He cut him a year later and he ended up playing in Canada for a few years. A player like that needs someone in his corner on cut-down day. He needs time to develop. After I left I don't believe he had that. Maybe he couldn't play. I wasn't there. But I don't think he got much of an opportunity. That was the old NFL at work there.

Looking at the Patriots' draft, I thought whoever was doing the picking had done a good job getting Julius Adams, a defensive lineman from Texas Southern. They didn't get much else, but that was a good pick. I found out later it was Rommie Loudd who made it, so I created the position of pro personnel director for him and promoted him. That made him the highest-ranking African American in the league at the time, but that's not why I did it. I did it because he was good at his job.

I took the contract Sullivan sent me to Duval Farrar, Rosenbloom's financial person who'd helped me try to buy the Eagles. The terms were more than I asked, but I had trouble with the hiring and firing clause. Duval finally told me I was going to have to take Billy at his word because it wasn't going to change. So what was I going to do, call my new boss a liar first shot out of the box?

I could have refused to come, but we're back to the owners and renters. Even if they give you power, you don't totally have it. You always have to convince the owner. Not even Belichick or Shula could just say, "Here you go!" without talking to the owner. I could have that clause and tell him I wanted to fire someone and he could always say, "I don't think so." If that happens, that person is still working and maybe you aren't, so I reconciled myself to it and Billy kept assuring me it wouldn't be a problem.

You can only force so many decisions on an owner who is signing your paycheck. What you hope is that the owners ask themselves, "Why did we bring him in if we're not going to listen to him?" But most owners don't have a board of directors to hide behind. I learned later that none of those other directors picked Clive Rush or George Sauer. That was Billy. He had them all conned.

I knew what it was but I took it. It was a three-year contract for a big raise, so I couldn't complain about that. I was making $30,000 at the Colts. I got $45,000, $50,000, and $55,000, no cut. Now it's millions but at that time, that was serious money. According to the Department of Commerce, the median income in 1971 was $9,636. Of 66.7 million households, only 21 percent were making $15,000 or more. I was making three times that.

I could have had a longer deal. Billy offered me five years, but I felt I'd do a good job and after three years I'd get paid more. I'd be like a player cashing in on performance or I'd become a free agent and go to another team. So much for planning.

Before I left Baltimore, Ernie warned me of one thing. He told me Mazur was a Notre Dame man (he'd been a quarterback there) and an ex-Marine. Sullivan loved that. He knew him. Sullivan had been the PR person at Notre Dame when Frank Leahy was coach. I didn't know anything about Mazur, and Sullivan always presented him as an interim person, so I didn't really consider that.

The day I arrived, I opened one of the Boston papers and the headline was: "The B.S. Patriots." Because they were moving to suburban Foxboro, halfway between Boston and Providence, they'd changed their name from Boston Patriots to Bay State Patriots. That was Billy's idea. I saw trouble there, and I quickly convinced the board to change it to the New England Patriots to appeal to a five-state area. You could see where B.S. Patriots was headed.

That day Cliff Keane, an irascible old Boston sportswriter, came to interview me. People had warned me about him. He must have known that because the first thing he told me was, "The enemy here isn't the press. It's the guy you're working for." What was I to think?

I didn't hate Billy, but I recognized early on what the problem was. It was the way he ran things. He didn't want anyone else to really run it because if they were successful they'd get credit for it with the press, and he didn't like that. That was the real problem. This was a boiling cauldron I'd walked into.

I never went back to Baltimore, but I did get a glimpse of what Lenny Moore complained about many years later at that Colts' team reunion. My wife, Anne, stayed back with our young son, Christopher, to sell the house. She called and told me there was a problem. The highest bid was from a black family and the neighbors didn't like it. I said, "Sell it to them."

It was a nice Colonial right around the corner from Loyola College in a beautiful section of town. She said the neighbors were objecting. I told her I didn't give a damn. If she wanted me to fly back and tell them, I would. We sold it to that couple. As we should have.

Before that first press conference, Billy was dictating letters to his secretary. He answered everybody. One of his secretaries told me he even answered junk mail and thank-you notes. He'd send fifty to a hundred notes a day. I got one every day, it seemed. The only day I didn't was the day I got fired.

Just before the press conference, Billy was trying to get Carroll on the phone to tape him saying something nice about me. Meanwhile the press was out there waiting to consume me as the next person to die with the Patriots. When I finally got to the podium, I went to grab the microphone and someone hollered, "Don't touch the mike!" I jumped back in confusion. Only later did I learn that two years earlier when they introduced Clive Rush as head coach, he was nearly electrocuted by a short circuit when he grabbed the mike. I avoided that, but there were a lot of shocks to come.

Our office was a dump next to a bowling alley, behind the left field wall at Fenway Park, the famous Green Monster. It was so cramped my assistant Peter Hadhazy ended up with his office in the men's bathroom in back. Literally. We put a desk in there, and between flushes we said "excuse me" a lot.

I don't know why exactly, but from my desk I could look up and see baseballs that had hit the screen above the left-field wall and fell down behind it. I always wondered how they got there and if maybe the old Baltimore-born slugger Babe Ruth put one there. The place was cramped and cluttered with papers stacked everywhere. It wouldn't be long before that gave us a problem so serious I nearly lost my whole team.

My first hire was Herman Bruce as business manager. Sauer's major job had been handling our travel, but he'd resigned the day I was hired, although he ended up scouting for us in the Southwest, where he was from. But my major focus was scouting. It had to be fixed immediately.

Rommie had been doing everything from his office at Curry College, a half hour away. That's where the coaches were and where we practiced. We'd all be moving to Foxboro soon, but it was a disjointed operation at the time, and that breeds problems. To try to avoid some, I tried to get us into BLESTO, the scouting service, because they didn't share reports, but I couldn't get in. At the time the Patriots weren't in any scouting service, so I spoke with Wellington Mara about getting into CEPO and he agreed.

I called Ernie the day of my first press conference and told him I had Billy on the phone and we'd love to have him as assistant general manager. I called Steve Rosenbloom for permission, but he said he didn't think C.R. would allow it. Ernie told me later he didn't feel he was ready, but I didn't care. He knew how to make up his mind. He could have learned the other stuff, as he proved later.

I told Steve the real reason I was calling was I didn't know how bad it was here. There was no discipline. It was such a small operation that people's duties overlapped, which cannot be in a strong football organization. Football is a team of specialists. I had so many fires to put out, I needed someone like Ernie to bring a semblance of order. It was a good argument but I couldn't convince Steve. I was desperate.

I was interviewing other people for what I felt was the key position in the organization, the personnel director's job. I tried to hire Bobby Beathard, who was scouting for the Falcons at the time, but he was leery of the Patriots' ownership situation. I later recommended him to Shula in Miami. After Beathard turned down the offer, I considered one of the best young scouts around, Ron Wolf, who was the personnel director of the Oakland Raiders and now is in the Hall of Fame, as he should be. During that time, my secretary told me, "You have a collect call from a Francis Kilroy. He's calling from a phone booth in Dallas." I said go back and ask the operator if he's Bucko Kilroy. If he was, I'd take it.

Bucko wanted to talk about the personnel director's job, but he didn't want the Cowboys to know. He kept saying, "I don't know if they'll let me go." I hung up and called Tex Schramm, because I really needed to get permission, and Tex basically said, "Be my guest."

When somebody says something like that, you wonder, because Bucko had been Dallas's super-scout. I wondered, why were they willing to let go of someone that valuable who had all the information and all the computer stuff I didn't have?

I wondered why Bucko would leave Dallas for New England, too. They'd just been to the Super Bowl and had a great young team and the best scouting system in football, but the more I thought about it, it all made sense. He'd once been the personnel director in Washington and he wanted to be a head guy again. Simple as that.

I knew Bucko from 1947, when my father fined him for rough play but promised Bucko's wife if he behaved the rest of the season he'd give the money back. He did and my father did. Then I'd watched him scouting on the road. I knew the good and bad of him. He was a little eccentric but much smarter than he let on.

I started thinking, there's a twofer here. I'm getting a terrific scout who is very detailed and I'm also going to get Dallas's information. So I brought him in as personnel director and told him I wasn't going to tell him what to do, but I didn't want a bunch of old-time scouts coming in. I wanted something different.

I wanted young scouts who hadn't already been exposed to the "he looks pretty good to me" mentality. We hired Tom Boisture, Bob Terpening, Mike Hickey, and Gary Glick. The next season we added Dick Steinberg. Every one of them but Gary ended up as a general manager or personnel director. Same was true with George Young, Fred Schubach, and Dick Szymanski in Baltimore. I don't know if there's such a thing as a personnel tree the way they talk about coaching trees, but if there is, I grew some pretty strong branches in those places, scouts who later would build their own successful teams. I'm proud of that.

At our first meeting Bucko told me he'd need a place to store his antiques. He said we were building a new stadium, so there must be room somewhere, which there was. I figured how much room can a couple tables and a clock take?

Not long after he arrived, I get a call from one of the construction supervisors asking me why all these antiques were there. Bucko must have had $100,000 worth of antiques stored in our stadium. How he went from Eagles tough man to antique collector I don't know, but I didn't care as long as he could scout.

We installed everything like I had it in Baltimore and Bucko had it in in Dallas. I had magnetic boards up for every team's personnel so we could move the names up and down as our evaluations changed. We had another set up with all the top college prospects and computerized printouts of all the information. Everything was there.

The scouts we hired were young with a sharp eye for talent. I believed in them. I'd learned from Shula and Rosenbloom not to be afraid to give young people a chance. Steinberg and Terpening had no scouting background. Neither did Mike Hickey, who was the son of 49ers head coach Red Hickey. But they were smart and you could mold them the way you wanted.

The last person I hired was Peter Hadhazy from the league office. His job there was to run the waiver wire and make sure every transaction conformed to league rules. He knew that rulebook better than the people who wrote it. Since we had first pick of anyone on waivers, I wanted someone who understood the nuances.

Peter was only twenty-six, but he was the best I'd ever seen with the waivers. Running waivers in the league office is a difficult job. Everybody is yelling at you. I wanted someone who knew every part of it because I wanted to manipulate the waivers and avoid problems. It didn't take long for that decision to pay off.

I wanted to know every day what was going on and if anything looked suspicious, because everybody played games with the waiver wire. Peter came to me late in the summer just before the final cut-down date and said Kansas City had put Mo Moorman on waivers injured. Moorman had been a No. 1 pick in 1968 and started for the Chiefs when they won Super Bowl III. If you've ever seen the NFL Films show on that game, Moorman was the guard who threw the trap block on Mike Garrett's touchdown run where Stram, who was miked-up, kept hollering "65 Toss Power Trap" like he knew it was going to score.

I had scouted Moorman when he was playing at Kentucky, and I knew Hank. I figured he'd waived Moorman to open a roster spot for a couple weeks and then he'd bring him back because nobody would claim an injured player. I didn't think Moorman was really injured long-term, which it turned out he wasn't, because he started eight games that year and for three more years after that.

For a team as downtrodden as the Patriots were, there are two ways to build: through the draft and by picking up every available veteran player who can breathe. Every position was open for competition except quarterback, and Moorman was a 6-foot-5, 252-pound former All-Pro and a proven starter at right guard, so I told Hadhazy to put in a claim.

In those days, waived injured really meant nobody claimed him. That was the shorthand message. It was a gentlemen's agreement I'd never agreed to. Hadhazy said, "You sure?" I was.

Hank Stram called immediately, but I told Peter to tell him I was unreachable. I wanted to make him wait and get anxious. We had seventy-two hours to play with, but after a couple days of him calling and me not being available, Billy told me his good friend Lamar Hunt, the Chiefs' owner, had appealed to him for me to take Stram's call.

I told Hank I'd give Moorman back for a No. 1 choice. I still had some time to release my claim. He said, "You can't claim an injured player." I said, "I just did." Then he started in on how

Moorman's got a terrible ankle injury and I said, "So what? Have you seen my offensive line? He could have a broken ankle and it's an improvement."

I really did want to keep him. He could have stepped in and been All-Pro, but instead I made another offer. I said I'd accept his best receiver, Elmo Wright, instead. I think Hank was ready to pull the rug off his head, but I was the first personnel director to go from that job to becoming a GM, and that gave me an advantage. I knew every player in the league because I'd scouted them. Teams couldn't take advantage of the Patriots in personnel anymore. If somebody went on waivers, I knew what he was.

The Mo Moorman thing was a game everyone played, but I didn't have a second thought about it. Hank was hiding him. Claiming him sent out a warning. If you're going to try hiding players, Bell is going to claim them. Some writer called me "The East Coast Al Davis." I hoped he was right.

Meanwhile Billy kept telling me Lamar was a good friend and implying that's more important than Mo Moorman. He wasn't ordering me but he was pressuring me to relent. If I was the owner, I would have kept him or got a No. 1 pick, but I wasn't, so I told Billy we had to build; and if everyone in the league thought they could take advantage of us, as they had, we were going to pay a terrible price. In the end I settled for a second-round pick when I should have gotten a first. I didn't want to, but I can be a good politician when need be.

So Billy told Lamar. They were hot about it but that was the deal I got. I think we were the first to ever claim an injured player and get a draft choice for him. Some people accused me of breaking the "code," but so what? Look at the people they'd stuck us with, like Joe Kapp. There was a pattern there and it was a loser's pattern.

It only took a month for that pattern to resurface because we had no safeguards in place yet. We still had no organization, and a month after I got there we nearly paid dearly for it.

Before I left for the annual owners' meetings in Palm Beach in March, I told one of our secretaries not to forget to send the option letters out. There was paperwork stacked everywhere, but I thought everything was fine. It was standard procedure.

The option clause had been put in by my father to protect the club so the player couldn't take off. The commissioner signed every contract then, and I remembered hearing him say on the phone a thousand times, "Make sure that option is signed."

The way it worked was in the final year of a player's contract we had to send notification we were picking up his option, whether we kept him or not. If a player had a two-year contract, the club had an option for a third year, which I could pick up. If it sounds like a perpetual contract, it was, although it really was only a one-year option. That's how Ted Hendricks left Baltimore for Green Bay. He played out the option. He was one of the few who ever did it. They usually signed a new deal, with a new option, instead.

So a two-year deal was really a three-year deal for the club, plus we got compensation for the player if he signed with someone else. Later it was called restraint of trade, which of course it was. That was the whole idea. It eventually led to a limited form of free agency, but nothing like baseball has.

Well, someone forgot to send the letters out. I didn't know it until I got a call from Phil Olsen's agent after I got back, thanking me for making Phil a free agent because he wanted to get to the West Coast to play with his brother, Merlin, on the Rams. I was dumbfounded.

His agent, Edwin Masery, also sent me a letter notifying me I hadn't picked up the option and therefore Phil was free. I looked into it and learned Sauer used to send those letters out himself. The secretary seemed confused by the whole thing. Nobody knew what I was talking about.

I got all our contracts ready to send out, and we had all these players now without an option letter. None of the letters had gone out. Thirty players were now free agents. I'd lost my entire team!

When I explained the situation to Hadhazy and Bucko, I thought they were going to pass out. Hadhazy suggested we send letters out immediately, but it was too late. The deadline had passed. If we sent them now, at least some players would realize what had happened and try to leave. Fortunately, it never became public. Today it would get out in ten minutes, but very few players had agents then and that helped us.

Peter Hadhazy told me there was nothing we could do about it, but in trying to come up with some way to stop it, I went down to the league office with one of our lawyers to plead our case. Our lawyer said he thought we had one last shot with something called an estoppel. It's a legal principle that precludes a person from asserting something contrary to what is implied by a previous action or statement. In other words, Olsen knew there was an option and we always exercise it, so it was reasonable to infer we would again and he didn't need notification about that. It seemed like a Hail Mary, but sometimes you have to throw one. Or say one. The league said it wasn't too sure. Neither was I.

Billy couldn't have been better about it. I think he was used to these kinds of things happening, even though I wasn't. He didn't blame me. Carroll would have called the person in and put him in front of a firing squad, but it never would have happened at the Colts in the first place.

Every day for two months I woke up knowing if this got out, I'm a dead man walking. I kept waiting for someone like Will McDonough at the *Boston Globe* to discover it. Thankfully, Phil and his agent never told the media.

What I decided was we'd send the other players new contracts, most with a small raise. I'm sure some of them wondered why they were getting raises for going 2-14, but none asked. Every day I'd contact three or four more players, feeling like there was a death sentence hanging over my head every morning. Jon Morris was our starting center and the player rep. He was a smart man, so I was surprised he didn't notice, but maybe his option wasn't up.

Commissioner Rozelle finally stepped in and declared Olsen a free agent but said the Rams had to give us compensation, and we ended up with their No. 1 pick in 1972 because Olsen was a former No. 1. Today that wouldn't happen. The agent would holler. The union would step in. It would be all over social media and we'd be dead, which legally we should have been. We didn't send the letter. The Rams didn't owe us anything.

Even after it became public, not one player came to me and said, "You screwed me." I didn't con them. I just didn't tell them they were free agents. They just thought Phil was the only one.

Considering how contentious everything is today between the union with DeMaurice Smith as its director and the league with Goodell as commissioner, you're probably wondering why the NFLPA didn't demand all those players become free agents or threaten to sue. That's where we got a break. As much turmoil as we were in, so was the NFLPA.

Ed Garvey had just taken over a year earlier in 1971 as executive director and the union was going through a merger with the AFL Players Association. The problem was that Garvey was negotiating a new four-year deal with the owners and preparing what would become a landmark antitrust case involving John Mackey. Had Garvey known what was going on, he would have been all over it, because it was a clear example of the kind of antitrust violation he would later use to ease restrictions on player movement. But the union was in a state of flux when Pete stepped in.

The whole issue was never fully explained until now. Today it would be analyzed over and over, but information didn't flow as quickly then. I called it a technicality and all the media wanted to know was that the Patriots' No. 1 pick of 1970 was out the door.

I took the blame but said Olsen used a loophole to get out of his contract. He'd hurt his knee in the College All-Star Game and never played a down for the Patriots, so if he didn't want to be here we didn't want him. What are the reports the next day? Dissatisfied Olsen skips out on team. Billy loved that. So did our fans.

I took the public fall, because what am I going to do? Throw my secretary under the bus? It would look like a first-year person coming in and copping out at the first problem. Imagine the headline: "Bell Blames Secretary." It was a legitimate mistake. Hell, my assistant GM's desk was in the bathroom. You could lose anything in those offices.

Today they call it spin. I called it damage control. Turned out that was just the beginning of a lot of damage control. Damage out of control was more like it. Olsen was the tip of the iceberg.

Every week there was a problem that on other teams would happen once every five years. The next one involved quarterback Joe Kapp, who had been the league's MVP in 1969 for taking the Vikings to the Super Bowl with a lot of machismo and a rag arm. It was amazing what he did, but not as amazing as what was coming.

A month or two after the Olsen fiasco, the league office called asking for Kapp's signed contract. We couldn't find it and one of the secretaries told me Sullivan had it, so I called Billy, because he'd negotiated the deal the previous season.

Kapp had refused to sign a new contract with the Vikings because there was no raise in it, and he played out his option in 1969. He was now a free agent, but no team contacted him until Billy called a week into the 1970 season. Kapp would later charge in a lawsuit that this lack of interest was because of the Rozelle Rule, the compensation rule he dubbed the Ransom Rule. He had a point, frankly.

Billy offered Kapp a three-year contract on October 6, 1970, and paid him $154,000 to go 1-9 as a starter, which made him the highest-paid player in the league and cost the Patriots their 1972 No. 1 pick and defensive back John Charles, who'd been a No. 1 pick in 1967. Kapp signed a memorandum of agreement but not a standard player contract on the advice of his attorney, John Elliot Cook. In reality, he played 1970 without a contract and now the league was demanding he sign a standard one, which Kapp wouldn't do.

Rozelle sent us a letter on May 28, reminding us Kapp could not play or practice without a signed contract. Kapp showed up at training camp out at the University of Massachusetts in Amherst, but I had to tell him to leave, although he remained in our control on the reserve list. Kapp sued, claiming an antitrust violation, and four years later won a judgment but no compensation because a jury ruled he had not been harmed, even though he never played another down in the NFL and never got the rest of the $600,000 he'd been promised. In 1977 the "Ransom Rule" was renegotiated to be less restrictive, and a multi-million-dollar settlement was paid to the union. Kapp got nothing. None of that helped me in 1971.

Earlier that spring, I spent a day driving to a team function in New Hampshire with Kapp, and I liked him. He seemed like a throwback player. He was a natural leader. What was clear to me immediately was Kapp was never going to sign that contract. It went on and on until the first day of camp, which was one of the most embarrassing scenes I'd ever seen.

I'm the GM but Billy is meeting with Kapp. I'm not involved and I didn't want to be involved. I would have told him if you don't want to sign, see you later.

We'd been told he couldn't practice if he didn't sign, so all the cameras are outside waiting. At one point Billy and Kapp walk out of Kapp's apartment with Billy carrying Kapp's bag. I was so pissed. We never saw Joe Kapp again, and I was relieved. It was one of the few things Mazur and I agreed on. The future was Plunkett.

A month later I thought I'd found a way to help Plunkett greatly. Duane Thomas had been Rookie of the Year in 1970, rushing for 803 yards for Dallas. Despite starting only eight games, he ran for over 100 yards four times and twice more in the playoffs on the way to Super Bowl V, but he was unhappy because he had a bad contract. Tex had really screwed him with a series of one-year deals, to the point one of the best players in the league was only making $21,000, and Thomas blasted them in the press. I figured I'd make a call because Bucko told me Dallas always liked Carl Garrett, who was a good player for us, but I thought Thomas was better.

I was heading to Canton, Ohio, to the Hall of Fame ceremony on July 31 to present Bill Hewitt, who had played for my father. I'd been in contact with Tex by phone and told him if Thomas's only problem was the contract, maybe we could make a deal. In my mind he was the 1970s version of Jim Brown. We'd taken Norm Bulaich in that draft, who never took a play off and was a solid blocker, because Duane was already taken. If he wasn't, Thomas would have been a Colt.

I saw it as an opportunity to get a bigger player and run him thirty times a game to take pressure off Plunkett. We'd also heard Garrett had drug issues, which it turns out he did, although his play didn't show it.

I could tell Mazur didn't like the deal. He loved Garrett to the point he let him take days off the next season until I suspended him after he'd missed his twelfth practice, but that's another story. Garrett was a problem just like Thomas but it was mostly off the field, so John looked the other way.

What I didn't know was that Thomas had drug problems too. During the 1970s that would become a significant issue for the NFL, but it was just starting and we didn't have any idea yet. That's what Tex was hiding.

Friday night in Canton was a big banquet with the Hall of Fame inductees in the audience. The presenters made their speeches that night and then did it again on Saturday at the actual induction. I started negotiating with Tex Thursday night. At the banquet the next night, who is sitting next to me? Richard Nixon. The president of the United States. Say what you will about him, Nixon was a real football fan.

We started talking about players and I told him I was trying to trade for Thomas. He said, "Make the deal." Now we had presidential approval! I figured the president likes the deal, I like the deal, so why not?

That night Tex and I negotiated on the phone until we made the deal around 4 a.m. That morning I was supposed to be in a big parade with Hewitt's family, but I didn't make it because I was barely awake. I called Mazur and told him we got Thomas, a young lineman named Halvor Hagen, and Honor Jackson, a defensive back, for Garrett and a No. 1 pick.

It wasn't like today when you can find everything out. They didn't know much about Garrett's problems and we didn't know Thomas's beyond the contract. I could tell John wasn't too enthused, but I didn't care. Thomas had produced even when he was disillusioned.

Bucko flew in and told me when Thomas arrived from LA he fell down the stairs. What was he doing in LA? Somebody claimed he was with a woman who was supplying him drugs, but I didn't have any idea if that was true.

When Duane arrived he had to pass a physical, but I wanted to make sure he didn't take all the tests in case we needed to flunk him. With the rumors about drugs floating around, I wanted to be careful. He never refused to take the physical. That's what was said later but it wasn't true. We never asked him to take a blood or urine test, even though at one point publicly I said he "declined to complete the physical exam."

When I got back I met with Duane and could see he was disillusioned because of his contract. I assured him this wasn't Dallas. I'd look at the contract and see if we could find a way to make him happy. He didn't say much. He was just observing.

Then he asked if we could go out to a field and talk. He said he felt uncomfortable in the office. Very few GMS would sit in the middle of a field with a player in 1971. I did whatever it took. I didn't care.

The press had descended by now. We were sitting outside and not too far away were a bunch of TV cameras. A local sportscaster named Don Gillis tried to get closer with his camera crew, and Duane walked over and hollered, "Don't come any closer!" Don looked shocked. It was the most demonstrative Duane had been since he arrived. I told Thomas I'd meet him after the afternoon practice and he went to get dressed. A little later Bucko walked in and said, "We got a problem. Mazur threw Thomas out of practice."

I heard later Duane went off by himself at the start of practice. Who cares? Raymond Berry did it every practice in Baltimore. Anyone with any quirks couldn't play for John Mazur, but there was more to it.

In retrospect I think it was all a setup. That was the beginning of the end of the relationship between me and Mazur. He didn't want this person from the beginning. This was a way to send the message he was in charge.

What happened was Duane lined up in the I formation behind Jim Nance and couldn't see around him. I must admit Nance was broad in the beam. Duane wanted to stand up with his hands on his knees rather than in a three-point stance and Mazur screamed at him to get down. It became a power play and he threw Thomas out.

I understand there couldn't be two more opposite men than John Mazur, the ex-Marine, and Duane. Mazur was a product of a time when it was the coach's football field and you stand where he tells you and how he tells you. From being on those college campuses in the sixties, I knew those days were over. That wasn't going to work anymore. Certainly not with Duane Thomas.

Here's the thing. Tom Landry was one of the most demanding coaches in the league and not a barrel of laughs. Yet he got along with Thomas well enough to give him the ball. Thomas's problems were never anything more than "somebody screwed me on my contract and I'm so bitter I'm not going to do anything you tell me but carry the ball." Fine.

In the end none of that mattered. He'd come in with baggage and got thrown out of his first practice. Mazur later claimed when he told him to get into his stance, Thomas said, "I'm me, man. I do what I do, man." So Mazur threw him out. If I wanted to be tough I could have said, "John, you've embarrassed everybody in the organization. Do your job. Coach him." Instead I got rid of Thomas and got the team a good deal, but I didn't like it and I didn't forget it.

I met with Thomas. I called Hadhazy and Bucko. Then I called Rommie and told him to get Duane out of there. We didn't need the media hounding him. We needed to figure out a way to send him back to Dallas.

Duane couldn't understand what happened. He said that's how he positioned himself to let him see the field better. A lot of AFL backs ran that way. Mike Garrett played his whole career that way with the Chiefs. Duane didn't say, "I'm not getting down in that fucking stance!" Mazur took it where he wanted to take it and now the well was poisoned.

Our team doctor, Dr. Burton Nault, was close to Mazur. He came out and said publicly he had concerns about how Thomas looked and that "officials" told him when he arrived at UMass that

Thomas had refused to take blood or urine tests. "Refused to do anything" is how he put it in the papers.

The truth was we never asked him to. If we'd given him the complete physical and he passed, I would have told Mazur "tough luck," but it would have been a problem all season. The writers would have become the Mazur camp and the Bell camp and maybe the Duane camp, and it never would have ended. Same could have happened with the board of directors. So I tried to make the best of it.

Hadhazy and I talked to Rozelle, and he helped save the day. He knew it was a bad situation because there was a question about drugs, which was new to the league in some ways. There was enough talk around that Dallas had to sweat it, because we assumed they knew there was a problem when they made the trade.

All we said was he didn't complete his physical. Technically, it was true but he never refused to do anything. We didn't complete it and people took that where they took it.

Duane flew back to LA the next morning wearing a dashiki. In Boston, that passed for shocking news.

Nobody saw me for four days. I never left my office. Not even to eat. I didn't go to practice as I usually did. I couldn't say anything until we made a deal, and Tex was pissed so I was in avoidance mode.

Tex liked Garrett and wasn't inclined to be helpful. I mentioned people said Thomas had been doing drugs and the Cowboys were aware of it. Then I dropped the bombshell. I told him Thomas didn't pass the physical and I'm sending him back. I didn't mention drugs. I just left it at that, but there was a suspicion hanging out there.

The collective bargaining agreement wasn't specific the way it is today about drug testing. It is fair to say I don't know if Duane ever refused to do anything. Rumors were around that the reason Thomas was acting strange was because he was using drugs. I don't know if he was or he wasn't. Didn't then and don't now. But I do not believe he ever refused to do anything we asked except get in a three-point stance. You can't negate a trade over that. So we just said he hadn't taken the full physical.

Duane raised a good question when he finally got back to Dallas and helped them win the Super Bowl that season. "How could I pass my physical in Dallas and not pass in New England?" We never answered it.

Rozelle voided part of the deal involving Garrett and Thomas, so what we ended up doing was we traded Thomas and our second- and third-round picks to Dallas for Garrett, a lineman named Halvor Hagan, and Honor Jackson, a defensive back. It was a high price, but it was high noon and Tex accepted.

Six weeks into the season we went to Dallas and they killed us, 44–21. Duane scored the first touchdown on a 56-yard run. He had his hands on his knees when they snapped the ball. He got a pretty good view of our defense from there and then he ran over it. I was not happy.

Thomas refused to speak to his coaches or teammates in Dallas all season, but he had a great year. He rushed for 793 yards and eleven TDS and the Cowboys won the Super Bowl, but Dallas never fixed his contract, and that unhappiness ruined his career. What happened to Duane Thomas is one of the real shames of pro football from that time. He put his hands on his thigh pads and got run out of town. Nobody understood the long-term effect of that on me, Mazur, or our team. He was soon traded to San Diego and suspended a year later, and his career dissolved.

Duane Thomas wasn't a bad person. He was a twenty-three-year-old kid disillusioned because he saw the bullshit of life and wasn't able to ignore it. How does that make you a bad person? Thomas straightened his life out and became involved in real estate in Arizona and Texas, and in fact Dallas, the very team that he rejected, ended up helping him in business. I tried to keep in touch with him over a period of time. The last time I talked to him was a radio interview I did with him about twenty years ago. I never had a problem with him. Other people did. Today, Bill Belichick wouldn't be arguing with him about his stance if he was eighth in the league in rushing like he was in 1970.

It was the times. It was a bad time in this country for a young person, especially a young black person. They saw demonstrations and took part. They saw radical change and protests on campus. They were no longer the good old boy football player. I told Billy and our other owners that players coming out of college then were different from what they were used to, but they didn't believe me.

These players took drugs. They challenged authority. They were coming off campuses in turmoil and didn't trust management. It was a difficult world for coaches to understand. In their world the coach was king, but now he had to negotiate. Duane and Mazur were the worst combination: someone coming in with new ideas and someone clinging to the old ones.

Later that summer some black players led by Darryl Johnson were complaining about two of Mazur's assistants, who had a reputation of not dealing well with African Americans. I was hearing more and more complaints about them. The players should have been going to Mazur and I told them so, but they didn't. They kept coming back to me.

Coaching isn't the most sensitive profession, especially in those days. Some of those men could be pretty coarse. Lot of hollering, not much cajoling. I told Mazur he had a problem and he told me not to listen because players always complain, but it persisted, so I finally agreed to meet with the African American players away from campus at a motel at night.

We'd already had enough problems with Olsen, Kapp, and Thomas. We didn't need a racial problem, so I took a chance, but I told them if this got out there would be bigger problems than they already had. I was willing to listen but this had to stay in-house. I was surprised how deep their complaints were. They felt they were being treated differently. Some complained about Mazur but I told them I didn't buy that, because Mazur screamed at everybody.

I didn't see those two coaches as being racist, but I wasn't being coached by them. I did think the players had some valid points and told them that. I thought they had legitimate complaints, but I explained I wasn't far from their age and I thought they were dealing with two men from a different era. I thought it would probably do no good to talk with Mazur, but I did tell him the players were still complaining and after the season I wanted those coaches fired. That would become a problem later.

Somehow we made it to our first home exhibition game at our new stadium. There had been some problems because they'd built it in 322 days on a piece of land by a harness track that the movie house magnate E. M. Loew offered in exchange for a split of the parking lot revenue.

Fine and Billy even got $150,000 in naming rights from the Schaefer Brewery at a time when few teams were being paid for that. Today they get millions, but then it was unheard of. Somehow they got it finished enough to open on August 15, 1971, against the New York Giants, but when it did the plumbing backed up.

We'd gone from around nine thousand season tickets in 1970 to over forty-five thousand, and it was a night of celebration, especially since we won, 20–14. It may have been a meaningless game, but not to a team that was 2-14 and homeless a year before. But while things went well on the field, they didn't go so well in the bathrooms, where the sewers backed up and overflowed.

The Board of Health was threatening to close down the stadium before our next game against the Falcons because of concerns over the plumbing, so Billy came up with the Great Flush to convince them we could function. On Saturday, September 4, he had groups of media, employees, and team officials stationed all over the stadium. They sounded a horn from the scoreboard and we all ran around like crazy flushing all the toilets as fast as possible to prove the plumbing worked. We had some urinals that were only a couple feet off the ground for some reason. They were for our three-foot fans, I guess.

While we were flushing toilets, the Falcons were waiting at the Atlanta airport to learn if we had a place to play them. The Great Flush worked, but the plumbing still didn't always.

It was just as rough in our dirt parking lots, which emptied out onto a two-lane road. The stadium designers forgot that moving 60,423 people onto Route 1 was impossible. People were stuck in those lots and on the road for hours. Some never got to the game and others thought they'd never get home. It was the largest traffic jam in Massachusetts history. In fact, the Department of Public Works made us change our games from night to day, and when I called the Rams to tell them our exhibition game would be played in the afternoon, they tried to get a draft choice out of me. You know what I told them!

It was such a rush job it was chaos. We probably should have played someplace else for another year, but in their minds they could get it finished and they did.

When the regular season opened on September 19, it was like heaven. We were playing the Oakland Raiders and nobody in the league thought we stood a chance, including Commissioner Pete Rozelle, who flew up for the game and sat in a small box with Hadhazy and myself. It was a grand occasion. We upset the Raiders, and Jim Plunkett threw two touchdown passes, including one to a player I drafted in Baltimore, Roland Moss. We cut him later because that's how we were building the team, a player at a time.

I brought in 180 players that year. If I was interested in killing the coach, you know how many I would have brought in? None. But I was trying to find players for him anywhere I could, including at Disneyland, which is where a rookie wide receiver named Randy Vataha was at one point before he was released by the Rams earlier in the summer. Vataha had been Plunkett's teammate at Stanford and was terrific that season. He caught fifty-one passes for 872 yards and nine touchdowns. The biggest one came in the final game of the season against the Colts.

Before we got to that point, we were up and down all season. We finished 6-8, which they considered a winning season in New England in those days, but we could have been 7-7 or 8-6. That's where I began to judge Mazur as a coach.

We'd have a great win followed by a terrible game. No consistency. Even if we lost, it wasn't just a loss. It was often ineptitude, like 34–7 to Detroit and 23–3 to the Colts at home right after that Raiders' win. We beat some of the better teams and lost badly to poorer teams. The only one on that staff I thought much of was

Sam Rutigliano, who was a successful head coach in Cleveland later in his career but was just starting out in the pros.

As the end of the season approached, we had a chance at a .500 record, were averaging around 58,700 fans, and had enough season ticket requests that we knew we'd sell out every game in 1972, which we did. We were homeless no longer, even if most of the seats didn't have backs. They were just aluminum benches that got hot in the sun and cold in the snow. But at least no one was forgetting anymore to shovel the snow off the seats, as happened at Harvard Stadium in 1970. Fans showed up and had to push piles of snow onto the steps so they could sit down and watch the Patriots lose to my Colts, 35–14. Being hearty New Englanders, they had their fun despite the score.

The whole game, Unitas kept moving up and down the bench trying to avoid bombardments of snowballs. Maybe I should have thought about what I saw that day before I left Baltimore two months later, but now things were getting better in New England. By the final game of the year I knew there were still problems, but I thought we could win. I knew we had better talent and I knew I could keep improving it if they left me alone. The truth of the matter was, even with all the complications, I would have done it until I dropped.

As it turned out, I didn't have to wait that long before I did . . . or rather before Billy Sullivan dropped me.

13

Everybody's Got to Serve Somebody

Sometimes a failing football organization has to be taken down to its foundation before it can be rebuilt. It's a process that requires time, patience, and discipline. There wasn't enough of that in New England in 1971 to survive what was about to happen. It was a classic example of why some teams consistently fail, as true today as it was then.

By late in my first season it appeared to the outside world we were well on our way to a rebirth. In reality the dry rot that had so debilitated that organization for over a decade remained. Soon it would cause the situation and the team to implode.

When an organization consistently loses, it is most often because it can't get out of its own way. That was true in Foxboro in 1971 and it's true in Cleveland today, where the Browns have been floundering for more than twenty years. Someone has to be in charge and that someone has to be a football man, but that doesn't mean he doesn't answer to someone. Bob Dylan had it right in 1979 when he wrote a song called "Gotta Serve Somebody."

In my case it turned out to be more the devil than the Lord, but I wasn't serving one person. I was serving a board of sixteen plus a head coach I didn't feel was up to the job but couldn't get rid of. What flowed from that was dysfunction and defeat.

Odd things happen when a pro football franchise is fractured and at war with itself, and we had one odd thing happening after another. The game is difficult to succeed at even when everyone is pulling in the same direction, because the margins for error are so thin. The talent difference between the worst franchise in the NFL and the best is far less than the scoreboard often indicates, so what separates winners from losers is often the kind of self-inflicted wounds now familiar to me in New England.

Although we were 5-8 as the final game approached and had upset Shula's Dolphins two weeks earlier, the rift between me and Mazur and the growing conflict between me and Billy Sullivan were being publicly debated almost daily. Ownership was getting pounded by the media, and that is seldom good for management. One of the city's highest-profile TV men, Clark Booth, kept calling it the "Foxboro Follies" and the "Patsies."

They all knew I didn't want Mazur back, but our differences were on a low boil until Billy did what bad organizational leaders always do. He made a public power play for short-term gain.

Although I knew what my contract said, I told the press over and over I'd make a decision on Mazur after the season. Let him coach and we'll see where we are. Then Billy came out just before Thanksgiving on a weekly Patriots television show I'd helped arrange and said I didn't have that authority.

Around the league people were shocked. At the time we still had a chance to go 7-7 or even 8-6. Why say something like that at such a crucial time? Because power was more important to him than winning.

That may sound strange, because we all understand the owner has the ultimate power, but I'd begun to get a lot of positive press for the turnaround, and Billy didn't like it because it seemed to him to criticize the past. He liked the positive headlines but he wanted credit. In any NFL organization, if getting credit becomes more important than success itself, you're doomed.

I got a call from a reporter asking what I thought about Billy's statement. I mumbled something about joint decisions and then called Billy and told him it was bullshit what he'd done, because he and I had talked about how to settle this thing. What was the need for him to cause a public firestorm?

He could have just said the board will take Upton's recommendation because he's the football man and then decide. I would have been fine with that. Instead he sent a message to me and to Mazur. If you and the coach don't agree and he knows you can't fire him, why would he listen to you? He won't. And he didn't, which is why Duane Thomas was running the Cowboys to the Super Bowl and not for the Patriots.

The thing Billy did better than anyone was separate and conquer. Pit the coach against the GM. Pit the coach against the players. Pit the various owners against each other. In the beginning it was Bell's team to rebuild, but what's a better story? Everyone getting along or Bell won't talk to Mazur and Mazur won't talk to Bell and Billy will make the decision?

From that moment on we had dueling columns daily because the newspapers were fighting for readers. One writer says Bell is doing a terrific job. The other says he's at war with the coach or the owner. It was like a talk show in the newspapers. I understand if you're the owner, you may not want people writing every day that the new man has done the job and all the years you were running it sucked, but the way to do that is not to divide and conquer your organization. But that's what he did. We lost three of the next four games. Shocker.

We were set to play the Colts in the season finale when "the call" came. I'm going back to Baltimore for the first time with my new team with a chance to go 6-8 despite all our problems. If we win, we will have beaten two of the AFC's best teams, Miami and the Colts, in a three-week span, which would be a good way to end the season. Then the phone rang.

It was Billy inviting me to a board meeting at one of the best restaurants in the city, Anthony's Pier 4, six days before that game. It turned out to be a high-class place to walk the plank.

He said they didn't normally do this but the board wanted to hear from me. Usually I dealt with Billy directly or a few of the others individually. I'd never been in front of the full board, and I'm sure Billy didn't want me speaking to them without him filtering what I said. We were winning some games and selling some tickets, but I was making waves and they were being blamed, so they wanted to hear from me directly, which I had no problem with. I welcomed it.

Somehow it was leaked to the press, of course, because that was the Patriots in those days. Under Belichick you can barely find out what time the game is, but in those days every board member had a writer and every writer had a source. I liked some of the board members, and some I didn't know well. They were always fighting each other because nobody had a majority. They don't allow that today but the NFL was different then. They still took owners where they found them, and in the Patriots' case Billy was running the team despite only owning about 20 percent of the stock. Today the principal owner must own at least 30 percent and have full control to avoid just what we were going through.

When I arrived, it looked like someone had called a newspaper convention. The media was everywhere and the door to the meeting room was closed. I opened it and walked in and there they were, sitting on a little raised platform.

I'm standing below them like a defendant at a jury trial. The idea was to give me the feeling I was not on the same level they were. Billy said they were there to discuss the future of the team, and they knew I had strong opinions.

I told them I thought we'd done some good things but I didn't believe the future was with John Mazur. I said they had to ask themselves one key question, which I asked myself every day: "Is this the man we want to lead the team for the next three or four years?"

I said if the answer was yes, rehire him with a long-term contract. If it's no, whether we win or lose the last game is not important. But it can't be just that he deserves another year if you don't think he's the long-term answer.

I also told them we had a problem with a couple of coaches, so if the decision was to keep Mazur, he had to understand those assistants had to go. When I said that, no one asked which two or what the problem was, which were logical questions. That told me they knew what the problem was because Billy had told them. If they didn't know, they would have asked. If they knew, why hadn't something been done?

Someone did say, shouldn't the head coach be able to hire his own assistants? I told them that was true, but that brought up a good point: If enough of them aren't good, shouldn't the coach go?

The only time I saw Don McCafferty really assert his authority in Baltimore was when he saw his line coach, Lou Rymkus, wasn't working out. Often a head coach covers that up because he brought him in. McCafferty didn't. After a couple of games, he replaced Rymkus with my personnel assistant, George Young. I brought that up as an example of leadership that was missing here.

Bob Marr said if I was thinking about replacing Mazur, who was I thinking about bringing in? It was a reasonable question, but I knew those names would be out in the press the next day, so I only mentioned Howard Schnellenberger, who was Shula's chief assistant in Miami. I first noticed him when he was Bear Bryant's chief assistant at Alabama. That's another advantage of being a scout: you have a chance to evaluate coaches too.

They started arguing that we'd upset Oakland, we'd upset Miami. I told them not to be fooled. We'd made progress, but watch the week after those upsets. We beat Oakland and got killed by the Lions. We beat Miami and stunk out the joint against the Jets.

I didn't see consistency. There are the normal ups and downs of a team being turned over, but what I saw was win-satisfaction-lose. Over and over. It's the coaches' responsibility to prevent that.

You could tell from the discussion there were people in the room blaming Billy for the bad publicity about the coach and the GM. Now they were sitting there with a GM expressing his dissatisfaction to them directly. I'd made up my mind when I went in there that if they wanted to fire me, fire me. I never said it but that was my thinking.

Someone asked if this was an "either/or" proclamation and I said no. I never threatened to quit. I was just appealing to let me do my job. I was giving them my recommendation going forward. I was not threatening them, because you don't challenge authority when you don't have the authority. I was told later that, after

I left the meeting, Hessie Sargent told the rest of the board, "If we hired Upton Bell to be our general manager and to make the football decisions, then we should let him do his job." In the end, they didn't heed what was a very good point.

I was used to dealing with people who had real power, so I knew when you could challenge it and when you couldn't. Not everybody is going to be Shula, where you can go in and get into an argument and he can say, "Screw you," and the next day it's over with no grudges. That's a good football organization, and it's true in any well-run business organization. Healthy debate, often contentious debate, then a decision is made and we all move on. When people can't work that way, the organization dies.

So the question was what do we do? The suggestion was made that if we didn't play well against the Colts, we'd let Mazur go. I added if the decision was to retain him, it had to be clear he fire those two assistants. Billy agreed. The rest of the board didn't say anything.

How do we determine this? It couldn't be based on a certain score, because we could play well and still lose by two touchdowns. It had to be how we looked. If we really looked bad as we had in the past after a big win, we would replace Mazur. Later people wrote if we lost by more than a touchdown Mazur was out, but that was never the case. That would have been ridiculous. If we lose embarrassingly, Mazur is out, but who defines what that is? I didn't know but I was sure it wasn't me.

I felt it was a fait accompli. Billy was going to get him another year, whereas I believed if he came back the game was up. It didn't mean I wouldn't try to help him, but you know when a situation is not solvable. I'd begun to feel this was not an organization where I could get anything done. I was like Sisyphus pushing that rock up the hill and it would always roll back down.

Under the ownership structure, their long-term success was impossible, and I was proved right. You can build a scouting staff and get better talent, but organizationally things had to change. I was looking toward the future and I felt the board was looking at the past. I just saw a team that was never getting out of the past. Or out of its own way.

What I decided after I left was that, regardless of their decision on Mazur, I'd do my best for another year and then look to get out. Had I been on my own I would have quit that day, but I had a wife, a young son, and a lot of people I'd brought into the organization. What about them? This wasn't going anywhere, but I didn't feel I could just walk out and leave those people I'd brought to New England with me on their own.

If Sullivan had met me halfway and said he wanted to give John another year because he took over a team from a person with mental problems, and we went from 2-14 to 6-8, I would have understood. I would have disagreed but I would have accepted it. That wasn't what this was about. It was about power, not about winning or even fairness.

In my previous job in Baltimore not everybody wanted to fire Weeb, but Rosenbloom did, as was his right. You could make a case for it either way. In New England it wasn't about that. It was a fractured ownership with factions fighting for power or having different agendas. That has always been a disastrous scenario in the NFL.

What is the greatest lesson I ever had about multi-ownership? Bert Bell having to step in and run the Los Angeles Rams because Dan Reeves, Fred Levy, and Edwin Pauley were fighting every day. How does Pete Rozelle rise? Why does Tex Schramm leave LA for CBS? Because he'd had enough of it. Finally, my father picked up the phone and told those owners from now on he'd break all ties and make binding decisions if they couldn't agree. Only time in history a commissioner has said that. He told them the person representing him was Rozelle. That would never happen today. So my lesson about multi-headed organizations was they always have problems. Look at any team that ran that way.

After that meeting you may wonder how I was feeling that next Sunday in Baltimore. Mazur later claimed I was rooting against the team, but that was never the case. I never went to a game in my life not wanting to win. Truth was it didn't matter what happened in Baltimore. I'd already lost. The die was cast.

I could see when I walked out of that meeting, I was never going to have enough authority to pick my own coach. It would be a Billy Sullivan cross-country publicity-seeking routine if we fired Mazur, which it became a year later after I was gone.

Once you knew that, you understood those Patriots were never going to run the way a winning organization should. You interview some candidates quietly, sit down with the owner, and make a decision. With all our board members everything would be public. It was like social media before social media. They were their own Twitter accounts, and I say that in the best of humor. Looking back, it's comical, although not so much at the time.

Billy loved to say, "Well, Upton, you know even the president of the United States has to deal with Congress." I always answered, "Tell that to Vince Lombardi, Billy."

I'd become the divided self the Jesuits talk about. On the one hand I wanted to win. It would be a great victory over my old team, but if you win, you actually lose. That's the divided self.

So the game comes and Jim Plunkett audibles to a pass play with about two minutes left on third-and-11 and hits Randy Vataha, who makes a fantastic catch and goes for an 88-yard touchdown when the defender falls down. Now we're up by 11. Basically, we've won the game and I can feel people are looking at me. From my training as a kid, I didn't react one way or the other. I didn't believe it was appropriate to be rooting in the other team's press box. Later some people, including Mazur, claimed I looked disappointed or I was upset and hollering after Vataha's catch. First off, how would Mazur know? He was on the sidelines and I was in the press box. Second, if you know me you'd know I never reacted during a game. It goes back to what my father told me. I was neutral, even when I didn't have to be.

The next day we had a press conference to announce John Mazur was coming back. There was a famous picture in the papers of me, Mazur, and Billy and somebody wrote, "They're all smiling but they don't look happy."

That was because Mazur had refused to fire those assistants and Billy let him get away with it. Instead of saying your contract depends on it, he just suggested it and when Mazur said no, he didn't press him. Billy backed down. It was another lack of organizational discipline.

Two months later I made what I thought was a blockbuster trade to help our defense. It should have really improved us. In the end it collapsed. Why? Billy Sullivan.

I went to the Senior Bowl and began talking to Wellington Mara about acquiring the compensation rights to Fred Dryer, who was one of the league's best defensive ends. Dryer had played out his option and was free to sign with anyone, but compensation had to be arranged with the Giants. It was what Kapp had called the "Ransom Rule."

I didn't talk to Mazur about it. We hadn't created that duality of purpose. I think he just wanted to run his coaching world and nobody was going to be part of it. He didn't want it with George Sauer and he didn't want it with me.

He also understood I'd tried to get him fired, so how much was he going to like me? All he kept saying was, "Get me the players," and Dryer surely was one, so there was nothing to talk about.

By this point, my relationship with Billy was not good, but I understood part of the GM's job is to sell, so I told him I thought we had a chance at Dryer. Billy said he loved the idea. I let him know exactly what I was doing, we made the trade, and after the draft I headed to LA to make the deal.

My feeling was Dryer would anchor our defensive line and give us a pass rush with him on one side and Julius Adams on the other. We'd have youth, power, and speed and we had Dave Rowe inside as well, whom I'd acquired from Houston. I felt it was a weak draft in 1972, especially in the defensive line, and that was our number one priority. There was no one we could have drafted better than Dryer, as the first two picks that year proved. They were Walt Patulski and Sherman White, both defensive linemen. Neither did much in the NFL. Dryer did a lot. Just not for us.

I traded our first- and sixth-round picks plus a second in 1973 to the Giants, but we actually gave them less because we'd already traded them that sixth the previous year for a young receiver from Boston University named Reggie Rucker. We shouldn't have had to, but Mazur told the press that we were claiming a Giants quarterback who was going to be waived named Dick Shiner before it happened. But Shiner got hot and walked out on the Giants.

When we claimed Rucker later that year on waivers from Dallas, the Giants claimed him too out of spite and kept him for several weeks. I was incensed, mostly at Mazur. It was payback for the Shiner incident and it cost us a draft pick, but I didn't mind helping Wellington look better by saying they got that sixth as part of the Dryer deal. That would be exposed in five minutes today, but not many people outside of football paid attention to the draft in those days. You could say pretty much what you wanted and we did.

Now I had to sign Dryer, who had been critical of the Giants' management because he didn't think they were doing enough to win. They had a fractured ownership too because Wellington and his nephew Tim were at odds. Same fractures as the Patriots. Same consistent losing.

Dryer had also refused to comply with the Giants' dress code, which didn't concern me. The only thing he wore that I cared about was his uniform. The days of dress codes were over with the way society was going.

I knew there was a fail-safe in this. If someone else signed Dryer, we'd either get our No. 1 back or another team's No. 1, so there was no risk. He could go where he wanted but we got compensation. Wellington agreed to the deal and I announced it at 10 a.m. on the first day of the draft, February 1, 1972. I believed we would get him for less money than I felt he'd get if there was a bidding war. I thought we'd hit this one perfectly.

Shortly after the trade was announced, Dryer said in an interview, "The only way I'd go to Boston is if they gave me a Bean Soup franchise or Upton Bell came out here and told me 'Here, take all the money you want.'"

A few weeks later I went to LA and made the deal. I met with Dryer's agent at his office in Beverly Hills, and he told me Dryer preferred to sign on the West Coast. I told him I thought he'd like New England. We both knew the real factor was money. It almost always is about the money with free agents. We agreed to a one-year deal for $75,000 with a club option for a second season. It was about a $25,000 raise but worth it for a team in our position.

I didn't go back to my hotel that day thinking about anything else. I wasn't thinking about Mazur or problems. I was thinking of the defensive line we'd have with Steve Kiner behind them at linebacker. Visons of sugar plums danced in my head until I called Billy.

When I told Billy, his reaction shocked me. He said he wasn't sure he could get the finance committee to agree to that. You talk about a downer. Are you kidding me? Did he take Jim Nance and Joe Kapp to the finance committee when he grossly overpaid them? I don't think so.

I could tell from his voice we weren't going to do it. I should have gone back and signed Dryer that day and said, "Tough shit. He's signed." What's he going to do? Fire me?

I told him I'd given them my word. My first thought was they might sue me. I couldn't believe it. I felt like someone on a high wire who takes one too many steps and crashes without a net.

I didn't want to call his agent back and say we didn't have a deal, so I waited. I talked to Billy several more times and he kept saying he didn't know. That was the last straw. They weren't going to pay him. Internally that was it for me. Whether we got to the Super Bowl or not, I was gone.

I had to go back to Dryer and his agent and tell them the team wouldn't do it. They were good about it and he ended up signing with the Rams for more than the $75,000 we offered. We got the Rams' No. 1 pick for the second year in a row as compensation, but we didn't have a pass rusher and I didn't have any more hope.

People asked what happened, of course. What was I going to say, my owner screwed me? I couldn't say that. I just said we couldn't get together on the contract and we got a No. 1 pick back for a player we never had under contract. That's how I sold it publicly. It's also why the NFL's whole option system was later taken down in court. It was obviously a restraint of trade, but those were the rules then. I used them the best I could for my club's benefit.

The Rams got one of the best defensive ends in the NFL for a draft pick. They weren't going to argue against a system that was locking up players and getting you compensation if you lost one who played out his option. The teams still controlled the situation, so the only ones complaining were the players. But we had begun to lose control of them in other ways.

They were coming out of college from a counterculture world into a militaristic operation where most coaches still expected orders were given and followed, end of discussion. Management thought the same way in most places, but we were getting players who no longer blindly trusted management. These were the children of the sixties. They didn't trust authority the way previous generations had. They had their own opinions and wanted to express them. And then there was the growing drug culture, which was about to invade us.

When training camp opened that summer, expectations were high. I'd traded one of our three No. 1 draft picks for next year against my better judgment to the 49ers for a tight end named Bob Windsor. Mazur kept saying we didn't have a tight end and I agreed. I thought Windsor was only worth a second- or third-round pick, so I should have said I wasn't giving up a No. 1 for someone who isn't worth it. But I acquiesced, which is what happens in that kind of organization: you lose the discipline to try to smooth over a bad situation. It was like a Greek tragedy.

That off-season our best young linebacker, Steve Kiner, got busted for having marijuana in his car in Tennessee. He'd been a terrific player for us after we acquired him from the Cowboys for a fourth-round draft choice, but he was always a little bit odd. When he got back to training camp that summer, he was not staying in the dorms with the team; he was living in his trailer with his girlfriend.

I didn't care where he was living, but the marijuana was a problem. It wasn't a surprise but it was a problem, as it still is today in the NFL. We didn't know how to handle it then and the NFL still doesn't know how to handle it.

Recreational marijuana is legal in many states in the country today and that trend isn't about to change, but the league is still suspending players for testing positive for weed. That can't continue. At some point you have to get in step with the times. On the marijuana score, the league still hasn't.

Kiner had also become a vegetarian and he was down to just over 200 pounds and didn't seem to be the same player he'd been in 1971. He was never really a problem except he would stare at you in a way that made some people uncomfortable.

We had him on a TV show once with four Boston journalists and they asked him a question, and he just sat there in a pair of wooden shoes staring at the camera. Never said a word. He looked like somebody out of a Hans Christian Andersen story. They kept asking questions and he kept staring into the camera and not speaking. It got a little eerie.

The year before, there was also an incident in a game that became legendary around the league. We were playing the 49ers in Kezar Stadium on Halloween, October 31, 1971. When they snapped the ball, twenty-one players were on the move, but Kiner just stood stock-still in his stance. Never moved a muscle.

I saw it from the press box and later we all saw it on film. Oddest thing I'd ever seen in a football game. We asked him about it later and he told one of the coaches, "Man, it's crazy out there." Funny thing was other than that play he had a tremendous game: ten tackles, a sack, and a 14-yard interception return.

Kiner's agent was one of the most powerful in sports, a Boston attorney named Bob Wolff. He'd called me that spring while I was at a banquet and said Kiner was in his house and upset about his contract, and he was a little afraid of what he might do.

He said he was just sitting there staring at him. I told him, "That's just Steve." I got on the phone with him and told him we'd work it out. No answer. Not a word. That was a preview of coming attractions.

Now it's training camp and he looks like a defensive back. Off his first season with us, I thought he was part of our future, but our coaches thought he couldn't play anymore, so I called Shula and explained the situation. Shula said, "You're not trying to send me a stiff, are you, Upton?" I told him he had some problems but in an atmosphere like his, coming off the Super Bowl, he might help. Kiner was like Nick Buoniconti, whom the Dolphins got from the Patriots a few years before. A small, quick linebacker who was good in pass coverage.

I knew I wasn't getting much in return but it wasn't working out, so we made the deal and I called him into my office. I also called Bucko, in case I needed some muscle, and started to tell him we'd traded him to Miami.

He never said a word. He just stared straight at me. I told him it would be great for him. For twenty minutes, nothing but a fly buzzing around him while I'm talking. All of a sudden—WHAP! Kiner reached out and squashed that fly in midair, got up, and walked out. I never saw him again.

Shula got rid of him in a week or so and called and said, "You sent me a stiff." I said, "That makes us even because you sent me one too."

Kiner didn't play that year but came back to New England and started all of the 1973 season for Chuck Fairbanks, then went to Houston and played pretty well for the Oilers for about five years. He started nearly every game there. He was a good player, just a little lost at the time, like a lot of young people then.

We opened the '72 season against the Bengals at home and it was frightening. Every gain we'd made in 1971 had disappeared. We played so poorly we got booed. Fans were tossing beer bottles at our team when they ran off the field at halftime and at the end of the game. People tried to run on the field. At one point I told Hadhazy to call the state police because we couldn't continue to have people running on the field. It was really bad.

Cincinnati tore us apart, 31–7. It was 10–7 at halftime after Larry Carwell blocked a field goal and returned it 45 yards for a touchdown, but we fell apart in the second half. We allowed 246 yards rushing. Terrible performance.

The next Sunday we had police ringing the field. It looked like we were waiting for demonstrators, but somehow we won. Then we won again. We beat the Falcons and Redskins by 1 point each and were tied for first place in our division heading to Buffalo with reason to think we had a chance.

What happened? Same pattern. We got blown out, 38–14, in a game where O. J. Simpson only rushed for 31 yards. Just what I'd warned the board would happen. The difference this time was we got in a rut. It seemed like there wasn't any life left in us. We became a team looking to lose. Instead of playing poorly one game and doing well the next, we lost nine straight and were blown out in six of them.

We got trampled 41–13 by the Jets the next week and then had to play the Steelers. Carl Garrett disappeared all week, then showed up for the flight to Pittsburgh. When we arrived, there were no buses to meet us. Nobody knew why.

Plunkett was sacked six times that day and we had players laughing on the sidelines. The wheels were falling off when we went to New York to play the Jets. Plunkett was 7 for 28 that day before Mazur pulled him for a former Yale quarterback named Brian Dowling. We lost 34–10, and a local TV sportscaster suggested we were giving ineptitude a bad name.

Somehow I'd managed to persuade the league to give us a Monday night game that season, which they did against the Colts. We brought in this act, Jumpin' Joe Gerlach, who was a former Hungarian Olympic team diver and now a daredevil who jumped out of a hot air balloon from one hundred feet above the ground into a huge air mattress. If he missed that air mattress, he got squashed. I thought it was a great act, so I told Hadhazy to see if we could book it. I thought it would be a great thing for ABC. Even if the game was terrible, they'd have something to talk about.

I told Peter this would be the summation of a disastrous season if he missed the mattress. He didn't, but when he landed, a cannon boomed, so you had to wait until the smoke cleared to be sure. In the midst of it, F. Lee Bailey, the infamous trial attorney, came down from Billy's box. He said he wanted to let me know Billy said if Jumpin' Joe had splattered it would have been the end of us. Then he disappeared. Pretty soon I'd join him.

A week later we went to Miami and were destroyed, 52–0. It was our sixth straight loss. On the plane home, Mazur allegedly quit. At least that's what Billy said but I never believed him. I think he fired Mazur but wanted to make it look like he didn't.

Mazur looked exhausted. The pressure was mounting because of the one-year contract, but he was also an ex-Marine who prided himself on his toughness. I don't believe he would ever quit although he said he did.

I never said, "I told you so," but it was a self-fulfilling prophecy. I kept thinking, "They got what they deserved." The organization wasn't put into a position to win. My hands were tied as his were. He was coaching for his job every week. You can't rebuild that way. He never had a chance.

Tom Beer, an erudite backup tight end of ours, later wrote a book called *Sunday's Fools* about life in the NFL. He claimed the players hated to see me coming, but I don't know about that. He claimed some of the coaches called me Napoleon, but later he wrote me a Christmas card I still have that said, "Upton: A lot of the guys were behind you. It's unfortunate what happened . . . You turned the team from a 'can of worms' to a 1st class organization."

With Mazur gone I suggested we bring in Phil Bengston, who was with San Diego's front office and had been Lombardi's defensive coordinator and later head coach in Green Bay, as a consultant and interim head coach. Billy agreed and also asked for my list of coaching candidates.

He wanted college coaches so I gave him Fairbanks, Joe Paterno, and Barry Switzer, and Billy wanted to talk with John McKay, who was still at USC. That was the new kick: college coaches. I gave him one from the pro side too with Schnellenberger at the top. What I didn't know was that he was going to use that list but I wasn't.

Billy said he'd talk with Bengston because he knew him from

the navy, so I actually never spoke with him before he got there. It didn't make any difference to me anymore, but can you imagine making a move like that without the general manager talking to him?

Bengston and I got along fine, and agreed something had to be done about Garrett, the running back I'd traded for Duane Thomas but had to take back the year before. Whatever problems Garrett had, they seemed to be getting worse, but Mazur ignored them.

John protected people when he shouldn't. That was one thing I objected to. He was letting Garrett get away with not showing up for practice and then playing him.

In a meeting with the players, I explained not only the Garrett situation but also why Mazur had resigned. I told them we all bore responsibility for what happened and that Bengston would be evaluating them all for the rest of the season. The same day Garrett missed practice for the twelfth time that season and I suspended him. It had gotten ridiculous. We sent a letter to Carl and his agent informing them. They said we couldn't do it but we did it.

Garrett, channeling his inner Allen Iverson, told the press, "I don't think you have to practice to be perfect. I can do my thing on Sunday without practice. It doesn't say in any contract that you have to practice. All it says is you have to play those fourteen games."

Not quite, but he brought a grievance and I flew to New York to argue our case, and who shows up on Garrett's behalf? Our captain, Jon Morris, who was the player rep. He was pleading his case with one of the union's lawyers, and it pissed me off. He was making excuses for a player who wouldn't practice, claiming his wife was sick. I asked them which one? I told Morris the one he said wasn't feeling well wasn't the one he was living with. He didn't have much of a response.

Three weeks later we were playing the Dolphins at home on December 3. I'm in my box before the game and see professionally printed signs across the stadium: "Fire Upton Bell." I never found out how they got there, but there were people who told me Billy planted them. I don't know that and couldn't prove it.

After another loss, Shula came up to my office, which was very unusual after a game. Usually you just go to the locker room and then get on one of your buses and leave. He said he wanted to make sure I was okay. He saw those signs and was disturbed by them. We could both sense when someone was in trouble.

The next morning Billy called and asked me to come to a meeting at the Red Fox Motel on Monday morning. I knew what it was about. We had two games left but I didn't.

When I arrived that morning, Billy was there with the executive committee. He said I'd done a good job but they'd decided to go in another direction. He told me they thought it was a one-man job, coach and GM. Then Billy said he hoped I wouldn't go away mad, and I stopped him right there and pointed a finger at him and said, "I think you, Billy, have hurt my career." I looked right at him. Then I pointed to the rest of the board and said, "That goes for the rest of you, too."

When I walked out there was a sense of relief, not anger. This had been a two-year stations of the cross and now it was over. I returned to the stadium and thanked everyone at the stadium for the work they'd done under a lot of pressure and walked out with a few things. As I was coming out, I ran into that gnarly old sportswriter Cliff Keane.

"How you doing, Mr. GM?" is what he said to me. I wasn't sure if he knew what had happened or not, but I told him good. He said he'd come down to get a comment on the NFL reversing Garrett's suspension. Garrett was now free to come back.

I told him that was great but I had to go to a meeting. He never knew I'd been fired. I was leaving and a player who refused to practice was coming back. It was a fitting way to end things in New England.

Not long after the word got out, Hadhazy got a call from Carroll Rosenbloom, who had gotten a call from Billy saying he was concerned the people I had brought in would all quit. Rosenbloom told him not to quit and to tell the scouts I brought in not to. Then he told him, "I'll make sure that little SOB never works in the NFL again." The message was clear. Nobody was to leave Billy.

Carroll had been my father's friend. He'd given me and my brother our start in pro football. We had done a good job for him. But we were renters. I never spoke to Carroll Rosenbloom again. What was I going to say? Owners side with owners. He was probably still pissed I'd told John Steadman, the sports editor of the *Baltimore News-American*, the first year I was in New England that I didn't think season ticket holders should have to buy preseason tickets.

A day later, Don Klosterman, Carroll's GM, called telling me how terrible it was what had happened. He wanted to hear my side so I told him. He said not to worry about it. Things would work out. I didn't hear from him again for ten years. That was Don but it was also the new NFL. We'd gone from football first to finances first, and from no bullshit to all bullshit.

I didn't hear from Bucko immediately, but I understood. He grew up in an era where you were very careful. My other scouts called, but not Bucko. He was back in that phone booth like in Dallas. He understood you didn't survive in New England if you weren't Billy's man. That's why I never held it against him. Bucko was one of life's great survivors. He had the talent to do the job but he also had a great gift. He knew how to survive working for Billy Sullivan for twenty years.

Bob Terpening told me later Bucko had our draft information packed up and asked him to help carry it to their cars. Bob asked why he was doing that. He said, "Leverage!" That was Bucko. I loved Bucko.

On the surface I was fired because we went from 6-8 to 2-12, but that wasn't the real reason. Neither was the rift over Mazur. The real reason was about power.

He didn't want to win because if somebody wins, Billy is out of the picture. He was always stepping in to save the franchise from a bad coach, bad management, bad players. That's the propaganda he was selling the board.

That off-season they hired Chuck Fairbanks as head coach and general manager. He used those two No. 1 picks I'd left behind to draft John Hannah and Sam Cunningham and complete the rebuilding process I started. The Patriots began winning two years later, but by 1978 he and Sullivan were at odds just as I had been. Billy and his son Chuck refused to honor a deal Fairbanks struck with Hannah and Leon Gray, the team's best linemen, to end their holdout.

Fairbanks announced he was leaving at the end of that season for Colorado, but Sullivan fired him before the final game and appointed two assistants as co–head coaches. Two days later, under pressure from the league and his lawyers, Billy reversed his decision and Fairbanks returned for the first home playoff game in the club's history, but the team got blown out 31–14. Billy sued Fairbanks for breach of contract and Fairbanks was forced to admit working for Colorado while still with the Patriots. Colorado bought out the remainder of his contract. Fairbanks was gone.

Pretty soon the Patriots were losing again. They couldn't sustain anything because Billy's way of operating wouldn't allow it, but it did allow him to survive even after the board of directors fired him as managing partner two years after I left. He blamed me for starting his problems. In the end he beat them too, but they never won anything until he was gone. They did reach the Super Bowl in 1985, which is a feat in itself, but were blown out by the Chicago Bears, 46–10. It was one of the worst defeats in Super Bowl history.

14

A New League, a Second Chance

By early in my second season in New England, I remembered what it was like to operate with a solid owner and sound organization behind me and what life was like with the opposite in place. Although there were significant differences, in both cases one thing was constant: All employees serve at the whim of the owner.

It didn't matter if you're Don Shula or John Mazur or Simple Simon, there was no real security. The better the organization the better the chance of winning, of course, but you have only limited control over the environment unless you have the final word, and that resides with the owner. And so an old desire festered not far below the surface until my cousin George Bell approached me with another chance to do what I most wanted: to own an NFL team.

George was working at Dillon, Read, one of the most powerful investment banks in New York. Its chairman at the time was Nicholas Brady, the future treasury secretary under Ronald Reagan. When Dillon, Read called a captain of industry, the captain picked up the phone.

George had always told me if I ever wanted to try again to put a franchise offer together, he'd work with me, so when I heard the league was planning to expand to Tampa and Seattle, I called him. What I proposed didn't interfere with the job of rebuilding the Patriots, so I told him let's pursue it.

We met with many Dillon, Read clients who might have an interest, including Marshall Field's people in Chicago and potential investors from Tampa as well as a wealthy investor Shula suggested. We got many meetings because of Dillon, Read's connections but nobody was committing, because the franchise fee was $16 million.

I kept telling anyone who would listen that the day was coming soon when the television money would be worth so much that $16 million would be a drop in the bucket. The investors looked at me like I was crazy. They couldn't see where the NFL was headed.

My cousin and Bill Ford, who owned the Lions, were classmates and friends at Yale, so George kept calling to ask him about the expansion plan and who we were up against. Ford told him it wasn't a great investment. When George told me that, I said, "Then why's he in it?"

Our idea was we'd get a small percentage of the team in exchange for serving as managing general partner. That was the same kind of arrangement Al Davis started out with at the Raiders.

I called Joe Robbie for advice. Like me he had very little money but had put a group together and bought the Miami Dolphins. I could see franchise values increasing, so buying a team the way I would have to do it wasn't going to be possible much longer. You can find a partner willing to put up $16 million and let you run it, but it's not so easy to find a partner willing to put up $116 million and let you run it.

Several months after I was fired in New England, I was invited to a symposium on the future of sports and met a young man from Babson College, a business school outside Boston. His name was Edsel Ford II, the son of Henry Ford II. His father was running the Ford Motor Company, and his uncle had bought the Lions ten years earlier for $4.5 million. Now franchises were selling for $16 million. The uncle, Bill Ford, was telling us it wasn't a good business, but it looked pretty good to me.

Edsel was only about twenty-five at the time, and we hit it off. He was interested. I felt if we had Edsel as the major partner, we would only need to add a local partner from Tampa. So George and I went to Detroit to meet with Pierre "Pete" Heftler, the Ford family attorney. If we didn't get by Pete Heftler to okay it, it wasn't happening.

After we explained our proposition, it came down to two or three things. I wanted 2 to 3 percent of the stock plus a lifetime contract. They could fire me, but I wanted some security since I wouldn't have much ownership. He was really bothered by that.

He kept looking at the financials and saying he didn't see it as a good investment. He said he thought football was a risky game. Whether he was just there to say no or not, I'll never know, but he kept saying, "Why do it?"

I told him the future of pro football wasn't in the stands. It was on television. Television revenue had never gone anywhere but up and no franchise since the late 1940s had sold for a loss. I explained how cable TV was coming and that would only create more value. He looked at me like I was speaking in tongues.

I still remember him saying, "Who's going to pay for TV? We can't do it."

That was it. The gatekeeper had locked the gate to the NFL on me for a final time, but the way things turned out proved I was right about revenues and escalating franchise values.

A Philadelphia developer and construction magnate named Tom McCloskey, who also tried to buy the Eagles back in 1968, ended up having the franchise awarded to him, but there was an economic downturn that concerned him and he was going through a divorce and got cold feet. He missed the first down payment on the $16 million and on December 5, the league, growing worried, asked for the full $16 million. He refused.

That left the league in an embarrassing position, so it turned to a Jacksonville tax attorney and developer named Hugh Culverhouse who'd already been screwed once by Rosenbloom but now was going to benefit from that experience.

In 1972 Culverhouse thought he had a handshake agreement to buy the Rams from Dan Reeves for $17 million only to learn Reeves sold him out for an additional $2 million to Robert Irsay, who immediately swapped franchises with Carroll. Carroll got the Rams, Irsay got the Colts, they both got a tax break, and Culverhouse got a lawyer.

He reached a settlement that included a promise from Carroll to help him secure a franchise when the league expanded. Culverhouse was offered the Seattle franchise in 1974 but didn't want it because it was three thousand miles from home. When McCloskey backed out, Art Rooney and his expansion committee turned to Culverhouse again.

When Rozelle called, Culverhouse did what businessmen do. He negotiated better terms, which turned out to be paying the $16 million over seven years. Culverhouse then sold 48 percent of the team to a Cincinnati financier named Marvin Warner for $9.6 million. He was already going to receive $2 million a year from the league's television deal, and by 1978 that had ballooned to $5 million a year per club.

Culverhouse quickly bought out Warner, and the Buccaneers became one of the most profitable franchises in the league. That was partly because Culverhouse was not a sportsman. He was a businessman-investor, which isn't the same thing by a long shot. He was a tough negotiator with the union, notoriously cheap, and far from obsessed with winning. His team payroll was regularly near the bottom of the league but his profit margin was near the top.

In 1989, for example, the Bucs went 5-11 but were the NFL's second most profitable franchise at $6.3 million. That year the San Francisco 49ers won the Super Bowl but lost $16.2 million. The Bucs won nothing with the second lowest payroll in the league but made $20 million more than the 49ers. Culverhouse was a new breed of owner who generally put profit ahead of performance.

After he died in 1994, Culverhouse's estate sold the team to a Palm Beach businessman named Malcolm Glazer for $192 million. It was the largest fee ever paid for a sports franchise at the time and $176 million more than Culverhouse paid twenty years earlier. In 1995, the same year Glazer bought the Bucs, expansion franchises in Jacksonville and Charlotte sold for $206 million each, nearly a $190 million rise in entry cost to the NFL in the twenty years since I tried to buy the Buccaneers. When I read those numbers, I wondered if Bill Ford and Pierre Heftler would still say pro football was a risky investment.

That was the end of my efforts to buy an NFL franchise. That dream was dead. It simply was no longer possible to do it the way so many had at the start—without any money. The last ones to do it were Robbie, Al Davis, and Billy Sullivan. They were all AFL men. The NFL was already past doing business that way. Now you had to have your own money or you didn't have a chance at ownership.

You weren't getting in anymore for $2,500 cash like my father or the 1974 equivalent of that. This was the new NFL. It was more and more centered not on how good the football people were but how good the tax attorney, marketing and sales people, and businessmen were. That drives the value of franchises today.

Around that time I was having dinner with Bob Schmertz, who owned the Boston Celtics, and I asked him why sports people weren't running sports leagues any more. He couldn't have been more forceful in his reply.

"All sports are changing," he told me back in 1974. "Lawyers are going to be running all these leagues. The game now has more to do with the finances and the legal part of it than it does with people who know sports."

He was certainly right. In fact, he told me future commissioners would not be sports people. They would be lawyers and businessmen. Soon the NFL commissioner's office would reflect that change. After Rozelle retired unexpectedly in 1989, he was replaced by a Washington lawyer, Paul Tagliabue, after a bitter battle. That was the point of no return.

The commissioner had gone from an ex-football player in my father to a former GM in Rozelle to a Washington lawyer to a marketing executive today in Roger Goodell. Jim Finks, who was a pure football man, looked like he was next in line after Pete retired, but he got his legs cut out from under him by the Chicago Eight, a group of new-guard owners led by Jerry Jones, who had just bought the Cowboys. That group had enough votes to block Finks and enough stamina to hold out. Eventually the other owners caved and settled on Tagliabue when it should have been Finks.

That would have been three great executives in a row running the NFL, men who understood both the game and the business. Instead that speeded up what was already happening in the 1970s. The league was going from a football organization that did business, to a business organization that does football. I would argue that despite its unprecedented popularity today, much of its problems are a result of having forgotten what product they're really selling.

Despite those kinds of changes and my own disappointment at how things ended in New England, my intention was to remain in pro football. Not long after I was fired, I was told by a few NFL people that I might be out for a couple years because some of the owners were upset with me for getting into a public fight with Billy. I didn't think a lot about it, but as things went along that was pretty accurate.

I met with the Cardinals' owner, Billy Bidwell, about becoming director of football operations. I met with Art Modell in Cleveland and George Allen in Washington about GM jobs. Bidwell hired Larry Wilson, who had been a Hall of Fame safety for him. Larry became director of scouting that year and later general manager, so that made sense.

I never heard back from the others, but Bidwell did say to me, "Maybe you should have talked less about Billy Sullivan." At thirty-five you don't think you may never get back in, but it was becoming obvious something was going on.

All I'd ever said was that things in New England were impossible. Their track record was my defense. The other owners knew what the problems were, but it's such a small industry that if you get in a beef with a powerful person, especially an owner, you may not work. They can put you on ice, which is what happened to me.

It was many years before I spoke with Billy again, but that didn't mean things were settled.

When I was first named general manager, I'd arranged a deal with Chrysler for most of our front office and coaches to get cars. Sullivan had Hadhazy call me saying he wanted my car back. I told him I would not return the car until the contract was finished. The Patriots leaked that to an iconoclastic sportswriter named George Kimball, who wrote a column at an alternative weekly called the *Boston Phoenix*. Billy told Kimball the board of directors discussed buying me a Toyota if I gave the car back. It was a pretty funny column.

What wasn't funny was they started missing paychecks. Instead of every two weeks it would be once a month. I finally had to go to the management council to adjudicate it. In the end I kept the car but I also bought a Toyota. I got paid, too. Rarely on time but I did get paid. Life is seldom huge victories. Life is small victories and sometimes big disappointments.

I'd had my share of both in New England but now I was out of the NFL family. I still thought I'd get back in, though, so I turned down a chance to become executive director of the Boston Ballet and kept looking for my next team. Around that time, the late spring of 1974, a Boston attorney named Bob Caporale, who worked for the law firm that helped set up Stadium Realty Trust for the Patriots, and a young entrepreneur named Howard Baldwin called with a proposition.

Baldwin owned the New England Whalers of the World Hockey Association (WHA) and now was part of a new summer football league that was already in motion, the World Football League (WFL). They wondered if I'd be interested in a team.

I'd heard of the league of course, so when Baldwin asked me to fly to Newport Beach, California, to meet with its founder, Gary Davidson, I agreed. I wasn't interested yet in saying no to football.

The first thing that struck me was that Davidson had some pretty fancy offices for a league just starting out. He'd already started the American Basketball Association and the WHA and in both cases been given a franchise and quickly sold it for a profit. He'd done the same thing in the WFL with the Philadelphia Bell. He knew how to make a buck and run a hustle.

I had a lot of questions about the WFL's financial stability, because it wasn't supposed to start until 1975 but had been rushed into existence a year ahead of schedule when the NFL went on strike, and there were rumors another league might start up. While NFL players were wearing T-shirts that said "No Freedom No Football," the WFL was playing games.

Davidson said he had some franchises available, which didn't sound good to me since their season had already begun, but the NFL had twenty-five franchises go belly up between 1925 and 1946, so I understood how it worked.

Davidson never once talked about football. He talked about prices of franchises and big crowds for their early games. He was like a football hustler's version of Donald Trump. He was fast-talking, but you couldn't be quite sure about what. I didn't know that soon they'd get caught wallpapering the house in a lot of cities, but I knew there was trouble, because there's always trouble at a start-up.

What was clear was he wanted me in the league because of my father's name and what I'd done with the Colts. He felt the Bell name had some value and added some legitimacy to the WFL. Maybe it did, but I didn't like the idea of Davidson being commissioner. I thought he was a salesman who belonged on Wall Street. He was a hustler.

Davidson wanted a team in New York for the TV market. The team played out on Randall's Island, which was barely accessible from most of the city, but that didn't matter to Davidson. It was in New York and that was good enough for him.

Caporale said he'd look around for a troubled franchise and see if I was interested. The first was the Detroit Wheels, but the wheels were already coming off, so I passed. Then he asked if I might be interested in the New York Stars because Schmertz, who'd bought it and then partnered with Baldwin when Baldwin's Boston team couldn't get off the ground, was having financial problems.

Schmertz had lost a lawsuit involving ownership of the Celtics, and his major asset, a business called Leisure Technology, had been hit hard by the recession. Its stock had fallen from $34.75 a share in 1970 to $2.25 by August 1974. Add a divorce in there and you're looking at a motivated seller.

I said I might be interested but only if I could take the team to

Charlotte, North Carolina. Baldwin thought he had a better shot convincing David Merrick, the Broadway producer, to buy the team for $4 million, so he went to him first. In his recent memoir, *Slim and None*, Howard claimed that would have cleared all the debt but left no profit so Schmertz refused the offer. When Schmertz's situation worsened, he asked Baldwin to revive that deal, but Howard claimed Merrick told him, "You tell that partner of yours I wouldn't pay a dollar for that team. He had his chance. It's over."

With that avenue closed, another one opened for me. I could get a six-month option to buy it for $1 million and I wouldn't have to put up a nickel! I'd have to go find investors, but I was used to that.

Caporale and I flew to Charlotte to meet with John Belk, who was the mayor and one of the richest men in the South and whose family owned the Belk Department Store chain, which was all over the South. I'd spent years scouting Charlotte and thought it was a ripe environment for pro football.

When I first got to the Colts, there was something called the Continental League and I told Moley I wanted to scout it. This was 1964. I went to Charlotte to see a wide receiver named Winston Mapp and I was impressed by the city. There were big banks there and no competition.

Belk said they'd welcome us and gave me a key to the city. I remember thinking, what locks will this open? As it turned out, quite a few.

By now it was September and the twenty-game WFL season was nearly 75 percent complete. It appeared the league might be as well. In the first few weeks of a season that began in July, WFL attendance exceeded that of the early days of the AFL, averaging around forty-three thousand a game. But it quickly came to light that teams in Philadelphia and Jacksonville had given away or steeply discounted nearly all their tickets.

In Detroit the thirty-three investors who owned the Wheels were in desperate shape and being forced to pay in advance to fly their team to games. The Florida Blazers in Orlando, which were run by my former scout Rommie Loudd, couldn't meet payroll.

The Houston team had already moved to Shreveport, Louisiana, and now the New York Stars were ready to pack their bags. Attendance was down, expenses were up, and in many places the players hadn't been paid in weeks and in some cases months.

So why did I sign on? Although I was realistic about the league's chances, it was football and football was my life.

Charlotte had a good market and an available stadium that held about twenty-four thousand people. The Stars had a competitive roster and I figured if we sold out the last four games, the revenue would pay the payroll and I'd have time to find backers.

After I got the lay of the land in Charlotte, some weeks later I flew back to New York and met with Schmertz in his apartment on Fifth Avenue. I didn't intend to put any money down but I told him I'd take an option to buy for six months at $1 million. If I sell it, I sell it. If I don't, I don't. You could see this was a man whose empire was failing but he agreed. Then he did a remarkable thing. I joked about loaning me $15,000 to get started and he took out his checkbook and handed me $10,000. Unbelievable.

I called a press conference for the next day, September 25, 1974. That's the day I sort of became owner of a professional football team. I didn't really own it but I didn't need to. I had the option and the first thing I'm doing is packing up the Stars and moving them out of New York. It was like George Halas buying the Decatur Staleys in 1921 and moving them to Chicago. It was the early days of the NFL repeating themselves, because this was the eighth franchise shift since the twelve-team WFL was founded a year earlier. Pro football had come full circle. It was the Wild, Wild West again. At least in the WFL it was.

So we shook hands and I went back to Howard's hotel and we scheduled the press conference to announce the Stars were leaving. I assumed no one would show up. Then we called our coach, Babe Parilli, around midnight to tell him he was moving to Charlotte. He was in shock. I told him he and I were going down the next day and it would be great. He didn't seem reassured.

Next morning I walked into that press conference and there was media from all over. If the team's games got that much coverage, it would still be in New York! Even Howard Cosell was there. I couldn't believe it.

Baldwin explained why we were leaving and then introduced the person who was taking over. Me.

Cosell starts snorting, "You are leaving the greatest city in the world for Charlotte, North Carolina? Are you kidding me?" He was like a one-man thundering herd.

I said we had to decide if we were going to stay in New York and take a bath or move to Charlotte where we had a chance of making some money. The Stars had only drawn 8,050 fans for their last two home games, 3,830 in a rainstorm and 4,220 two nights earlier against the Wheels. Cosell didn't care, he kept banging away at the whole idea. He kept asking, "Where's Schmertz?" I had no idea nor did I give a damn. I was heading to Charlotte.

I needed to secure a place to practice and play because our first home game was October 9, just fifteen days away, but I had that in motion. When we finished I met Babe at the airport and he looked shell-shocked. I told him they want the franchise down there. No one wanted them at Randall's Island.

When we got to Charlotte that afternoon for a packed press conference, it couldn't have gone better. We announced that tickets for our first home game against the Memphis Southmen, one of the best teams in the league, would go on sale that night. We didn't have a ticket office so we sold them out of six rooms and in the lobby of the Manger Motel, and people started lining up. In a day we sold 6,500 season tickets for the remaining four games and around 5,000 individual game tickets. The Chamber of Commerce, headed by Bill Hensley, was taking ticket orders too and sold over 600. It was like the people felt it was their civic duty. It was like Baltimore in 1953.

The city auditor, T. L. Bent, showed up with $570 and bought nineteen sets of season tickets at $7.50 a game. There literally were lines around the corner. We sold out the Memphis game in a couple of days.

The team came down a day later and we got them out to Belmont Abbey, a small college a few miles from downtown. It was a beautiful practice facility and we got everything for next to nothing.

The two papers started a contest to name the team, and 564 different names were submitted. I settled on the two most popular, the Metros and the Hornets. There were 252 nominations for the Metros and 188 for the Hornets, but I liked the latter because it went back to the American Revolution when the British general Charles Cornwallis called the area a hornet's nest because of how fiercely the people opposed the British. I thought the name was more appropriate.

Our first game was on the road, and I was in a state of euphoria when the team left for Chicago to play the Fire in my first game as owner. I insisted we change the Stars logo and told our equipment man, Tiger Ferraro, to come up with a temporary one. When the team landed in Chicago, he and his son went around to some print shops but couldn't come up with anything. We were still the Stars for another week, but we needed to get that "NY" off our helmets.

Being resourceful, Tiger finally called the equipment manager of the Bears, explained his plight, and bought one hundred letter "C" Bears logos for $150 and stuck them over the "NY" on our helmets. Maybe we weren't the NFL, but that night we had something in common with the Bears—their logo. Try that in today's marketing-driven NFL and see how many lawyers call you.

TVS, a small network that televised the WFL's Thursday Night Game of the Week, decided not to show the Detroit Wheels as scheduled because the stands would be nearly empty and opted to do our game in Chicago. Unfortunately, it was scheduled for Wednesday night, not Thursday night. No problem. The league moved the dominos the way my father used to on our kitchen table when he was making up the NFL schedule.

Back in Charlotte, we were selling tickets like mad. In the span of a week I'd signed a deal with WBT Radio to have our games broadcast too. They were going to do play-by-play and a pre- and postgame show. I'm not sure they paid for it but I just wanted us on the air.

I still hadn't found any investors because I was too busy finding a stadium, a practice field, an office, and a logo. My first move
for an investor came after we beat the Fire. Dick Thigpen, my
attorney, and Bill Hensley of the Chamber of Commerce suggested I meet with Gar Laux, who was managing Arnold Palmer's business affairs. He later arranged for me to meet Arnold,
who owned one of the biggest Cadillac dealerships in the area. I
invited him to our game.

I was in no hurry to get an investor at that point because there
was so much to set up first. You can't just go in and say, "How
about investing in this thing that doesn't exist?" But as part of
welcoming us, Arnold and Gar arranged for me to have the use
of a gold Cadillac. It had Arnold's name on the back. They figured if I'm going to be driving all over the city, why not advertise?

On October 9, American Legion Memorial Stadium was packed.
My team's first home game had sold out: 25,133 fans jammed the
place to watch us lose a close game, 27–23, to the Memphis Southmen. We fell behind and then rallied but fell just short. The fans
didn't care. Pro football had come to Charlotte and they loved it.

Arnold showed up that night for the game and later for a big
party we threw for many of Charlotte's VIPs. In fact, the *Charlotte
Observer* had as much coverage of the party and Arnold as they
did of the game. The good news is that Arnold and his company
later invested $5,000 in the team. He said he'd be at future games
with his salesmen, but he didn't want any television cameras on
him. I told the TV people that I didn't want any cameras put on
Arnold. Meanwhile I was about to learn that Schmertz owed the
league money, which I was not aware of when we shook hands
in New York.

The next day I met with Luther Hodges, who had become chairman of the North Carolina National Bank at the age of thirty-eight.
The meeting was arranged by a former classmate of his at the
Harvard Business School, Bob Kenney, who at the time was head
of the Boston Redevelopment Authority. Hodges would enter politics three years later and be replaced by another young man on
the rise, Hugh McColl, who would transform NCNB into the giant

that is now Bank of America. Both men wanted to help Charlotte grow and saw the Hornets as potentially a part of that growth.

Within a week or so, we had rent-free office space in one of the bank's buildings. Luther gave it to us. People treated you differently in Charlotte than in New York. They wanted to help you succeed.

Nobody wanted that more than Schmertz, who kept calling looking for his money. He wasn't alone. I was getting calls from businesses around New York claiming Schmertz owed $15,000 here, $20,000 there. I didn't want to be sued so we reincorporated, but that didn't end the calls.

I was spending most of my time trying to raise money while stories were breaking about the league collapsing. My feeling was the sooner we got Davidson out the better. He was like the Wizard of Oz. There was nothing behind the curtain. We needed a visionary, not a huckster.

The same month we arrived in Charlotte, the league folded the Wheels and the Jacksonville Sharks, so we were down to ten teams. We also had to relocate World Bowl I, which was supposed to be played at the Gator Bowl in Jacksonville. The league's credibility was suffering, but the Hornets were not.

We drew 20,333 the next week and shut out the Fire and had another near sellout of 23,613 lined up for October 23 against the Florida Blazers. We were proving Charlotte was a viable place for pro football. If the worst-case scenario happened and the league folded, I believed we'd have a shot at NFL expansion or being absorbed into the league the way teams from previous leagues had been. That's the reason I agreed to pay the Blazers' salaries that week.

That may sound odd, but Davidson told me the Blazers couldn't afford to fly up and hadn't made payroll in weeks. No airline would take their check and a judge was ready to serve an injunction to stop the game. I told Davidson to pay it but he said the league was out of cash.

Dick Thigpen, my attorney, and I then negotiated directly with the judge from Thigpen's office. We came up with an agreement to pay the Blazers' traveling expenses and guarantee each of their players $1,000 to avoid canceling the game. What came into my mind? Art Rooney sending money to my father to keep the Eagles going. That's why I didn't get discouraged. It was pro football history repeating itself.

After I confirmed those facts with the Blazers, I called Davidson back, but one of his assistant said he wasn't available. When I asked why, he said he was playing tennis. The WFL is falling down all around us and the commissioner is working on his backhand? Was he out of his mind or was I out of mine?

I finally got a call back from Davidson's office saying they needed a certified check for $60,000 to cover the flight and the player's salaries. I got it and joined perhaps the smallest fraternity in professional sports. I had just financed my opposition.

When the game was over, they'd beaten us 15–11 and I'm handing them paychecks. Their quarterback, Bob Davis, thanked me. He said it was the first one he'd seen in a month. You had to feel sorry for them, but I was also feeling sorry for myself.

Financially we were able to manage that, but the mortal blow came a week later when I got a call from Davidson's office saying Schmertz owed $100,000 in league fees and if we didn't pay they were going to pull my franchise. I didn't care if Davidson ever got paid, but he had a legal document. Somebody had to pay it.

Paying it would cut our margin to the bone with three games to go, but what choice did I have? The league's associate legal counsel, Tim Grandi (whom I called the bag man), flew in. It was like seeing the hangman coming, but I gave him the money. I tried to convince him to take fifty cents on the dollar, but no way. Obviously, if they pulled our franchise, how could I raise any money? Even if I got an injunction to play, who would invest then? I was between a rock and a hard place, which is a lot like life. I'd just hit another rock.

We drew 19,436 for our last home game, but now we weren't making payroll and didn't have enough cash on hand, so I called a meeting and told my players the truth. I didn't think we could make the payroll because the league came in and took $100,000. I already had problems with withholding taxes so the best I could do was pay them $1,000 a game for the rest of the season.

I told them I appreciated what they'd done and if they didn't want to play they didn't have to. Finally Gerry Philbin, who had been a fine defensive lineman on the Jets team that beat my Colts in Super Bowl III, got up and said he'd agree to it but he wanted to see the books. When's the last time any team let a player see the books?

I had no problem with it, because I knew what they said. They were written in red ink. He took a look and just said, "Okay," and left. So that's how we finished that season. The players knew I hadn't paid myself anything. Maybe that's one reason they stayed.

I didn't make the trip to Shreveport for our game with the Steamers on November 6, because I was busy trying to find investors. I was sitting at home, listening to our game on the radio, when our business manager, Ken Bogdanoff, called me after the game, which we lost. He said that at halftime the Caddo Parish sheriff, Jimmy Goslin, showed up in the locker room with a court order to seize our uniforms and equipment for failure to pay $26,216 in cleaning fees and security costs run up by the Stars in New York. Sheriff Goslin had our uniforms and equipment under house arrest.

It turned out Goslin had received a federal court order during the day and could have shut down the game, but he waited because he wanted it to go on. I told Ken to put the team on the plane and come home. Our players did get to keep one piece of equipment. They kept their cleats because they'd paid for them.

I got the uniforms back after agreeing to honor the debt, because they were worthless to that cleaning person as collateral. It wasn't like he owned a football team. Of course neither did I.

By that time, Davidson had been forced to resign after a run-in with Chicago Fire owner Tom Origer and growing disillusionment with him among ownership. I was happy to see him go, but I also understood it didn't solve the WFL's problems. What I also felt was I had the right city, the right TV market, and the right players. If I couldn't raise the money, I believed I had the right kind of option too, which is one where I didn't have to pay Schmertz anything. So I wasn't really sweating it. I believed Charlotte would find a home in the NFL at some point. It did but it came twenty years too late for me.

Even though we'd finished with a four-game losing streak, we were 10-10 and preparing for a rematch with the Blazers in the playoffs when John Bassett, who owned the Memphis team and was on the WFL's executive committee, called me three days after the regular season ended. By then I'd come to hate Alexander Graham Bell for inventing the telephone. It was 3:30 in the afternoon. It's frozen in time in my memory.

Bassett informed me the Blazers had sold less than 1,000 tickets for the game, so there was nothing there for us. It would cost us money we didn't have just to show up, so the league replaced us with the Philadelphia Bell and put that game on TVs instead. I assumed this was about the size of Philadelphia's television market. It was a reminder that pro football was in some ways becoming a prisoner of a box in people's living room.

The executive committee had changed the playoff format to include only teams that were financially solvent plus the Blazers, who weren't but who had the best record in the league. We'd been eliminated from the playoffs because our opponent was broke and couldn't sell any tickets. We hadn't been knocked out, we'd been voted out. There wasn't anything I could do about it, so I hung up.

Considering all that happened that season, it would have been fitting if we'd renamed our league championship game Broke Bowl I. It featured the indigent Florida Blazers versus the insolvent Birmingham Americans on national television. It only took place because the IRS agreed to accept a portion of the gate receipts in lieu of $237,000 in federal taxes owed by the Americans.

The Americans agreed to the arrangement, but their players hadn't been paid in weeks and threatened to boycott. The Americans' owners settled matters by agreeing to buy them championship rings if they won. It says a lot about football players that they accepted. Most would play for nothing. In this case they did.

Birmingham jumped out to a 22–0 lead, but the Blazers rallied to cut it to 1 when the final gun sounded. I don't know if the Americans ever got their rings, but after the game their uniforms were seized and their office furniture was repossessed the next day. Alice in Wonderland had nothing on me at that point. My first season as an owner had ended. Who knew if there would be another?

15

No More Fish in the Sea

Had Chris Hemmeter been the original commissioner of the World Football League instead of Gary Davidson, it might have survived long enough to achieve its primary goal, which was to merge in some form with the NFL. Historically, that has always been the goal of rebel leagues in professional sports.

It had been achieved by the All-America Conference in the 1940s and the American Football League in the 1960s. It had been achieved by Davidson's two other fledgling leagues of the '60s as well, the American Basketball Association and the World Hockey Association. The AFL was a rarity, though, in that the entire league was absorbed into the NFL, an act that seemed to sate the marketplace for expansion for a decade.

In Charlotte we had a prime market and a loyal fan base despite the WFL's many problems and franchise failures. Ultimately it would become a far more viable NFL market than Jacksonville. Both came into the NFL at the same time, but while Charlotte has thrived since its NFL inception in 1995, Jacksonville continues to struggle with stadium and corporate revenue problems many small markets face.

The WFL also had Memphis and Birmingham, which were two football hotbeds, but what we didn't have by the end of the 1974 season was a sound plan or a TV contract. In the end we got the former too late and the latter not at all, in part because the NFL had learned its lesson after its long war with the AFL.

The AFL survived for a decade and finally forced a merger

because it landed a large television contract with NBC in 1965 and had some form of a TV deal from its inception. What the NBC deal made clear to the NFL establishment was that the AFL wasn't going anywhere, but it was going to cost owners on both sides a lot of money in increased player salaries as bidding wars for talent escalated. Faced with that reality, the NFL made a deal.

A decade later, in a lawsuit involving the defunct USFL, a 1973 memo written by the NFL surfaced during discovery. What it said was the league made a tactical mistake in the 1960s by not locking up all three major networks and thus freezing out the AFL. It did not intend to make that mistake again with the World Football League or any league that followed it. It has never merged with nor absorbed any portion of a rebel challenger since. They have all withered away for the same reason the WFL did. Without a lucrative broadcast deal, you can no longer survive.

By 1974 the NFL had exclusive broadcasting contracts with NBC, CBS, and ABC, thus monopolizing the three major networks. For the WFL there was nowhere to turn but the far smaller TVS network, because this was well before the cable industry explosion that gave us ESPN and FOX as alternatives.

TVS gave each WFL team some initial revenue in exchange for a *Thursday Night Game of the Week*, and all things considered our ratings exceeded expectations. According to an NTI rating summary, the WFL was shown on 117 stations and reached 80 percent of the country. TVS Network had hoped to achieve a 5 rating and initially reached a 6, but as the credibility issues resulting from collapsing franchises like Detroit, Jacksonville, and Florida spread, ratings plummeted. TVS made money but opted not to pick up its option for 1975, claiming many of the independent stations it dealt with had informed them they had no interest in carrying the games of a league with shaky underpinnings.

The one ray of hope was an ironic one. The renamed Chicago Winds announced it was ready to sign Joe Namath, even changing uniform colors to the Jets' familiar green and white to accommodate him. TVS said if Namath jumped leagues it would pick up the option. The irony was that it was Namath's decision to reject the NFL and sign with the Jets in 1965 for a then record $427,000 that convinced NBC to hand the AFL the five-year, $36 million broadcast rights fee that ensured its continued survival.

The first AFL game NBC televised was the Jets versus the Houston Oilers at Rice Stadium. Joe Namath was on the bench, but no one cared. All that mattered was that he was in uniform. If the Winds could achieve the same thing, the WFL had a chance for survival.

Already saddled with bad knees and limited mobility, Namath had become a target for NFL pass rushers. That was not going to be the case in the WFL, however, because there was a growing consensus among our club owners that if Namath signed, we would make a gentlemen's agreement to keep him upright. Exactly how that could be enforced in the midst of a game remained to be seen, but many of us felt defensive coordinators and even pass rushers could be reasoned with if the league's existence was at stake.

Winds owner Eugene Pullano offered Namath a three-year contract for $600,000 per season, a princely sum in those days. If he took it, we all knew, the WFL was in business. For a time it seemed he would, until Pullano and the league made a short-sighted tactical blunder.

Namath's agent, Jimmy Walsh, was driving a hard bargain, which was his job. He demanded a three-year deal worth $1.5 million plus a $500,000 signing bonus, a $2 million annuity, and a favorable deal for Namath to own a WFL franchise in New York at some point. In his definitive biography *Namath*, writer Mark Kreigel said TVS executive Eddie Einhorn told Hemmeter his affiliates were waiting to see if Namath signed before agreeing to carry the games, so everything was riding on that decision.

Things seemed to be falling in place until Walsh, according to Kreigel's biography, demanded 15 percent of the television package revenue for Namath as well, which frankly wasn't illogical, since there was only going to be a television package if Namath jumped leagues. Instead of seeing the WFL's cup as 85 percent full, the league and Pullano saw it as 15 percent empty and declined, hence ending up with 100 percent of zero. I told many of our owners that this was not the smartest financial move in pro football history, but it would prove to be the most fatal.

Five weeks into the season the Winds were extinguished in Chicago. The entire league lasted only a month longer, strangled to death for many reasons, but a major one was a lack of the shared television revenue Namath's presence would have provided. Before that came about, I had my own fiscal adventures in Charlotte beginning in an empty room at Fort Bragg, the largest military facility in the world.

Not long after World Bowl I, Hemmeter came up with a financing plan based on stability and reality, two things missing the previous year in the WFL. It was discussed at several meetings as were some more exotic financing options.

Rommie Loudd, who was still running the Florida Blazers, got up at one of our league meetings in Memphis before we accepted the Hemmeter Plan and said he was going to get some Saudi Arabian sheiks involved. I laughed out loud. I knew reality and that wasn't it. The Hemmeter Plan issued a January 15, 1975, deadline for all teams to deposit at least $650,000 into a league account to ensure solvency. In addition, player salaries would be based on a percentage of actual revenues, with the average salary 1 percent of team income after taxes. To pay more, the money had to be deposited into an escrow account in advance, thus assuring no repeat of players going months without a paycheck. The projected average player salary was $20,000. That may sound like pocket change compared with today's NFL, but at the time the NFL average was only $30,000.

The plan allocated 42 percent of revenue to player salaries, 10 percent to stadium rental costs, 6 percent to the league, and 3 percent to an injured reserve pool. That left 39 percent for more variable costs like office rent as well as for a profit margin. If you couldn't deposit the minimum amount, you were out.

Around this time the bank moved our offices to the new NCNB Plaza building. It was the best office I ever had, sitting on the thirty-sixth floor overlooking a section of I-77 where ten years earlier a proposal had been made to build a new football stadium. Every day I looked out at a dream.

Luther Hodges liked the Hemmeter Plan and eventually I got five investors to agree to invest, but we didn't make the deadline. The league agreed to extend it to February 15 when I proposed a public offering, selling shares for $100 each with a goal of raising $1.5 million. Mayor John Belk stepped up immediately and pledged his $11,000 salary, which had to be the only time a politician offered to pay for anything.

Also around that time, I had convinced Eastern Airlines to fly our players in for a private meeting with me, Dick Thigpen, and a financial planner. The proposal was to have the players, along with myself, own a percentage of the team. This way they would be investing in their future, and it would not only help solidify us financially but also give them a real sense of ownership. The one sticking point was if a player was traded or picked up by another team, would he still retain his ownership? That proved to be the failure of the plan.

The news of a public offering was all over the papers in North Carolina, which led to some odd encounters. The first was the one at Fort Bragg.

One morning I got a phone call from an officer who wanted us to come to Fort Bragg for a rally. He said he was going to organize a big meeting and thought he could raise five thousand people, maybe even ten thousand, to invest at $100 a share. It didn't take long to say yes.

Upon arriving, I was met by an army officer who took me to a huge arena. I heard this roar like I was entering Boston Garden with Larry Bird. I couldn't believe it. I'd brought some stock forms and thought we wouldn't be able to write fast enough.

I turned to go in the door and he said, "Oh, no, that's another event. Your room is down here." So we came upon this closed door. I opened it and there was no one inside. No one but a writer from the local paper, which was the worst thing that could happen.

Invitations had been sent out but no one had confirmed, although the officer was sure they were coming. The reporter asked what my thoughts were that nobody was here. There was no way to talk my way out of that question.

Not one single person showed up. None. The story made the papers up there and in Charlotte. It didn't deflate me, though. I'd survived a lot by then. There's always hope.

Hope fulfilled is what I thought walked into my office a while later when an investor from Memphis named Paul Sasso showed up. He'd flown into Charlotte on a private jet after calling and telling me he wanted to invest $1 million because he thought the franchise was worth it and the WFL would prosper.

Sasso had a stadium plan and wanted to become the majority owner. He arrived with a beautiful replica of the stadium that we took over to Mayor Belk. It was amazing. I thought we were on our way when Sasso said he would make a good-faith deposit of $100,000 before Memorial Day. My ship had finally come in.

Over the next few days I started getting calls about this man Sasso bragging all over town that he owned the Hornets. A reporter named Bill Ballinger from the *Charlotte News* covered our team. He went on the plane with Sasso and they were flying to Memphis and then on to Toronto, where Sasso said he was going to meet with John Bassett, the WFL's most powerful owner.

Now I learned Sasso's a mystery man, but he's a mystery man with several associates brandishing guns on the plane. That made Ballinger very uncomfortable, and I was starting to wonder about him. I didn't have to wonder long.

I received a call from Larry Tarleton, sports editor of the *Charlotte Observer*, saying he had been picked up by two associates of Sasso and driven to a place outside of Charlotte where he was taken in to meet him. Sasso told him all his plans for the Hornets. Larry thought it was a very strange encounter. In fact, he felt as if he had been kidnapped. The *Observer* later wrote a story about this very strange evening.

A few days later federal agents showed up looking for this man, whose real name was Paul Sassone. He'd been in the Witness Protection Program in Memphis, but they threw him out because his information on the Brooklyn Mafia was unreliable at best and unbelievable at worst. Who gets thrown out of witness protection?

It turned out the man known to us as Paul Sasso had once tried to commit suicide on the Verrazano-Narrows Bridge in New York because some loan sharks were after him. Geraldo Rivera showed up with a film crew and talked him down. His son said that's why he went into witness protection. The only problem was he'd never witnessed anything. He was a con man.

For three or four days there were screaming headlines in both papers. The feds took him back to New York and I quickly lost track of him, but in 1988 he surfaced again, sort of.

Police in Altamonte Springs, Florida, found him dead at fifty-six in the trunk of a 1980 Buick. All his life he'd tried to convince people he had Mob ties and now it appeared he did, but the police concluded it was a suicide. An obituary in a local paper quoted Lieutenant George Hagood of the Seminole County Sheriff's Department saying his death was a mystery that "goes along with every other weird thing he did."

That included his two-week stint in the Witness Protection Program in Memphis, conning a lot of people out of a lot of money and even once using a washer and dryer to clean thousands of moldy dollars dug up in either the Ocala National Forest or at a local drug dealer's backyard. The police weren't sure which. Paul Sasso was the most bizarre character I ever met in or out of sports, but for a couple of days he was the Hornets' savior. That's how desperate things became.

Actually, though, Sasso was a blessing. That incident triggered the bank to feel bad for us. This mystery man had come to Charlotte and tried to hustle their Hornets. The Chamber of Commerce organized a meeting on March 4 of what it hoped would be one hundred possible investors. Only twenty-nine showed up. Eventually around $755,000 in cash and pledges was raised, but on March 31 I announced we were still $345,000 short of the cash needed to meet the WFL's requirement.

It looked like it was over, but on April 15 the WFL again lowered the threshold and North Carolina National Bank covered the remaining $40,000 or so and we were in. I was elated because I still felt strongly about Charlotte. In four games at the end of the 1974 season, we'd shown up out of nowhere and drawn 88,515 fans, an average crowd of 22,129. I still needed to find investors to pay Schmertz, who was still waiting because he had no other option, but we only needed to draw around 14,000 a game at home to otherwise break even.

Other clubs were not in the same circumstance, however. We only had two of the original twelve owners still in the league when our second season began, and many of the new franchise holders had tighter margins than the Hornets. With no television deal to lift our profile, odd ideas surfaced. One of the worst was the "Pants Plan."

On June 30 the league announced we would try a four-game experiment with "color-coded pants" at every position. Offensive linemen wore purple. Running backs green. Receivers were in orange, defensive linemen in blue (wouldn't black and blue have been more appropriate?), linebackers in red, defensive backs yellow, and quarterbacks, of course, in white. Some were also adorned with stars or pinstripes.

It was an idea thought up by William Finneran, the management consultant in New York who came up with the "action point" a year earlier, which allowed you to run or pass for 1 point after scoring a touchdown. Touchdowns were worth 7 points, not 6, and no extra-point kick was allowed. That was a great idea. The Pants Plan? Not so much. We abandoned it after one game.

Before the start of our second season, I let our head coach, Babe Parilli, go, and ironically he ended up in Chicago and would have been Namath's coach if the league wasn't so stupid about signing him. In the meantime, I hired Bob Gibson from Memphis who in turn hired Lindy Infante. Both would go on to be coaches in the NFL. In fact, Infante was a head coach in both Green Bay and Indianapolis. I was very pleased with our coaching staff as well as our roster.

After two exhibition games, our season began in San Antonio, a new franchise, on July 26, in front of 12,375 fans. We lost and then traveled to Memphis to face Bassett's Southmen, which now had NFL refugees Larry Csonka, Jim Kiick, and Paul Warfield. All three had been signed away from my old friend Don Shula, who didn't blame me but wasn't exactly rooting for the WFL to survive.

One of the more bizarre parts of the evening was an invitation to meet Elvis Presley, whom Bassett had convinced to invest a small amount in his team. I was ushered by more security people than the president has to a small box off the press box. What I saw was an overweight, profusely sweating person who seemed to be a shadow of himself. He was very nice and talked in very low tones, but he didn't seem to be paying attention to anything.

We led 11–0 at halftime but ended up losing 23–11, and we headed back to Charlotte for our first home game. Because we'd averaged over 22,000 a game the previous season and only needed 14,000 to break even, I was thrilled to get back to American Legion Memorial Stadium. Apparently my feelings weren't shared by our fans. Only 8,447 showed up. Considering that we only had 3,200 tickets sold by 3 p.m. on game day, I considered it a success, but like most of our successes it wasn't a financial one.

That was the first of four straight wins, and by the time we returned to Memorial Stadium on September 27 our fans were back. We drew just over 17,000 on the kind of beautiful fall night that has people flocking to retire to North Carolina. We lost but came back the next week on the road to beat Shreveport. That night I was happy to see 20,407 in the stands and Sherriff Jimmy Goslin not among them. We left the way we came. With our uniforms.

What turned out to be our final home game came the next Sunday when we faced the Jacksonville Express. We improved our record to 6-4 but I was stunned when only 7,750 showed up to watch. By now it was clear the whole league was in trouble.

Unseen anywhere but on local television, the WFL was disappearing from the collective sports consciousness. Chicago had folded and many of the remaining ten teams were in financial trouble again when we arrived in Philadelphia to play the Bell at Franklin Field on October 18, 1975. It was the same field where my father had been a star quarterback at Penn and where he died in the stands in 1959. It was where he and I had shared many hours of enjoyment as father and son watching the game we both loved and where we shared a final hour of despair together.

I convinced my mother to come, along with five of our investors and Mayor John Belk of Charlotte. It was a damp, dreary night made worse when we entered the stadium and saw only 1,293 fans in the stands. It was a season-low attendance figure, as most Philadelphians were home, warm and dry, watching the defending Stanley Cup champion Flyers on television.

There was an engineers' strike in Philadelphia at the time too and pickets surrounded the stadium. That prevented our local television crew from setting up the equipment needed to broadcast the game. The last game we'd ever play was never seen in Charlotte. We had disappeared.

There was my poor mother, who had sat in so many stadiums watching my father's teams struggle in front of small crowds on dreary nights like this, and now here was her son repeating the same song. She understood when it came to football the Bell boys had no choice. She understood we had fallen in love with a game that refused to love us back quite as much. There's that circle of life again.

I'm not sure what she must have been thinking but I knew what I was thinking. This was the stadium where my father died. Now it was the stadium where his son's struggling team had come to die as well.

Four days later, on October 22, 1975, Hemmeter and representatives of the league's ten teams joined a conference call to discuss the future. After losing an estimated $20 million combined in 1974, we'd already lost another $10 million among the clubs. Players were quitting, coaches like my friend Ron Waller had left in disgust, and the fans were no longer to be found in most cities. We had been effectively delegitimized by virtue of bad management, under-capitalization, greed, and the failure to secure Namath's name on a contract.

We talked for two hours, and by 3 p.m. it was done. A vote was taken to disband and it carried, 6–4. I supported playing on, but I can't say I was shocked. I'd seen my own club's attendance figures plummet. We were averaging 10,940 fans after four home games, less than half our average of the year before. Although I came up with five small investors, I was nowhere near raising the $1 million I needed to fulfill the option, and we were in considerable debt. It was over.

Realizing bad news travels fast, I called our practice facility at Gus Purnell Day Camp, where we'd moved from Belmont Abbey, and pulled our head coach, Bob Gibson, off the practice field to tell him. He met with the team and later so did I. The first thing I told them was that the Charlotte Hornets had not voted to fold. We were ready to play on but were outvoted.

I spoke from my heart. I told them those two years had been the best thing I'd ever done with a group of players. It was what football really was at one time. Some of the players were in tears.

As bad as things got at the end, it was the noblest league I was ever involved with. Players and coaches loved the game. It's a cliché to say they would have played for nothing, but in this case it was true because they did. They would have played with uniforms or without uniforms. They were the purest form of the game. They played for love.

With my wife and son Christopher still up in Boston, I drove home that night to an empty house and told myself this was the end of it. My time as an owner was over.

I've always been a voracious reader, and the character of Santiago from Hemingway's great novel *The Old Man and the Sea* kept coming to mind. Santiago had gone out every day to fish and seldom came back with anything. When he finally caught his great fish, sharks attacked it, and by the time he got back to shore all that was left were bones. Exhausted from the fight, he went home and fell asleep, knowing he would go out again the next morning. I was not Santiago. My fishing for a football team was done.

At thirty-eight years old, I'd come to understand the reality of the modern NFL. The only chance I ever really had to own a team was with Tampa. I could have afforded the WFL, but the reality was the NFL had grown too big for it, or any other league that followed us, to survive.

I had the right town, the right team, and a bank willing to give us an office for next to nothing. You think that would ever happen again? They all knew, deep in the back of their minds, that we weren't going to make it, but they did it anyway just to help us try.

When I got back to the office, I spent a long time looking down on that site near I-77, where the city once had proposed to build a football stadium ten years before the Hornets arrived. That was still the city's dream but it was no longer mine.

I'd worked as hard as I could for sixteen months. I'd lost $100,000 and was as close to broke as I would ever be. If I had it to do over again, I would have done the same thing. Difficult as it was at times—and sometimes it was a nightmare—I loved having my own football team.

The very next day I called Dan Rooney, head of the NFL Expansion Committee, and told him I thought Charlotte was a great city and should be the first one considered for expansion. While I realized I would never be the person, I knew that this city would be a great place for the NFL.

Thirteen days later we filed for bankruptcy protection. We listed $49,132.70 in assets and $267,847.07 in debt. That didn't include Schmertz's $1 million because I didn't have to pay him. It didn't include a loan from Luther Hodges's bank to help us pay off the creditors either. Creditors who were owed $400 or less, which were mostly ticket holders, were paid in full. Those owed more got $400 or 30 percent of the debt, whichever was larger. I personally guaranteed that in the settlement. That was how my time owning a pro football team ended.

Six weeks later, my mother passed away. It was Thanksgiving Day.

16

Scouting for QBs, the Most Important Position in Sports

If I learned anything in all my years searching for football talent, it's that the most difficult thing to find is the quarterback who can make a championship difference. There's a reason so few of them have won so many Super Bowls.

As a scout, you can find a thrower. You can find a runner. You can find a leader with charisma. You can find a lot of players with shotgun arms. But finding the one who can make you a consistent winner is like the Ford Modeling Agency signing a beautiful woman. There are a lot of them, but only a few have "it."

Four quarterbacks have won 31.3 percent of the fifty-one Super Bowls played. Twelve have won 63 percent of them. Twelve out of all the quarterbacks to play since the game was born in 1966. Why so few?

Quarterback is the most important position in any team sport, even though he is surrounded by more players than anyone else. The reason why is he has to do more than simply pass accurately and command the huddle. The great quarterback must also instill fear in the defense yet know no fear himself.

What I learned being around football players for forty years is that if they sense even an inkling of fear or indecision in their quarterback, your team is dead. Forget the opposition. The quarterback first has to convince his own team that he is a man of steel when under pressure. It's not something you can teach or learn. It's a gift and very few players have it.

A competent scout can find a great tight end. He can find a

great wide receiver or running back or lineman. He can even find a great pass rusher or cover corner, although those are rarer. But finding a great quarterback is like searching for King Solomon's Mines. They're enormously valuable and very well hidden.

That's because quarterback is less about the physical and more about the mental than any other position in sports. To me the three greatest guessing games are chess, the pitcher versus the batter, and the quarterback versus a defense. In two of those you only have a few seconds to make your decision, but in only one is there an added factor that separates quarterback from any other position in sports. You're going to get hit. You're going to get hurt.

Al Davis always used to say one of the key elements in winning was that early in a game "the quarterback must go down. He must go down hard. That sets the tone for the game." How the quarterback reacts to that often decides the day.

The snap of the ball means somebody is going to get hit. There's going to be a lot of violence all around you. I don't care how immune you are to being hit, it still hurts. That's what separates football from the other games and quarterback from the other positions.

Can you still think clearly? Can you still process information quickly? Can you still be patient inside the closing confines of the pocket?

That's when you find out what you really have and that's why, in my opinion, there are two who stand out above all the quarterbacks I've seen in my lifetime.

That's one of the great sports debates, isn't it? Who is the greatest quarterback? It's a difficult question, because when you've seen everyone from Sammy Baugh and Sid Luckman in the 1940s to Tom Brady and Peyton Manning today, you understand we're talking about not only different eras but a different game. The game they played in Baugh's day or in Unitas's day or even fifteen years ago is so different from today because of the rules. They've effectively outlawed aspects of defense, or at least they've tried to, in order to protect the quarterback.

So when you're analyzing quarterbacks, there's a factor missing today from most of the eras that preceded this one, and that's the level of violence the quarterback must cope with. You can't minimize that factor.

To me the clear line of demarcation is January 18, 2004. That's the soggy, snowy afternoon the Patriots beat the Indianapolis Colts in the AFC Championship Game, 24–14. Manning was intercepted four times that day, and his receivers were mauled and manhandled by the New England secondary in the great tradition of defensive assault and battery. Ty Law intercepted Manning three times and knocked future Hall of Fame receiver Marvin Harrison around like he was a piñata. Once he literally threw him out of bounds into the Colts' Gatorade bucket. Ty laid down the law, but soon his actions led to the laws being rewritten.

In the ensuing days and months, the Colts, among other teams, complained bitterly that the officials had not enforced the rules on illegal contact, pass interference, and defensive holding on the Patriots' secondary. That led to an instruction going out in the off-season to more strictly enforce those penalties, and that led to a number of rule changes that reduced the defense's ability to hit the quarterback or his receivers, while expanding what has become legalized holding at the line of scrimmage by offensive linemen.

When you add that together, it explains many of the remarkable passing numbers of recent years. That doesn't mean today's quarterbacks aren't incredibly efficient and accurate, but they are playing a different game than Unitas or Baugh or Joe Montana played.

Consider this: Sammy Baugh retired in 1952 after sixteen years in the NFL. His prime seasons were between 1937 and 1948. His career completion percentage was 56.5 percent, which would get you fired today.

Otto Graham, who was the greatest winner in sports history, retired in 1955 after ten years in which he took the Cleveland Browns to ten consecutive championship games and won seven (he also won an NBA title in his only season playing for the Rochester Royals, when the league was known as the NBL, by the way). His team won 81 percent of the time with him at quarterback

(57-13-1 in the NFL and 106-17-4 if the All-America Football Conference years are added, a .835 winning percentage) yet his completion percentage was only 55.8 percent. Today that would have a scout like me looking for his replacement.

Johnny Unitas began his career in 1956 and played eighteen seasons. His career completion percentage was 54.6 percent despite being widely considered the greatest quarterback in NFL history.

Terry Bradshaw won four Super Bowls in the 1970s but completed only 51.9 percent of his throws, and his great rival, Dallas's Roger Staubach, retired after eleven seasons with a 57 percent completion percentage.

The career accuracy numbers were similar for John Elway (56.9 percent) and Dan Marino (59.4 percent), who came into the NFL together in 1983 and played to the edge of the new millennium, retiring in 1998 and 1999 just as Brady and Manning were entering the NFL and just prior to what became a change both in the aim of the passing game and in the tightening of the restrictions on all forms of defensive contact.

The outlier in those decades between Baugh and Brady was Joe Montana, who retired in 1994 after fifteen seasons and four Super Bowl victories with a 63.2 percent completion percentage. Troy Aikman would complete 61.5 percent as well during his twelve-year career, retiring in 2000, another departure from the long-held passing efficiency norm.

So for six decades the best quarterbacks in the NFL were completing between 55 and 59 percent of their passes with the exception of the outlier, Montana, who was to make Bill Walsh's West Coast offense popular by changing pass offense from the vertical game it had been to what Walsh called "the extended handoff." That meant an increasing reliance on short passing in safe areas rather than attacking defenses with deep but less accurate throws.

Couple that strategic shift with the rule changes and you end up with quarterbacks who are seemingly more accurate than their predecessors. But are they? I would argue not, even though Manning retired after winning his second Super Bowl in 2015 with a career completion percentage of 65.3 percent, while Brady entered

2017 with a career 63.8 percent completion percentage and five Super Bowl victories.

Are we really to believe Manning and Brady are 10 percentage points more accurate passers than Johnny Unitas, Sammy Baugh, and nearly all the quarterbacks who preceded them into the NFL for six decades? Or is the difference more a reflection of changed rules designed to open up the passing game to please points-hungry fantasy football fans?

The scout's eye tells me the latter. Eras make a difference in football, especially when evaluating quarterbacks. In many sports the games haven't changed all that much. They may have improved the equipment, as in golf, and the conditioning, as in all sports, but the basics are the same. Not so in pro football when it comes to the quarterback and the passing game. That's why you can only fairly and fully judge a quarterback in his own time.

Look at one last set of facts on this matter of quarterback accuracy. Within two weeks of each other in 2015, the McCown brothers, Luke and Josh, passed for a total of 767 yards. Luke, playing for the Saints, completed 81.58 percent of his throws on September 27 against the Carolina Panthers. Barely two weeks later, on October 11, Josh, starting for the Browns, threw for 457 yards and completed 70.6 percent of his throws against the Baltimore Ravens. No knock on the McCown brothers, but can you look at those numbers from two journeymen quarterbacks and not agree something's going on in pro football today when it comes to the passing game that has nothing to do with the ability of the quarterback? You're not talking about the same game Baugh, Unitas, Graham, Staubach, and even Marino and Montana played. Today it's pinball. In those earlier decades it was Demolition Derby.

You could probably argue Montana was more accurate than Brady because he was his equal (63.6 percent) while playing in an era where both he and his receivers were hit far more often. It's the kind of debate that can rage on for time immemorial.

To an extent, the same holds true for the extended high-performance levels of many of today's athletes. Compare the numbers in the last years of Barry Bonds and David Ortiz with Hank Aaron or Willie Mays, or compare Brady and Drew Brees at thirty-nine and thirty-eight with Unitas and Bradshaw at the same age. The differences are stark reminders how much things have changed.

Their peak performances lasted considerably longer than their predecessors, who mostly began to slip by their mid-thirties. This was most often due to cumulative injury. Why is this so?

Improved training methods and nutrition are clearly part of it. Few athletes obsess over their fitness and labor to preserve it more than Brady. But Brady could eat all the avocado ice cream and munch on all the kale he wants and it wouldn't make a difference in 1960 or 1970 or even in the 1980s or 1990s, because by thirty-five, thirty-six, he would have had no knees left, his arm would be hanging by his side, and his nose would have been broken ten times. That is the difference in the physical nature of the game then and now.

He could still swear by eating cold food when it's hot and hot food when it's cold or reject tomatoes as co-conspirators in our physical demise, but when Deacon Jones or Dick Butkus or Reggie White could legally decapitate the quarterback before, during, and after he threw, you would not be at thirty-nine what you were at twenty-nine, which seems to be the remarkable case of Tom Brady today. He deserves credit for that, because all the work he puts in has something to do with it, but not as much as how the game has changed.

You could hit Unitas before he threw, when he threw, and, most importantly, after he threw. Do that today and they drag the defender off in handcuffs and leg irons. There's a big difference knowing you're safe after you throw it or that you can dump the ball into the ground on a lot of occasions to avoid the rush and not be called for intentional grounding because of how the rules have changed, and knowing this ferocious pass rush can turn you around like a top and hit you in the face and not only is there no whistle but nobody even notices. Or cares . . . including your teammates.

They damaged quarterbacks in previous eras. Today they try to preserve them. That's just part of playing the position. Brady or Manning might well be tough enough to have played then. I don't doubt it, but we don't know. What I do know is Unitas could play today under these rules and flourish, and if Brady and Manning were playing under the rules Unitas faced, they would not be getting up and playing as well at thirty-eight or thirty-nine, because their bodies would have been broken in too many places.

Every time you go down hard you leave a tiny bit of yourself on the field. It's hard to know what hit does it, but one time you get up and too many pieces are still on the ground and you're not the same player anymore. You may still be able to play. You may still be able to lead, like Unitas could right to the end. But you're not really Unitas anymore. You're a shadow. It happened to Manning too. It just took five years longer.

Brady would have won games in the '40s or the '60s or the '90s, but he'd also be like all those quarterbacks back then completing 54 percent, 55 percent. But how would he hold up? How long could he last? Unitas was still the best quarterback in the league well past his physical prime not just because he was smart. It was because he was tougher than everyone else.

In 2008 Brady blew out his ACL and MCL in the first quarter of the season opener on a hit by Bernard Pollard that would be illegal today. Brady was back a year later as good as new. In 1968 if you blew out an ACL and MCL, you were finished in most cases, and in all cases you were never the same. Not even close.

Those differences are a result of the tremendous improvements in surgical techniques, medicine, and rehab. If all three are handled properly today, you have a far better chance of retaining your physical skills than you did facing shoulder or knee surgery in 1965. That's simply reality. You still have to do the work and Brady did every bit of it, but today it can be done. In 1965 there was no surgery or rehab that could put you completely back together. No one was claiming your knee was stronger than ever or your shoulder after Tommy John surgery was stronger than before because there was no such thing as Tommy John surgery. There was ice.

So the only question I would have is, could Brady take the beating—game in and game out—that those earlier quarterbacks faced? I don't know, but he seems to complain to the officials every time he gets hit. Maybe it's just the way it is today because they get the calls. I don't doubt if you knock him flat he's getting up and coming right back at you. You can see that in him. But how many times?

As far as being productive, he might get six or eight years at prime performance if he's lucky. Then what? Can you still find ways to win when physically you're no longer the same player? Unitas did it for a long time but not many could. Namath couldn't. Bradshaw couldn't. Most of them couldn't.

They are better conditioned today, but part of the reason for that is nobody is beating the shit out of them all season long. If J. J. Watt can hit you after you throw one week and Von Miller can cut you down at the knees the next and Khalil Mack can hit you right in the head the week after that, do you really think you're going out to the High Performance Center in Phoenix and work out a month after the season ends? No, you're not.

If you got hurt, until recently, they opened you up with a chain saw. I was surprised Unitas came back from his injuries in 1965, the season we lost him and Gary Cuozzo back-to-back and had to play with Tom Matte. The scout's eye is very doubtful Brady or Brees could duplicate what they're doing today if this was 1967.

That's not a knock on those players. It's just to point out different eras, different rules, different playing styles account for different performance levels and for longevity. Timing always matters.

Unitas passing today? He'd hold every record because he not only had all the skills to throw every pass, he also had the best football mind. He was playing at a time when he took a terrible beating and the defense could beat up his receivers at the line and all over the field. The middle was clogged because they could clobber receivers on crossing patterns and slants and they did. They used to call Bill Pellington, one of our linebackers, "The Hangman" because he'd clothesline players crossing the middle, putting his forearm out as they ran and getting them in the throat. They used to call the Redskins' Hall of Fame linebacker Chris Hanburger the same thing fifteen years later. You can't do that today, nor should you be able to, but it was pretty effective at slowing a receiver down. Someone like Julian Edelman would not be running free through the heart of the Colts' defenses Shula ran. He'd get blasted every play.

Yet Unitas went forty-seven straight games with a touchdown pass. That was the record for fifty-two years until Brees broke it in 2012 with fifty-four. The next two years Brady (fifty-two) and Manning (fifty-one) also passed Unitas. So for fifty-two years that record stood and then it's passed three straight years by three different quarterbacks. What that tells me is those players are all great, but the passing game is also easier today because of the rule changes. If Unitas was playing today with the limits on defensive contact, he might have thrown one in seventy straight games.

Certainly you can say the athletes are better, but I'd cancel that out by pointing out, my God, the defenses are a mile wide to throw into. The fact that athletes are better is canceled out by the fact you could beat the hell out of the receivers up until 2004. Because of that you didn't have to be as great an athlete. It helped if you were, but you didn't have to be a sprinter like today.

Back then a cornerback like Willie Brown or Mel Blount put his hands on you at the line or bumped you down the field and your route was over. Or at least the timing was blown. Not today. They'd be flagged on every play. So the receivers run freer now beyond 5 yards. That's a huge advantage in the passing game.

When I rank quarterbacks I think like a scout and look at them like a personnel director. I know no other way to do it. Having the advantage of having seen them all, since I first saw Baugh at the Redskins' training camp and Luckman at the Bears' in the 1940s to watching Brady and Manning today, my top ten are clear:

1. Johnny Unitas
2. Tom Brady
3. Dan Marino
4. John Elway
5. Joe Montana

6. Otto Graham

7. Peyton Manning

8. Sammy Baugh

9. Roger Staubach

10. Terry Bradshaw (with Aaron Rodgers closing in fast on the top ten)

A lot of people will quibble with Bradshaw and I understand that, but he won four Super Bowls. You don't win four Super Bowls if you aren't a great quarterback. I scouted him at Louisiana Tech. The first thing you saw was the arm, but he had more than that. He was a leader. That hit he took late in Super Bowl X, when he threw a 64-yard touchdown pass to Lynn Swann but never saw it because he got knocked out by a Dallas lineman named Larry Cole as he threw, was what separates the greatest from the nearly great and the almost great.

Many people who have never seen Graham will question his inclusion too, but he was the greatest winner in football history. Greater than Brady, as great as he has become. He had ten shots at the championship game and reached it every time. He won seven of those ten, the last one coming out of retirement to do it. He knew everything about running Paul Brown's offense and everything about what it takes to win. In the end, that's the quarterback's only job. To win.

It was true when the game began and my father was quarterbacking Penn to the Rose Bowl as it is today. Quarterbacks are judged by their jewelry, and no quarterback who ever played had more rings on his fingers than Otto Graham. That can't be ignored. Winning counts.

The air gets pretty thin the further up the list you go. I put Unitas and Brady in one category and the next five together, but the truth is if I drafted any of them he'd make my team a winner. We're talking about thin lines of difference here. If Manning had won a few more playoff games he'd be higher, but who can argue about his production? Same is true of Brett Favre, who isn't on my list but was a great quarterback in the tradition of Bobby Layne and Kenny Stabler. Those three were leaders, gamblers, brave to a fault. You want them on your team.

But as I've said throughout this book, the scout's job is to have an opinion. The personnel director's job is to listen to those opinions and make a choice. It's what you must do. It's what I looked for in the scouts I hired in New England. They all went on to do great things and a large part of the reason, beyond their judgment, was they weren't afraid to have an opinion. So here's mine on the most important position in the sport.

I'd pick Unitas first, but if you take either one you'd be fine with it. It's not like picking between Manning and Ryan Leaf, as Bobby Beathard had to do in 1998. In that case, there was no second choice really. He needed a quarterback and Bill Polian took the right one for the Colts, so he was left with the other one knowing he had holes and it didn't work out. Sometimes you have no choice. In this case neither do I, but the choice is easier. You win with either, but my life in pro football always came down to one thing: make a pick. Mine is Unitas.

Why? When I think of a football player, I don't think of Tom Brady or Peyton Manning. I think of Johnny Unitas. That's the separation for me.

From 1958 to 1964 or '65, there was nothing ever like him. His performance in the 1958 sudden-death championship game, I don't care if it had happened a hundred years ago, was a performance like watching Leonard Bernstein doing Beethoven's Ninth at the Berlin Wall. It was a virtuoso. He was an artist. You had to be there, and I was. It was like watching the greatest symphony you'll ever see performed. I can't ever remember seeing a quarterback as confident as Unitas was that day. Maybe Elway in Cleveland during "The Drive" in the 1987 AFC Championship Game is one.

One thing that separates Unitas from the rest of them is he controlled everything. He called the plays. I understand why coaches want to control everything today. Belichick is A-number-1 at that and Shula began doing some of it when he got to Baltimore. But if I were the coach, Brady would be more like Unitas. He'd run everything.

If Brady had more leeway to run the whole game, you wouldn't have to worry. He'd be like the great quarterbacks who had to do that, but the fact is he doesn't have to do it. He's got that headset and they're talking to him and telling him what to run. He may adjust it. He may change it completely. But it's still a relief from the pressure.

After Super Bowl LI, Brady told *Monday Morning Quarterback*'s Peter King that the last thing he heard before he took the snap and threw a critical late touchdown pass to Danny Amendola was offensive coordinator Josh McDaniels in his helmet headset saying, "Don't forget Danny! Don't forget Danny!" Danny, it turned out, was wide open.

It's not the same having someone in your ear as being in the situation Unitas was, working off his knowledge and his preparation and most importantly his feel for the game. It doesn't always go the way you planned it. Then what? Unitas knew what.

No one was in Unitas's ear before the snap in the 1958 championship game saying, "Don't forget Mutscheller! Don't forget Mutscheller!" He had to see what was going to be open on his own.

If you've got two minutes left to drive the length of the field, I'd say give me Unitas. If you tell me the lives of my children are on the line and we have to go the length of the field and Unitas has the ball, I think they have a pretty good chance of surviving.

My second choice would be Brady, and I'd feel the same way. Those kids would be safe because those are the two players who stand above the rest in that situation. The only things that separate them, in my mind, are the little things that are products of the eras in which they played.

Same thing is true with running the two-minute drill. Unitas invented that. Brady is great at it, but one player runs it and the other invented it. Watch that drive in overtime in the 1958 championship game against the Giants. Watch how Unitas sets up Alan Ameche's 23-yard run on a trap play the Giants never expected after completing a 20-yard throw on third-and-15 to Raymond Berry and then how, instead of handing off to Ameche on the 7-yard line, he throws it to Jim Mutscheller when an interception would have been fatal because he knew he'd be open. Knew it. Ball's at the 1 and he calls "Power 16," and before Ameche can plow through a huge hole to win the game, Unitas has already turned and is walking off the field.

Matter of fact. No celebration. No surprise to John. He knew what was going to happen. Game was over and he was heading home, like a steel worker at the end of his shift. That's John Unitas. That's a football player.

Until he began to get hurt, I never once doubted Unitas. Neither did his teammates. He was a football genius. He saw things no one else saw. Sometimes he couldn't really explain it but he knew. Brady is the same way. His teammates reflect that complete faith in him. You could see it during Super Bowl LI, when he led that remarkable 25-point second-half comeback against Atlanta. They had total faith that if they gave him enough time, Brady would do it. And he did.

Maybe in the end the other difference is toughness. I'm not saying Brady isn't tough, but the game is different. Alex Hawkins told me one time Unitas was like an offensive or defensive lineman playing quarterback. Sure he had great touch, great accuracy, a great arm, and great game intelligence. But he also was tough at a time when the game didn't do much to protect the quarterback. He was just another player getting hit.

I never saw him waver, no matter how much of a pounding he took. He never flinched. I never heard a player question Unitas. There's a reason they all believe we would have won Super Bowl III if Shula had put Unitas in sooner. I believe it too, even though his arm was shot and he couldn't throw the ball 10 yards with any zip on it that season.

I know Johnny Sample was with the Jets that day and had a great game, but he told his teammates when he saw No. 19 coming in that the game wasn't over. Unitas took us right down the field and made the right throw, but his arm was shot and the ball was picked off. Next time he took us down and we scored. Who thinks he wouldn't have done it again? Nobody in Baltimore.

Now look at Manning and Cam Newton. They both have a better arm than Unitas or Brady, but when their time came in the biggest games when they were actually older and more experienced than Unitas and Brady were when they first reached the championship, they were not successful. Players feared Unitas. They knew no matter what they did he'd never be rattled, even on a bad day. You don't see Brady rattled very often either. Contrast that with Cam Newton in Super Bowl 50.

Newton was under heavy pressure all day and he cracked. Many quarterbacks would when pressured twenty-one times and sacked six. He may have the tattoo but he's not Superman. He flinched.

When he was rushed by both Von Miller and DeMarcus Ware, he was 1 for 12 with four sacks and two fumbles. He completed only 31.6 percent of his throws when pressured that day. And he had ten overthrown passes on a day when he went 18 for 41 with no touchdowns and no celebratory dabs, which had become his controversial trademark.

Then look at Peyton Manning. He's 2-2 in four Super Bowls, but he threw more interceptions than touchdowns (3-5) in those games. He threw two pick sixes, including one that killed the Colts with 3:12 to go while driving to tie Super Bowl XLIV in a loss to the Saints. He was overwhelmed against Seattle four years later in a 43–8 loss in Super Bowl XLVIII and was little more than a game manager against the Panthers in Super Bowl 50, completing only 13 of 23 with another interception. Even when he beat the Bears in 2007, it was not a Manning-like performance. Add to that an overall playoff record of 14-13, and it's not what you expect from the game's best quarterback. Compare it to Unitas (6-2, .750 playoff winning percentage) and Brady (25-9, .735) in the playoffs, and there's no comparison.

I'm not knocking them. They have great ability. We'll see where Newton ends up. We know where Manning ended up. He was great, but when the history is written, it will not be the Manning Era. Despite all the numbers he threw up, it was the Brady Era. Why?

Because on the biggest stages, at the biggest moments, Peyton Manning came up short too many times and Brady did not. That's what separates them and always will. It's in the books. The history has been written. It's a thin line but it's a line that exists.

Manning flinched. Newton flinched, at least the first time. We all remember against the Broncos in Super Bowl 50 when the ball came loose and instead of going for it, Newton backed up. It was only for an instant and by then he'd taken a terrible beating, so there was a reason for it, but I never saw Unitas back up. I never saw Brady back up. From the first day you play football, you're taught if the ball's on the ground, you dive on it. You don't back up, although a lot of good players would have in that situation. But Unitas and Brady? No way. That's what separates them from Newton and Manning. They never backed up.

So why Unitas over Brady? To me, he's the quarterbacking father of modern football. He is to the modern quarterback what Paul Brown was to the modern coach.

If you're asking me just to draft the best pure passer, it's Marino, then Unitas, Manning, Elway, Baugh, and Sonny Jurgenson. Marino's release was so fast and his arm was so strong but he also had touch, and although he couldn't run, he had a feel to avoid people in the pocket. Not fast, but quick feet and a sixth sense of feeling pressure.

Who was better in pure throwing than Marino? I'd say when everything was right with Unitas he'd be just below Marino and Elway, who had a gun. I saw Baugh throw and Unitas throw. I'd take Unitas. As for Manning, I never thought he had a particularly big arm. Favre had a bigger arm, but Manning was so accurate and it got out of his hand nearly as fast as Marino, which made him nearly impossible to sack, so I'd take him above Favre.

Brady is different. He is not a great deep thrower. All his statistics show that. But he is one of the most accurate passers within 15 yards or so that I've ever seen and he may be the most accurate low thrower ever. It's amazing the way he can throw the ball low where only his receiver can reach it time after time without it being too low to be handled. Tremendous.

Now when it comes to accuracy, that's a little different to judge. Scouts can tell a big arm. So can everyone else. But how accurate is the passer when he's got to throw into very small windows? That's something you have to make a determination on when you're scouting and it isn't easy, because in college the windows are a lot bigger. Passing lanes in college and the NFL are like the difference between a bay window and a cellar window. One has a lot more glass to see through than the other.

As far as accuracy goes, I put six players above the rest. Unitas would be there. Marino would be there. Montana would certainly be there. The later version of Brady would be there—not the first couple of years, but by the second Super Bowl. It's hard to separate that group.

Graham and Baugh would be right there too. It's hard to separate them because it's not like arm strength, where you say Marino, Unitas, Baugh, and Elway and then the others are below that. In most of the categories that make a great quarterback over the past sixty years, it's the same five or six men in the end. It's not fifteen or twenty. We can argue about those five or six men, but don't try to tell me there are twenty, because there aren't. So let's take a scout's look at the top two, Unitas and Brady.

Unitas had the arm to make all the throws, long and short. He was accurate. He had high football intelligence. He had the ability to read defenses. High courage, high toughness, and he had leadership through the roof.

He was the most confident athlete I was ever around. Not cocky, just sure. Who stood in that pocket better than Unitas when you have three or four players coming at you and you have three seconds to make a decision before you get hit? That separates the greatest from the rest. That never changed, no matter how much he got hit. In the pocket Johnny Unitas never wavered, even in Super Bowl III when his arm was hurt and he couldn't throw.

What are the negatives? He was stubborn. That was his great strength and his great weakness. To coach him you had to be Weeb. You prepared Unitas for the game and then you let him run it. Weeb used to say you prepared Unitas well and when the game came there was no one better to run it than John. Including Weeb. Later Shula and the coaches who followed didn't believe that.

John would have had a problem playing for Paul Brown. As great as Brown was for Otto Graham, Graham admitted he hated Paul's running the game, calling every play when he could have done it perfectly well and maybe better. But Otto was an extension of the coach. Unitas was the coach on the field.

I remember once Shula and the staff thought they had information that would tell him when one of our opponents was going to blitz. So he had a signal he was going to give when they had it, and one of our tackles was to tell Unitas and he was supposed to throw deep.

Shula got it and sent it in and Unitas called it, and when he dropped back they didn't blitz. He had to throw the ball out of bounds. When the play was over, he just stared at Shula.

When Johnny came to the sideline, Shula told him they thought they had it but they were wrong, and Unitas barked back, "If you're not sure what you're doing don't send in a call that fucks up my game!" Shula was hot, but that was John. Direct.

That's why I think Unitas would have had a problem with Belichick and Josh McDaniels, the Patriots' offensive coordinator. He would never have accepted anyone in his ear on every play. How did we get to that, which I personally think is ridiculous? Paul Brown.

Brown was the greatest innovator the game has ever seen, but he also did one of the worst things for the game, which was take it away from the quarterback. Today there isn't a quarterback who comes into the NFL who ever called a play in his life. All the way back to high school. They probably couldn't do it today because they never had to, but Brady and Manning could. To a degree they do it at the line now but it's not quite the same thing. They have a crib sheet, that offensive coordinator in their ear in the huddle. All Unitas had was himself.

Now when it comes to Brady and the quarterbacks today, a scout also has to take into account that much of the time they're looking at the full field from the shotgun at the snap. For most of the history of football, the quarterback is turning his back to the defense and retreating. The minute you do that, the defense may change what they are showing. So the real decision for most eras came when you turned around after a three-, five-, or seven-step drop. That's a disadvantage they've eliminated today.

Couple that with those gaping holes in the middle and it's a different throwing game. It's why Brady has had so much trouble with Rex Ryan's defenses. He takes those gaping holes away. He hasn't always been able to do it, or do it well enough to compensate for some of his team's other weaknesses, but Brady has said many times he has a headache at the end of a game against Ryan. On those days, he was facing what Unitas faced every game. He wasn't a 64 percent thrower then.

So when I look at Brady, what do I see? When he first came into the league, it wasn't his arm. That's gotten better, which is unusual. It's because he worked so hard at getting stronger. He deserves all the credit for that. He took what he had and made it better. It's still not the arm Unitas had, but it would have been enough to play effectively in the 1960s when it was a more vertical game.

He's not a great deep thrower. He tends to overthrow when he misses, and I think it's because he's conscious of not having the strongest arm, so he puts too much leg into it sometimes. It's not effortless, so you'd have to account for that as a scout. But in the end he can make all the throws he needs to make. He couldn't have played for Al Davis and his vertical game but neither could Montana. Brady would have done it a little differently than John but I believe he would have found a way to be effective in 1965 or 2015.

Even though Unitas was cut by the Steelers and played sandlot football for a year before the Colts signed him, Brady has come a longer way than Unitas had to. If I was looking at Unitas in Louisville and Brady at Michigan, I would have drafted Unitas. I might not have drafted Brady and the Patriots nearly didn't.

If you watch Brady's combine workout, his arm is nothing special. He's skinny and not a particularly good athlete when being timed and measured. He was a catcher on the baseball team, not a shortstop. And he was always battling Drew Henson for play-ing time at Michigan. So you'd wonder about that.

But the Patriots' quarterback coach, Dick Rehbein, saw what the best scouts see. He saw it was Brady playing at the end of games when they needed to be won. So they finally took him on the sixth round as a developmental player, No. 199 in the draft on Rehbein's recommendation. Belichick has admitted it was Reh-bein's pick. That says a lot for Belichick. He trusted the judgment of the man who knew the position best.

Back when Unitas came out the draft would have been long over, but there are thirty-two teams now. Had Unitas been released today he would have been snapped up, but with only twelve it was easy to fall through the cracks.

Still, you have to give Belichick and his staff credit. They kept four quarterbacks Brady's rookie year, which is unheard of. They saw something and they were patient with him. A year later he got his chance and Drew Bledsoe never came back. Same story as Unitas in 1956 when George Shaw got hurt. Unitas wasn't an immediate star, but there was a point that season where someone asked when Shaw was coming back and Gino Marchetti, who was the alpha male in that locker room, said, "He isn't. It's Unitas's team now." Gino knew just like Belichick knew in 2001. Bledsoe wasn't coming back. It was Brady's team.

So their stories are similar, but in my opinion Brady came fur-ther than Unitas because he didn't have the arm. So what are Brady's assets?

His intelligence. His ability to process information quickly and then retain it. He may be better at that than anyone who ever played. That allows him to make the right decision so quickly, which is a key element of the offense he runs. If you can't do that, you can't play today's game. The ball has to come out fast.

One thing I learned as a scout is the importance of memory. Memory is a gift. A scout has to compare players he's looking at with ones in the past who made it or didn't and understand why and how that applies in the case in front of him. Brady has the same ability. He can see something at the line of scrimmage he saw three years ago and he's not fooled. Most quarterbacks don't have that kind of command. He sees things so quickly he says he knows where the ball is going most of the time before the snap. That speaks to both his mental preparation and his ability to retain information.

The interesting thing to me is when he was at Michigan, I bet if you put his film on, three scouts would give you three different opinions. One would say he can't do anything. Another would say he can do everything. But the great scout would see what the difference is. Some scouts can only see the negatives. Others only see the positives. The great scout sees the projection from where he is to what he might become. That's what you needed with Brady.

He's unflappable. That's an asset. He's intelligent and makes quick decisions. He's extremely accurate, which is really the most important trait of a great quarterback. You better be able to make the ball go exactly where you intend it to go or you're in trouble. He could do that.

Marino's arm? The best. How strong is Brady's arm? Strong enough. If you're open for the bomb, the ball won't be 10 yards short. If anything he overthrows people, maybe because he's over-compensating for not having the shotgun-blast of Marino, Elway, or Baugh. I don't know. You can see his long ball doesn't always look good, but if it's anything it's overthrown not underthrown.

Arm strength can be overrated. Obviously, there's a minimum you need but you don't need a cannon. You have to be more accurate today because you're throwing more and you're throwing shorter, and Brady is as accurate as anyone who ever played at a time when that's at a premium. Unitas might throw twenty-five times. Today it's thirty-five, forty, maybe fifty times. So if you're not accurate, you're not going to play long. You're not going to make it.

The last thing is, like Unitas, Brady has no fear but he makes defenses fearful. They know no matter what they do those two can't really be rattled even on a bad day. They're in command of themselves.

Wes Welker told a story to NFL Network about a play against the Dolphins where he was supposed to run an in-cut, but he and Brady had talked about if the defense played underneath he was to put his hand up and take the route deeper. They got the coverage and Welker said, "As soon as he saw it, he was right there. The ball was in the air and we got a big play out of it. His ability to see that so quickly (was critical). I feel like most quarterbacks would've waited and been like 'what's he doing?'"

That's the difference between the greatest quarterbacks and the rest. They don't wonder. They know what they're doing and what you're doing. That was Unitas. That's Brady. Others do it too but those two do it a little bit better and a little bit more often.

This is a little Hollywood, but it's like the famous scene in *High Noon*. I see Gary Cooper, Marshall Will Kane, walking down the dusty street. He knows there will be three, maybe four people and they're going to blow him away. You hear the train whistle and you see him walking. He knows what's coming and how to beat it. He never flinches. He is the same man who in the scene before was asking people to come out with him and nobody would.

I see that and I cut to Unitas or Brady after a touchdown pass to win the game. They're Marshall Kane after he's killed them all. Take off the badge and throw it in the dirt and just walk away. That's how I see them.

When I think of Manning, though, I recall how he performed in that playoff game against the Patriots in 2004. He was terrible. He wasn't good in the Super Bowls he won and worse in the ones he lost. I wouldn't use the word "choked," but he was terrible. I never saw Brady that way. I never saw Unitas that way.

If I have to win a big game, I take Brady over Manning every time. Great as Manning was. Great as Favre was. I'll take Brady. One way Brady benefits is by not having the Marino gift. There are throws he would not try because he knows he can't do it. Brett Favre would try it. It's a low-percentage throw, but he believed he had the arm to do it and sometimes he did. For Favre, everything was a high-percentage throw in his mind. Had he not done a few of those stupid things he'd be right there with the rest of them. What wasn't there to admire about the man? Except he was fearless and he paid for it.

Favre was a throwback player. No question he could've played in the 1960s. Courageous. Played with every type of injury and never missed a start, but something went dead in the head sometimes and he'd throw a pick when he didn't need to. He played a tremendous game for the Vikings against New Orleans in the 2010 NFC Championship Game. The officials let him take a beating that day. It was cruel. But he still had a great day until he tried that throw across the body with eleven seconds to go when he could have dumped it off for a 5- or 6-yard gain and set up a 48-yard field goal to win with seven seconds left. Unitas didn't throw across his body in that situation. Brady takes the short gain. Favre went for the juggler on a throw he didn't have to make and Tracy Porter intercepted it. No one was shocked.

He didn't need to do it, but that's him. "I can get it in there. Nail in the coffin." And what happened? He turned it over and they lost. That's what makes football better than anything. It's not best of seven. It's not best of three. It's one game that decides it. That's what decides where you rank. A lot of our opinions are based on, did they win the Big Game? Is it fair? No, but life isn't fair.

When Favre or Manning threw the killer pick, you weren't surprised. If Brady or Unitas did it you'd be shocked. That's the difference. That's what separates them. It's not much. It's a thin line. But the line exists.

That's what defenses feared the most about Unitas and Brady. They would not help them win the game. They would not stop themselves. You have to do it. That's the fear.

It's hard to say "fear" about a football player. It's not fear physically. But if you see a stoop-shouldered No. 19 trotting in at the start of the third quarter or No. 12 with one drive to win the Super Bowl and you're playing cornerback, how do you feel? I think you feel fear.

Unitas created that. Brady creates that. The opponent knows those players know what's going on better than you do. They know your vulnerabilities in every formation you have and how to exploit them. Opposing players revered Unitas in his day. That's not the same as liking him. I know a lot of players say they don't like Brady, but he's not running for student body president. You see those two running onto the field and think, "Now what do we do?"

It's what the Giants' defense was thinking in 1958 when Unitas had the ball in overtime and was driving the Colts toward the goal line for the win. It's what the Falcons' defense was thinking in Super Bowl LI when Brady had the ball in overtime and was driving the Patriots toward the goal line for the win. The only overtime games in an NFL Championship or a Super Bowl were won by the two best quarterbacks who ever played. Coincidence? I don't think so. They both put fear in their opponents' heart, and that includes the hearts of the opposing coaches.

That's an edge that has nothing to do with your arm. Brady never had Unitas's arm but he has the same edge. I'm not totally sure Manning had it. They respected Manning but there's a difference between respect and fear. They knew he had a history of making the big mistake. So did Favre. Doesn't mean they weren't great. They were, so that made you nervous, but if you play defense for a living in the NFL, you live in fear of Johnny Unitas and Tom Brady.

Nervousness makes you edgy. Fear makes you tentative, and that allows you to be beaten. A quarterback has to create that kind of fear, which those two did better than anyone else who ever played, although Montana did the same thing in a different way. It's not automatic just because you're a great passer. It's more than that.

You can win with the others. Everyone on my list won a lot. But not as often as you win with Unitas and Brady. When you talk about the total package, the tangibles like accuracy and intelligence and the intangibles like leadership and fearlessness and that attitude that "I will never back away," who had more of that than Johnny Unitas and Tom Brady?

No one.

So if I'm scouting those two, what do I report? I write what Don McCafferty wrote on his report to me about Dick Butkus in 1965: "Radar nose. Get him."

17

Only One Moses Wore a Whistle

I was fortunate to work with three Hall of Fame coaches and have the opportunity to closely observe nearly all the game's greatest minds over the past sixty-five years. So when I'm asked who was the best, it is both easy and difficult to come up with an answer.

The difficult part is there have been many coaches who won multiple championships and mastered the craft of building an organization. The easy part is selecting the one who left the most indelible mark on the game. That's Paul Brown.

To me, Paul Brown was football's Moses. All the rest of them carried the tablets. Whether you liked him or not, and many people didn't, Brown stands above them all, and that includes the three Hall of Famers I knew best, Don Shula, Chuck Noll, and Weeb Ewbank, as well as George Halas, Vince Lombardi, Bill Belichick, and anyone else you can name. What separates him? He was an innovator, although calling Paul Brown an innovator is like calling Einstein a physicist.

Brown didn't just build winning football organizations—he wrote the blueprint for how it's done. He changed how teams were organized, how they trained, how they scouted, and how they played the game. His teams went to the championship game eleven of the first twelve seasons he was in Cleveland. Two decades later when he ran the Bengals, they went there twice too. What more is there?

Shula, Belichick, Bill Walsh, and Lombardi are right there with him when it comes to coaching football, but none of them truly changed football. Paul Brown did. He hasn't coached a game in forty-two years, yet much of the way he operated the Cleveland Browns' dynasty of the 1950s remains how it's done today. Who else can make such a claim?

Although Brown understood the physical nature of the game, he turned it into a mental exercise as well. He was the first to test the intelligence of his players and to design a playbook and require each player to study it like a graduate student of football.

He was the first to incorporate film study into scouting opponents as well as his own players and the first to grade those players off that film on every play. He once described this approach as "a detailed scientific study. The pictures never lie."

He made his assistant coaches full-time employees during an era when most assistants held second jobs in the off-season. He professionalized the coaching of pro football and turned it into an academic as well as a physical exercise.

He ran his team with precision down to the smallest details. When running two-a-day practices in summer training camp, each practice was exactly fifty-five minutes long. During the season his teams practiced once a day . . . for exactly an hour and twelve minutes. How precise were the details? He strongly urged his players to refrain from sex after Tuesday night the week of a game. How many complied is impossible to know, but he consistently told them to follow that regimen to preserve stamina. Imagine trying to get away with that today!

He was a major force in integrating first the All-America Football Conference in the 1940s and then the NFL in the 1950s, not by talking about it but simply by doing it. A year before Jackie Robinson integrated Major League Baseball in 1947, Brown signed powerful black fullback Marion Motley and quickly added future Hall of Famers Bill Willis and Len Ford. They were three players who changed the complexion of the game literally as well as figuratively. He dominated opponents with them. He was an advocate of power and speed, and when he took over the Browns in their inaugural season in the AAFC in 1946, he realized there was an untapped vein of talent among black players shunned by the NFL. He struck gold with it and his success forced the NFL to finally follow suit.

I've always believed the best coaches were the ones who understood personnel. What's more important to a coach than the talent at his disposal? What's more important, evaluating personnel or a coach's strategic command? In my opinion, 100 to 1 it's personnel. I think it's more important now than ever. It's one of the things that separate Bill Belichick from his peers. He not only knows personnel, he understands value, which is important with the salary cap. You can be as great a strategic coach as you want, but if you don't have an understanding of personnel, you're going nowhere.

In most cases personnel beats strategy. No doubt in my mind about that. Talent beats coaching. Shula once told me, "Upton, if you want to be sure you're going to win, show up to the stadium with the best players on your bus. It's a player's game."

Look at Lombardi's Packers. Everyone knew what was coming. Nothing fancy. The Packer sweep. No one could stop it. Why? Because he had the best people.

Brown understood that and he understood talent evaluation. He was the first to make the 40-yard dash a measuring stick for football speed. He had an eye for talent and an instinct for it, but he also wanted objective measurements as well.

Paul Brown knew and understood personnel and especially the African American player. Never forget that. He was one of the first coaches to employ the battering ram fullback with speed in Motley. He had a tremendous mind and was the most innovative coach in football history, but first and foremost, he knew talent and understood that was what would make his ideas and theories flourish. Without players what do you have? A pile of jockstraps and tight pants. Talent makes it all work.

Brown was always looking for ways to develop talent, which is why he created the first "taxi squad" when he got to Cleveland. He kept promising players not yet fully ready for the NFL in reserve by stashing them on the payroll of the Browns' owner, Mickey McBride. McBride owned a cab company, so non-roster players were put on the cab company payroll. The only time they were in a cab was on the way home from practice. It was considered a gimmick of questionable legality at first, but today every team has a taxi squad or non-roster practice players.

Strategically Brown was also an innovator. He created the draw play, and he expanded the use of the passing game with Otto Graham in the late 1940s, a revolution I witnessed firsthand in 1950 when I visited the Browns' training camp for the first time and realized these refugees from the All-America Football Conference were playing a game with which I and the NFL were not familiar.

To allow the passing game to flourish, Brown developed pocket protection, surrounding Otto Graham with blockers who provided him time to throw. In short order, it was universally adopted. Some thirty years later in Cincinnati, along with assistant coach Bill Walsh, Brown created the West Coast offense for a quarterback with an accurate but limited arm named Virgil Carter.

Greg Cook had been Cincinnati's rifle-armed quarterbacking future. He might have become a Hall of Famer had an undiagnosed rotator cuff injury in his rookie season of 1969 not resulted in his career coming to a quick end. Forced to play Carter, Brown came up with a way to utilize his strengths with short passing that put a premium on accuracy and quick delivery and limited his exposure to the deep throws. Belichick often refers to what is now a staple of today's passing game as "Paul Brown's Ohio River Offense" rather than calling it the West Coast offense, as it came to be known after Walsh's success with it in San Francisco with Joe Montana. That approach is now the staple of nearly every passing offense in the game.

In his quest for total control, Brown also developed the messenger guard system by which he would send in every play by rotating his guards. Chuck Noll, who had four Super Bowl victories, was one of those guards who shuffled in and out like telegram delivery boys.

This was at a time when quarterbacks called every play from the huddle. Many critics claimed Brown was trying to turn football into human chess, and perhaps he was, but it was the forerunner of how offense is called today, completely from the sidelines.

Brown was also the first to adopt phone contact between a coach in the stands and the sidelines. He put his top aide and best friend, Blanton Collier, high above him to get a bird's-eye view of which plays were working and which were not and, more important, why. They would talk via a sideline telephone before Brown would send in his call or between offensive series, thus making it easier to attack opposing defenses. That is standard operating procedure today, but until Brown tried it no team even thought of it.

Like all innovators Brown was far ahead of his time. In 1956 he was approached by two Cleveland inventors, John Campbell and George Sarles. They had developed a tiny radio transmitter and suggested Brown mount it inside a helmet to communicate directly with his quarterback.

Brown liked the idea and secretly planted it inside the helmet of George Ratterman during an exhibition game against the Detroit Lions. It worked perfectly, but the Lions' coaches noticed Brown was no longer shuttling messenger guards in with a new call every play and became suspicious. One finally spotted a small radio transmitter on a light pole near the bench, and word spread quickly as other teams tried to develop similar technology.

None was as successful as Brown's, so after using it in three more games, my father stepped in and banned the device that October as an unfair advantage. Brown's idea was revived and implemented league-wide in 1994, first in the quarterback's helmet and then in the helmet of a defensive player of the coach's choosing so the sidelines could communicate freely on both sides of the ball. As was often the case, Paul Brown was forty years ahead of his time.

Brown even was involved in revolutionizing the equipment. During a late-season game against the San Francisco 49ers in 1953, Graham was punched in the face as he ran out of bounds by Art Michalik and his chin was badly gashed. This was at a time when no one wore facemasks on their helmets.

Graham fell right at Brown's feet, sustaining a cut that required fifteen stitches. Brown decided this was preventable and came up with a design for a wide piece of plastic that would attach to both sides of the helmet and run in front of Graham's face, chin to nose.

Graham was able to play the next week with it, but the plastic caused breathing problems and tended to fog up, so Brown spoke with the helmet maker Riddell. He asked them to design a rounded piece of hard plastic no wider than his thumb to put on the front of the helmet for protection. Soon nearly every player was wearing some form of the facemask Brown created. A defensive lineman named Jesse Richardson, who played with the Eagles and Patriots, was the last lineman to play without one in 1964. Wisely, Brown had patented it and for many years collected royalties from Riddell.

Shula, Noll, Belichick, and Tom Landry all credit Brown for today's game. Landry neither played nor coached for Brown yet once said Brown was the person who most influenced his approach to coaching. And Belichick, who could be a historian of the game if he wasn't still making history himself, told NFL Network, "There is no one in the game that I have more respect for than Paul Brown. His contributions, from the game to the way it's played, protective equipment to playbook—every film breakdown, every meeting. Everything that he did as a coach, fifty years later, everybody is still basically doing the same thing. I really think of him as the father of professional football."

While generally not considered a sentimentalist, when Belichick tied Brown for career NFL victories, he honored his memory by wearing a fedora to the stadium, Brown's trademark sideline attire. By any measure but one—most career wins—Paul Brown stands above the rest.

He won seven professional championships (four in the AAFC and three in the NFL), and anyone who tries to minimize the first four need only recall how the Browns dominated the 1950s after entering the NFL. I remember as a twelve-year-old knowing how badly the Browns were going to manhandle the Eagles, the reigning NFL champions, in the 1950 season opener after the two leagues merged. I'd seen the Browns at their training camp that summer. I knew they were a revolutionary force.

When they killed the Eagles, 35–10, NFL apologists of the time claimed the passing game Cleveland used wasn't really playing football. That was absurd excuse-making, but Paul Brown took it personally, as he did all criticism. When they played again later that season, the Browns beat the Eagles, 13–7. They had zero net passing yards that day. They'd beaten the NFL champions playing their game too. That was no accident. That was Paul Brown.

Most successful coaches have a controlling personality. I've come to believe it's what is demanded to be highly successful. You have to be in control of everything, although I have to admit Brown could take it too far.

He was unpopular with a lot of players because of his stinging criticisms during film study, when he often didn't just correct them but ridiculed them. He had a flinty approach to relationships, tolerated no deviation from his system, and was a tough contract negotiator. When the players began to unionize in 1954, it came as no surprise to my father that two of Brown's players, Abe Gibron and Dante Lavelli, were leading the way. Both had tired of Brown's hard-line approach to contracts and wanted, among other things, a minimum salary and notions as "radical" as per diem on the road and their uniforms being paid for and maintained by the teams.

For two years they met on Wednesday nights before formally announcing that 370 NFL players, a majority, had agreed to unionize in 1956. Their lawyer was Creighton Miller, a former Notre Dame player who had served as a Browns assistant coach in 1946 while attending law school.

My father supported their efforts, believing in the long run a players union would help the owners avoid charges of antitrust violations. He was right, but Brown and other owners disagreed.

The newly formed union hoped to meet with my father at the owners' meetings in January 1957, but no meeting was held. Later that year, Miller testified in front of Congress during an antitrust hearing and threatened a lawsuit if the owners did not recognize the union. Eventually many of the players' demands were met, but the owners refused to recognize the union as the players' bargaining agent until 1968.

The rise of the union so irritated Brown that he not only opposed many of their demands, he went so far as to have Miller's image erased from a picture of the 1946 championship team that hung on his office wall. That was the other side of Paul Brown.

In the end he was fired on January 7, 1963, after a long-running feud with his star running back, Jim Brown, and new owner Art Modell. Modell took a more hands-on approach from the ownership side than Brown expected, and when Brown traded Bobby Mitchell for the draft rights to Ernie Davis, some felt in a search for Jim Brown's replacement, the end was near.

Davis, the 1961 Heisman Trophy winner, contracted leukemia and died before ever playing a game for the Browns. Modell had urged Brown to allow Davis to play, but he refused. That was the final straw. His firing split the city into Brown backers and Browns backers and ended his relationship with Collier when he was named as his replacement, even though he'd given him his blessing to accept the job.

He lived in retirement in San Diego for five years but grew increasingly restless, finally becoming the third biggest investor in the Cincinnati Bengals, an AFL expansion team in 1978. He served as coach, GM, and potentate in all league matters. In other words, Paul Brown finally had what he always wanted and what I sought in New England and in the World Football League. He had total control of the football operation.

In a radical departure from the norm that proved brilliant, his first draft choice was center Bob Johnson, who would start for ten years in Cincinnati, anchoring their offensive line. Brown's explanation? "It all starts with the center snap." Brilliant.

Paul Brown went 158-48-8 in Cleveland, a .767 winning percentage. In eight years he built the Bengals from nothing into a three-time playoff team, retiring as head coach following the 1975 season after going 11-3 but losing in the first round of the playoffs for the second time in three years. His overall professional coaching record was 213-104-9, a .672 winning percentage. Couple that with his innovations and building an AFL expansion team into a two-time Super Bowl finalist that lost to Walsh's 49ers by less than a touchdown each time, and it's easy to see why he is held in such high esteem by everyone who knew him in professional football, including myself.

His coaching tree includes Hall of Famers Shula, Noll, Walsh, and Ewbank and his influence is everywhere in today's game. If I just went by what I saw, I'd think Belichick had to have worked for Paul as well (which he never did). He's exactly like him.

Now if you take Moses off the mountaintop, who else would I want coaching my team? Well, my top ten (plus one) looks like this:

1. Paul Brown
2. Don Shula
3. Bill Belichick
4. Bill Walsh
5. Vince Lombardi
6. Chuck Noll
7. Tom Landry
8. George Halas
9. Joe Gibbs
10. Tie—Bill Parcells and Curley Lambeau

Those are the best I ever saw or worked with, but my list has to have one more name added to it. I'd lump Shula, Belichick, Walsh, and Lombardi in one group, then the others, but you have to add 10A. You have to add someone I think is one of the most underrated coaches in the game. You have to add Weeb Ewbank.

A lot of people will say that's crazy because Weeb's overall record in twenty years as a head coach was 130-129-7, a .502 winning percentage, and he was only 5-4 in the playoffs. That's true, but he also won three world championships and arguably the two most important games in NFL history: the 1958 NFL Championship Game in sudden-death overtime with the Colts, which changed how the public perceived pro football, and Super Bowl III in 1968 against my Colts, which legitimized the AFL and the merger. Both were historic moments and Weeb was on the winning side each time.

Maybe that's a sentimental pick because I worked for him in Baltimore, but try to write the history of pro football without Weeb Ewbank's name in it. If somebody grades your report, you'll get an incomplete.

Great coaches can differ in many ways, but what I always saw in every great coach was a dominant personality. Sure you have to know what you're doing; you have to understand personnel and be able to make decisions. You have to know the game and be a sound game-day tactician, but first you have to dominate the situation. There can be no doubt and no doubters about who is in charge.

Certainly there was no doubt about that with Halas. I saw that up close when I sat in those meetings at the Bears' training camps when my father would leave me and my brother there. When I think of Halas I think of the Monsters of the Midway who ruled the NFL in the 1940s and of the six championships he won, but the first thing I think of is I'm not sure the game would have survived without him.

Halas kept pro football alive when he signed Red Grange and made him the NFL's first hero in 1925 at a time when pro football was on life support. He came up with a nationwide tour using Grange as the headliner, nineteen games in sixty-seven days that legitimized pro football.

Grange earned over $100,000 at a time when players were lucky to make $100 a game. Don't worry about Halas, he made plenty too. But more important, those games packed over seventy thousand people into the Polo Grounds on December 6, 1925, a live gate that helped keep the New York Giants afloat. Grange did the same thing in Detroit, Chicago, and throughout the country. Everyone wanted to see the Galloping Ghost they'd watched before only on news reels played at the movies.

It was so successful, Halas set up two tours, the second going into the South and out West. It may be hard to understand today, but that barnstorming tour truly made the NFL a national league for the first time.

Halas worked out the Grange deal with the first player agent, C. C. "Cash and Carry" Pyle, a movie house owner in Evanston, Illinois, who signed Grange while he was still at the University of Illinois. Grange was already a hero and that was the point. The heroes of college football didn't turn pro in those days. Pro football was looked upon by most people as slumming when compared to the college game until the Bears signed Grange.

Halas had an idea that kept a number of franchises afloat that were ready to fold. Add that to all his years as Papa Bear, growling on the sidelines in Chicago, running a new offense called the T formation, selecting Dick Butkus and Gale Sayers in the same draft, winning the 1963 championship almost exclusively by playing defense—put that all together and you've got a top ten coach.

Lombardi's on the list of course. You win five championships in seven years and go 9-1 in the playoffs and how could you not be? But he was never forced to change anything. He had the best players and he won with them, but when he saw them coming to the end, he quit. No disrespect to Lombardi, but those others did it in two or three different eras and with different quarterbacks, so I give them credit for that.

You have to add Landry in there somewhere. He was a very innovative coach with the Flex defense and signed Staubach even though he was in the navy for five years. And Gibbs is one of the most underrated coaches in history. He won three Super Bowls, and look at the quarterbacks he won with: Joe Theismann, Doug Williams, and Mark Rypien. None of them were close to being Hall of Famers. He and Parcells are the only ones who won without great quarterbacks, so you have to acknowledge that.

Walsh was another great innovator. Much of the foundation of the West Coast offense was developed by Sid Gillman and later Don Coryell, but Walsh refined it with Paul Brown and then perfected it in San Francisco when Brown wouldn't give him his chance in

Cincinnati. He ended up winning three Super Bowls before he retired, and if he'd stayed he would have won two more. George Seifert, his longtime assistant, got the last two on his resume, but he did it with Walsh's players and Walsh's offense.

I have nothing but respect for all the names on my list, but if you hired me to run your team and I had to pick a coach, I'd go with two I'm most familiar with, Shula and Noll, or Belichick, who is clearly the best coach of the salary cap era. No one really comes close since the salary cap and free agency came in.

It's a different game today. You can't do what Lombardi did, which was build a team and then keep it together for a decade. Players leave or they get too expensive and you have to let them go. So you have to understand the salary cap and how to manage it. You have to be able to turn over your roster more frequently because of the economics. That's where Belichick has the edge. He's put that degree in economics from Wesleyan to good use.

So let's take a look at my three finalists to coach the Upton Bells, starting with Noll.

I first met Chuck when I picked him up at the airport in Baltimore after Shula hired him away from the San Diego Chargers in 1966. He'd been Gillman's defensive line coach and later defensive coordinator on a team that went to five AFL Championship Games in six years. He was unlike any other coach I was ever around.

Chuck was a Renaissance man. He had a bunch of interests, not just X's and O's. He had an opinion on everything and he could usually back it up—football, food, wine, history. He once didn't know the difference between Steak Diane and Steak Dolphini and we had a hell of an argument over it before he gave in. That's why I began calling him Knute Knowledge. You'd never think he was a football coach . . . until you started talking football. No doubt after that.

Noll arrived in Baltimore after Shula's third year as head coach, just as I was taking over player personnel. I had enough observations of Shula to know one of his strengths was hiring coaches. He'd hired Bill Arnsparger, whom I'd never heard of. I remember thinking, "Who the hell is this guy?" He turned out to be a brilliant defensive mind. The same was true of Noll.

Chuck was the opposite of Shula. He was just as tough but not as confrontational. Shula would yell at you when he was younger. He'd yell when he was older too but not as often. Or as loud. He'd confront the quarterback right on the sideline. Even Unitas, which didn't go over very well with John.

Chuck was different. When he cut players, he'd call them in and tell them, "Son, it's time for you to pursue your life's work." That's how he looked at it. Football was not a career for a player, he felt. It was a means to an end if they handled it right.

He was very much his own man, and you could see the respect Shula had for his intellect. You hesitate to use that word in football, but it was true with Chuck. Once he got with Arnsparger in Baltimore, it was like you'd joined two great research scientists together and loosed them on the NFL. They created one of the greatest defenses in NFL history built around maximum blitzing and shifting alignments designed to confuse the offense or overpower it. Those Colts' defenses often did both.

Chuck's last year with us was 1968. It didn't end well, but we went 13-1 and tied the league record for fewest points allowed (144). Chuck was a big part of that because he was a teacher, as all great coaches are. He was meticulous in the detail with which he looked at every position. Footwork was important to him. How you got into and out of your stance, which is as basic as football can get, was important to him. One thing he liked to do was write down the techniques of every position and player. It became a teaching tool for him.

You could tell right away he would make a great head coach. As I was walking down from the coaches' box after the crushing disappointment of Super Bowl III, I ran into Dan Rooney, who was a friend of mine. I knew he was looking for a coach and I suggested Noll. I later heard Shula had recommended him too. Fifteen days later, on January 27, 1969, the Steelers hired him after Joe Paterno, Penn State's coach, turned them down. Chuck was thirty-seven years old and the youngest coach in the league, but we all knew he was ready. And he proved it.

In Baltimore he was always interested in personnel. His scouting reports in the spring were excellent. He understood talent, which he certainly showed in Pittsburgh, where he and Art Rooney Jr. combined to have some of the great drafts of the early 1970s. No one who ever scouted for a living will forget his 1974 draft when he selected four Hall of Famers with his first five picks (Lynn Swann, John Stallworth, Jack Lambert, and Mike Webster). A scout could retire on a draft like that.

Shula was different from Chuck. He could be overbearing at times, especially when he first came to Baltimore, but if a decision needed to be made he made it. Boom! He was decisive from the first day he arrived. We had a veteran team that had won a lot with Weeb, who was very different from Don, and that could have been a problem, but he commanded the respect of his players. Respect is not the same as liking you. It's that they listen to you and believe in what you're telling them. The Colts believed in Shula. So did the Dolphins.

Every great coach needs good communication skills. You've got to be able to get your ideas across to your players and your coaches. You must be able to teach your system. Don was a teacher.

He came in with a reputation as a defensive coach because he was the coordinator in Detroit who gave the Packers their only loss, on Thanksgiving Day 1962. He really understood the passing game—how to use it and how to defend it. It was no accident the Lions sacked Bart Starr ten times that day and limited him to 49 net passing yards.

Later he went to Miami and had the only team to go undefeated (17-0) in the modern era, and later his defense was the one that gave the 1985 Bears their only loss in a 15-1 Super Bowl season. Think about that. He's the only coach to go undefeated in a season and give two teams their only loss in a season. That's coaching.

But once Noll and Arnsparger took over the Colts' defense and he was confident with what they were doing, he ran the offense. He did the same in Miami. That was another of his strengths that most great coaches have. He identified great assistants and then he let them coach. The coaches who don't make it are the ones who try to run everything. They get in their own way. Their message gets muddled. Their assistants begin to resent it and the players begin to doubt them. Then it's over.

You have to let your coaches coach, but you can't be afraid to step in when they aren't doing it quite the way you want. There's a line there, a delicate balance between instruction and intrusion. You need to question your assistants, but you can't step on them to the point where they just sit there and nod their heads. They have to feel they can say something to you if they disagree.

Part of Shula's genius was the same thing Belichick has. Don knew everyone's job. He'd stop the film and say, "Chuck, why's he doing that?" He'd do the same thing to McCafferty and the offense and Sandusky with the line. Shula ran the offense and knew the defense. He knew everything those coaches were teaching.

He wasn't like Paul Brown but he wasn't Weeb either. He wanted to call some plays. Not all of them but more than Weeb and that grated on Unitas, even though he didn't really call that many. In fact, he never wore a headset. He knew what he wanted to run but he wasn't micromanaging everything. He coached the coaches so when the game came, they knew what the approach was, and it'd better be his approach.

Don listened to your opinion but he would press you when you gave it. He wanted to know you could defend what you said. He had a temper, but that never bothered me. He might scream at you but then it was over. He had a mind of his own, but if you convinced him about a player he'd go with your pick. He trusted you until you proved you couldn't be trusted. Then you weren't around.

When you think of Shula you think of winning. He won more games than any coach in NFL history (347), and his 328-156-6 regular season record was a .677 winning percentage over thirty-three years. We were together in Baltimore for seven years and he went 71-23-4, a .755 winning percentage. But the biggest thing about him as a coach isn't the numbers. It's that no coach in history won more different ways than Don Shula did.

Most coaches have a system and they ride it to the end. Usually that's to Death Valley because things change. Your staff changes and maybe they aren't as good as the teachers you had before. Your personnel changes and maybe they don't fit as well with what you've always done. Or the game itself changes and you refuse to accept that.

Don never suffered from that. He wasn't wedded to a system. He was wedded to winning. When he had Unitas or Marino, he threw. When he had Larry Csonka, Jim Kiick, and Mercury Morris, he pounded the ball and limited the amount of passes Bob Griese could throw. His biggest strength was that ability to adjust. Adjust to his personnel. To the style of the moment. To the changes in the game.

Griese was a handoff quarterback and very economical. Marino wanted to throw it every down. He won with Unitas but also with an aging veteran backup in Earl Morrall and a rookie quarterback like David Woodley. Hell, he won with Tom Matte, who was a running back masquerading as a quarterback in 1965 when we lost Unitas and Cuozzo. Don rewrote the offense to take advantage of Matte's running ability and we won then too. He was a very good coach in Baltimore and even better in Miami.

I remember one time when we were in Baltimore, Norm Van Brocklin, whom my father was going to make head coach of the Eagles if he'd lived to buy the team in 1960, came in during the off-season to talk football with Shula for a few days. He was coaching the Vikings at the time. I remember walking into the back of the room one day just to listen to them talking at the blackboard. It was like watching Stephen Hawking and Albert Einstein. Two great scientists talking football with each other. That's where I got great respect for Shula, because the thing I remember most clearly was that Van Brocklin was listening more to Shula than Shula was listening to Van Brocklin, who'd been a Hall of Fame quarterback. Van Brocklin understood he needed to listen.

The knock on him is he should have won more, because he went 2-4 in Super Bowls, 2-5 in championship games (losing to the Browns 27–0 in 1964), and 19-17 in the playoffs. Belichick has been the opposite of that. He's 5-2 in Super Bowls and 26-10 in the playoffs. Does that mean he was a better coach than Shula? I don't necessarily believe it does.

You need key assistants to keep winning, and Shula lost them. Noll left for Pittsburgh. Arnsparger left for the Giants. Those men are hard to replace. After those two left, what happened? He still won but it got harder. I think he had a tremendous football mind.

What does that mean? It means a lot of things beyond X's and O's, which he thoroughly understood. It meant telling me to sit in with him and his staff on Mondays so I'd understand the type of player they liked, which is very important for a scout. A lot of scouts don't understand that. It does no good to bring your coach Steve Largent if he wants Randy Moss. No good to bring him a five-foot-nine cornerback if he likes six-foot-two corners. It won't work. He knew that and taught it to me.

Noll was insistent on a certain type of athlete. Fast, quick, with good size. Shula was more open. He wasn't wedded to the size/speed thing. He believed good football players came in all sizes and shapes. He won with a big, hard-hitting defense in Baltimore that was one of the best ever built; he won with the No-Name defense in Miami in the 1970s and the Killer B's defense in the 1980s. He found ways to take the players he had and make them winners.

Same on offense. He won with power running and he won throwing the ball a million times with Marino. He got to the championship game with different types of offenses because he really understood offense as well as defense.

Some say he didn't win the big one often enough, but he won big games. How do you get to the big game without winning big games? If you lose every time maybe it's different, but he won two Super Bowls. The playoffs are single-game eliminations. Don was 2-4 in the championship game and he had to live with that, but I always felt John Madden, who lost five AFC Championship Games, got off the hook and Shula didn't because people liked

Madden personally more than they liked Shula. That's because they didn't know Shula. If you knew Shula and weren't bothered by a no-bullshit person, you liked him. Most people didn't know him. Not really.

The sad thing is there were four or five games during his time in Baltimore that if the outcomes were different, he's the Lombardi of that era. Four or five games that determined who won the NFL championship—reverse them and we win five championships. But that's life. The fact is he won more games than anybody else and he took six teams to the Super Bowl not because he had the same Hall of Fame quarterback for fifteen or sixteen years. His greatest genius was this: Don Shula changed with the times to the very end. In thirty-three years, he had two losing seasons. Go find me another person who did that.

This brings us to Belichick, who is to the new millennium what Paul Brown was to the old one. In the salary cap era, no one has created success like Belichick. This has led some to call him a genius. I tend to reserve "genius" for research scientists and brain surgeons, but certainly he's a football genius, especially as a game coach.

In seventeen years in New England, Belichick has won five Super Bowls and been to seven, meaning he's won 29.4 percent of those played since he took over the Patriots in 2000 and played in 41 percent. He's reached the playoffs fourteen times in seventeen years (82 percent) and got to the conference championship eleven times (64.7 percent of the time). That doesn't happen if you don't have control of personnel and command of the sidelines and the team on it. You can get lucky once. You can't stay lucky for seventeen years.

Belichick has many strengths, but his greatest is making changes during the game. He's a tremendous in-game manager, which not all coaches are. He's also Mr. Modern, like Brown was. He used to keep track of things on the sideline writing notes to himself with a pencil behind his ear. Now he has a handheld computer. Either way he's in control of his team in a way that's shared by few of his peers.

That was never more evident than in Super Bowl XLIX against Seattle. A lot was riding on that game for Belichick. If they lost he'd be 3-3 in Super Bowls. That's still pretty impressive for those of us who tried to make a living in the NFL, but the larger public looks and says, ".500 coach in the big games." Same way some people looked at Shula and looked at Landry for a long time until the Cowboys won a couple Super Bowls in the 1970s. America is a bottom-line country, and pro football has become much more of a bottom-line business. I don't agree with this, but today a lot of people believe there's one winner and thirty-one losers every year.

If they understood all that goes into building and maintaining a team or all the vagaries of why you win or lose a game, they'd see it differently. Did we lose that playoff game to the Packers? Not if the official doesn't blow the call on Chandler's missed field goal. But when you pull up Shula's record, what does it say? Loss. There's no asterisk for a blown call or a fumble or a quarterback missing a wide-open receiver on a flea flicker in a Super Bowl game played forty-eight years ago.

That's part of what we love about sports. It's why we're attracted to it. There's an obvious conclusion that's written on the score-board. Most of life isn't like that, but like Parcells used to say, "You are what your record says you are."

So here's Belichick in Super Bowl XLIX. He knew the consequences of losing that game. If he did it would have been ten years since his last Super Bowl victory. He hadn't won since Spygate, when Belichick was charged with illegally videotaping opposing coaches' hand signals from the sidelines despite having been warned to cease and desist.

That resulted in a $500,000 fine, the biggest ever assessed against a coach at the time, and the franchise was fined $250,000 and lost a No. 1 pick. The weight of that penalty and a decade-long championship drought had to be on his shoulders.

He also hadn't won since his top aides, offensive coordinator Charlie Weis and defensive coordinator Romeo Crennel, left to become head coaches following New England's third Super Bowl championship in 2004. He was approaching the same problem

Shula faced and never totally solved—the drain on you when you lose your top assistants. His critics were starting to say he only won when the stars were aligned and opposing hand signals were on tape, even though he'd taken two other teams to the Super Bowl. It was ridiculous, but his team didn't beat the Giants in Super Bowls XLII and XLVI, so the critics began to say, "What is he really?"

He understood that, yet he never wavered at the end of the game. He looked across the field at Pete Carroll and admitted he saw some chaos. There was no chaos on his sideline.

He knew what they were going to do at the goal line and he'd prepared his defense for it, so he sent in a fifth defensive back because he felt they'd throw it not run it, even though they had a runner called "Beast Mode." He believed they weren't going to give it to Marshawn Lynch again, so he sent in Malcolm Butler and told his defense to expect what they'd prepared for.

He changed from a pure goal-line defense to five defensive backs, believing they'd go back to what they'd done so many times that season in that situation—run a quick slant, even though New England was back on its heels and looked ready to succumb to the moment.

He was sure of what he was doing. His opponent was unsure. That's the thin line between winning and losing in the NFL.

"We had it," Seattle linebacker Bruce Irvin lamented after that game. "I don't understand how you don't give it to the best back in the league on not even the 1-yard line. We were on the half-yard line, and we throw a slant. I don't know what the offense had going on, what they saw. I just don't understand."

Few people did beside Belichick, who sensed what was coming and reacted to it without hesitation. After Butler intercepted Russell Wilson's pass by playing the technique he'd been corrected on by Belichick four days earlier at practice, I remember thinking that was the dumbest call in Super Bowl history. New England had come back to take the lead, and then Seattle's young receiver Jermaine Kearse made one of the greatest catches under pressure I'd ever seen flat on his back, and Belichick's defense had snapped. Seattle is on the half-yard line and the Patriots are desperate, but Belichick isn't. If he loses, he's a .500 coach in The Big Game, not a genius. But he didn't lose. He didn't lose because his defense was prepared for the very play it faced at the most crucial moment of the game. The player still had to make the play, but having him ready for it? That's coaching.

Then Belichick comes back two years later, in Super Bowl LI, and leads his team on the biggest comeback in Super Bowl history to beat the Atlanta Falcons in overtime. There had never been a Super Bowl overtime until then, and it took a 25-point comeback in the second half after falling behind 28–3 to do it. A lot of things had to go right for the Patriots, and the Falcons had to be co-conspirators in their own demise for it to happen, but in the end, Bill Belichick found a way for his team to win. He was the leader.

The closeness of those two Super Bowl wins, though, is why I'm very careful judging someone based on one playoff game. If you lose them all, like Marvin Lewis in Cincinnati, that's different. You can make a fair assessment if you're 0-7 in playoff games. But if your career is determined by who won the last game, then everything is a waste of time. What I know is if I were running a team, I'd take Shula or Belichick and we'd win a lot of games. Big ones and small ones.

Beyond tactical command during the game, Belichick also understands personnel, which I believe is the most valuable talent a head coach can have. You won't always be right, but you'll be right a lot if you do. If you don't, you're only guessing and that won't work for long. He possesses the ability to keep a lot of moving parts in the air, which is more important now than it ever was. Tactics, personnel, the salary cap, ownership relations, media control. It all falls on the head coach today.

First of all, there are thirty-two teams today. You release a Unitas today and five teams claim him. In 1955 most of the teams had no clue who Unitas was. Paul Brown did. He spoke to him about coming to training camp the next summer. But Weeb and Don Kellett knew too, which is why they spent eighty cents on a phone call that changed the history of the Colts and pro football. Belichick would have known who he was too.

Free agency and the salary cap changed everything when it comes to team building. Sometimes he uses the cap like a bludgeon. It allows him to tell a player anything he wants. It's in his favor. It's in everyone else's favor too, but he's smart enough to understand the economics of team building today better than his opponents. Because of that, he builds a better team. Even when they beat the Rams in Super Bowl xxxvi, he had the better team.

At the time it looked like it would be a blowout and later it was seen as a big upset, but if you went on to watch what those two teams did going forward, New England had the better team, especially on defense. It wasn't the upset we thought it was. They went on to win two more Super Bowls the next three years. They were better than the Rams. We just never realized it at the time.

In 1968, if the Super Bowl ran like the World Series, we wouldn't have lost another ballgame to the Jets, but that's the great equalizer. In pro football it's one game. We were the better team but not on that day. In the case of the Patriots and the Rams, the Patriots went on to prove they were the better team. It wasn't magic, like the Jets beating the Colts. The Patriots were better defensively, better prepared, and they had the better coach that day. So they won.

They weren't yet the complete team they became. They had holes, but Belichick is a master at two things: taking away what you do best and making you beat him with something you're less comfortable doing, and hiding the deficiencies of his players. All players, except maybe Jim Brown, have deficiencies. Belichick knows that and does all he can not to expose them.

He is one of the few head coaches today who fully understand roster building in the salary cap era. Generally he doesn't make the big mistake. He goes for the second-day bargains in free agency, not the big splash that can sink a franchise. The times he tried the latter, he's 1-1. Darrelle Revis worked for a year; Adalius Thomas was a big miss. But usually if he misses, it doesn't hurt that much long-term; and if he hits, he's gotten value beyond the norm, which helps his cap.

Shula never wanted to get involved in salary negotiations and the economics of the game. He felt it was the primary way to get players to dislike you and it could affect your judgment of them as players. Today it's different. You have to be involved in that aspect of the game.

Belichick sits there and says this is what we're going to pay. That can cause great resentment, but when you're winning there's nothing the player can say about it. Once he decides who he is going to play with, he does not put those players in positions to fail. He doesn't ask them to do what they can't. He'll hide your weakness and emphasize your strength as a player. There's a genius to that.

He drafted Devin McCourty to be a starting corner, but when McCourty showed he couldn't do it, Belichick didn't argue with the facts the way a lot of coaches would. He didn't try to justify the pick or say, "We brought you here to play corner, so play it!" He was a little stubborn at first but then he moved him to safety and McCourty became one of the best in the league. Some coaches would have kept trying to prove when they drafted him to be Ty Law that he could do it. They'd want to prove they were right, and they'd both go down with the ship.

Belichick has an ability not to get caught up in that. He doesn't concern himself with things that are not important where other coaches might. Before Super Bowl XXXVI, for example, Lawyer Milloy came to him early that week complaining about the rooms being too small at the Fairmont Hotel in New Orleans—an older hotel with cramped rooms—while Belichick and some of his coaches had suites.

Belichick understood immediately this wasn't a power issue. It was a potential distraction. A possible excuse not to play well. So he gave Milloy his suite. Not many other coaches would have. All week, he kept asking Milloy if he was sleeping all right. The message to me was, "You've got no excuse now."

He told somebody else, "What the hell do I care about how big my room is?" It had nothing to do with doing his job, so he didn't care, but it might have affected one of his players, so he gave them the best room. When you win, that's genius. If you don't win, no one mentions it.

It's a different era today, but Shula never left until everything was done. Belichick is the same way. Both correct you immediately if there's a mistake; or if there's some confusion, they deliver their message until you understand it. They correct everything because the little things, like Butler not playing the goal-line slant aggressively enough in practice Super Bowl week, can decide your future.

Noll would practice huddling up. What did it matter? It was about the players focusing on the little things. More games are lost than are won in the NFL. That's always been true. The great coach doesn't have teams that conspire against themselves.

There are many examples of this with Belichick's Patriots, but one stands out. In a divisional playoff game against San Diego on January 14, 2007, Brady threw a killer interception on fourth down with the Chargers leading by 8 late in the fourth quarter. All safety Marlon McCree had to do was go down and San Diego could have worked the clock down, but instead he tried to return it and had the ball poked free from behind by Troy Brown. Five plays and a 2-point conversion later and the game is tied. New England won it on a field goal with 1:10 left, and a month later Chargers coach Marty Schottenheimer was fired. He'd gone 14-2 that season, but a day after the game McCree said he would have done the same thing if they played again. So did New England win the game or did San Diego find a way to lose it? I'd say both.

Belichick seems to believe in creative tension. He asks his players questions that seem meaningless, like where did the gunner on your opponent's special teams go to college? He seems to believe if his players home in on the small things, they will be homed in on the more important ones the way Noll was. "Questions and answers," like first-year law students at Harvard. Shula wasn't into that as much as Belichick but they both held you accountable, both the coaches and players, for what happens.

Coaching at the NFL level is a twenty-four-hour-a-day, seven-day-a-week, twelve-month-a-year job today. It wasn't always that way but now I think it has to be. I don't think you need all the assistants they have now but the hours are required. There's always something to do. I saw personnel the same way. There's always something you can do to help your team get better if you know what you're doing.

Belichick turned sixty-five in 2017. He's the longest-tenured coach in the NFL, eighteen years with the Patriots and twenty-three as a head coach. He came into the league in 1975, so that's over forty years of coaching. How much longer can he do it? I don't know. Shula was sixty-five his final season and they pushed him out because they weren't winning enough. They fired Paul Brown. Walsh was emotionally spent after ten years and quit. It was time to go. It happens. It's a corrosive job.

I believe Belichick will do it until they tell him to leave too. My guess is it may not be nice at the end, the same way it wasn't nice for Shula or Paul Brown. A lot of people will be waiting for Belichick if it turns bad. A lot of the media. A lot of his opponents. They're lying in the weeds waiting because of the way he's operated all these years. So if he falls, it could be steep. If you win a lot for a long time, you create enemies. You create jealousies. If you slip, they come after you. What great player or coach didn't face that?

But once he's gone they'll have to admit Bill Belichick dominated his era. So did Paul Brown and Don Shula. The others on my list did well, but everything they do today stemmed from Brown. Shula won more games than anyone else and had the fourth-best winning percentage among NFL coaches with at least one hundred wins (.677). Belichick has won the most Super Bowls and has the fifth-best winning percentage among coaches with at least one hundred victories (.673), and he isn't done yet. NFL life is about the bottom line. We're all evaluated the same way; whether it's Halas in the 1940s or Belichick today or Upton Bell picking players for two Super Bowl teams, it's the same: How often did you win?

Yet in the end, just like in the Bible, there's only one Moses. In the NFL, that's Paul Brown.

18

Out of the Frying Pan, Into the Fire

Six weeks after the collapse of the World Football League, my
mother passed away at the age of seventy-one. At the funeral, both
Wellington Mara and Art Rooney showed up. They were there as
family friends, not NFL representatives, but their presence was a
reminder that the NFL wasn't totally out of my life. I was still, at
heart, a football man.

As we were walking out of the church, Wellington came up and
asked how I was doing and if I was going to be all right. What
was I going to say?

My team and league had just gone out of business. My mother
had passed away. I didn't have a job and I was in debt and intended
to pay back every penny I could. Naturally I said I'd be fine.

It took about six months to clear up the issues in Charlotte.
Then I returned to Boston and went on to New York to prepare
to get a stockbroker's license. The fact was I had to make some
money to take care of my family and clear up those debts.

I wasn't really depressed about it. This was the football life,
at least for the Bells. In football, you gain ground and you lose
ground. Sometimes you win when you don't expect to. Other
times you lose. Either way, you play on.

I had a million contacts, and brokerage houses like people with
contacts, especially ones with money. I didn't have any money but
I knew people who did, and I landed a job at Shearson, Hayden,
Stone back in Boston.

I didn't come in as a traditional broker. I was a rainmaker, someone whose job was to connect investors with brokers. It didn't take long.

The first deal I made was with the Bert Bell Pension Fund to manage part of its assets. At the time I think it was worth almost $200 million. A couple weeks after I passed my securities exam, a manager at Shearson told me that Shearson's management company landed $100 million of it to manage. The commission wasn't a fortune, but it was pretty good.

After bringing that in, I started to drift in an unexpected direction. I began moonlighting on radio and television. I kept looking for pensions, but not every pension happens as quickly as that first one did. It can take years. It wasn't like scouting a player, making a decision, and signing him.

In that spring of 1976 I also wrote Wellington and told him I felt I was being kept out of football. A lot of people from the WFL, a lot of my own players and coaches, had gotten NFL jobs, but I hadn't heard a word despite a successful track record of finding and drafting talent. One of Wellington's sons was at Boston College, and he told me when he came to visit we'd meet and we did.

Exile is not a comfortable existence, but that's what my sense of things were. We had a long discussion about my football future. I laid out what I thought was going on and told him I'd appreciate his help. He said he'd see what he could find out.

Maybe a month later I received a letter from Wellington, which I still have. He said what I felt was basically true. However, it wasn't Billy Sullivan who was actively keeping me out of the NFL. I questioned then who his surrogate was. Wellington said it was Billy's son, Chuck, who was telling NFL people I was a difficult person to deal with. Chuck was quite powerful at the time. He was on the Management Council and was a lawyer whose views a lot of people listened to.

I also spoke with Rozelle. We had a good conversation and he said he'd look into it, but he also told me I had to understand he had no control over the owners. The league was too big now. I never knew if Pete talked to some of the other owners in the league or not. Maybe he did but I think it unlikely.

Later that year I got a call from Bob Gibson, who had been my second head coach in Charlotte. He was now the Giants' offensive coordinator under John McVay, two refugees from the WFL assimilated into the NFL. I was happy for them both. They knew what they were doing and deserved that chance.

Gibson told me he'd heard Andy Robustelli, the Giants' general manager, was close to retiring and Wellington was seriously talking about me as a candidate. Gibson was a not a bullshitter. He was a very direct person. He said he thought it could happen. It was the first I'd heard of it.

I soon got a call from someone in the league office who told me Wellington had been asking questions about me and what was I like to work with. He wanted the opinion of a disinterested third party, which was smart.

When we'd met in Boston, he kept asking about operating under difficult financial circumstances in the WFL. I think he was interested in how I'd run an operation without any money, because he remembered what the NFL was like in the early days. He was impressed too that every one of my coaches and many of my players in Charlotte had been hired immediately.

At the time the Giants had played at Yale Bowl and then Shea Stadium while their new stadium at the Meadowlands was being completed. It didn't open until October 10, 1976, and in the interim the Giants were facing a lot of organizational change.

Robustelli had been a Hall of Fame player for them and returned in 1974 to run most of the football operation. At the time there was a lot of turmoil with the franchise after Wellington's brother, Jack, died.

Jack had always run the business side and Wellington ran the football side. It was a 50-50 partnership that worked well until Wellington's nephew, Tim, took over. They clashed over a lot of things and Wellington was ultimately forced to give up some of his authority, because it was still a 50-50 partnership and he needed Tim's approval to do anything. It got to the point where they weren't even talking to each other. They were at odds over every decision, and that began to affect the franchise on the field.

They had the same kind of internal bickering and resulting turmoil I'd dealt with in New England, and it led to the same result. When Robustelli arrived, he took over a 2-11-1 team. He was there for six years. They never had a winning season.

Wellington not only knew me through my father, he knew me professionally. He'd been in all those meetings with me at CEPO, the scouting service. We did that deal together for Fred Dryer. Now he was asking about me. I thought I had a real chance to run a great NFL franchise again.

I don't know this to be true, but I was told when my name came up there was a strong voice that wouldn't agree to anyone who was a friend of Wellington's. Certainly something happened, because you don't go from being a leading candidate to never hearing from anyone, and it stands to reason they may not have accepted me because Wellington's family and mine had grown up together. They needed someone both sides could agree upon, which meant the person had to come from outside their circles.

Ironically, George Young, my assistant in Baltimore, ended up there and he brought in Ernie Accorsi. George not only had to deal with the football operations, he also had to spend a lot of his time refereeing Wellington versus Tim and later Bill Parcells versus Tom Boisture, my old scout in New England who became the head of personnel. Whoever got the job had to get along with everybody and that was one of George's great strengths.

George didn't have a close relationship with either of the Maras, and Shula had suggested him to Rozelle one day when they were playing tennis. Eventually I got a call from someone in the league that it wasn't going to happen. Timmy was fearful I'd side with Wellington. If I hadn't been a friend of Wellington's I might have had a chance, but George was a good choice because he was good politically. I would have been back in the same position as the Patriots, trapped between warring factions. I had a lot of respect for Wellington, so it would have been hard to be in that position. Looking back I can't say for sure what I would have done if the job was offered, but I'm glad it wasn't.

Around the same time, I did the first televised NFL draft show.

As with many things in my career, it was an odd situation. The show was on public television. Imagine the NFL draft on PBS?

I'd gotten a call from a PBS producer at WGBH in Boston named Greg Harney. He'd talked PBS into doing tennis and hired Bud Collins to do it, and the rest is history. For decades, Bud went on to become synonymous with tennis coverage all over the world.

Harney was a great idea man. He felt the draft was a unique event no one had ever really delved into. He wanted to do both days with cameras in New York with Kim Prince, a tennis commentator, doing cut-ins as they announced the picks while I'd be the expert analyst back in Boston. We'd also have other guests talking about the players. He also hired Curt Gowdy Jr. to co-produce and direct it.

Harney told me since my father invented the draft I should be in the middle it. That's how I ended up co-hosting the draft's first national telecast in 1977 on PBS. It still amazes me. Not that we did a draft show but that it started on public TV.

Harney was a crazy genius. He convinced PBS in Boston that sports was an important part of the larger world and deserved its attention. Because WGBH was one of the most powerful PBS stations in the country, this was a gigantic production. PBS had obtained film of many of the top players, which was unusual in those days. It was really a landmark broadcast, but Harney could only put it on the air if he could raise the money to do it. Somehow he did, although we only did it that one year.

As important as the draft has been to the survival and growth of the NFL, I never once thought it could become prime-time television. To turn four days of people sitting around conference tables picking players into prime-time TV entertainment like it is today is like saying an amoeba one day will become an elephant and would you like to watch. It shows how great a hold on the public the NFL has established. They've hooked the rabid fan, the fantasy football geek, and the casual observer and convinced them all of the idea they could have been the one picking those players like I once did.

Today fans study draft guides, watch the combine workouts

on NFL Network, see video of all these college players, and try to find that diamond in the rough out at Eastern Montana or Western Carolina or Tennessee A&I. They think they can scout from the living room. It's brilliant!

Fans have that sense of both discovery and having inside information. They forget three-quarters of these draftees will be failures. The league has done a great job of masking that. They sell dreams. They've always sold dreams.

That's truer now than it ever was. In 2016, 208 of 253 drafted players made opening day rosters. Counting undrafted college free agents, 277 rookies made it that year. Another 20 were on injured reserve.

That meant 81 percent of drafted players were on opening day rosters, which was a record. In 1995, the first year of the salary cap, it was 71.1 percent, so it's a 10 percent increase and I believe mostly a result of financial decisions, not football decisions.

That speaks to the economic changes in the game. If star quarterbacks, pass rushers, and cornerbacks are going to be paid a huge portion of the salary cap, then it demands cheap labor in the bottom third of the roster. Maybe even higher. Where do you find it? With inexperienced young players.

A lot of veterans who can still play end up with their salaries cut to the minimum or find themselves released not because they can't contribute anymore but because they cost too much. The more young players not ready to play have to be put on the field, the more the product suffers. That's a part of salary-cap reality nobody wants to talk about, but I drafted players for years, and I know 81 percent of them in any year do not belong in the NFL. But here they are and fans are spending hours and hours watching the selection process. It's amazing. The NFL's marketing people deserve a pat on the back. It's a phenomenon I never saw coming in 1977 on PBS.

At the same time I was working on that draft show, I began doing college football games on local television in New England, and one day WBZ Radio called to ask if I would be part of its Patriots pre- and postgame shows as well as do some fill-in work. It turned out to be my first big break, and in a backhanded way I had Billy Sullivan to thank for it.

In 1977, my first year working Patriots broadcasts, Billy got into a spat with the coach and general manager who replaced me, Chuck Fairbanks. He refused to honor a contract Fairbanks had promised John Hannah and Leon Gray to end their holdout. My first thought was, "Hello, Fred Dryer."

Hannah and Gray were the best guard-tackle tandem in the league at the time. Hannah is considered the greatest guard to ever play, and Gray at one point was voted the best offensive lineman in the league. Both were All-Pros playing at their peak and felt woefully underpaid.

Hannah still had three years plus an option left on his rookie contract and Gray had two plus an option, so they decided to take teamwork to the negotiating table with an agent representing them named Howard Slusher. Howard was a brilliant but difficult negotiator, so much so that some teams got to the point they avoided his clients altogether. He became known as "Agent Orange" because of his red hair and scorched-earth approach to negotiating.

Slusher convinced a number of clients to hold out, and that included Hannah and Gray. The previous season, the Patriots had averaged 210 rushing yards a game and 5 yards per carry on 591 runs, much of it gained behind those two. Without them the Patriots were not a playoff contender, as they'd been in 1976.

The two of them launched a holdout prior to the season's final exhibition game on September 11. My thought was to ask Chuck or Billy to come on the postgame show to discuss the situation. I decided no matter what our relationship was in the past, I wanted them on to explain their side of it because they were getting slaughtered in the media. I'm pretty sure it was Billy who agreed to do it.

I had no compunction asking him about the situation. I didn't feel nervous about it. I didn't say, "Hi, Billy, isn't this like when you screwed me on Dryer?" I just asked how it had come to this.

His replies were a replay of what he'd said to me six years earlier. He couldn't say it was the board anymore because by then he'd bought 100 percent of the team, although a class-action suit had been filed challenging how he handled the transactions that eventually cost him a lot of money.

He said he was sorry it all became public, but he had to be a responsible shepherd for the organization. He was looking out for the greater good. I just listened. I didn't get emotionally involved because I didn't want to lose control of the questioning. I didn't have to say, I think you screwed Fairbanks the way you screwed me. I just let him reveal himself.

We took calls on the postgame show and people were going crazy. The phone lines were all flashing. I told him that although I might agree with him, the public didn't.

I didn't agree but I was trying to get the story. My reaction to the whole situation told me I had a future in the media. I was able to detach myself from what had occurred between us and just ask questions I thought the public would have asked if it had the opportunity. The interview wasn't personal. I'm sure Billy didn't share that opinion, but it wasn't. What it became was my real start in the media business.

Listening to Billy explain why he didn't back Fairbanks was a reminder of how things can go off the rails. Unless it was a winning situation, I wasn't going to run back to pro football to be in it for two or three years and get fired again. I was beginning to understand that while you may have a dream, that doesn't mean the people around you share it.

The morning of Super Bowl XII, I'm at home waiting for the game to begin and I get a call from Bob Lobel, who was a sportscaster at WBZ Radio on weekends. He was in studio for four or five hours and knew no one would be calling, so he asked if I'd come in.

My first reaction was, I want to watch the game, but then I thought, "Why not?" It was the kind of decision that can change your life without you realizing that possibility exists. That show was like Cinderella putting on the glass slipper. I knew immediately it fit.

We did three or four hours like it was nothing. The station's general manager had been listening and decided to take a chance on me. We started on the weekends and then moved to weekdays later that year. It was a big gamble for WBZ because they had to replace a man named Guy Mainella, who was a pioneer in sports talk radio but who had begun doing a general news talk show. Prior to that he'd done *Calling All Sports* since its inception on July 15, 1969. Now Lobel and I were replacing him. Who knew if we would make sense or nonsense five nights a week? We were about to find out. That was the summer of 1978, the summer of the Red Sox collapse, which we covered both at Fenway and at Yankee Stadium.

Calling All Sports was really where things took off for me in Boston. Lobel and I were like Oscar Madison and Felix Unger—very different from each other, but it worked. We got the most fascinating people and put them on. One was former San Francisco 49ers running back Dave Kopay, who played with five NFL teams before becoming the first pro football player to come out as gay in a 1977 best-selling book, *The David Kopay Story*. It shocked the world.

He had been a hard-nosed player for nine years in the NFL, which didn't fit the prevailing stereotype. He came on and spoke of living this hidden life in the toughest sport there is. We were the only show in Boston dealing with things like that. During the show Kopay gave a rather graphic description of his life that had to be bleeped out. Thank God for the seven-second delay! The phone lines lit up.

We were on for a year before I changed stations when the program director was fired and they brought in a new general manager from Pittsburgh, who decided why pay two when I can pay one? I went to WEEI, CBS, and did *Sports Line* and Bob went to WBZ television as the weekend anchor. Years later, a former Patriot player named Tim Fox told me, "Upton, just remember, you're only as good as your next program director." That was a lesson that would be learned many times over.

Of all the people we interviewed, one of the most fascinating was Woody Hayes, the legendary Ohio State football coach. Lobel was from Ohio and Woody was one of his heroes as a kid. I knew him from my scouting days and always thought he was a bully, so I kept baiting Lobel about him. I told him Woody doesn't recognize that the forward pass exists. He's a Neanderthal. Let's get him on.

We did and Bob is going on and on, telling how great he is. Then I begin to question everything Woody does. That was the great yin and yang of the show. It was one of the most amazing interviews we ever did because Hayes spent the whole time talking about Ralph Waldo Emerson's essay "Self-Reliance" and *The Ethics of Authenticity.* That is a philosophy described as individuals seeking the good life for themselves on their own terms. That was Woody explaining himself in a way I never anticipated.

Instead of talking about Ohio State–Michigan or the Rose Bowl, he said Emerson was the real deal when compared with Henry David Thoreau. He never spoke about football. He kept talking about the significance of Emerson's philosophy.

What became clear from that interview was this was much more than a football coach. That was the kind of surprise we wanted to bring out on the show, and we often did.

There were also insane moments too after we began doing a spinoff of the radio show once a week on PBS called *Sports Weekly.* One time we brought on Marvin Hagler, who is considered one of the two or three greatest middleweight champions in boxing history. He had a hard time getting his first break, so he was talking about his hopes and dreams when Lobel said, "Why don't we get up and you show me the punches you use?" They get into the fighter's stance and Marvin is explaining the uppercut, the hook, and next thing I know Lobel sucker punches him with a big glove on. Marvin took a dive and I'm thinking Hagler is going to beat the crap out of him when he gets up. Instead he was laughing, but what a reaction it got.

Another wild character was Don Cherry. People know him in Canada today as the broadcaster with the loudest sports coats, but he was the Bruins coach at the time and a very funny, colorful man. He was always talking about his dog, Blue. So I said let's get Blue on the show.

Cherry arrives with this huge bulldog wearing a fancy blanket.

He's talking about his problems with Harry Sinden, the general manager and former coach. I look down and the dog has taken a crap on the set. Live on air. It's not like regular TV where you have ads to go to. It's PBS. They didn't have ads but they had a mess on their hands.

As *Calling All Sports* was ending and *Sports Nightly*, a five-nights-a-week show created by Harney, was beginning, WBZ did give permission for Bob to do both broadcasts. Lobel eventually became a local legend as the weekday sports anchor at Channel 4. He became the highest-paid local anchor in America at one point and Boston loved him for over two decades. With Bob gone, Harney and I were scrambling. Harney had created a regular PBS version and we needed a co-host. Harney turned to his close friend Bud Collins, who was an erudite man.

On our first show the teleprompter broke, but no one realized it but us. Bud was trying to remember the sports updates and he kept waving his script, hoping someone would notice. We looked like two men lost at sea. Someone finally figured it out and went to a promo, but we got savaged by a local critic. It was the last time Bud appeared on the show, as he'd done Greg a favor to at least appear on opening night. He wanted nothing more to do with it so we brought in a young man named Brian Leary, who ended up having a long and successful television career. He was just starting out at the time but the chemistry worked

I'd always wanted to interview John Wooden, the great basketball coach from UCLA. I thought his philosophies on winning and team play were fascinating, even though he often came off as pretty dry.

He was in Boston one year to promote a book and we had him all set up when he called about a half hour before the show was to begin to say he wasn't feeling well and couldn't make it. What do you do? It's live TV.

I asked a producer if he could get a tree stump and wrap a chain around it, which he did. We put it in the chair where Wooden was supposed to sit for the second half of the show. Here's our special guest—John Wood-en.

I kept asking the questions and the camera would pan to the stump for thirty to forty seconds and there would be nothing but dead air. Then on to the next question. Finally I said, "Coach, great to have a wooden personality on the show." Viewers loved it.

When *Sports Nightly* came to an end, as all shows do, I got the Harvard Band to march in to open the final show and march out to end it. I toasted Brian Leary with champagne, which was a no-no on TV at the time, and we all marched out with the band. Never happened before. Never happened since.

When I was doing my show on WEEI Radio, I was approached by my producer to do an interview with a young actor about a new comedy show on television based on a former Red Sox pitcher running a local bar in Boston. I was singularly unimpressed. I told him I couldn't care less about some bar show.

He convinced me to do it, though, and Ted Danson was on the phone line and was very entertaining. The show, of course, was *Cheers*, proving once again no scout gets it right every time.

Around this time I began to see the media was changing. There had always been this great divide between the print media and the electronic, but now newspaper guys wanted to get paid to go on the air, and deservedly so. TV and radio producers wanted them to legitimize things. Thus began the "insiders" syndrome we have today.

It has been fed by the rise of cable television and the 24-hour news cycle that demands constant feeding of the beast and an endless supply of shows, but the early pioneers of that, like my friend Will McDonough at the *Boston Globe*, Peter King from *Sports Illustrated*, and Bud Collins, who wrote at the *Globe* for many years, were all newspapermen. They provided the gravitas. As McDonough used to say to callers, "The difference between you and me is you think and I know." He usually did.

One thing I realized about radio and TV was it wasn't much different from professional sports in one area. There's always someone younger waiting to take your job. In both cases, you want to protect your turf.

You didn't want to be Wally Pipp, the Yankee first baseman

who took a day off because of a cold and let Lou Gehrig play, and then Gehrig didn't come out of the lineup for 2,130 consecutive games. It's a fear of replacement I'd first seen in Baltimore and it was the same in broadcasting. There's a shelf life for everyone, so be careful, which oftentimes is why you aren't careful about some things.

The brother of Tenley Albright, the Olympic gold medalist figure skater, was my doctor. In the early 1980s, he'd taken a biopsy and found the final stages of a malignant melanoma. He told me it had to come out immediately because if it spread I could be dead in a couple of weeks. I had a show to do. I didn't want people to know about it.

I went to his office, where he numbed my arm and performed the surgery right there. It was a scary hour. He found a second spot and took that out too. Then I had to get to work. In those days you didn't tell anyone you were sick. Somebody starts thinking, if he's got cancer we'd better look to replace him.

He strapped me up, I put on a long-sleeve shirt, and I headed to the studio. People today would have said take the time you need, but you didn't feel that way then. Maybe they still don't, because they can replace you in a minute and they will.

In 1989 I was part of what became a groundbreaking television panel show called *Sports Beat*. It was four men sitting around talking sports: myself, Lobel, Bob Ryan of the *Boston Globe*, and Joe Fitzgerald from the *Boston Herald*. It was the forerunner to shows like *Sports Reporters* on ESPN.

It was the idea of a very talented general manager named Dan Berkery and producer Nate Greenberg, who became vice president of the Boston Bruins. At the time the station, Channel 38, carried the Red Sox and Bruins telecasts, so the ratings were gangbusters. The show just took off because there was nothing like it on local TV or national TV: three men with me as moderator debating three sports issues a show.

It went up on the satellite so it was seen all over the country, but that's not why it was successful. It was successful for the same reason most things in the media are. It was real.

Today there seems to be a hundred shows trying to be like we were. They argue and fight, but many of them don't come across as real. That's what we did on that show because we had some of the most knowledgeable personalities in Boston, many of them writers who have gone on to great careers in radio and television. It really changed local TV because everyone wanted to create a show like it, which, if you turn on television today, they have.

A few years later Will McDonough and I were offered a spot doing televised debates on Channel 7, the local CBS affiliate in Boston. One of our skits in 1985 got a reaction from Shula, the year his Dolphins were playing the Patriots in the AFC Championship Game.

The Dolphins always beat the Patriots in those days. It was the reverse of how it is now, so we went to Salem, Massachusetts, the site of the famous Salem Witch Trials, and had a séance with a self-proclaimed witch named Lorie Cabot. We wanted to know who was going to win the game.

She's divining this and divining that and finally says it's going to be the Patriots' year. Shula called me and said, "I heard about you guys. Billy told me you were with some witch and picked the Patriots over me."

Billy called him? I told him we weren't analyzing the game. It was a spoof. It was just entertainment. Today it would be expected, but not in 1985.

When the Celtics lost the NBA Finals to the Lakers in 1987, I got a friend who owned a funeral home to loan us a casket and a hearse. We filmed us pulling up to the funeral home. They pull out this closed casket and we go inside with organ music playing. Inside it's an open casket. We move the camera in as Will and I are peering in with sad faces. When they pan to the casket there's a Celtics basketball inside. The station got a lot of reaction from it because it was different from what was being done on local TV, and different sells if it's also entertaining.

Over the years I came to see running a football team and being on radio and TV weren't that different. Both jobs were affected by decisions made by many different people, and some of them didn't know enough about their own business. Others were brilliant and those people won everywhere they went, so your own success was only partly in your hands.

Over my forty years in the media, I never got another nibble from the NFL after the Giants didn't happen, although from time to time some writer would call from a town where his team was struggling and ask why no one called me. John Steadman wrote about it in Baltimore and all but said he thought I'd been blackballed. Dave Klein, who was an influential football writer at the *Newark Star-Ledger,* wrote a piece with a headline that read: "Why Can't Bell Get a Job in the NFL?"

This was six years after I'd been fired by the Patriots and three after the WFL had collapsed. The point he raised was funny if it hadn't been so true.

Klein opined that many successful people were also disliked. He described me as "a somewhat harsh, somewhat abrasive man. He is also somewhat brilliant in the fields of drafting and trading."

I enjoyed the article and others like it. When people called to ask why I was no longer in pro football, I told them I didn't really know but I'd moved on. I had no choice. Life's too short to stay stuck in one place.

I understood radio-TV was as dangerous a business as sports management, but I was enjoying it and making a living and it became the next adventure, like the day I got in my car and drove off to Baltimore.

As the years went along, the NFL as an occupation began to recede from my mind. Everything in the NFL was changing. The owners I knew were fading out and the new ones had a different attitude. The general manager didn't have the authority he once had. It was becoming what they called narrow casting in the media business. Responsibilities were being broken up so the general manager had less organizational control. As the game grew into a bigger business and began taking over Sundays, Monday nights, and Thursday nights as well as most of the off-season, the importance of the game itself organizationally seemed to begin to recede in my opinion.

The last fifteen years or so I moved away from doing sports exclusively. It seemed to me you were beginning to beg sports personalities to come on your show unless they had something to sell. People were starting to pay them to come on. That was a change I didn't like. I didn't want to beg people to reveal a little of themselves to their public, so I moved on to general news talk and got to do some of my favorite interviews.

People thought I was crazy when I first made the move, but I was used to that. In 1991 Dave Maynard was the big name in morning talk radio in Boston. Maynard was retiring and I applied for the job. No one thought I had a chance. I was a sports personality, but the decision changed my career path once again.

I did a fill-in show and lined up Yo-Yo Ma, the greatest cellist in the world; Harry Ellis Dickson, the great Boston Symphony and Boston Pops conductor; and U.S. Attorney Wayne Budd. Yo-Yo drove over to WBZ on the Fourth of July to do the interview. That's the interview that got me the job replacing Dave Maynard. The general manager heard the show and decided he was going to put me in the competition. I owe Yo-Yo Ma a lot for that interview.

I've been blessed to have lived an interesting life. My years in pro football were some of the greatest times in my life, but so was sitting on the White House lawn under a tree asking President George Herbert Walker Bush how sports helped relieve the pressure for him in times of crisis.

That interview came about in the odd way so many things seem to happen in my life. I was riding the subway in Boston one morning and ran into an old friend, Nancy Bush Ellis, President Bush's sister. I told her I wanted to interview the president about the importance of sports in his life. She said she was going to the White House and if I got her a letter she'd give it to him.

One day my phone rings and a voice says, "This is the White House. President Bush will do the interview with you." What?

I deflated a WFL football because he was dealing with an inflation problem at the time as well as Kuwait and brought it with me. He had lots of meetings so they said they'd whisk me through.

The press was clamoring to interview the president, and Lesley Stahl of CBS saw me going through the press room and wanted to know who I was and what I was doing on a day the president wasn't doing interviews.

While we were waiting, an aide came in and said President Bush may not be able to do it, as he's meeting with his cabinet about Kuwait. I'm thinking, "Oh, God. It's not going to come off," when someone else came back and said the president told you he was going to do it so he's going to do it.

They took me outside near a little pond on the grounds and President Bush came out. The first thing he said was, "Anybody who ever tells you your uncle was a great governor, you remember he was only governor for seventeen days." He was laughing and so at ease and so able to put you at ease. None of it was put-on.

The interview was about how he dealt with the pressure of the presidency. He talked about playing baseball at Yale and what a joy it was. He spoke of playing against Babe Ruth in an exhibition game and he talked about Nolan Ryan and his own son, George W., running the Texas Rangers. As the president was talking, the man next to me kept looking at his watch, which was his job I guess. He was the off-camera timekeeper, who monitored all presidential interviews, ready to end the round like in a boxing match.

The president always has meetings waiting, and at some point an aide told him he had something else on his schedule. Very politely but very firmly President Bush said, "I told him I was going to give him the time, and that's what we're going to do. Resume the interview." It went on about thirty minutes. I'll never forget his humanity.

I asked him how he wanted to be remembered and he said, "As someone not worried about his image or what I did or didn't do, but I don't want anyone to say they felt sorry for me because it was a hard job." He emphasized that. Don't feel sorry for him.

That interview ran for five nights in Boston, and you can still watch it today on YouTube. Google it and you'll find Uppie under a tree with Bush 41. If you want to see a gracious man comfortable with who he is, go watch President Bush talking with me about how sports shaped his life.

I also did one of the final interviews with Pete Rozelle. He was ready to retire and he looked so tired. He'd fought a lot of battles by then with the union, the new breed of owner, and his old nemesis, Al Davis. We talked about the history of the game and its growth. He talked about how my father influenced his life. You could tell he was a man who saw the end coming.

In the last part of the interview I asked him why he was retiring. He told me he'd seen my father die in office and he didn't want to die that way. He didn't, but he died less than six years later. I'll always believe building the NFL into the colossus it became contributed to that.

When he announced his retirement at the 1989 league meetings, it shocked a lot of people. He was in tears at the press conference. Football is hard to walk away from, even if it's time. You think you have a grip on it, but it turns out that it has a grip on you.

I think the same thing was true for Don Shula when the end was approaching for him in Miami. He wasn't winning as often as he once had and people began criticizing him. In his last ten seasons in Miami, the Dolphins missed the playoffs six times, and he only won three playoff games during that stretch before retiring after the 1995 season.

Maybe his teams weren't quite what they had been, but there are a lot of reasons for that. One was not that Don Shula forgot how to coach. He was as great a coach as pro football ever had, which is why he won more games than anyone who ever coached. What measuring stick is there but winning games?

When I came to interview him late in his career, we didn't really talk about football. Not directly. We started off talking about it, but we'd been through so many ups and downs together we began talking about him leaving practice early to be home with his wife, Dorothy, who was dying from cancer.

He talked about how that had changed his life. He was very forthright. It was one of the most honest interviews I ever did.

He still had this great football team with Dan Marino at quarterback, but he was talking to me about his wife's struggles. Of all the people I'd spoken with, that was the most difficult interview because it was about life and death. Reality, not games. There is no one I respect more in pro football than Don Shula.

When Bill Clinton was first running for president, he was up in New Hampshire when my producer lined him up as a guest. This was right after Gennifer Flowers went public about her affair with him while he was governor of Arkansas. Clinton was in third or fourth place in the race and getting killed over this affair and no one was expecting him to be a factor, but after we were done talking, I told my producer he was going to be president. He could talk his way around anything. He made you think you were the only person in the room. No one can define "it" but you know when someone has it. Bill Clinton had it.

So did Howard Cosell, but it was a different kind of "it." He was someone people loved to hate, but he was as big as any sportscaster in broadcasting history. He was acerbic, polarizing, interesting, and entertaining. I interviewed him at the end of his career and he'd become a bitter man. He wasn't the same man who grilled me when I was taking the New York Stars to Charlotte in 1974 or the one who when he used to see me would say, "The brilliant young GM Upton Bell! He's done many things but what has he done lately!" Then he'd laugh. He wasn't laughing much anymore.

The last time we spoke I was doing a series of personality interviews for WBZ TV, and he agreed to come on. I went to his office in New York, and it was a little cubbyhole. He'd had a falling out with Roone Arledge, who ran ABC Sports, and he'd written a memoir that deeply offended a lot of his colleagues, including Frank Gifford, who was as beloved as Cosell was vilified. Those things put him on ice with many people in the business, and TV is a small business.

Now he was in this little office in New York with few adornments. I felt sorry for him but it was a reminder of what life is. He talked about his demotion and the deterioration of his relationship with Arledge and he railed about what he called the "jockocracy," which he saw as former athletes given broadcasting jobs they neither earned nor deserved. He'd become a kind of sad Shakespearean character, a king brought low by hubris, human frailties, and his own ego.

His fatal flaw was he thought he was bigger than his business. Bigger than the sports he broadcast that made his name a household word. It's a great business, but it's just as deadly as pro football if you start thinking it can't go on without you. Both can and will. Sometimes people forget that.

Unlike Howard, I'm among the lucky ones. I've been blessed in my life to know two careers and love them both. One of them, pro football, allowed me to live out my boyhood dreams and spend many years at the highest level of the greatest game there is.

Pro football is still that. When I think about the game and what it has become, I think of two quotes that seem to explain its place in American culture today.

The great political reporter Mary McGrory once said, "Baseball is what we were. Football is what we've become." I think she was right. As much as I love baseball, it is a game out of a slower past. It's a game of subtlety that can take a long time to develop and, in theory, can go on without end. Football is about speed, power, dominance, and instant gratification. It's what society has become. You don't grind it out much on the ground anymore. You throw it and keep throwing it and people seem to love it.

The other important thing about pro football today is something Michael MacCambridge, the author of the definitive history of the sport, *America's Game*, wrote: "At the dawn of the 21st Century, pro football was one of the few solid pieces of common ground left on the increasingly balkanized map of modern American popular culture."

Football brings together people who might otherwise have nothing in common the way few other things do today. It transcends race, politics, religion, and other agendas. It's communal even if that community is the fantasy football crowd. There are so many channels now there is no common denominator television show we all watch except the Super Bowl.

I was present at the creation of all that pro football has become. Through my father I fell in love with the game, and even with all the ups and downs, that has never waned. Even with its problems today, pro football is still the great game my father and mother introduced me to and made a part of my life. Maybe because it's still about your team.

It's difficult to explain to people, but there's nothing like the feel of a team like the Colts were. Unlike most work environments, in pro football there is a clear goal once a week. As Herman Edwards, the old Jets coach now on ESPN, put it so well, "You play to win the game!"

In other work environments there are a hundred goals and a hundred agendas. In football I may dislike you, but I will make the block so your sorry ass gets in the end zone and we win. In other walks of life maybe someone's not so anxious to make that block.

My biggest adjustment going from football to radio-TV was I'd been schooled in the idea we do it together. Despite the turmoil I had to deal with at times and the personality and philosophy clashes in the NFL, the hardest thing I had to face after football was the idea of having to go out and promote myself. It was totally the opposite of the way it was done in the NFL in the 1960s and 1970s. That whole idea of self-promotion was bothersome to me. People who know me may not think that, but it was.

If I did that when I was with the Colts, somebody like Shula would say, "Stop trying to be a big shot and just do your job." Everyone was reminded of that. The irony is what do we hear the most successful coach in the NFL today say over and over? What is Bill Belichick's mantra? The same as Shula's was in 1968: "Do your job." We should all take something from that, because it works pretty well in New England.

There is nothing better than being part of a team. It's a group striving for one thing: to win on Sunday. You get your report card every week. There's a final score for everyone to see and there's a fairly level playing field to compete on. In pro football, if you're No. 1 at the end of the season, you know it through your performance. The same is true if you're No. 32. It's all right there.

If you win, you keep playing. If you lose, you sit down. That's the way life should be. It's the way sports is and that's why I've loved it all my life. You win, you keep playing. You lose, you go home. It's as simple as that. Or at least it should be.

EPILOGUE

Having survived the ups and downs, the great peaks and valleys, of pro football and radio and television as well as a near-death experience from an automobile accident, I can truthfully say I cherish the life I've led. I am a true believer in these words of playwright Edward Albee: "If you have no wounds, how can you know you're alive?" I have seen all of the great teams from the 1940s until today. I have seen most of the great performers in baseball, basketball, hockey, and particularly football. I saw the great movements in this country such as civil rights, the turbulent '60s, turmoil in the South, deaths of presidents and great leaders. I have been exposed, through my second career in radio and TV, to many of the greatest people in the world, many of them in Boston and New England. I want to thank my parents, particularly my father, Bert Bell, for exposing me to the great melting pot that is America. He taught me about sports, politics, and the vicissitudes of life and, most important, how to treat people. I am lucky to be able to do this book with Ron Borges, who brought the passion and research through his long history in the game. So with a bow to my lifetime friend Ernie Accorsi, and in no particular order, I am borrowing from Ernie's and Jimmy Cannon's "Nobody asked me, but . . ." to let you know how I feel:

Bert Bell's great quote, "On any given Sunday," lives in perpetuity.

Bert Bell's idea of the draft saved pro football.

Thanks to the Baltimore Colts organization for giving me a home and a sense of family that I lost when my father died.

Despite our great difficulties and bitter ending, in my mind Billy Sullivan was the only reason that the Patriots were founded and remained in New England.

Sid Luckman was the first great quarterback I saw as a nine-year-old at the Bears' training camp in 1946. He won four championships, and no one in today's generation saw him play. If Twitter was around, it would have been splashed all over the place that his father went to prison for murder.

Green Bay coach Curly Lambeau was one of the most underrated great coaches of all time.

The two most important positions in America are the president and the NFL quarterback.

Having said that, I never should have taken President Nixon's advice in 1971 to trade for Duane Thomas.

It saddens me that many NFL quarterbacks have become game managers. The reason is too many coaches think they're the managers and they are. Nobody calls their own plays on offense or defense.

Head coaches in the NFL are more important today than ever. Bill Belichick would be my coach if I had to win one game. Belichick and Don Shula did the best coaching jobs I've seen under extreme circumstances. I'll never forget Don Shula taking running back Tom Matte in 1965 after John Unitas and Gary Cuozzo went down and making Matte the quarterback for the last game against the Rams. We needed to win that game in order to get into the playoff game against the Packers, a game that we actually won but lost because of a blown call on a Don Chandler field goal. Belichick lost two quarterbacks, Brady followed by Jimmy Garappolo followed by Jacoby Brissett, yet won his first three games in 2016, despite missing many of his other best players as well.

Greatest combination player and GMs: Jim Finks—QB of the Steelers and GM of the Vikings, Bears, and Saints. He should have been commissioner. John Elway—QB of Denver and GM of the Super Bowl Champion Broncos. Former Cleveland Browns tight end and Hall of Famer Ozzie Newsome of the Super Bowl–winning Baltimore Ravens.

Greatest GMS I've seen: Tex Schramm—LA Rams, Dallas Cowboys. He was the best all-around football and business manager in the game. In fact, many people thought he was Pete Rozelle's alter ego. Jim Finks—Vikings, Bears, and Saints. Ron Wolf—Oakland Raiders, Tampa Bay Buccaneers, Green Bay Packers—both as a scout and a GM and now rightfully in the Hall of Fame. Ernie Accorsi—Baltimore Colts, Cleveland Browns, New York Giants, and NFL League Office. Bill Belichick—he is really the GM as well as coach of the Patriots. Paul Brown—he was a great coach as well as being a GM of the Cleveland Browns and Cincinnati Bengals. Al Davis—he was coach, GM, and owner of the Oakland Raiders and briefly AFL commissioner. At the height of his power, he was as smart and as shrewd as anybody in the game. George Young— Baltimore Colts, Miami Dolphins, New York Giants. He came into one of the most difficult situations in pro sports and helped resolve a very bitter situation in the Mara family.

If I owned a team and wanted to hire a GM who would always give me a frank and unvarnished opinion, it would be ex-Giant GM Ernie Accorsi.

The first time I went to the Cleveland Browns' training camp in 1950 and saw the Paul Brown operation, I knew football would be changed forever.

I was lucky enough to sit in the Philadelphia Athletics' dugout with Connie Mack pregame and see Bob Feller, Joe DiMaggio, Jackie Robinson and the Boys of Summer, and Willie Mays in their prime.

The greatest baseball player I ever saw was Willie Mays.

Sweeney's Bar in Baltimore was the greatest bar I've ever been to.

The back bar featured some of the most interesting and famous players and personalities of their time. Many of the people I met there became lifetime friends and acquaintances: Tommy Heinsohn and Johnny Most; Fr. Jordan, one of the great characters in Baltimore; John Sterling, now the longest-running play-by-play announcer in New York Yankees history; Steve Stonebreaker; Alex Hawkins (they should do a movie of his life); Hank Bauer, manager of the Orioles; Sammy Goldstein, who ended up in the trunk of a car; Mickey Mantle, who never knew what closing time was; Frank Sinatra; Bill Bradley; and Dave DeBusschere of the New York Knicks. And, of course, the one and only Irma the Body.

Best sports bars in America: Sweeney's and Gussie's Downbeat in Baltimore, P. J. Clarke's (there were tables reserved for the immortal Dan Jenkins and Jack Whittaker, but you could also see Walt "Clyde" Frazier, Woody Allen, and Edward Bennett Williams), and Toots Shor's in New York (where if Toots had enough drinks, he would lock you in; in fact my father had to escape through the men's room window at 6:00 a.m. to get out). Toots Shor had a special table for Joe DiMaggio and Toots's favorite bar partner, Jackie Gleason. He lovingly called everybody a "crumb bum." Lew Tendler's in Philadelphia was a great hangout for umpires and players after night games. It was great to sit up to two in the morning listening to stories from umpire Cal Hubbard (who is in both the baseball and football Hall of Fame), and Charlie Berry. The 1614 Club in Philly, owned by Footsie Stein, who always knew the numbers and was rumored to have either a knife or a gun in his boot. And any bar in Green Bay that featured Paul Hornung.

There's only one place in America for breakfast and that's the Fells Point Diner in Baltimore.

Coaches who saved their franchises: Bill Parcells, New England Patriots; Don Shula, Miami Dolphins; and Vince Lombardi, Green Bay Packers.

The greatest TV sports executive, who breathed life into the AFL: Roone Arledge of ABC.

My one long meeting with Ted Turner in 1974 was a conversation with a genius. He wanted to put my Charlotte Hornets' games on TV throughout the South and told me about a national cable news network he was working on called CNN. I asked him, "Do you think people will watch it?" They did.

Whether you liked him or not, Howard Cosell changed the way we looked at sports.

Cosell, Don Meredith, and Frank Gifford changed our Monday night habits and were the most entertaining group of their time.

If there's a sweet hereafter, I hope Art Rooney is there to get me in.

Red Smith of the *New York Times* was the Shakespeare of sports.

A football player's life is shorter than a mosquito's.

The death of Ed Garvey, the first executive director of the NFL Players Association, reminded me of a chilling speech he gave to NFL owners in 1972. The only thing missing was Nikita Khrushchev's banging his shoe and saying, "We will bury you!"

It is ridiculous to think that the NFL is considering removing the kickoff from the game. *It's called football.*

But it's time to get rid of the extra point. My father proposed to eliminate it in the 1940s.

If I were a player today, I'd want Bill Clinton representing me.

Wellington Mara, owner of the Giants, was the best owner/football man I've known. Before his brother Jack died, he was the person who ran the football end of the Giants. He was the scout, the trader, the drafter and had a brilliant football mind, but when his brother died, he had to take on the burden of the business side, which changed the way the Giants were run.

Adam Schefter of ESPN is the Walter Winchell of today's NFL.

Greatest scouts I've known: Eddie Kotel—Los Angeles Rams. He belongs in the Hall of Fame. He and Dan Reeves really invented scouting in the NFL. Gil Brandt—Dallas Cowboys. He computerized scouting and changed the way it was done. Ron Wolf—Oakland Raiders. Bobby Beathard—Kansas City Chiefs, Atlanta Falcons, and Miami Dolphins and later GM of the Washington Redskins and San Diego Chargers. The most underrated and near the top of any list, Art Rooney Jr., who belongs in the Hall of Fame for the drafts that built the Steelers' dynasty. Art, along with his top scout Bill Nunn, helped Pittsburgh become one of the great powerhouses in NFL history. Bucko Kilroy—Eagles, Redskins, Cowboys, Patriots. I always believed if the CIA was looking for a director, Bucko was their man. Bill Polian, who was the director of player personnel of the great Buffalo teams, then became GM of the Carolina Panthers and Indy Colts. He is in the Hall of Fame and justifiably so. Milt Davis of my Colts team, Lloyd Wells of Kansas City, and I could go on forever. But how could I forget the greatest character, Fido Murphy, who worked for everybody.

Greatest one-day draft: Chicago Bears 1965—Dick Butkus and Gale Sayers. Two of the greatest players of all time and both in the Hall of Fame. Pittsburgh Steelers 1974—Lynn Swann, Jack Lambert, John Stallworth, and Mike Webster.

Best all-time drafting: the Pittsburgh Steelers' drafts that produced Mean Joe Greene, Jack Lambert, Terry Bradshaw, Franco Harris, Mike Webster, L. C. Greenwood, Jack Ham, John Stallworth, Lynn Swan, and Mel Blount. All but L.C. are in the Hall of Fame, and he belongs in there too.

Five greatest dynasties: Cleveland Browns, Baltimore Colts, Green Bay Packers, Pittsburgh Steelers, and New England Patriots.

Greatest team I've seen: four-time Super Bowl–winning Pittsburgh Steeler teams of the '70s.

Someday, Woody Allen will immortalize Bill Belichick.

Next to watching the new installment of *Star Wars*, my favorite movie is played each week when Bill Belichick has his postgame press conference.

The most questionable move by a commissioner was when Paul

Tagliabue appointed Dr. Elliot Pellman, a Long Island rheuma-
tologist with no previous expertise in brain research, to be in
charge of concussions.

Meeting the profusely sweating Elvis Presley at a football game
between my team, the Charlotte Hornets, and the Memphis team
with Larry Csonka, Jim Kiick, and Paul Warfield in the WFL was a
shock. He had more security than the president of the United States.

Two of the greatest African American coaches of their time and
two coaches who had more prospects than half of the NFL: Eddie
Robinson of Grambling and "Big John" Merritt of Tennessee A&I.
They were great friends to me when I scouted with the Colts.

Most people won't remember Lindsay Nelson on play-by-play
and Red Grange as the color man on early NFL telecasts, but I'll
never forget them.

George Raveling, who was my teammate in the Narberth basketball league and a star at Villanova, went on to become one of the
great basketball recruiters and coaches in America. What most
people don't know is that he stood behind Martin Luther King at
his "I have a dream" speech and asked for his copy of the original speech as Dr. King was leaving. He flipped it to George and
today it's in a safety deposit box somewhere.

A great scene at the NFL league meetings my first year with the
Patriots in Palm Beach: Atlanta head coach Norm Van Brocklin threatened to punch Will McDonough for listening into our
conversation.

Will McDonough in my mind was the best football writer in America and broke more stories in Boston and around the country
than any other writer I've known. When I first came to Boston,
McDonough seemed to be the only full-time football writer. But
that has changed. Today, there are many good and knowledgeable football writers covering the Patriots. In fact, in those days,
most writers never bothered coming to practice, let alone Foxboro.

If I want to listen to or watch a football game, it would be a Curt

Gowdy with anybody, Chuck Thompson from Baltimore, Ray Scott of Green Bay, Al Michaels, John Madden, Chris Collinsworth, and Pat Summerall of cbs, Gil Santos and Gino Cappelletti, Bob Socci and Scott Zolak (he's as knowledgeable and colorful as they come).

A man for all broadcast seasons: Sean McDonough of espn.

My mother and Willie Mays. I'm riding in a cab with my mother in Philadelphia. She spots Willie Mays walking down the street. She stops the cab and yells out the window, "It's the Say Hey kid!" She jumps out of the car and drags me with her and has this short conversation about stickball with Willie. Do I need to say more?

My mother and the Whiz Kids. September 1950. The Whiz Kids Phillies are playing their last game at Ebbets Field. The winner goes to the World Series. Dick Sisler hits a three-run homer in the tenth inning. My mother, who has been arguing with my father all day long over watching the Phillies or the Eagles on tv, drags my brother, sister, and me out in front of the statue of the Blessed Virgin in our front yard to say prayers and thanks. It was one of my most embarrassing moments.

The greatest teams of each era: 1940s—Chicago Bears and Philadelphia Eagles. 1950s—Cleveland Browns and the 1958–59 Baltimore Colts. 1960s—Green Bay Packers. 1970s—Pittsburgh Steelers and Miami Dolphins. 1980s—San Francisco 49ers and Washington Redskins. 1990s—Dallas Cowboys. 2000 to present—(the ultimate) New England Patriots.

Two greatest football dynasties: Steelers and Patriots.

My greatest players of all time: Jimmy Brown, Johnny Unitas, Dick Butkus, Lawrence Taylor, Lenny Moore (one of the great combination rb/receivers), Jerry Rice, Joe Montana, Tom Brady. One of the greatest could have been Bo Jackson.

If I was going to remake the movie *The Wild Bunch*, it would feature Bill Parcells, Don Shula, Abe Gibron, Vince Lombardi, Alex Karras, Dick Butkus, Jimmy Brown, Lawrence Taylor, and John "The Tooz" Matuszak.

My scariest moment in television was when The Tooz had a melt-down and threatened me during the taping of a sports anthology for Disney.

The greatest sports books I've read: *Semi-Tough* by Dan Jenkins, *Friday Night Lights* by Buzz Bissinger, *North Dallas Forty* by Pete Gent, *The Best Game Ever* by Mark Bowden, and *The Boys of Summer* by Roger Kahn.

Greatest opening line by a columnist: Jim Murray in his column on the Indy 500, "Gentlemen, start your coffins."

I'm glad to see that not only the NFL but all major sports have begun to employ more and more women in key announcing positions.

What's the difference between college football and the NFL? Nothing. It's all about money.

I recommend that the NFL accept the University of Alabama as its next expansion team.

Will the NFL, many years from now in order to keep interest in the Super Bowl, suggest that the losing team offer one of their players as a human sacrifice?

Many people won't remember that the great athlete NBA All-Star Wilt Chamberlain was once offered a tryout by Hank Stram of the Kansas City Chiefs. Stram thought he would make a great tight end.

Fred Dryer, the defensive end I lost to the Rams, had a success-ful career in television playing the lead role in *Hunter*, a crime drama during the 1980s.

Greatest back-to-back NFL commissioners in sports history: Bert Bell and Pete Rozelle. Bert Bell saved the game and Pete took it to new heights.

Thanks to Bob Lyons of the Associated Press for resurrecting my father's life with his biography *On Any Given Sunday*. Both he and Ray Didinger, Hall of Fame writer from NFL Films and now Comcast, wrote the best book on an NFL team, which was the history of the Philadelphia Eagles. It sold over forty thousand copies.

Of the great cities I've lived: Philadelphia, Baltimore (an unforgettable experience), Charlotte, North Carolina (great civic leadership in trying to make my team go), and Boston, home of the most passionate and knowledgeable fans in all of sports as well as the best media in the country.

Washington should drop the name Redskins. It's about time.

My most moving interview: U.S. House Speaker Tip O'Neill discussing his bout with cancer and lamenting that ordinary citizens could not afford the medicine needed each month because they didn't have the great insurance coverage that Congress was afforded.

Please. Stop the overuse of instant replay. The games will take five hours.

Celebrating and taunting have gotten out of hand. Every tackle and block is not orgasmic.

I first became afraid of heights at a young age when the wrestler Man Mountain Dean took me on his shoulders and walked me into a pounding surf.

What happened to the great nicknames in football: "Concrete Charlie," "The Blade," "The Hangman," "Wild Man," "Captain Who," "Bucko," "Deacon," "Lou The Toe," "The Tank," "The Galloping Ghost"?

Are football stadiums just excuses to have restaurants, shopping centers, and supermarkets?

Steve and Ed Sabol of NFL Films changed the way that we looked at football.

I still can't figure out why Frank Sinatra sent me a letter asking me for a Patriots jersey. We were 2-10 at the time.

I'll never forget Jack Lemmon telling me about filming his 1966 movie *The Fortune Cookie*, in which he played a sideline photographer who gets run over by a fictional Cleveland Browns running back, Luther "Boom Boom" Jackson. They used Hall of Famer Leroy Kelly and then his backup, Ernie Green, to make it look authentic.

Chuck Noll taught me as much about life's finer things as he taught me about football.

Rex Ryan is really Shakespeare's Falstaff.

There are only two sacred places: The Cathedral of Notre Dame and Fenway Park.

The greatest competition I've seen on television was in Boston in the 1980s when Bob Lobel, Mike Lynch, and John Dennis squared off each night on sports.

Novelist William Martin knows as much about the Patriots as anybody.

If Nick Saban of Alabama says, "Good morning," I immediately put my PJs back on.

A little-known fact: Bert Bell saved the Packers by getting advance money from CBS to keep them going and start a new stadium.

The politicians that were the most fun to interview were former Massachusetts governor Bill Weld and then Senator Ted Kennedy doing his version of Tennessee Ernie Ford's "Sixteen Tons."

Three of my most memorable interviews: Sir Edmund Hillary, Stephen Hawking, and Annie Leibovitz.

I was fortunate to have spent a couple hours with the great Arnold Palmer. He defined charisma for an entire generation.

The most corrupt sports organizations: FIFA, IOC, and the NCAA.

What business other than football requires you to take a shot before you come to work?

My greatest concerns regarding the NFL today and its future:

Will the golden goose of television eventually hurt the product? With four major networks plus the Red Zone continually feeding us games on Sunday, Monday, and Thursday (and who knows, if they have their way, other days), will the public get tired of watching a product that basically has, in my opinion, at least ten teams that I don't want to watch? It is mediocrity at its best. They're just not enough good players to go around for thirty-two teams.

There's no question that the NFL has become a quarterback/receiver-dominated league. The only problem is there are only about eight or ten really great quarterbacks, and the irony is some quarterbacks are making $18 million and look like they'd have trouble in the Boston Park League.

Fan Duel and Draft Kings are not games of skill but games of chance. They're absolute rip-offs and out-and-out gambling. The NFL, which since the 1940s has been fearful of gambling, including staying out of Las Vegas, now has a franchise there and spends much of its telecast promoting gambling through Fan Duel and Draft Kings. Jerry Jones of the Cowboys and Bob Kraft of the Patriots are investors. The continual promoting of fantasy football is a very clever move by the NFL, since it ties the fan to the game based on statistics and not necessarily the actual game. The solution is to legalize sports gambling.

TV, the Internet, social media, streaming—although making a lot of money for the owners—spells overexposure to me. The difference between the old NFL owners and the new NFL owners is simple—money.

Count me among those who think an eighteen-game regular season schedule is very dangerous to the players' health. I know because it's what we had in the WFL. Even if you cut down preseason games from four to two, you're still putting the players in a dangerous position.

Thursday night football is another example of money over serious injury. There is no way the body recovers from the severe beating it takes every Sunday in three days. The normal recovery time for a player is five to six days. Figure it out for yourself.

The NFL Players Association is the weakest association of the four major sports leagues. No matter how they paint the picture, they have done a poor job of taking on the owners, the commissioner, and, more importantly, their own safety. Unlike baseball, they didn't have enough guts to sit it out and, if necessary, to cancel a season to get the things they need to protect their safety and their money. Their excuse is the rank-and-file wouldn't have enough money to hold out. Well, baseball did and now the Players Association, not the owners, rules baseball. The worst thing for an NFL player? He has no guaranteed contract and, unlike any other sport, can be cut. He also doesn't have true free agency and has given up many of his rights through collective bargaining.

Don't blame Roger Goodell for doing his job. He is paid by the owners and is only the "front guy" for fulfilling their wishes. In their mind, he's doing their bidding, which brings me to Tom Brady. I do believe he had some knowledge of what was going on with the footballs and could have easily ended the whole ridiculous two-year "Deflategate" fiasco by simply saying this was the way he wanted the balls and paid a $25,000 fine. On the other hand, the four-game suspension is ridiculous and overkill on the part of the league and commissioner.

The NFL changed for good when it voted in free agency and, particularly, the salary cap, which has penalized older players who still have some good years in front of them but have to be cut. So now you have the stars and the high-priced players at the top and the rest of the team are young players who don't make much money. The rule changes have also penalized the defense entirely too much, and the offense has become a passing game with essentially the running back becoming extinct. At times, it reminds me of pinball.

I think fans are being screwed by having to buy tickets to preseason games. I propose more padded practices, more scrimmages, and more joint practices with other teams like the Patriots have recently done with New Orleans, Philadelphia, Washington, and Chicago. What has happened with the new safety rules is there's less hitting and fewer padded practices and, as a result, the first three regular-season games look like exhibition games.

Has the game become too violent and have the players become too big and should there be some weight limit? How soon will the average offensive or defensive lineman be 400 pounds? Imagine being hit with that speed and power and not being seriously injured.

Each week, more and more players are going down. Every week and every year, the list gets longer and longer. The one reality of an NFL player is that he knows that from the very first day he goes to training camp to the very last day of his career, he'll always be hurting in one way or another. In summing it up, will the NFL be greatly diminished by the growing problems of concussions, CTE, player suits, TV overexposure, and owners' greed? That remains to be seen.

The greatest performance by a football player: O. J. Simpson at a spring practice scrimmage at Southern Cal, 1967.

My greatest interview other than President George H. W. Bush: Muhammed Ali at his training camp.

Best quotes: Jim Thorpe, after the king of Sweden called him "the greatest athlete in the world"—"Thanks, King." Pedro Martinez— "Wake up the Bambino and have me face him. Maybe I'll drill him in the ass." Roger Angell talking about athletes—"They are what they do."

I was at the 1948, 1958, and 1968 championship games. I only went to the 1958 sudden-death championship game because my father said Joe DiMaggio was going to be there.

Three best sports shows on TV: *Real Sports*, HBO; *The Sports Reporters*, ESPN; and *Sports Beat*, which I moderated and which included Bob Lobel, Bob Ryan, Joe Fitzgerald, Dan Shaughnessy, Kevin Paul Dupont, Clark Booth, and many others.

Boston sports icons: Bobby Orr, Milt Schmidt, Bill Russell, Bob Cousy, Larry Bird, Teddy Ballgame, Yaz, Doug Flutie, Tom Brady, Pedro Martinez, and Big Papi.

Thanks to Lesley Visser and Jackie MacMullen, who brought

women sports reporting into the twenty-first century, and Dusty Rhodes, who became the first female general manager in pro football with the New York Stars and Charlotte Hornets.

Thanks to Jack Johnson and many of my boyhood friends who taught me as much about life as sports.

Theo Epstein could run any business for me.

My mother, Frances Upton, was invited to a dinner with Al Capone. She naively asked Capone why all the women were sitting with their backs to the door.

Many of the greatest life lessons I learned about race were on the playgrounds of Philadelphia. Later, in the 1960s, I saw it at its worst when I scouted in the South. The treatment of African Americans there was disgraceful. It changed me for life.

I will take to my grave the admiration I have for the great African American players of the 1960s and '70s, who suffered so much to blaze a trail for today's NFL players.

Sammy Baugh, Otto Graham, and Red Grange were in the movies during the 1940s and '50s.

When the Colts once played the Eagles, the Baltimore Colts Marching Band, a great American original, was led into Shibe Park by running back Buddy Young.

Domestic violence was always present in the NFL, but years ago there was no social media around to expose it. The NFL is still trying to tiptoe around the issue instead of confronting it. The public is aware that stronger action is still needed.

What is the NFL's greatest enemy, concussion or overexposure?

Football is Family? It's really about the NFL selling jerseys.

I worked in radio and television with a tennis genius and great human being, Bud Collins.

Carly Simon to the NFL: You're So Vain.

John Mackey is still the greatest tight end in NFL history with his speed and blocking ability. Gronk would be in second place.

Picasso and Matisse changed art. Two-time Pulitzer Prize–winning cartoonist Paul Szep changed social commentary.

One of my favorite people, John Madden—player, Hall of Fame coach, TV commentator—is the last of the triple threats.

My friend Howard Baldwin, founder of the Whalers, should be remembered as much as the producer of *Hoosiers*, *Ray*, *Sahara*, and *42*, about the life of Jackie Robinson.

How can anybody say that Tom Brady, or Peyton Manning, or any quarterback is the greatest of all time unless they've seen all the greats from the '40s on? Each era has its great quarterbacks and different rules.

Bert Bell brought the Dempsey versus Tunney fight to Philadelphia. He was also asked to check with Al Capone (who was in prison at the time) if the Lindbergh baby's kidnapping was the work of the Mob. Within forty-eight hours, Capone got back to him that it was not.

I tried to pass my accounting course twice, the first time with my classmate at LaSalle, Jim Binns, who became an international lawyer as well as counsel for the WBA and then boxing commissioner for the State of Pennsylvania. He also raised the money for the Rocky statue in Philadelphia and appeared in the movie *Rocky V*.

The second time I tried to pass accounting was in summer school at Villanova with the great Olympian Charlie Jenkins (from Cambridge Rindge and Latin), who in 1956 came from way behind to win the 400 meters.

My brother, Bert, nicknamed Blackie, was really Peter Falk as Colombo.

My former WFL team, the Charlotte Hornets, still maintains a fan club forty-one years after the team's demise. It's run by Richie

Franklin. The players from that team were among the greatest people I have been associated with.

Tom Moore was an assistant coach for my Charlotte Hornets team in 1974. Forty-two years later at the age of seventy-eight, he is still coaching in the NFL with the Arizona Cardinals. He coached the Steelers for two Super Bowls and was Peyton Manning's coach at Indy for the 2006 Super Bowl.

I will miss Hocky, Wingy, and Frisco Legs.

One of the most ironic conversations: John B. Kelly telling my father, "Bert, Gracie's first movie is a low-budget western called *High Noon* with Gary Cooper. I hope it does okay."

Most iconic snapshot of a great champion: John Unitas turning his back to the field and walking off after engineering two of the greatest drives in NFL history in the 1958 sudden-death championship game.

My last radio show was at WBIX where the owner sold the station and threw a big celebration, then went home and tried to commit suicide. He was unsuccessful and went to prison for running a $32 million Ponzi scheme and started a jazz band there.

There's no business like show business. And the beat goes on . . .

In looking back at more than seventy years of being in and around the game, I hope for its survival. If you grew up loving something, that doesn't mean you can't be critical of it. So, from the frozen tundra of New England to the frozen tundra of Lambeau Field, On Any Given Sunday, I will be pulling the curtains, turning on my three TVs, gorging on the pregame shows, watching all the replays, and taking to Twitter. You see, I'm hooked . . . for the time being.

BIBLIOGRAPHY

Bagli, Vince, and Norman L. Macht. *Sundays at 2:00*. Centreville MD: Tidewater Publishers, 1995.

Baldwin, Howard. *Slim and None*. Toronto: House of Anansi Press, 2015.

Beer, Tom, with George Kimball. *Sunday's Fools*. Boston: Houghton Mifflin, 1974.

Callahan, Tom. *The GM*. New York: Crown Publishers, 2007.

———. *Johnny U*. New York: Three Rivers Press, 2006.

Daly, Dan. *The National Forgotten League*. Lincoln: University of Nebraska Press, 2012.

Felser, Larry. *The Birth of the New NFL*. Guilford CT: Lyons Press, 2008.

Freedman, Lew. *Clouds over the Goalpost*. New York: Sports Publishing, 2013.

Gildea, William. *When the Colts Belonged to Baltimore*. New York: Ticknor & Fields, 1994.

Hawkins, Alex. *My Story (and I'm Sticking to It)*. Chapel Hill NC: Algonquin Books, 1989.

Lyons, Robert S. *On Any Given Sunday*. Philadelphia: Temple University Press, 2010.

Olesker, Michael. *The Colts' Baltimore*. Baltimore: Johns Hopkins University Press, 2008.

———. *Front Stoops in the Fifties*. Baltimore: Johns Hopkins University Press, 2013.

Patterson, Ted. *Football in Baltimore: History and Memorabilia*. Baltimore: Johns Hopkins University Press, 2000.

Price, Christopher. *New England Patriots: The Complete Illustrated History*. Minneapolis: MRI Publishing, 2010.

Schultz, Brad. *The NFL, Year One*. Washington DC: Potomac Books, 2013.

Steadman, John. *Baltimore Colts: A Pictorial History*. Virginia Beach: Jordan, 1978.

———. *The Best (and Worst) of Steadman.* Baltimore: Press Box Publishers, 1974.

———. *Days in the Sun.* Baltimore: Baltimore Sun, 2000.

———. *Football's Miracle Men.* Cleveland: Pennington Press, 1959.

———. *From Colts to Ravens.* Atglen PA: Schiffler Publishing, 2012.